Computational Intelligence Applications in Business and Big Data Analytics

Computational Intelligence Applications in Business and Big Data Analytics

Edited by
Vijayan Sugumaran
Arun Kumar Sangaiah
Arunkumar Thangavelu

CRC Press
Taylor & Francis Group
Boca Raton London New York

CRC Press is an imprint of the
Taylor & Francis Group, an **informa** business

CRC Press
Taylor & Francis Group
6000 Broken Sound Parkway NW, Suite 300
Boca Raton, FL 33487-2742

International Standard Book Number-13: 978-1-4987-6101-7 (Hardback)

Visit the Taylor & Francis Web site at
http://www.taylorandfrancis.com

and the CRC Press Web site at
http://www.crcpress.com

Contents

PART IV APPLICATIONS OF COMPUTATIONAL INTELLIGENCE

Editors

 **Vijayan Sugumaran** is a professor of management information systems and the chair of the Department of Decision and Information Sciences at Oakland University, Rochester, Michigan, USA. He is also a WCU visiting professor at Sogang University, Seoul, South Korea. He received his PhD in information technology from George Mason University, Fairfax, Virginia, USA. His research interests are in the areas of Big Data management and analytics, ontologies, and semantic web, intelligent agent, and multiagent systems, and component-based software development. He has published more than 150 peer-reviewed articles in journals, conferences, and books. He has edited 12 books and serves on the editorial board of eight journals. He has published in top-tier journals, such as *Information Systems Research, ACM Transactions on Database Systems, Communications of the ACM, IEEE Transactions on Big Data, IEEE Transactions on Engineering Management, IEEE Transactions on Education, IEEE Software*, and *Healthcare Management Science*. Dr. Sugumaran is the editor-in-chief of the *International Journal of Intelligent Information Technologies*. He is the chair of the intelligent agent and multiagent systems minitrack for the Americas Conference on Information Systems (AMCIS 1999–2016). Dr. Sugumaran served as the chair of the information technology committee for the Decision Sciences Institute. He has served as the program co-chair for the 14th Workshop on E-Business (WeB2015) as well as the International Conference on Applications of Natural Language to Information Systems (NLDB 2008, NLDB 2013, and NLDB 2016). He also regularly serves as a program committee member for numerous national and international conferences.

 **Arun Kumar Sangaiah** received his M Eng in computer science and engineering from the Government College of Engineering, Tirunelveli, Anna University, India. He received his PhD in computer science and engineering from the VIT University, Vellore, India. He is presently working as an associate professor in the school of computer science and engineering, VIT University, India. His areas of interest include software engineering, computational intelligence, wireless networks, bio-informatics, and embedded systems. He has authored more than 100 publications in different journals and conferences of national and international repute. In addition, he is an editorial board member/associate editor of various international journals. In addition, he has edited a number of guest editorial special issues for various journals, including *Applied Soft Computing (SCI), Computers and Electrical Engineering (SCI), Future Generation Computer Systems (SCI), Engineering Applications of Artificial Intelligence (SCI), Neural Network World (SCI), Intelligent Automation & Soft Computing (SCI)*, and *Scientific World Journal (SCI)*. Also, he has organized a number of

special issues for Elsevier, Inderscience, Springer, Hindawi, and IGI publishers. He has acted as a book volume editor for various publishers including Taylor & Francis Group, Springer, and IGI.

 **Arunkumar Thangavelu** is currently associated with Vellore Institute of Technology University as a senior professor and as the dean of the School of Computer Science and Engineering. He has more than 21 years of academic and R&D experience in industries. He has managed and initiated multiple international-level projects, including QoS for WiFi forum. He is an active consultant in R&D planning and proposal evaluation as well project guidance and review of PG projects and PhD works. Dr. Arunkumar Thangavelu's area of research interest focuses on soft computing algorithms, ad hoc high-performance networking (MANET/ VANET/PANET), Big Data, data mining/analysis, ambient intelligence, and aspect-based network management, which includes mobile, context-aware middleware. He has published multiple papers in international conferences and journals. He has served as the chair and a committee member as well as an editorial board member for international journals and international conferences. He plays an active role in IEEE/ACM and CSI professional bodies and also works toward the upliftment of society and rural people development.

Contributors

S. Abirami received her PhD in the area of document imaging from Anna University, Chennai. Currently, she is working as an assistant professor in the Department of Information Science and Technology, Anna University, Chennai. She has more than 10 years of research experience. She has authored more than 90 research publications in international journals and conferences and two book chapters. She has mentored many sponsored research projects from Amazon, Tamil Virtual University, and the Center for Technology and Development. Her current research area focuses upon the use of machine learning, data mining, computational intelligence, and video analytics.

R. Baskaran received his PhD in computer science and engineering from Anna University, Chennai. Currently, he is working as associate professor in the Department of Computer Science and Engineering, Anna University, Chennai. He has more than 13 years of research experience. He has served as an editorial board member and technical program committee member for reputed journals and conferences. He has received the IBM Best Faculty Award, Shiksha Ratan Purashkar, and Certificate of Excellence in the year 2011. He has authored more than 155 research papers in international journals and conferences. His research interests include artificial intelligence, robotics, video analytics, and data mining.

Dr. Siddhartha Bhattacharyya received the BS degree in physics, the BS degree in optics and optoelectronics, and the MS degree in optics and optoelectronics from the University of Calcutta, India in 1995, 1998, and 2000, respectively. He completed his PhD degree in computer science and engineering from Jadavpur University, India in 2008. He is the recipient of the University Gold Medal from the University of Calcutta for his MS degree. He is the recipient of the coveted National Award Adarsh Vidya Saraswati Rashtriya Puraskar for excellence in education and research in 2016. He is also the recipient of the Distinguished HoD Award and Distinguished Professor Award conferred by the Computer Society of India, Mumbai Chapter, India in 2017.

He is currently the professor of information technology of RCC Institute of Information Technology, Kolkata, India. In addition, he is serving as the Dean (Research and Development and Academic Affairs) of the institute. He served as the head of the department from March 2014 to December 2016. Prior to this, he was an associate professor of information technology of RCC Institute of Information Technology, Kolkata, India from 2011 to 2014. Before that, he served as an assistant professor in computer science and information technology of the University Institute of Technology, The University of Burdwan, India from 2005 to 2011. He was a lecturer in information technology of Kalyani Government Engineering College, India during 2001–2005. He is a coauthor of four books and a coeditor of eight books, and has more than 170 research publications in international journals and conference proceedings to his credit. He has obtained a patent on intelligent colorimeter technology. He was the convener of the AICTE-IEEE National Conference on Computing and Communication Systems (CoCoSys-09) in 2009. He was a member of the Young Researchers' Committee of the WSC 2008 Online World Conference on Soft Computing in Industrial Applications. He has been a member of the organizing and technical program committees of several national and international conferences. He served as the editor-in-chief of the *International Journal of Ambient Computing and Intelligence (IJACI)* published by IGI Global, Hershey, PA, USA from July 17, 2014 to November 6, 2014. He was the General Chair of the IEEE International Conference on Computational Intelligence and Communication Networks (ICCICN 2014) organized by the Department of Information Technology, RCC Institute of Information Technology, Kolkata in association with Machine Intelligence Research Labs, Gwalior and IEEE Young Professionals, Kolkata Section and held at Kolkata, India in 2014. He is the associate editor of the *International Journal of Pattern Recognition Research*. He is a member of the editorial board of the *International Journal of Engineering, Science and Technology* and *ACCENTS Transactions on Information Security (ATIS)*. He is also a member of the editorial advisory board of *HETC Journal of Computer Engineering and Applications*. He has been the associate editor of the *International Journal of BioInfo Soft Computing* since 2013. He is the lead guest editor of the Special Issue on *Hybrid Intelligent Techniques for Image Analysis and Understanding of Applied Soft Computing* (Elsevier, BV). He was the general chair of the 2015 IEEE International Conference on Research in Computational Intelligence and Communication Networks (ICRCICN 2015) organized by the Department of Information Technology, RCC Institute of Information Technology, Kolkata in association with IEEE Young Professionals, Kolkata Section and held at Kolkata, India in 2015. He was the lead guest editor of the Special Issue on Computational Intelligence and Communications in the *International Journal of Computers and Applications (IJCA)* (Taylor & Francis, UK) in 2016. He has been the editor of the *International Journal of Pattern Recognition Research* since January 2016. He was the general chair of the 2016 International Conference on Wireless Communications, Network Security and Signal Processing (WCNSSP2016) held on June 26–27, 2016 at Chiang Mai, Thailand. He was the general chair of the 2016 IEEE Second International Conference on Research in Computational Intelligence and Communication Networks (ICRCICN 2016) organized by the Department of Information Technology, RCC Institute of Information Technology, Kolkata jointly with IEEE Young Professionals, Kolkata Section and held at Kolkata, India on September 23–25, 2016. He is a member of the editorial board of *Applied Soft Computing* (Elsevier, B V). He has been serving as the Series Editor of the IGI Global Book Series Advances in Information Quality and Management (AIQM) since January 1, 2017.

His research interests include soft computing, pattern recognition, multimedia data processing, hybrid intelligence, and quantum computing. Dr. Bhattacharyya is a fellow of the Institute of Electronics and Telecommunication Engineers (IETE), India. He is also a senior member of the Institute of Electrical and Electronics Engineers (IEEE), USA; the International Institute of Engineering and Technology (IETI), Hong Kong; and the Association for Computing Machinery (ACM), USA. He is a member of the International Rough Set Society; the International Association for Engineers (IAENG), Hong Kong; Computer Science Teachers Association (CSTA), USA; and the International Association of Academicians, Scholars, Scientists and Engineers (IAASSE), USA. He is a life member of the Computer Society of India, Optical Society of India, Indian Society for Technical Education, and Center for Education Growth and Research, India.

Fadwa Bouhafer is a first-year doctoral student in computer science at the University of Oujda. He received his Master's degree at the University of Paul Sabatier in Toulouse, France. His research is focused on data mining and incremental clustering.

Zakaria Boulouard is a third-year doctoral student in computer science at the University of Agadir. He received his engineering degree at the National School of Applied Sciences. His research is focused on parallel and distributed algorithms, and data visualization.

Nihal Chouati is a second-year doctoral student in computer science at the National School of Applied Sciences in Tangier. He received his engineering degree at the Faculty of Sciences and Technologies in Tangier. Chouati's research focuses on information retrieval, the semantic web, and Big Data.

Deepthi P. S. is working as an assistant professor at the LBS College of Engineering, Kasaragod, India. She is pursuing a PhD in computer science and engineering at the University of Kerala. She has more than five years of experience in teaching and three years in research. Her areas of interest include data mining, machine learning, and swarm intelligence. She is an active ACM professional member and has served as a secretary of ACM Trivandrum Professional Chapter. Deepthi is a recipient of the SPEED-IT research fellowship instituted by the Department of Information Technology, Government of Kerala. She has published a few papers in international conferences and has received an ACM travel grant for presenting a paper at the Second IKDD Conference on Data Sciences (CoDS 2015). She has served as a reviewer for many international conferences and a few international journals.

Bernard Dousset received his PhD degree in 1978 from Toulouse III University. Currently, he is a professor at the University Paul Sabatier, Toulouse. His research interests include data mining, pattern recognition, data mining and knowledge discovery, text mining, web mining, and Big Data.

Ankur Dumka received his B.Tech in computer science from Gurukul Kangri University, Hardiwar, in 2007 and completed a postgraduate diploma in advanced software design and development specialization in Java from CDAC in 2008. He is currently pursuing his PhD in networking from Uttarakhand Technical University, Dehradun. He is currently working as an assistant professor in the computer science department at the University of Petroleum and Energy Studies, Dehradun. His current research concerns areas including IoT, Big Data, networks, SDN, and NFV.

Anass El Haddadi received the Doctorate in Business Intelligence from the University of Toulouse (France) and the University Mohammed V of Rabat (Morocco; 2011). He joined ENSA of Agadir in 2013. He is an associate professor at the Department of Computer Sciences at the ENSA of Al-Hoceima. He gives lectures on databases, data warehousing, and business intelligence for decision making. He is a co-president of the International Conference on Scientific and Technological Strategic Intelligence. He is a member of the French Research Group in Competitive Intelligence. Since 2014, he has been a co-president of Competitive Intelligence Day in Morocco; since 2015, he has been the president of the VSST Association Chapter Morocco; and since 2016, he has been the vice-president of ISKO-Maghreb (Morocco). His research interests include decision-support information systems, Big Data analytics, data visualization, and unstructured data management. He is also carrying out training, research, and consultancy work for private and public sectors in Morocco, Europe, and South America.

Amine El Haddadi is a third-year doctoral student in computer science at the University of Paul Sabatier in Toulouse, France and Faculty of Sciences and Technologies in Tangier. He received his engineering degree at the National School of Applied Sciences (2008–2013). His research interests include parallel and distributed algorithms, massive data processing, and collective intelligence.

Abdelhadi Fennan received his PhD degree in 1995 from Centrale Lyon School, France. Currently, he is a professor at Abdelmalek Essaâdi University, Tétouan, Morocco. His research interests include artificial intelligence, software engineering, and information systems (business informatics).

Amit Goel is an accomplished technology leader with hands-on capabilities and senior executive level experience with multiple-size companies globally. Starting his career as a computer software programmer in the 1990s, Amit gained diverse experience over three decades, spanning software engineering and research. He has spearheaded 5- to 100-person teams with US\$ 1–50 million budgets. Amit leads with a strong customer service-oriented focus on providing advanced solutions with scientific problem-solving methods. An avid champion of Agile methods, Amit promotes and utilizes continuous integration, test-driven development, build–deploy automation, scrum sprints, code reviews, and related Agile tools to manage delivery time and cost.

Chuanping Hu received his PhD degree from Tong Ji University, Shanghai, China, in 2007. He is a research fellow and the director of the Third Research Institute of the Ministry of Public Security, China. He is also a specially appointed professor and a PhD supervisor with Shanghai Jiao Tong University, Shanghai, China. He has published more than 20 papers, has edited five books, and is the holder of more than 30 authorized patents. His research interests include machine learning, computer vision, and intelligent transportation systems.

Deepthi P. Hudedagaddi is a second year MTech (by research) student at VIT University, Vellore. She completed her bachelor's degree in engineering at Dayananda Sagar College of Engineering in Bangalore in 2013. She specializes in data mining and is working on developing spatial uncertainty-based algorithms for image segmentation. She is working under the guidance of Dr. B. K. Tripathy.

Her research interests include soft computing, image segmentation and spatial algorithms, uncertainty, and hybrid intelligence. She has four Scopus indexed papers to her credit and has been active in several national and international conferences. She also has some book chapters to her credit.

Goran Klepac, a university college professor, works as head of the strategic unit in the sector of credit risk at Raiffeisenbank Austria d.d., Croatia. In several universities in Croatia, he lectures on subjects in the domain of data mining, predictive analytics, decision support systems, banking risk, risk evaluation models, expert systems, database marketing, and business intelligence. As a team leader, he successfully completed many data mining projects in different domains such as retail, finance, insurance, hospitality, telecommunications, and productions. He is the author or a coauthor of several books published in Croatian and English in the domain of data mining. E-mail: goran@goranklepac.com

Robert Kopal, an assistant professor and vice dean for R&D at University College Algebra Zagreb, Croatia, is also the board advisor for R&D at IN2 Group, a chief science officer at IN2data Data Science Company, and a lecturer at several university colleges in Croatia and at the Croatian

Managers' and Entrepreneurs' Association (CROMA) EduCare Program. He is also the author or a coauthor of 10 books (on competitive intelligence analysis, game theory, etc.), numerous chapters in books by various authors, and more than 40 scientific and professional papers. He is a workshop manager and teacher at more than 100 business and intelligence analysis workshops; a designer of several specialized IT systems; a certified trainer in the area of structured intelligence analysis techniques; and a SW, SCIP, and IALEIA member. He has held presentations at various national and international conferences and participated in and led a number of national and international intelligence analysis projects. E-mail: robert.kopal@in2data.hr

Yunhuai Liu is a professor in the Third Research Institute of Ministry of Public Security, China. He received PhD degrees from Hong Kong University of Science and Technology (HKUST) in 2008. His main research interests include wireless sensor networks, pervasive computing, and wireless networks. He has authored or coauthored more than 50 publications, and his publications have appeared in *IEEE Transactions on Parallel and Distributed Systems, IEEE Journal of Selected Areas in Communications, IEEE Transactions on Mobile Computing, IEEE Transactions on Vehicular Technology,* etc.

Lin Mei received a PhD degree from Xi'an Jiaotong University, Xi'an, China, in 2000. He is a research fellow. From 2000 to 2006, he was a postdoctoral researcher with Fudan University, Shanghai, China; the University of Freiburg, Freiburg in Breisgau, Germany; and the German Research Center for Artificial Intelligence. He is currently the director of the Technology R&D Center for the Internet of Things with the Third Research Institute of the Ministry of Public Security, China. He has published more than 40 papers. His research interests include computer vision, artificial intelligence, and Big Data processing.

Leo Mršić is an experienced top-level corporate executive, entrepreneur, college professor, assistant research scientist, and certified court expert witness with deep expertise in the application of technology in different areas of business and government, a strong background in different areas (law, finance, technology, math) and fields (retail, project management), with focus on analytic methods and data management and data usage with the ability to extend its approach from the operational through the strategic level. He possesses a strong organizational skill set (teams or companies up to 1,000+ employees) developed during 15+ years of management experience. He is the head of chair for data management and analysis at University College Algebra Zagreb, active in the edu community with a wide range of different experiences (editor, lecturer, reviewer, editorial board member, advisor, book author), and able to provide a deep and usable approach in many areas especially related to technology, math, structured decision making, and educational methodologies. E-mail: leo.mrsic@in2data.hr

Muthu Ramachandran is currently a principal lecturer in the Computing, Creative Technologies, and Engineering School as part of the Faculty of Arts, Environment and Technology at Leeds Beckett University, UK. Previously, he spent nearly eight years in industrial research (Philips Research Labs and Volantis Systems Ltd., Surrey, UK) where he worked on software architecture, reuse, and testing. His first career started as a research scientist, and he worked on real-time systems development projects. Muthu is the author or a coauthor of the books *Software Components: Guidelines and Applications* (Nova Publishers, 2008) and *Software Security Engineering: Design and Applications* (Nova Publishers, 2011). He has also authored and published nine books, hundreds of journal articles, more than 50 book chapters, and more than 200 conference papers on various advanced topics in software engineering, software security, cloud computing, and education. Muthu has been leading conferences as the chair and as a keynote speaker on global safety, security and sustainability, emerging services, IoT, Big Data, and software engineering. Muthu is a member of various professional organizations and computer societies such as IEEE and ACM; a fellow of BCS; and a senior fellow of HEA. He is also an invited keynote speaker at several international conferences. Muthu has worked on several research projects, including all aspects of software engineering, SPI for SMEs (known as a Prism model), emergency and disaster management systems, software components and architectures, good practice guidelines on software developments, software security engineering, and service and cloud computing. Project details can be accessed at www.se.moonfruit.com and at soft-research.com.

Jhuma Ray (MBA, M.Phil) received the BS degree from University of Calcutta, India in 2000 and the MBA degree in finance from F.M. University, India in 2002. She is presently pursuing her PhD.

She is currently working as an assistant professor in the Department of Engineering Science and Management and is the former head of the Department of Basic Science and Humanities of RCC Institute of Information Technology, Kolkata, India. In addition, she is acting as a Nodal Officer of Equity Assurance Plan Committee under TEQIP-II (Technical Education Quality Improvement Programme), a World Bank–funded Project.

She has several research publications in international journals and conference proceedings to her credit. She has also authored chapters in books published by reputed publishers. Her research interests include portfolio management and risk optimization procedures.

William A. Rivera has more than 15 years of experience in the software industry and is currently working as a senior software architect for BCA technologies, where he provides leadership and guidance for analytics and software teams. His research interests include predictive modeling, machine learning, software architecture, and engineering and data mining with emphasis on implementing artificial intelligence into software applications. He holds a masters and PhD in engineering, modeling, and simulation from the University of Central Florida and a masters in computer science from the University of West Florida.

R. Sasikala received the BE degree from Kongu Engineering College, Tamilnadu, India in 1994, the ME degree from Government College of Technology, Coimbatore, Tamilnadu in 2003, and the PhD degree from Anna University, Chennai, Tamilnadu in 2011. She is currently an associate professor in the School of Computer Science and Engineering at VIT University, Vellore, Tamilnadu, India. She published more than 20 papers in various reputed journals and international conferences. She is the reviewer of many international journals. Her research interests include cloud computing, Big Data, wireless networks, body sensor networks, and optical switching networks. She is a life member of Computer Society of India and Indian Society for Technical Education.

M. Sivarathinabala received her ME in communication systems in 2007. Currently, she is undertaking research in the field of video processing in the Department of Information Science and Technology, Anna University, Chennai. Her research interests include different aspects of multimedia systems and video processing.

Sabu M. Thampi is an associate professor at the Indian Institute of Information Technology and Management–Kerala (IIITM-K), Trivandrum, India. His research interests include network security, security informatics, bio-inspired computing, very large databases, image forensics, video surveillance, cloud security, secure information sharing, secure localization, and distributed computing. He has authored or edited a few books published by reputed international publishers and published papers in academic journals and international and national proceedings. Sabu has served as a guest editor for special issues in a few international journals and as a program committee member for many international conferences and workshops. He has co-chaired several international workshops and conferences. Sabu is a senior member of the Institute of Electrical and Electronics Engineers (IEEE) and a member of the IEEE Communications Society, IEEE SMCS, and ACM.

B. K. Tripathy has received three gold medals for topping the list of candidates at the graduation and postgraduation level of Berhampur University. He was a professor and head of the Department of Computer Science of Berhampur University until 2007. Dr. Tripathy is now working as a senior professor in the School of Computing Science and Engineering, VIT University, Vellore, India. He has received research/academic fellowships from UGC, DST, SERC, and DOE of Govt. of India for various academic pursuits. Dr. Tripathy has published more than 380 technical papers in different international journals and proceedings of reputed international conferences, and has edited research volumes. He has produced 25 PhDs, 13 MPhils, and four MSs (by research) under his supervision. Dr. Tripathy has published two textbooks on soft computing and computer graphics. He was selected as an honorary member of the American Mathematical Society from 1992 to 1994 for his distinguished contribution as a reviewer of the *American Mathematical Review*. Dr. Tripathy has served as a member of the advisory board or as a technical program committee member of several international conferences inside India and abroad. Also, he has edited two research volumes for IGI publications and is editing three more research volumes. He is a life/senior member of IEEE, ACM, IRSS, CSI, ACEEE, OMS, and IMS. Dr. Tripathy is an editorial board member/reviewer of more than 60 journals. He has guest-edited some research journals. Dr. Tripathy has technical grants for research projects from various funding agencies, such as UGC, DST, and DRDO. His research interests include fuzzy sets and systems, rough sets and knowledge engineering, data clustering, social network analysis, soft computing, granular computing, content-based learning, neighborhood systems, soft set theory, social Internet of things, Big Data analytics, theory of multisets, and list theory.

Zheng Xu received diploma and PhD degrees from the School of Computing Engineering and Science, Shanghai University, Shanghai, in 2007 and 2012, respectively. He did postdoctoral work at Tsinghua University from 2014 to 2016. He is currently working in the Third Research Institute of the Ministry of Public Security, China. His current research interests include public security, surveillance systems, mobile crowd sensing, and social media. He has authored or coauthored more than 90 publications, including *IEEE Transactions on Fuzzy Systems*, *IEEE Transactions on Automation Science and Engineering*, *IEEE Transactions on Emerging Topics in Computing*, *IEEE Transactions on Systems, Man, and Cybernetics: Systems*, *IEEE Transactions on Big Data*, etc.

Zhiguo Yan received his PhD from Shanghai Jiaotong University in 2008 and accomplished postdoctoral research at Fudan University in 2013. Now he is a vice professor of the Third Research Institute of Ministry of Public Security. His scholarly interests focus on video intelligent analysis, Big Data techniques, IoT techniques on public security, etc.

INTRODUCTION

I

Chapter 1

Computational Intelligence Paradigms in Business Intelligence and Analytics

Vijayan Sugumaran,[1] Arun Kumar Sangaiah,[2]
and Arunkumar Thangavelu[2]

[1]*Department of Decision and Information Sciences, Oakland University, Rochester, Michigan, USA*
[2]*School of Computer Science and Engineering, VIT University, Vellore, Tamil Nadu, India*

Contents

Abstract

In business intelligence (BI) and big data analytics, computational intelligence (CI) paradigms have been adopted as an intelligent decision support system for prediction and optimization in a variety of applications. The traditional data analysis approaches are lacking in efficiency, have a limited computational capability, and have an inadequate and imprecise nature of handling unstructured data. However, CI methodologies have a high computational efficiency to integrate, explore, and share a high volume of unstructured data in real time, using diverse analytical techniques for enhanced decision making. Further, CI has the capability to implement complex data via sophisticated mathematical models and analytical techniques. This chapter illustrates a short overview of CI approaches and its noteworthy character in BI and data analytics. The focus of this chapter is to study and analyze the effect of CI for the overall advancement of emerging intelligent decision support systems.

1.1 Introduction

This chapter provides a brief overview of computational intelligence paradigms and their significant role in the application of business intelligence and Big Data analytics. Humans are intelligent—that is, they have the ability to acquire and apply knowledge and skills during the decision-making process of any application. In the same way as humans, machines are also intelligent, but the intelligence is artificial and hence known as artificial intelligence (AI). Artificial intelligence is exhibited by machines to complete their assigned tasks and emulate human behavior. Machines apply AI by using cutting-edge technologies to perform cognitive functions, such as learning and problem solving that are associated with humans. Moreover, a human mind constitutes a set of cognitive faculties, such as consciousness, perception, thinking, judgment, and memory. In addition, humans have brains and nervous systems that act according to these facilities. Unlike humans, machines don't constitute any biological organs to apply the intelligence. The machines can understand only binary language, which is the basis for AI. Until the past few years, this was a limitation for AI, which is based on hard computing techniques that work with binary logic (0 and 1)—that is, it can solve only simple and some complex problems with a traditional process by translating it into binary language. So AI is incapable of solving some complex real-world problems, which cannot be translated into binary language and have some uncertainties during the process. This incapability gives rise to the evolution of a new approach called computational intelligence (CI, a subset of AI) to diminish those limitations. Further, CI is the successor of AI and is considered the future of computing. CI techniques and their applications in business intelligence and analytics are addressed in this chapter and are also the focus of this edited book.

1.2 Computational Intelligence

CI paradigms have the ability to gain knowledge about a specific task from given data. A system is called computationally intelligent if it deals with low-level data, such as numerical data during the decision-making process of any application. In general, CI is similar to AI in terms of seeking goals. It is designed to solve complex real-world problems for which AI or traditional modeling

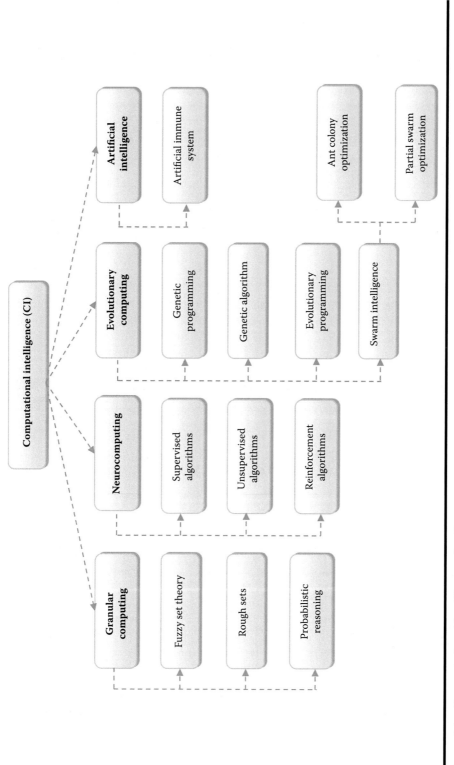

Figure 1.1   Computational intelligence family tree.

is inadequate because of the uncertainty or stochastic nature of the problem and the difficulty in translating to binary language.

CI approaches have been used to handle nonexact and subjective vagueness of knowledge to take control of actions in an adaptive fashion similar to the human reasoning process. CI consists of various branches that are not limited to granular computing: neurocomputing, evolutionary computing, and the artificial immune system as shown in Figure 1.1. In addition, CI mainly constitutes the combination of the following five techniques: fuzzy logic, artificial neural networks, evolutionary computation, learning theory, and probabilistic methods. All these methods in combination with one another help the computer to solve a problem in the following way: (a) fuzzy logic—understanding natural language, (b) artificial neural networks—learning from experiential data by operating similar to biological ones, (c) evolutionary computing—the process of selection, (d) learning theory—reasoning, and (e) probabilistic methods—dealing with uncertainty imprecision.

In addition to these main principles, there are some other approaches that include genetic algorithms; biologically inspired algorithms, such as swarm intelligence; and artificial immune systems. Recently, there has been an interest in fusing CI approaches with data mining, natural language processing, and AI techniques. As stated earlier, CI and AI methodologies seek similar goals; however, there is a unique distinction between the approaches.

CI is a subset of AI as machine intelligence can be distinguished among two types of computing: AI is based on hard computing techniques, and CI is based on soft computing methods, and it can be adapted according to the situation. Hard computing techniques are mainly based on binary logic, which consists of two values, only 0 and 1, and the computation takes place using this binary logic. This is also the basis for the modern computer. This binary logic gives rise to the problem that natural language cannot always be converted easily into absolute terms of 0 and 1. Although the soft computing techniques are based on fuzzy logic, they usually differ from binary logic. Fuzzy logic works by aggregating data to partial truths, which is similar to the human brain, and this logic is one of the main principles of CI. Both AI and CI approaches move forward with a similar goal to accomplish general intelligence—that is, the intelligence of a machine that may perhaps achieve a particular intellectual task that a human being can carry out.

1.3 Big Data Analytics

Big Data can be described in simple terms as a data set of large size that contains both structured and unstructured data from different sources. In general terms, Big Data is a data set that is large or complex and to which traditional data processing applications, such as analysis, capture, data duration, search, sharing, storage, transfer, visualization, querying, data mining, updating, and privacy are applied to extract value from the data. In Big Data, extraction of more accurate values of relevant parameters may lead to efficient decision making, which results in superior operational efficiency, cost reduction, and reduced risk. Big Data within an organization involves terabytes of data flowing into the organization both internally and externally as well as from other sources of data using technology resources.

The increase in numerous information-gathering sources, such as information-sensing mobile devices, computers, cloud devices, software logs, cameras, microphones, and wireless sensor networks has led to rapid growth in the size of these data sets. The "3Vs," namely, volume, variety, and velocity, became the basis for defining or describing Big Data in the past few years. These 3Vs are the key management challenges for any business organization. Big Data analytics is the analysis of large data sets that helps in finding new information that will be useful to the organization, for example, to be able to spot business trends, prevent diseases, combat crime, etc. People and organizations may regularly face difficulties with analyzing these large data sets in areas including finance and business informatics, Internet search, etc. It is not easy for relational database management systems, data warehouses, visualization software, and data marts to handle Big Data. Analyzing Big Data requires a lot of tools running on parallel systems, which help to aggregate, transform, and analyze the data to find the hidden patterns. Big Data diverges, depending on the capabilities and tools of the users, and expanding capabilities make Big Data a moving target.

1.4 Business Intelligence

Business intelligence (BI) covers a variety of tools and methods that can aid organizations in making effective decisions by analyzing "their" data. Thus, data analytics is a big part of BI. Of late, Big Data is also being used for the purpose of analytics, which falls under BI. Business intelligence and analytics (BI&A), in the context of Big Data, is increasingly being applied in critical and high impact application domains, such as e-commerce, market intelligence, e-government, health care, and security. Further, recent reports point out that advanced analytics for Big Data with BI marks a significant step in research, which has a great impact for organizations and facilitates increased return on investment (ROI). The increasing demand for CI applications in different fields entails a serious challenge for developing BI&A applications in order to deal with imprecision and uncertainty in information. Hence, there is a significant need for research and sharing of recent developments in BI and Big Data analytics in conjunction with CI approaches. The synergy between the four different streams of research shown in Figure 1.2 has the potential to deliver significant results as discussed in the following:

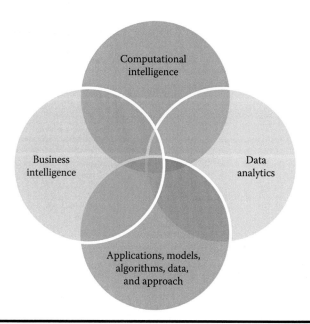

Figure 1.2 Research streams contributing to business intelligence and Big Data analytics.

a. BI&A covers a variety of techniques, technologies, systems, practices, methods, and applications that can explore business "data on store" to support an organization in understanding its business and making effective decisions toward market. However, Big Data, being part of analytics with research and support from CI, falls under BI as shown in Figure 1.2.
b. Exploration of business data with an emphasis on statistical and/or CI is referred to as business analytics (BA). BA utilizes the predictive power of CI approaches to explore data to find new patterns, create relationships, evaluate results, and test previous decisions. CI can greatly support this process and facilitate the predictive and descriptive analysis of outcomes.

The primary aim of this book is to help practitioners, researchers, designers, and developers understand the power of CI approaches and build appropriate BA systems that support computational models (fuzzy sets, artificial neural networks, and genetic algorithms) with different real-world case studies and applications.

1.5 Importance of Topic

CI approaches and optimization algorithms have paved the way for effective design, and implementation of business applications and successful integration of business disciplines. The CI paradigms applied to Big Data analytics and BI systems have been receiving much attention recently. In addition, hybridization of CI techniques, such as neurofuzzy approaches, artificial neural networks, evolutionary computation, swarm intelligence, and rough sets can be incorporated to handle uncertainty and subjectivity in the decision-making process. However, the fusion of CI approaches and optimization techniques has not been adequately investigated from the perspective of Big Data analytics and BI. Hence, there is an opportunity for implementing an enterprise-wide BI&A process to gain a competitive advantage and meet the business challenges in the marketplace by harnessing the power of CI.

This book attempts to explore the application of CI in various domains and answer the following questions:

1. Which types of learning and knowledge-based approaches can be adapted to support the various aspects of the BI&A process?
2. What are the general principles to be adopted when we attempt to employ a specific CI approach in implementing a business process?
3. What are the different types of state-of-the-art methods that are followed in business data analytics & CI?
4. How do we apply CI techniques for predictive analysis of venturing into new business models and improvement of data analytics in business applications?
5. What types of CI approaches would be beneficial for common business problems, such as forecasting next year's profit or turnover?

1.6 Need for a Book on the Proposed Topic

a. CI techniques are more suitable for handling uncertainty and the complexity of enterprise business processes compared with the traditional statistical approaches and tools presently being utilized.

b. Research in the field of CI and BA as part of design, analysis, and development modeling has gained rapid momentum among industry members, but a book with an in-depth coverage of all the functional components still remains to be published. Hence, this book and its topics may command a broad audience because of its practical value and variety of application domains.

c. Recently, CI approaches have been applied to a wide variety of complex problems, including engineering, science, and business. However, because of the complexity and uncertainty in these problems, it becomes difficult to find the optimal solution. Hence, there is a great need to explore in depth the various CI techniques in conjunction with data analytics to support BI and adaptive computational models for solving real-world problems.

d. The main objective is to explore novel contributions that bridge the gap between applying CI to BI, data analytics processes, and the overall business success of the organization.

e. The major outcome of this book, namely, hybridization of CI techniques and advances in the design of computational models, algorithms, and case studies, may help in proposing novel solutions to contemporary engineering problems.

1.7 Future Research Directions

From the analysis of open research problems related to CI in BI&A, several future research directions can be identified. Among them, we have highlighted a few in the following paragraphs.

Earlier researchers (Chen et al., 2012; Lim et al., 2013; Minelli et al., 2012) have classified BI&A activities into three broad research directions: (a) Big Data analytics, (b) text analytics, and (c) network analytics. Also, a number of studies (Anandarajan et al., 2012; Rouhani et al., 2012) have handled the BI&A complexity and uncertainty via various CI approaches (artificial neural networks, genetic algorithms, and fuzzy systems). Earlier studies (Gao et al., 2016; Sangaiah & Thangavelu, 2013, 2014; Sangaiah et al., 2015a,b,c) investigated the various CI approaches for organizational decision-making problems. However, there is a great need for constructing effective prediction and classification models for large business applications that don't rely on statistics. Also, a number of studies (Azar and Hassanien, 2015; Cheng et al., 2013; Jin and Hammer, 2014; Zhou et al., 2014) have identified the significance and research direction of CI in Big Data:

- Data size and feature space adaption
- Uncertainty modeling in learning from Big Data
- Distributed learning techniques in uncertain environments
- Feature selection or extraction in Big Data
- Sample selection based on uncertainty
- Uncertainty techniques in Big Data classification and clustering
- Active learning on Big Data
- Random weight network on Big Data

The research on the development and application of evolutionary computational algorithms and other metaheuristic approaches can provide effective solutions for optimization problems, specifically, dealing with incomplete or inconsistent information and limited computational capability. The future research directions for data-driven decision making (notion of Big Data) and optimization problems using CI are briefly mentioned here. Future CI-based applications would focus more on real-world problems that need a paradigm shift of paying attention to improving computational efficiency; understudying theoretical foundations and frameworks; and most essentially, supporting real decision making in complex, uncertain application contexts. Moreover, conventional data analysis approaches and computational models concentrating on small or large data and executing on a single processor are insufficient to handle data repositories of massive size. As a result, novel approaches and technologies are needed for analyzing and handling Big Data.

Many theories and methodologies have been created to deal with a variety of uncertainties as shown in Table 1.1. Further, quantified uncertainties would assist while constructing a high-performance learning system. At this point, focusing on learning from Big Data, one of the significant challenges is how to adapt CI approaches and paradigms for massive data. As a result, further research on CI application in business and Big Data analytics is needed in order to face these challenges and develop potential new applications that can deal with uncertainty in learning from Big Data.

Recently, hybrid metaheuristic systems have been becoming attractive because of their predictions and their decision capabilities in exploring and handling complex problem environments. Studies on hybrid systems are focusing on extending hybrid intelligent systems and the synthesis of computing tools, such as knowledge-based certainty theory, Bayesian, neural network, fuzzy logic, genetic algorithms, particle swarm optimization, etc. Consequently, there is evidence from recent studies (Bahrammirzaee et al., 2011; Lin et al., 2012; Tkáč & Verner, 2016; Yeh et al., 2010; Zhiqiang et al., 2013) that hybrid intelligent systems can play a significant role in many important practical applications in science, technology, BI systems, etc. Based on the above elucidation, it can be concluded that CI paradigms have a powerful ability to be applied effectively in BI and Big Data analytics.

Big Data could be the source of future data-driven, decision-making approaches. Big Data is a core research area, which has received more attention among researchers and companies around the globe. The appropriate management of a high volume of structured and unstructured data is the major challenge for future research. Decision makers could utilize CI paradigms for Big Data analytics, which can lead to effective and optimized solutions or decisions with respect to a specific application domain. The integration of CI approaches and models in handling Big Data will have major benefits to an organization. Future research should address novel approaches, theories, techniques, and tools that adopt the application of CI in BI&A. Some of these topics that need further exploration are the following:

■ Machine learning algorithms for Big Data analytics
■ Intelligent decision support systems for Big Data

Table 1.1 Underlying Principles of Evolutionary Computational Approaches

Methodologies	*Underlying Principle*
Fuzzy set theory	Imprecise or uncertain information
Probability theory	Randomness
Rough set theory	Approximation of concepts
Classification entropy	Impurity of a set
Conventional artificial intelligence (knowledge-based systems)	Generate patterns or rules from large data sets

- Classification and regression techniques for Big Data
- Supervised or unsupervised learning approaches over Big Data
- Learning or prediction methods for Big Data applications
- Handling real-time, distributed, large-scale data sets
- Evolutionary computing over Big Data
- Swarm intelligence and handling uncertainty in Big Data
- Applications of fuzzy set theory in Big Data

Recent trends in machine learning and evolutionary computational approaches focus on more complex problems that involve high dimensionality. Previously, machine learning techniques have been challenged by the inadequacy of data to infer predictive models or classification labels. In contrast, nowadays, there is a huge volume of data accumulating from various sources. Hence, we need to improve the computational capability of CI tools and techniques, particularly to be able to handle the large-scale problems with very high dimensions. Taking ideas from evolutionary computing that relate to BI and Big Data analytics and bringing them into computational models can help researchers in this field to develop novel approaches and establish new research avenues to pursue.

1.8 Organization of Book

This book is divided into four parts. The first part contains this introductory chapter by the book editors. The second part, titled "Computational Intelligence in Business Intelligence and Analytics," covers the fundamentals of CI approaches, metaheuristic approaches, and related research in Big Data analytics. "Data Analytics and Prediction Models" is the third part dedicated to the issues and tools related to data analytics of various applications and some methodologies and processes used during organizational decision making. It also covers several tools for data analytics, such as Hadoop, NoSQL, MongoDB, etc., for BI and its applications. The fourth and final part, "Applications of Computational Intelligence," highlights the use of CI paradigms in several applications and the employment of heuristic approaches and other data analysis technologies in various domains. Examples of real-life applications of data analytics in areas such as video surveillance, medical informatics, smart home environments, business process intelligence, and decision making are included. The following section is a brief summary of the salient aspects and contributions of each chapter.

1.8.1 Part I: Introduction

Part I contains this single introductory chapter. We briefly outline the significance of CI paradigms in BI, data analytics, and the state-of-the-art in the application of CI in various domains.

1.8.2 Part II: Computational Intelligence in Business Intelligence and Analytics

Part II contains four chapters. In Chapter 2, Jhuma Ray and Siddhartha Bhattacharyya illustrate the three different soft computing-based metaheuristic approaches to risk minimization with respect to portfolio optimization of an organization using particle swarm optimization (PSO), ant colony optimization (ACO), and differential evolution (DE) techniques centering on optimizing the conditional value at risk (CVaR) measure in different market conditions based on several objectives and constraints. In addition to comparative application of the proposed approach, the value-at-risk approach is demonstrated on a collection of several financial instruments. A distributional assumption for employing a particular type of financial assets for developing a much more generalized framework is reported in this chapter.

Chapter 3 by Zheng Xu et al. presents three aspects, including (a) the intelligent analysis of video surveillance systems, (b) the Big Data analysis of the video surveillance system, and (c) the application of the video surveillance system. The semantic-based model named video structural description (VSD) for representing and organizing the content in videos has been proposed. Moreover, visual information or content knowledge distilled by a VSD system can be shared conveniently in the mobile computing framework, so more general information mining and social trend forecasting could be further addressed.

In Chapter 4, Deepthi P.S. and Sabu Thampi give an overview of how structured and unstructured data in the form of electronic health records (EHRs), patient reports, clinical images, genomic data, etc., are managed and analyzed. In addition, the general architecture of Big Data in health care has been outlined. Consequently, with the increase in opportunities for Big Data analytics in health care, security and privacy concerns have also loomed. This chapter also discusses the state-of-the-art Big Data analytics and data mining in health informatics and the related privacy and security issues. Finally, this chapter provides an outline of health care and biological Big Data, conceptual architecture of Big Data analytics, and case studies that showcase the capabilities and applications of data mining in health informatics and issues such as threats to privacy and security.

In Chapter 5, William Rivera and Amit Goel address the computational challenges in group membership prediction of highly imbalanced Big Data sets. In addition, this chapter presents a formal definition of imbalance along with an understanding of what levels researchers should consider alternative approaches for when faced with large imbalanced data. The authors have proposed the parallel noise reduction a priori oversampling (PNRAP) method to combat these issues and highlight the performance of this technique compared with competing approaches. Consequently, using neural network classifiers, the PNRAP method has statistically significant improvement compared with popular oversampling methods SMOTE, local neighborhood SMOTE, borderline SMOTE, safe level SMOTE, safe level OUPS, and OUPS. Similar results were seen when using support vector machine classifiers, although in some cases it was not statistically significant over the SMOTE method.

1.8.3 Part III: Data Analytics and Prediction Models

Part III consists of four chapters. Chapter 6 by Goran Klepac et al. proposes a new paradigm in fraud detection modeling using predictive models. Moreover, the proposed approach integrates predictive models, fuzzy expert systems, social network analysis, and unstructured data, taking into account structured data from databases and data warehouses, social network data, and unstructured data from Internet resources within one solution. This chapter illustrates fraud detection on the basis of various case studies. Further, the presented case study results show the importance of the proposed methodology efficiency and integration of different analysis concepts based on traditional data sources and big data sources for successful fraud detection solutions.

Chapter 7 by R. Sasikala presents speedy data analytics through automatic balancing of Big Data in MongoDB sharded clusters. This chapter illustrates the NoSQL database, MongoDB, for three different sharding techniques: range-based sharding, hashed sharding, and tag-aware sharding techniques with case studies, implementation commands, and detailed result analysis. Moreover, the step-by-step practical implementation of sharding with different shard key algorithms gives great insight into Big Data research in a distributed environment. The results concluded that although identifying the sharding algorithm for specific application is difficult, tag-aware sharding and predicting the right tag for the database is a standard technique for any type of application. Further, this chapter assists the readers to extend this work on different data mining, data analytics, and machine learning algorithms on Big Data with distributed environments.

In Chapter 8, Ankur Dumka describes smart metering as a service using Hadoop aimed at analysis of past and present electricity use based on data received from smart meters and thus help for predicting the future analysis of electricity consumption and taking adequate steps for management of electricity. Hadoop can be used for determining real-time analysis of electricity consumption based on customer-based segmentation, area-based segmentation, usage-based segmentation, or purpose-based segmentation, all based on the type of parameter analysis that needs to be done. Thus, using a data analytics platform for the smart grid is capable of analyzing slowly and rapidly changing data using a combination of batch and real-time data processing techniques and is therefore useful in calculating data on a real-time basis on various parameters and can be used for efficient power management.

Chapter 9 by Muthu Ramachandran provides a systematic approach to service-oriented architecture (SOA) design strategies and business processes for Big Data analytics. The proposed approach is based on the SOA reference architecture and service component model for Big Data applications known as SoftBD. In addition, a large-scale, real-world case study demonstrating their approach to SOA for Big Data analytics is discussed. SOA Big Data architecture is scalable, generic, and customizable for a variety of data applications. The main contributions of this chapter include a unique, innovative, and generic softBD framework, a service component model, and a generic SOA architecture for large-scale Big Data applications. This chapter has also contributed to Big Data metrics, which allows measuring and evaluating when analyzing the data.

1.8.4 Part IV: Applications of Computational Intelligence

Part IV contains four chapters. Chapter 10 by B. K. Tripathy discusses rough sets and neighborhood systems on knowledge acquisition from Big Data analysis on the basis of two approaches. The first one uses the basic rough sets, and the other one uses neighborhood rough sets for the purpose. Moreover, the concept of neighborhood covering reduction has led to a decrease in processing time as the number of rules has come down, which becomes quite significant especially in a big data set. However, this reduction in the number of rules generated comes at the cost of accuracy and coverage computed.

In Chapter 11, Deepthi Hudedagaddi and B. K. Tripathy discuss some of the fuzzy techniques of clustering in Big Data. Clustering is a technique to handle a massive amount of data. Using fuzzy clustering algorithms makes the data analysis more realistic. The authors address the future research directions of several uncertainty-based clustering algorithms, such as IFCM, rough C-means, and hybrid family of these clustering algorithms to be implemented on Big Data.

Chapter 12 by M. Sivarathinabala et al. presents the learning models with respect to human behavior analysis for large-scale surveillance videos. The objective of this chapter is to recognize human behavior analysis (HBA) in the context of Big Data. HBA plays a major role in the video surveillance system. The aim of human activity recognition is to automatically analyze the ongoing activity from an unknown video. In this chapter, the problem with respect to the learning method in large data sets from big video data is discussed. Mainly, this chapter focuses on different learning approaches that can handle big video data synchronously.

In Chapter 13, Anass El Haddadi et al. explore a new analytical model of big unstructured data for the competitive intelligence system. Moreover, this chapter provides a study on the state-of-the-art methods concerning mining unstructured data and large graph visualization. In addition, this chapter also introduces a case study representing the performance of XEW. In this case study, we present the ability of XEW to extract up-to-date data from the Bio-Space online database, analyze its contents, and then display the current strategic alliances between biotechnology companies as a 3-D graph.

References

Anandarajan, M., Anandarajan, A., & Srinivasan, C. A. (Eds.). (2012). *Business intelligence techniques: A perspective from accounting and finance.* Springer Science & Business Media, New York.

Azar, A. T., & Hassanien, A. E. (2015). Dimensionality reduction of medical big data using neural-fuzzy classifier. *Soft Computing, 19*(4), 1115–1127.

Bahrammirzaee, A., Ghatari, A. R., Ahmadi, P., & Madani, K. (2011). Hybrid credit ranking intelligent system using expert system and artificial neural networks. *Applied Intelligence, 34*(1), 28–46.

Chen, H., Chiang, R. H., & Storey, V. C. (2012). Business intelligence and analytics: From big data to big impact. *MIS Quarterly, 36*(4), 1165–1188.

Cheng, S., Shi, Y., Qin, Q., & Bai, R. (2013, October). Swarm intelligence in big data analytics. In International Conference on Intelligent Data Engineering and Automated Learning (pp. 417–426). Springer, Berlin Heidelberg.

Gao, X. Z., Sangaiah, A. K., & Ramachandran, M. (2016). Soft computational approaches for prediction and estimation of software development. *The Scientific World Journal, 2016*, 3905931, http://dx.doi .org/10.1155/2016/3905931.

Jin, Y., & Hammer, B. (2014). Computational intelligence in big data. *IEEE Computational Intelligence Magazine, 9*(3), 12–13.

Lim, E. P., Chen, H., & Chen, G. (2013). Business intelligence and analytics: Research directions. *ACM Transactions on Management Information Systems (TMIS), 3*(4), 17.

Lin, W. Y., Hu, Y. H., & Tsai, C. F. (2012). Machine learning in financial crisis prediction: A survey. *IEEE Transactions on Systems, Man, and Cybernetics, Part C (Applications and Reviews), 42*(4), 421–436.

Minelli, M., Chambers, M., & Dhiraj, A. (2012). *Big data, big analytics: Emerging business intelligence and analytic trends for today's businesses.* John Wiley & Sons, New York.

Rouhani, S., Ghazanfari, M., & Jafari, M. (2012). Evaluation model of business intelligence for enterprise systems using fuzzy TOPSIS. *Expert Systems with Applications, 39*(3), 3764–3771.

Sangaiah, A., & Thangavelu, A. (2013). An exploration of FMCDM approach for evaluating the outcome/ success of GSD projects. *Open Engineering, 3*(3), 419–435.

Sangaiah, A. K., & Thangavelu, A. K. (2014). An adaptive neuro-fuzzy approach to evaluation of team-level service climate in GSD projects. *Neural Computing and Applications, 25*(3–4), 573–583.

Sangaiah, A. K., Gao, X. Z., Ramachandran, M., & Zheng, X. (2015a). A fuzzy DEMATEL approach based on intuitionistic fuzzy information for evaluating knowledge transfer effectiveness in GSD projects. *International Journal of Innovative Computing and Applications, 6*(3–4), 203–215.

Sangaiah, A. K., Subramaniam, P. R., & Zheng, X. (2015b). A combined fuzzy DEMATEL and fuzzy TOPSIS approach for evaluating GSD project outcome factors. *Neural Computing and Applications, 26*(5), 1025–1040.

Sangaiah, A. K., Thangavelu, A. K., Gao, X. Z., Anbazhagan, N., & Durai, M. S. (2015c). An ANFIS approach for evaluation of team-level service climate in GSD projects using Taguchi-genetic learning algorithm. *Applied Soft Computing, 30*, 628–635.

Tkáč, M., & Verner, R. (2016). Artificial neural networks in business: Two decades of research. *Applied Soft Computing, 38*, 788–804.

Yeh, C. C., Chi, D. J., & Hsu, M. F. (2010). A hybrid approach of DEA, rough set and support vector machines for business failure prediction. *Expert Systems with Applications, 37*(2), 1535–1541.

Zhiqiang, G., Huaiqing, W., & Quan, L. (2013). Financial time series forecasting using LPP and SVM optimized by PSO. *Soft Computing, 17*(5), 805–818.

Zhou, Z. H., Chawla, N. V., Jin, Y., & Williams, G. J. (2014). Big data opportunities and challenges: Discussions from data analytics perspectives. *IEEE Computational Intelligence Magazine, 9*(4), 62–74.

COMPUTATIONAL INTELLIGENCE IN BUSINESS INTELLIGENCE AND ANALYTICS

II

Chapter 2

Conditional Value at Risk-Based Portfolio Optimization Using Metaheuristic Approaches

Jhuma Ray[1] and Siddhartha Bhattacharyya[2]

[1]Department of Engineering Science and Management,
RCC Institute of Information Technology, Kolkata, India

[2]RCC Institute of Information Technology, Kolkata, India

Contents

Abstract

Of late, the field of portfolio optimization (the process of selecting the proportions of diverse assets existing within a portfolio and building the portfolio to be the best in relation to some criterion) in the modern capital market has assumed paramount importance as a field in business intelligence thanks to the evolution of the multiobjective optimization of the market risk–return paradigm. The downside risk can be ascertained with a very common method within a portfolio known as value at risk (VaR), which, in turn, can be explicated as the pth percentile of return of a defined portfolio during the termination of the planning skyline. The conditional value at risk (CVaR) is a more robust expedient for determining the defined unit of risk of a portfolio in volatile market conditions. The soft computing paradigm is efficient in handling real-life uncertainties. It entails several tools and techniques, namely, neural networks, the concept of fuzzy logic, and evolutionary computation measures. Applications of three different soft computing-based metaheuristic approaches to risk minimization leading to portfolio optimization using particle swarm optimization (PSO), ant colony optimization (ACO), and differential evolution (DE) techniques centering on optimizing the CVaR measure under different market conditions based on several objectives and constraints are reported in this chapter. The proposed approaches are proven to be reliable on a collection of several financial instruments as compared to their VaR counterparts. The results obtained show encouraging avenues in determining optimal portfolio returns.

2.1 Introduction

With the existence of excitability (volatility) in the present day's real work-a-day world financial transactions, an impartial balance between risks and returns has to be controlled by any investor to deduce a conclusion at the best standpoint (Brown, 2004; McNeil et al., 2005). In spite of the current excitability, the advantage lies in the correlation of the combination of financial instruments or assets in a financial portfolio under specific market conditions. Lately, portfolio management has been employed because of the requirement to reach a resolution in investment opportunities in a sequence of events involving high risk, thus showing that current scenario risks and returns are inevitably interlinked, culminating in significance in the decision-making system in the investment opportunities accordingly. The risk–reward trade-off in distribution of investments requires a wide variety of assets, in turn, maximizing returns or minimizing risks within a given investment period. According to Markowitz (1952), an asset should not be chosen by counting its features only, but also by considering its comovement with other assets. Estimation of risk as a standard deviation of returns by Markowitz along with its diversification into different investment factors was done, which, in turn, have limited or negative correlations in terms of their movements with a reduction in the overall risk structure. This can be measured by a correlation coefficient varying between +1 and –1 according to Markowitz.

Several models for portfolio selection have been promoted over the years, which comprise the early mean variance models in addition to Markowitz's (1952) work. Once again, moderation of stochastic optimization methods based on the market scenario has counterfeited the significance (Bhattacharya et al., 2010; Ray & Bhattacharyya, 2015). It doesn't matter to which model one resorts; the underlying principle or notion lies in the denigration of some measures of market risks coupled with focusing on increasing the portfolio return. It has been claimed that the risk metric is simulated to be a performance of the likely portfolio returns in almost every model.

The most extensively used method for gauging downside risk (financial risk correlated to losses, which is the risk of the actual return being under the expected return or else considered to be the uncertainty of the extent of that very difference) in a portfolio is the value at risk (VaR), which is labeled as the pth percentile of portfolio return at the edge of the planning perspective. Incidentally, for low values of p (as low as 1, 5, or 10), it analyzes the "unconditional" fallout of portfolio returns. VaR is said to be (a) a terminology for risk, (b) giving space to efficient and coherent risk management, (c) administering an enterprise-wide approach for market regulation, and (d) delegated for risk evaluation.

On account of the existing literature concerning the diverse approaches for the computation or estimation of a portfolio's VaR, one of the appealing perspectives of VaR derivation is to determine how it can be practiced for appropriation of portfolios in a multifinancial instruments situation. Based on VaR, if business organizations are to accomplish their various financial transactions, then it is a vital issue in designing the plan of action for proper investment selection. Furthermore, if organizations make decisions in a VaR context, then the implications of the organization's risks are to be taken into account. Because VaR is rather discrete in nature and is strenuous to assimilate in conventional stochastic models, very few efforts have been outlined in the literature as regards the optimization attempts. Rockafellar and Uryasev (2002) suggest looking into a scenario-based model for portfolio optimization. They have adopted the conditional value at risk (CVaR) for this purpose. CVaR serves as an example of the anticipated value of losses outstripping VaR. Their model lessens CVaR in the course of scheming VaR. It was observed that the minimum CVaR is tantamount to the minimum VaR in the case of normally distributed portfolio returns.

Thus, for weighing the financial worth of an asset or of a portfolio of assets in a specified market structure, declining over a specific time period (usually considered to be more than one day or 10 days) subservient to typical market situations, VaR (Jorion, 2001; Holton, 2003; Dowd, 2005) is shown to be an impressive mechanism. This, in turn, is also exceptionally valued for being assimilated within industry regulations (Jorion, 2001) regardless of the fact that it suffers from instability as well as the problem of working with numerical values in the case of normal distribution of losses because loss distribution often tends to display "fat tails" (a statistical phenomenon showcasing large leptokurtosis, representing a higher probability of the ultimate occurring identically to the financial crisis) or factual discreteness.

VaR (Jorion, 2001) at a confidence level is thus treated as the maximum loss not surpassing a given probability over a stipulated time period. VaR is regularly determined by the framework of the three parameters, which include (a) the time horizon (typically 1 day, 10 days, or 1 year), which is determined by the time period over which any organization should hold its portfolio or the time period needed for liquidating its assets; (b) the confidence level (common values are 99% and 95%), which is the evaluation of the interval in which the VaR would not likely exceed the unit of VaR in currency; and (c) the maximum probable loss structure.

In contrast to VaR, CVaR is positioned to be a risk-weighing approach in cases in which risk involves cogent advantages for the derivation of loss distribution in financial structures involving discreteness (Rockafellar & Uryasev, 2002). Due to the commonness of different structures that have been proposed, which are found in varied scenarios and finite sampling, the applications of such distributions, in turn, have become an important property in the financial markets.

CVaR can be defined as the weighted average of VaR along with CVaR⁺ (the values themselves are contingent on the decision along with the weights), with which no value of VaR and CVaR⁺ stands to be coherent. The specific technique of estimating CVaR in terms of probability of VaR brings out the value of weights in the existence of the other.

Computational advantages of CVaR over VaR have become the major impetus in the CVaR methodology development procedure in spite of substantial efforts toward finding the efficient algorithms for the process of optimization of VaR in high-dimensional environments, which are still unavailable. CVaR stands to be a new coherent risk-measuring structure having distinct advantages when compared with VaR (Rockafellar & Uryasev, 2002), quantifying risks beyond VaR, consistent at different levels of confidence α (smooth with respect to α), and also being a static statistical estimate with integral characteristics. CVaR has thus been entrenched as an excellent tool in the risk management procedure and optimization of portfolios accompanied by linear programming, which has huge dimensions in the company of substantial numerical implementations. At various time periods with different levels of confidence, distributions are also shaped for multiple risk constraints along with the previously mentioned tasks, which, in turn, stand as fast algorithms for online usage. Rockafellar and Uryasev (2002) have considered CVaR methodology to be a consistent one, having a mean variance method taken to be under the minimal portfolio (with return constraint), which can also be considered to be a variance minimal in case of normal loss distribution.

2.2 Contribution

In this chapter, algorithms exercising particle swarm optimization (PSO), ant colony optimization (ACO), and differential evolution (DE) have been used for evolving optimized portfolio asset allocations in a volatile market condition. The proposed approach is centered on optimizing the CVaR (Rockafellar & Uryasev, 2002) measure in different market conditions based on several objectives and constraints. Other than achieving the general definition of CVaR and its associated minimization formulas, the authors have concentrated here on dealing with fully discrete distributions, enhancing the usefulness and properties of CVaR in the case of furnishing the elementary way of calculating CVaR directly. The results are compared with those obtained with the optimization of the VaR measure of the portfolios under consideration. A comparative application of the proposed approach along with the VaR approach is demonstrated on a collection of several financial instruments, enabling a distributional assumption for employing the particular type of financial assets for developing a much more generalized framework.

2.3 Motivation

A novel approach by the authors for the accomplishment of an optimized solution to the portfolio asset allocation problem is presented, centering the optimization of the CVaR measures of a portfolio being composed of numerous financial instruments within various market situations, which, in turn, are established on several objectives and constraints. The results are, in turn, set side by side with those obtained with the optimization of the VaR measure of the portfolios under consideration. Application of PSO, ACO, and DE for CVaR optimization is embellished, relating to the minimization of the risks convoluted in the portfolios under consideration, thereby minimizing the portfolio losses incurred. Although PSO, ACO, and DE provide superior performance, there are some drawbacks, such as dropping into regional optimum, that need to be rectified. We intended to find out the structure of the algorithm against different functions, comparing the determined values in accordance with them.

2.4 Background

Contemporary management methods have been broadly committed to the management of portfolio asset allocations in disparate spheres of operations. Financial portfolios, information technology portfolios, human resource allocations, and acceptance and investment strategy management are included among the common examples. Analysis of a financial portfolio associates a comprehensive treatment of the interrelation between time, money, risk, and return. This can often be characterized in terms of the correlation between the compatible assets existing within a specific market condition. Thus, preferring an appropriate portfolio is therefore contingent with respect to the risk–reward trade-off (the trade-off experienced by an investor between risk and return considering investment decisions in turn) in the distribution of investments to a divergent group of assets. The aim of such a selection procedure through management of the underlying assets is to maximize the returns of investment or to minimize the risks in a stipulated time period. Numerous efforts have been devoted to accomplishing one of the aforementioned goals in a volatile market condition (Markowitz, 1952; Zenios, 1996; Boyle et al., 1997; Crouhy et al., 2001).

2.5 Related Literature

Jacobs et al. (2005) describe some actual short sale arrangements, which vary from time to time. The usage of a general mean variance problem and solution to the general problem is stated along with critical line algorithm tracing out a linear set of efficient portfolios subject to any finite system of linear equality or inequality constraints meant for any covariance matrix and expected return vector.

Within his work, Filho (2006) provides an investor with a portfolio that is optimal for the worst case scenario and guarantees performance improvement if there are no worst cases. It also protects the investor from errors that arise from uncertainties in the expected return values for assets. There is the usage of a mean variance approach. VaR is depicted by the parametric method, historical simulation method, and Monte Carlo method. Coherent risk measures along with the genetic algorithm (GA) are also applied.

Lim et al. (2011) use the mean variance optimization along with mean CVaR optimization, and the coherent measures of risk are reported within the literature.

Krokhmal et al. (2001) extend the approach to the optimization problems with CVaR constraints with which maximization of the expected returns is done under CVaR. Multiple CVaR constraints with various levels of confidence are utilized for shaping the distribution of profit and loss. Any of the optimization formulations can be used for the purpose. The work is able to handle instruments and scenarios large in number, which can be used in applications under various conditions for binding the percentiles of loss distribution.

Deng et al. (2011) depict the problems of VaR taken under consideration while being applied. A covariance matrix with the GARCH model is also calculated. The modified version of the memetic algorithm is then applied in order to deal with the computational problems. This results in a much better approximation of the conditional volatility structure rather than a simple historical estimate. The mean CVaR model, pair Copuk-GARCH-EVT model, is used along with a pair

Table 2.1 Literature Surveyed

Sl. No.	Works Done	Authors	Source
1	Portfolio optimization with factor, scenarios and realistic short positions	Bruce I. Jacobs, Kenneth N. Levy, & Harry M. Markowitz	*Operations Research*, Vol. 53, No. 4, pp. 586–599, 2005
2	Portfolio optimization with conditional value at risk objective and constraints	Parlo Krokhmal, Jonas Palquist, & Stanislav Uryasev	*Journal of Risk*, Vol. 4, No. 2, pp. 43–68, 2001
3	Portfolio optimization via pair Copula-GARCH-EVT-CVaR model	Ling Deng, Chaoqun Ma, & Wenyu Yang	*Systems Engineering Procedia*, 2011
4	Conditional value at risk in portfolio optimization: coherent but fragile	Andrew E. B. Lim, J. George, Shanthi Kumar, & Gah-Yi Vahn	*Journal of Operations Research*, Vol. 39, No. 3, pp. 163–171, 2011
5	Portfolio management using value at risk: a comparison between genetic algorithms and particle swarm optimization	Valdemar Antonio Dallagnol Filho	Master Thesis, *Informatics & Economics*, July, 2006
6	Portfolio optimization under VaR constraints based on dynamic estimates of the variance–covariance matrix	Katja Specht, & Peter Winker	*Computational Method in Financial Engineering*, 2008
7	Risk measures and portfolio optimization	Priscilla Serwaa Nkyira Gambrah, & Traian Adrian Pirvu	*Journal of Risk and Financial Management*, Vol. 7, No. 3, pp. 113–129, 2014
8	Ant colony optimization approach to portfolio optimization—A lingo companion	Kambiz Forqandoost Haqiqi, & Tohid Kazemi	*International Journal of Trade, Economics and Finance*, Vol. 3, No. 2, pp. 148–153, 2012

copula decomposition of multivariate distribution and parameter estimation. However, adjusting the portfolio to the dynamic approximation of a conditional volatility structure also results in some overconfidence with regards to risk constraints.

Specht and Winker (2008) show VaR-based estimates of the conditional covariance matrix along with the "principal components GARCH model." The recent advances in heuristic optimization, which, in turn, is a modified version of the memetic algorithm, are also applied. The article also depicts the PC GARCH model. All the related works are listed in Table 2.1.

Haqiqi and Kazemi (2012) use the ACO approach to portfolio optimization, which we have also used in our study along with the DE and PSO approaches.

Gambrah and Pirvu (2014), in their research work, have shown portfolio optimization under VaR, average VaR, and limited expected loss constraints during a continuous time framework, in which stocks follow a geometric Brownian motion. The analytic expression for VaR along with the derivation of average VaR and limited expected loss is also done.

2.5.1 Objectives

This chapter is devoted to an understanding of the concepts and practices of the applications of three different soft computing-based metaheuristic approaches to risk minimization leading to portfolio optimization using PSO, ACO, and DE techniques centering on optimizing the CVaR measure in different market conditions based on several objectives and constraints. The application perspectives of these algorithms are also discussed with reference to a case study on portfolio optimization as it applies to the emerging field of industrial informatics (knowledge-based factory mechanization for enhancing industrial fabrication).

2.6 Metaheuristics: Concepts and Principles

Metaheuristic approaches are considered to be a higher level of operation or heuristic constructed to create, develop, or elicit a heuristic (a partial search algorithm), which may present an adequately satisfactory answer to an optimization issue, chiefly with inadequate or flawed data or restricted computing scope in the field of computer science and mathematical optimization (Bianchi et al., 2009). Metaheuristics pattern a definite number of results enormously huge in nature to be entirely fragmented or patterned. Metaheuristics may create hardly any hypothesis about the optimization problem being resolved, and so they may be subject to an array of complications (Blum & Roli, 2003).

Metaheuristics do not ensure that a universally optimal justification is constructed on a few categories of issues if compared to optimization algorithms and iterative methods (Blum & Roli, 2003). Abundant metaheuristics enforce the shaping of stochastic optimization in order to find the answer, which, in turn, is contingent on the spawned set of random variables (Bianchi et al., 2009). Metaheuristics are often helpful in finding good solutions with less computational effort than optimization algorithms, iterative methods, or simple heuristics by probing a huge set of feasible solutions proving to be beneficial for optimization problems (Bianchi et al., 2009). Most of the research work on metaheuristics remains unproved in terms of its attributes, along with breakthroughs except for a few explicit philosophical outcomes, which are ready to use and often result in finding the global optimum (Blum & Roli, 2003). For developing a local search heuristic, many metaheuristic ideas are projected in order to achieve excellent results. Such metaheuristics include simulated annealing (SA), tabu search (TS), iterated local search (ILS), variable neighborhood search (VNS), and GRASP (Blum & Roli, 2003). These metaheuristics are not at all restricted to local search bases or global search metaheuristics but are considered to be both at the same time. Within the other global search metaheuristics, those are not at all barred from the local search base and are usually population-based metaheuristics, which incorporate ACO, evolutionary computation (EC), PSO, DE, and genetic algorithms (GAs) (Blum & Roli, 2003).

Single solution approaches aim attention at altering and reconstructing a single candidate solution as has already been stated in SA, ILS, VNS, and guided local search (Talbi, 2009). Population-based avenues help in controlling and improving multiple candidate solutions, generally with the usage of population characteristics mentoring the search, in turn, as previously mentioned in EC, GAs, and PSO (Talbi, 2009). Swarm intelligence is that very class of metaheuristics that is based on a unified attitude of a dispersed, self-confessed operator within a population or swarm. ACO (Dorigo, 1992), PSO (Talbi, 2009), social cognitive optimization, penguins search optimization algorithm (PeSOA), and artificial bee colony (Karaboga, 2010) algorithms are set as examples of this class of optimization theories. DE algorithms are used quite often as metaheuristics for optimization globally along with limited analysis based on the generation of their initial population, which stands to be an important factor because of their influence on the search for various iterations, and it generally has an impact on the ultimate result. The initial population gets randomly selected in the case of no prior information about the optima, and is ready to use with the help of pseudorandom numbers.

Real-time financial transactions include the correlation between the perception of the ideas of time, money, and risk. This interrelation in terms of the correlation between the assets existing within a specific market situation can be described by a financial portfolio. According to Markowitz (1952), an investor needs to consider the comovement of one asset with all other assets at hand without choosing the assets only by their characteristic features. Risk was quantified by Markowitz and was also defined as the standard deviation of returns, showing how diversification occurs in the field of investments having limited or no positive correlation in their movements reducing overall risk. In the view of Markowitz, risk is thus measured by a correlation coefficient varying between +1 and –1. As stated by him, two investments with a correlation of +1 thus will move in lockstep with one another, and at the same time, those having a correlation of –1 will move in exactly the opposite direction. Because of the correlation coefficient that is used for estimating the variance of a portfolio, any coefficient less than +1 will ultimately lessen the overall variance of that portfolio.

According to Elton and Gruber (1997), an investor can create a portfolio showing a lesser risk structure by considering the above comovements rather than a portfolio constructed without paying any heed to the interaction between securities at the same expected yield or return. This model was modified by Black et al. (1972) for allowing the short selling of assets or negative weights of assets for constituting a closed-form resolution to the problem.

Measuring the value of an asset in the market or the value of a portfolio of assets can be done by calculating VaR (Jorion, 2001; Holton, 2003; Dowd, 2005), which is likely to decrease over a certain period of time (usually over 1 or 10 days) under typical market conditions. VaR is used by banks, broker dealers, and investment banks for calculating the market risk for their proprietary owned assets. Depending on the various market conditions, class of assets, factual accomplishment of the assets, volatility or standard deviation obtained by downside risk, and expected shortfall, the value of VaR varies widely. In the field of risk management, the VaR approach aims to fortify, in a rational manner, at the organization or entity level, the risks connoted in a portfolio of various classes of financial instruments. The outcome is articulated as the VaR, which is obtained in terms of the maximum expected loss, the confidence interval of the loss, and the number of days in the risk period.

2.6.1 *Particle Swarm Optimization*

One among the two well-known swarm-encouraged approaches in the computational intelligence field is PSO, which has been popularized as a simulation of a simplified social system. The initial motivation was to graphically simulate the choreography of a flock of birds or a school of fish. Yet it was identified that the particle swarm model could be used as an optimizer. PSO (Eberhart & Kennedy, 1995) is a population-based stochastic optimization approach that encounters a multitude of affinities when related to the ways of evolutionary computation, such as GAs. The system is booted up with a population of random solutions and seeks out optima along with the updating of generations with no evolution operators, such as crossover and mutation. In PSO, the potential solutions are known as particles, which usually fly through the problem space by following the current optimum particles.

Thus, PSO is a biologically exhilarated evolutionary computing pattern, which is a population-based stochastic optimization procedure stimulated by the sociocognitive behavior of birds in a flock or fish in a school (Holland, 1975; Glover, 1977; Yang, 2011) with an intention to graphically simulate the choreography of a flock of birds or school of fish starting with random solutions and searching for the most favorable by repeating through generations. However, in contradiction to other evolutionary findings, PSO is not able to apply any evolution operators, such as crossover and mutation, through which possible elucidations known as particles fly over the disputed space pursuing the prevailing optimum particles.

All along the process, each and every particle carries a record of its match correlated by the outstanding solution (fitness) that has been accomplished hitherto in the problem area. The reserved fitness worth attributes to the p best. Additional "best" values obtained hitherto by any particle within the surrounding community of the particle are also traced with the help of the PSO. Such condition is indicated as the l best (Yang, 2011). Although a particle assimilates the whole population as its topological neighbors, the supreme value is a global best and is termed as the g best. The regional interpretation of PSO constitutes, at every time step, developing the impetus of (accelerating) every particle toward its p best and l best locations. Acceleration is rated by a random term along different random numbers being produced for furtherance against p best and l best locations (Yang, 2011).

The efficiency of every particle in a PSO is ascertained by its closeness arising out of the global optimum. The cadent is usually utilized for the previously stated intention, which is the readiness role of the optimization issue. Each particle within the swarm retains the present position of the particle along with the present velocity of the particle and the personal best situation of the particle.

PSO has a favorable application in numerous application fields because of its competence in procuring improved outcomes in a quicker and more reasonable manner if compared with other methods.

2.6.2 *Procedure*

PSO simulates the behavior of a flock of birds, where it is presumed that a group of birds are randomly searching for food within an area having only a single piece of food. The birds are unaware of the presence of the food in that particular area. But they are aware of how far the food is in each iteration. Now the question arises for finding the best strategy to find the food, and the best answer would be to follow the bird that is nearest to the food. PSO studied these sequences of events and utilized them to solve the optimization problem. In PSO, each single solution is a "bird" within the search space, and is called a "particle." Each of these particles has fitness values, which are estimated by the fitness function, which is optimized, having velocities that, in turn, supervise the flying of the particles. By following the current optimum particles, the particles fly through the problem space. PSO is initialized along with a group of random particles (solutions) and then afterward starts searching the optima by updating generations. In each and every iteration, each particle is updated by following the two "best" values.

PSO Pseudocode

Step 1: For every particle
    Initialize particle
END
Do
Step 2: For every particle
    Calculate fitness value
    Whenever the fitness value is found to be superior to the best fitness value (*p best*) in history,
    then the new *p best* has to be set for the current value.
End
Choose the particle with the best fitness value of all the particles as the *g best*
Step 3: For each particle
    Compute particle velocity as stated in the equation (a)
    Reconditioning particle position in conformity to equation (b)
End
Although maximum iterations or minimum error criteria are not attained.

The first value is the best solution (fitness) that has been achieved so far. (The fitness value is also stored.) This value is known as *p* best. The other "best" value that is traced with the help of the PSO is the best value, which is acquired hitherto by any particle in the population. This supreme value is a global best and is known as *g* best. When a particle becomes the component of the population as its topological neighbors, the best value is a local best and is known as *l* best.

After calculating the two best values, the particle updates its velocity and positions with the help of the following equations (a) and (b).

$$v() = v() + c_1 \times \text{rand}() \times (p \text{ best}() - \text{present}()) + c_2 \times \text{rand}() \times (g \text{ best}() - \text{present}()) \qquad \text{(a)}$$

$$\text{present}() = \text{present}() + v() \qquad \text{(b)}$$

where $v()$ stands for the particle velocity, present() stands for the current particle (solution), p best() and g best() are defined in a similar way as stated earlier, rand() is a random number between (0, 1), and c_1, c_2 are learning factors. Usually, $c_1 = c_2 = 2$.

The pseudocode of the PSO procedure is shown in Figure 2.1.

The velocities of particles in each dimension are fastened to a maximum velocity V_{max}. If the sum of accelerations would induce the velocity on that aspect to surpass V_{max}, which is identified as a parameter specified by the user, then the velocity on that aspect is restricted to V_{max}.

2.6.3 PSO Algorithm

In PSO, the swarm is composed of a set of particles $P = p_1, p_2, \ldots p_k$, and an objective function f is represented by a candidate solution of the optimization problem at hand. This is referred to as the situation of a particle in which at a time period t, p_i has a position $\bar{x}_i^t$ and a velocity $\bar{v}_i^t$ correlated to it. The personal best position particle p_i (concerning f) has visited anytime until time step t is characterized by vector $\bar{b}_i^t$. In addition, p_i has been received with the instruction from its surroundings $N_i \subseteq P$. Within the standard PSO algorithm, the topology of the population of the swarm is thus stated with the help of a graph $G = \{V, E\}$, in which every vertex in V is a complement to a particle within the swarm, and every edge in E points out a connection between a set of particles.

An initialization area within the PSO process, $\theta' \subset \theta$, is selected for generation of the random situations for the particles. Velocities normally get initialized within θ'. Still velocities can also be initialized to zero or to small random values to prevent the particles, in turn, from escaping from the search area during the phases of initial iterations.

Within the process, the acceleration and situations of the particles get updated iteratively up until and unless a stopping criterion is obtained (Holland, 1975).

The updating regulations are

$$\bar{v}_i^{t+1} = w\bar{v}_i^t + \emptyset_1 \bar{U}_i^t \left(\bar{b}_i^t - \bar{x}_i^t \right) + \emptyset_2 \bar{U}_2^t \left(l_i^t - \bar{x}_i^t \right) \tag{2.1}$$

along with

$$\bar{x}_i^{t+1} = \bar{x}_i^t + \bar{v}_i^{t+1} \tag{2.2}$$

where w stands for the parameter known as the inertia weight, ϕ_1 and ϕ_2 stand for the other two parameters known as the acceleration coefficients, and $\bar{U}_i^t$ and $\bar{U}_2^t$ are two $n \times n$ diagonal matrices in which the entries in the main diagonal are random numbers that, in turn, get evenly dispersed in the interval $(0, 1)$. The stated matrices get reestablished during every iteration. The vector l_i^t is stated as the surrounding best and is the best situation ever established by any particle within the surrounding of particle p_i, that is, $f(\bar{l}_i^t) = f(\bar{b}_j^t) \, \forall p_j \in N_i$.

For values that are chosen properly for w, ϕ_1, and ϕ_2, the particles' velocities do not evolve any infinite situation (Glover, 1986). Within the l best (Yang, 2011) miniature, a swarm gets split into coinciding surroundings of particles, and the most excellent particle is indicated as the surrounding's best particle. Various neighborhood configurations can exist (Robbins & Monro, 1951) in PSO relying on particle indices or topological composition. The g best thus is an exceptional situation of l best with $l = s$, where s is denoted as the swarm size. The l best accesses a greater diversity even if it is in a more reluctant manner than the g best avenue.

The velocity update rule is affected by the local behaviors in the three terms of the particles. The first term is stated as the inertia or momentum (Barricelli, 1954) term, serving as memories of the earlier direction for flying and, in turn, preventing the particle alternating the way in the immediate. The next term is known as the cognitive component term, which portrays the aspiration of the particles returning back to their formerly found best positions. The third term, known as the social component (Rastrigin, 1963; Matyas, 1965) term, helps in quantifying the accomplishment of a particle corresponding to its neighbors, thereby depicting an approved level that should be procured.

Through observations, it has been found that, in some circumstances, particles get captivated to regions outside the feasible search space θ. Nelder and Mead (1965) devised mechanisms for the preservation of the solution feasibility and proper swarm operations in this context. One of the enticing systems for conserving practicability is the one in which the particles going outside θ are barred from improving their personal finest situation. In such situations, they are drawn back to the achievable space in consequent iterations.

2.6.4 Advantages and Disadvantages

A PSO is believed to be a robust technique for determining the nonsmooth global optimization problem and is considered to be a derivative-free approach like different heuristic optimization techniques. It is an easier concept and also has easier coding application in comparison to other heuristic optimization approaches. Being less nature-sensitive and having a restricted number of specifications, the effect of specifications to the solution is supposed to be less sensitive in comparison to other heuristic algorithms (Eberhart & Shi, 1998). The PSO technique is able to create high-quality results within a short period of calculation and is considered to be a more substantial concurrence attribute than other stochastic approaches (Gaing, 2003). Like the other heuristic optimization approaches, the greatest drawback of PSO is that it lacks a rather solid mathematical foundation along with other limitations for real-life applications. Also, the PSO-based approach is believed to have a lesser negative impact on the solutions than other heuristic-based approaches. Moreover, issues lie within the dependency on the initial point and limitations, and complication in analyzing the optimal design limitations along with the stochastic features of the ultimate results.

2.7 Ant Colony Optimization

ACO algorithms (Dorigo & Stützle, 2004; Camp et al., 2005) are typically used in solving minimum cost problems usually in situations involving numerous nodes (considered to be N) and some undirected arcs (considered to be A many). The sole target behind this lies in establishing a minimum cost path from the source (i.e., the nest of the ant) to the destination (the food source of the ant).

The ants within the process of building a solution have the possibility of generating loops along with pheromone updating; these loops tend to become more attractive. Because of the problems created with forward updating, it appears to give the impression that the algorithm should be limited to only backward updating, but the algorithm is to remain inactive in this case. In fact, the artificial ants must retain properties of real ants, which will help them to solve the minimum cost problem. They are provided with a limited form of memory, with which they are able to store the partial paths that they have followed as well as the cost of the links that they have traversed. By using this memory, the ants can build solutions to the minimum cost path problem. These behaviors include the following:

1. Construction of a probabilistic solution biased by pheromone trails without forward updating.
2. Determining the backward path with loop elimination and pheromone updating.
3. Evaluation of the quality of the pheromones that get deposited, and it is known that the pheromones will evaporate with time.

There are two working modes for the ants:

a. Forward
b. Backward

The forward mode proves its effect when ants are moving from the nest toward food, and they are in backward mode while moving away from the food toward the nest. Once the ant reaches its destination where the food is available, it will immediately go into backward mode. The ant moves forward by probabilistically selecting the next node to move to among the nearest neighbors. The probabilistic choice is based on pheromone trails on which pheromones are only deposited in backward mode, which, in turn, helps in avoiding loops.

The memory of the ants allows them to repeat the path that they have already followed while searching the destination node while improving the system by loop elimination. Before moving backward on their memorized path, they eliminate any loops from it. While moving backward, the ants leave pheromones on the arcs they have traversed.

The ants are able to evaluate the cost of the paths they have traversed in terms of the modulated and the deposited pheromones. The shorter paths receive a greater deposit of pheromones, and the rule of evaporation gets tied with the pheromones, which, in turn, reduces the chance for poor-quality solutions.

2.7.1 Steps Involved in Solving the Problem by Usage of ACO

1. Representing the problem in the design of sets of components and transitions or by the usage of a set of weighted graphs on which solutions can be built by the ants
2. Defining the significance of the pheromone trails
3. Delineating the heuristic preference for the ant within the process of construction of a solution
4. Implementing an efficient local search algorithm for the problem to be solved if possible
5. Selecting a particular ACO algorithm and applying it to a problem that is to be solved
6. Tuning the framework of the ACO algorithm

It has already been proved that R_1, R_2, ..., R_n are stochastic return rates of assets 1, 2, ..., n, where we presume that $E[|R_i| < \infty]$ for all $i = 1, 2, ..., n$ for investing the capital in these assets in order to earn some charming attribute of the total return rate on the investment. Denoting by x_1, x_2, ..., x_n the fraction of the original capital invested in assets 1, 2, ..., n, the formula for the whole return rate is

$$R_1 x_1 + R_1 x_1 + R_1 x_1 + \dots R_n x_n \qquad (2.3)$$

Apparently, the set of feasible asset allocations can be determined as follows:

$$X = \left\{ x \in R^n : x_1 + x_2 + \dots + x_n = 1, \ x_i \geq 0, \ i = 1, 2, \dots n \right\} \qquad (2.4)$$

The two important criteria for portfolio optimization are expected return and risk at the time of setting the target by an investor for maximizing the first one and minimizing the second one.

As has already been explained, the ACO algorithm starts by initialization of pheromone values followed by solution of the problem of the probabilistic method and finally with the updating of pheromones. Further details bring in the different steps of ACO algorithms for financial use.

Initially, where the ant colony gets generated is when implementing Equation 2.5 for selecting fragment I from K possible choices. τ_k is the amount of pheromone related with fragment k.

$$\text{Prob}_i = \frac{\tau_i}{\sum_1^k \tau_k} \tag{2.5}$$

Evaluation is done through an evaporation phase (where the evaporation rate is denoted by γ) and a pheromone deposit phase.

$$(t+1) = \tau_i(t)(1-\gamma) + \delta_i \tag{2.6}$$

While in the process of updating the quantities of pheromone that get deposited on each solution and that, in turn, have a direct relationship to the operation of the algorithm, during the step of ant distribution, ants get distributed with respect to their distance and finally stop the iteration. Finally, repetitions of the last process come to an end until the maximum number of ants is obtained or there is a lack of optimal solutions.

2.7.2 Advantages and Disadvantages

Application of ACO can be done in areas with dynamic characteristics, where changes in the path distance, etc., are required to be incorporated within the solution. The complication with ant-based control arises whenever there is a significant topology change within the network involving a little time before the ants discover and mark the new routes with pheromones. The drawback lies in the theoretical analysis, which is difficult due to the usage of a sequence of random decisions of the algorithm and which are not independent, and the probability distribution might change over the iterations. Overall, the application of ACO is done multiple times, including assignment problems, scheduling problems, and dynamic network routing. ACO has been proven to be a good choice for constrained, discrete problems.

2.8 Differential Evolution

DE algorithms are usually put into use as metaheuristics for global optimization purposes with very little exploration carried out on their original population. Within a population-based heuristic optimization strategy, the choice of the original population is valuable due to its effects on the exploration for several iterations and repeatedly has an impact on the resulting solution. Without having a prior indication regarding the optima, the original population then gets chosen randomly with the usage of pseudorandom numbers. DE is a relatively modern extension to the collection of population-oriented search heuristics. However, it cropped up as a procedure most preferred by engineers to resolve endless optimization issues. DE involves numerous attractive characteristics in addition to being a noticeably simple evolutionary technique that is extremely fast and increasingly popular in the solution of algebraic optimization issues and is likely to achieve the function's valid global optimum. DE bears the characteristic of a compact structure involving a small computer code having a smaller number of control restrictions when compared with the other evolutionary algorithms. A single strategy for DE originally was proposed by Price et al. (2005), which was later extended by them to 10 different strategies. Regardless of having numerous extraordinary characteristics and favorable applications in numerous fields, DE at intervals is criticized for having a sluggish convergence rate for computationally expensive functions. If the control parameters are varied along with the convergence rate, DE may get increased without affecting the quality of solutions at times. Usually in population-based search techniques such as DE, an acceptable trade-off is to be sustained between convergence and type of solution, which, even if it is not a global optimal solution, should be satisfactory rather than converging to a suboptimal solution, which may not even be a local solution.

For an objective function $f: X \subseteq R^D \rightarrow R$, where the feasible region $X 6 = \emptyset$, the minimization problem is to find $x^* \in X$ such that $f(x^*) \leq f(x) \ \forall x \in X$, where: $f(x^*) 6 = -\infty$.

Global optimization is necessary in the fields of engineering, statistics, and finance involving many practical problems that have objective functions that are nondifferentiable, noncontinuous, nonlinear, noisy, flat, and multidimensional, or involve many local minima, constraints, or stochasticity. In a similar manner, problems are considered to be complicated if not futile to solve analytically. Thus, DE is utilized to acquire approximate solutions to such issues.

A mutation operator remains the elite driver of DE, which exercises this process that makes DE distinct from the rest of the evolutionary processes. The mutation operation of DE puts into use the vector differentials between the existing population members for deciding both the degree and direction of perturbation correlated to the individual subject of the mutation operation. The technique of mutation at each generation starts by selecting three individuals randomly within the population. Listed below are the predominantly used mutation strategies implemented in DE codes:

DE/rand/1:
$$V_{i,g} = X_{\underset{1}{r,g}} + F * (X_{\underset{2}{r,g}} - X_{\underset{3}{r,g}}) \tag{a}$$

DE/rand/2:
$$V_{i,g} = X_{\underset{1}{r,g}} + F * (X_{\underset{2}{r,g}} - X_{\underset{3}{r,g}}) + F * (X_{\underset{4}{r,g}} - X_{\underset{5}{r,g}}) \tag{b}$$

DE/best/1:
$$V_{i,g} = X_{best,g} + F * (X_{\underset{1}{r,g}} - X_{\underset{2}{r,g}}) \tag{c}$$

DE/best/2:
$$V_{i,g} = X_{best,g} + F * (X_{\underset{1}{r,g}} - X_{\underset{2}{r,g}}) + F * (X_{\underset{3}{r,g}} - X_{\underset{4}{r,g}}) \tag{d}$$

DE/rand-to-best/1:
$$V_{i,g} = X_{\underset{1}{r,g}} + F * (X_{\underset{2}{best,g}} - X_{r,g}) + F * (X_{\underset{3}{r,g}} - X_{\underset{4}{r,g}}) \tag{e}$$

At which point, $i = 1, ..., NP$, $r_1, r_2, r_3 \in \{1, ..., NP\}$ are randomly selected and satisfied. $r_1 \neq r_2 \neq r_3 \neq i$, $F \in [0, 1]$, where F is the control parameter.

After the completion of the mutation phase, the crossover process gets activated.

$$\text{The troubled individual, } V_{i,G+1} = (v_{1,i,G+1}, \ldots, v_{n,i,G+1}) \tag{2.7}$$

$$\text{The prevailing population member, } X_{i,G} = (x_{1,i,G}, \ldots, x_{n,i,G}) \tag{2.8}$$

These are accountable to the crossover operation that ultimately engenders the population of the candidates or "trial" vectors:
$U_{i,G+1} = (u_{1,i,G+1}, \ldots, u_{n,i,G+1})$, as follows:

$$
\begin{aligned}
u_{j,i.G+1} &= v_{j,i.G+1} \text{ if rand} \leq C_j vR_{j=k} \\
&\quad x_{j,i.G} \quad \text{Otherwise}
\end{aligned}
$$

At which point, $j = 1, \ldots, n$, $k \in \{1, \ldots, n\}$ are considered to be a random parameter's index, selected once for each i, and the crossover rate, Cr $\in$ [0, 1], the other control parameter of DE, is set by the user.

The selection scheme of DE is different when the population for the next generation is selected from the individual in the current population and its corresponding trial vector according to the following rule:

$$
\begin{aligned}
1q \\
x_{i.G+1} &= U_{i.G+1} \text{ if } f(U_{i.G+1}) \leq f(X_{i.G}) \\
&\quad x_{i.G} \quad \text{Otherwise}
\end{aligned}
$$

Thus, every individual of the temporary (trial) population becomes distinguished from its counterpart within the prevailing population. The one having the inferior objective function value will survive from the tournament culling to the population of the next generation. As a result, all the individuals of the next generation are as good as or better than their match within the prevailing generation. The vector is not compared against all the individuals in the current generation in a DE trial, but it can be done only against one individual, its counterpart, within the prevailing generation.

DE Pseudocode

Step 1: Random initialization of the parent population by generation of the population randomly, (say) NP vectors, each having n dimensions: $x_{i,j} = x_{\min,j} + \text{rand}(0, 1)(x_{\max,j} - x_{\min,j})$, where $x_{\min,j}$ and $x_{\max}$ are lower and upper bounds for the jth component respectively, and rand(0,1) is a uniform random number between 0 and 1.

Step 2: Calculation of the objective function value $f(X_i)$ for all X_i.

Step 3: Selection of the three points from the population and generation of the perturbed individual V_i by the usage of Equation 2.7.

Step 4: Recombination of the target vector x_i with the perturbed individual generated in Step 3 for generating a trial vector U_i by the usage of Equation 2.8.

Step 5: Checking whether each variable of the trial vector is within the range. If yes, then move to the next step or else make it within range with the usage of $u_{i,j} = 2 * x_{min,j} - u_{i,j}$, if $u_{i,=j} < x_{min,j}$ and $u_{i,j} = 2 * x_{max,j} - u_{i,j}$, if $u_{i,j} > x_{max,j}$, and go to the next step.

Step 6: Calculation of the objective function value for vector U_i.

Step 7: Selecting the better of the two (function value at target and trial point) using Equation 2.3 for the next generation.

Step 8: Checking whether convergence criterion is met and, if yes, then stop or else go back to Step 3.

2.8.1 Advantages and Disadvantages

DE is a technique for optimizing an issue by iterative trial to ameliorate a candidate solution under consideration to a given measure of quality, although DE is not helpful in assuring that an optimal solution is ever developed. DE thus is able to keep the multiplicity of the population involving unstable convergence, which is easier to drop into p best.

2.9 Portfolio Optimization: Case Study

The field of portfolio management can be cited as one of the most interesting applications of the evolutionary algorithms. To the extent to which industrial informatics is concerned, portfolio management refers to the fruitful utilization of the industrial resources at hand (portfolio) focusing on either harvesting the returns or mitigating the associated risks. Resources may be either in the form of raw materials (material management), human resources (human resource management), information (information management), intelligence (intelligence management), or finance instruments (financial management). The risk–return paradigm immanent in any portfolio management technique makes it amenable to the evolutionary algorithm-based optimization techniques. This section throws light on the aspects of industrial portfolio management with reference to proper selection of financial instruments in a financial portfolio management scenario. Applications of the standard PSO, ACO, and DE algorithms as well as their multiobjective versions of the problem of a financial portfolio selection mechanism (Bhattacharya et al., 2010; Bhattacharyya & Maulik, 2013) are presented with examples. The following subsections illustrate the common measures used for the evaluation of risks and returns of portfolios in real-life situations. The optimization techniques aim at handling these measures in achieving the desired objective of balance in the risk–return paradigm.

In this chapter, a PSO, an ACO, and a DE algorithm have been used to evolve optimized portfolio asset allocations in volatile market conditions. The proposed approach is pivoted on optimizing the CVaR (Engle & Ng, 1982; Rockafellar & Uryasev, 2000) measure within market conditions that are based on several objectives and constraints. The authors have concentrated here on dealing with fully discrete distributions, enhancing the usefulness and properties of CVaR in the case of furnishing the elementary way of direct calculation of CVaR. The results are compared with those obtained with the optimized VaR values of the portfolios under consideration. A comparative application of the proposed approach along with the VaR (Ying, 2001) approach is demonstrated on a collection of several financial instruments with a real-life data set of Tata

Steel during the months of August and early September 2015, enabling a distributional supposition, employing the particular series of financial assets for developing a much more generalized framework.

2.9.1 Conditional Value at Risk

The return risk management framework that was introduced by Markowitz (1952) has come a long way in the process of portfolio optimization. Of late, the alternative coherent technique is being used for the reduction of the probability of incurring a large amount of losses by a portfolio. This can be done by the assessment of the specific loss that will exceed the value at risk. The outcome risk measure is termed the CVaR (Rockafellar & Uryasev, 2002), thanks to the evolving fields of data intelligence management and archival techniques in industrial portfolio management. Simulation by two basic requirements, in turn, has developed in the portfolio optimization procedure by (a) risks, constraints, and adequate modeling of utility functions and (b) efficient handling of huge numbers of scenarios and instruments. In terms of mathematics, the derivation of CVaR is done by considering the values of the weighted average at the intervals of the VaRs and the losses exceeding the VaRs. Compared to VaR, CVaR not only traces several different loss distributions but can also be easily expressed in a minimization formula.

Measures of risk play a vital role, notably in grappling with losses that might have been incurred in finance under the cover of uncertain conditions. Loss, being derived as a function $z = f(x, y)$ of a decision vector $x \in X$, purports to depict the values of a number of variables, such as interest rates or weather data in terms of future values. If y is assumed to be random with an accepted probability distribution z, then it produces a random variable having its dependent distribution on the superior x. If any optimization problem shows the involvement of z in turn of the superior x, then it can be accounted not just as expectations but also as "riskless" x.

If percentiles of loss or reward can be measured by $f(x, y)$, which is taken to be the loss function relying upon the decision vector $x = (x_1, \ldots, x_n)$ and the random vector $y = (y_1, \ldots, y_m)$, then VaR can be calculated as α percentile, representing the loss distribution, which is considered to be the smallest value at which the probability that loss exceeds or is equal to the value is greater than or equal to α. In such a case, CVaR$^+$, which is also known to be the "upper CVaR," is the expected loss that strictly exceeds VaR (in turn known as mean excess loss) and expected shortfall. CVaR$^-$, in turn known as "lower CVaR," is the expected loss weakly exceeding VaR, which is the expected loss equal to or exceeding VaR. It is also known as tail VaR.

Thus, CVaR is the weighted average of VaR and CVaR$^+$ (Rockafellar & Uryasev, 2002). It can be derived from the following formulation:

$$\text{CVaR} = \lambda \, \text{VaR} + (1-\lambda) \, \text{CVaR}^+, \ 0 \leq \lambda \leq 1 \qquad (2.9)$$

where λ is the Lagrange multiplier.

Because CVaR is convex as shown in Figure 2.1, VaR, CVaR$^+$, and CVaR$^-$ can also be nonconvex. This shows credible inequalities as the following:

$$\text{VaR} \leq \text{CVaR}^- \leq \text{CVaR} \leq \text{CVaR}^+ \ (\text{Rockafellar \& Uryasev, 2002})$$

The features of CVaR represent the risks that are simple and convenient in nature, hence measuring the downside risks, and are applicable to nonsymmetric distribution of losses. Stable statistical estimates of CVaR appear to be its integral characteristics in comparison to VaR, which can get influenced by any scenario. CVaR yields values in a continuous process in terms of confidence level α, steady at different levels of confidence in comparison with VaR (VaR, CVaR⁻, and CVaR⁺ may not be continuous to α). CVaR portfolios coincide in the case of normal distribution of loss in optimal variance to the level of consistency in the mean variance approach. CVaR is variously acceptable due to its ease of control and optimization process for non-normal distributions, and even loss distribution is shaped using CVaR constraints for the first online procedures.

2.9.2 Value at Risk

In economics and finance, VaR is defined as the maximum loss that is not exceeded with a given probability (the confidence level) over a given period of time or horizon. VaR is most commonly used by security firms or investment banks to measure the market risk of their asset portfolios (market value at risk). It is widely applied in finance for quantitative risk management for many types of risk. However, it might be noted at this point that VaR does not give any information about the severity of loss by which it is exceeded.

Estimation of three parameters is required for the determination of VaR. The time horizon (period) to be analyzed relates to the time period over which a financial institution is committed to holding its portfolio or to the time required to liquidate assets. Typical time horizons are 1 day, 10 days, or 1 year along with the confidence level, which is the interval estimate in which the VaR would not be expected to exceed the maximum loss. Commonly used confidence levels are 99% and 95%. However, confidence levels are not indications of probabilities, and the unit of VaR, which is in currency, is taken under consideration.

Given a probability p and K days, where p and K must be predetermined by the risk manager, VaR is delineated as a number such that there is a probability p of exhibiting a worse return over the next K days. VaR is thus simply a quantile of the return distribution and thus does not reflect anything about the risk distribution. More important, it does not indicate how large the likely magnitude of losses is on those days when the return is worse than the VaR. On the other hand, expected shortfall (ES), which is defined as the expected return conditional on the return being worse than the VaR, has been suggested as an alternative to VaR. Needless to state, in spite of all these limitations, VaR still remains the most common risk metric used in practice.

A VaR-enabled given portfolio asset allocation model should possess the following characteristics:

1. The asset allocation model should be a fully specified data-generating and data-intensive one that can be estimated and implemented on daily returns for portfolios with a large number of varied assets.
2. It should allow the computation of VaR for any prespecified level of confidence (p) and for any horizon of interest (K) subject to the current market conditions.
3. It should also be flexible enough to allow for calculation of risk measures other than VaR. The model should reflect the following itemized facts of daily asset returns in order to deliver accurate risk predictions.
   - Daily returns should have little or no exploitable conditional mean predictability. The variance of daily returns should be predictable and should greatly exceed the mean return.
   - Daily returns are not normally distributed. Even after standardizing daily returns by a dynamic variance model, the standardized daily returns are not normally distributed.

Positive and negative returns of the same magnitude may have different impacts on the variance.
4. The correlations between assets should appear to be time varying.
5. As the investment horizon increases, the return data distribution should approach the normal distribution.

Thus, given these salient features of daily asset returns, a portfolio optimization technique involving the VaR reduces to building a dynamic market risk management model that contains only a few parameters to be estimated and that is easily implemented on a large set of assets.

2.9.3 Mathematical Formulation

As already stated, VaR is an important measure of the exposure of a given portfolio to different kinds of risks inherent in financial environments, which can be used for portfolio optimization purposes.

Given a portfolio P composed of k assets $S = \{S_1, S_2, ..., S_k\}$ and $W = \{W_1, W_2, ..., W_k\}$, the relative weights or portions of the assets in the portfolio, the price of the portfolio at time t is given by

$$P(t) = \sum_{i=1}^{k} S_i(t)W_i \tag{2.10}$$

where $S_i(t)$ and W_i are the value and importance level of the portfolio at time t, respectively.

The VaR of the portfolio P, which is the maximum expected loss over a holding period at a given level of confidence (α), can then be defined as the smallest number l such that the probability that the loss L exceeds l is not larger than ($1 - \alpha$), that is,

$$\text{VaR}_\alpha = \inf\{l \in R : P(L > l) \leq 1 - \alpha\} = \inf\{l \in R : F_L(l) \geq \alpha\} \tag{2.11}$$

2.9.4 Common VaR Calculation Models

All of the techniques and models for calculating VaR rely on a set of assumptions of their own. However, the most common assumption is that the best estimator for future changes in market conditions is the historical trace of market data. Some of the well-known models for estimating VaR include the following:

The variance–covariance (VCV) model assumes that the risk factor returns are always mutually and ordinarily distributed and that the portfolio return is also normally distributed, assuming the value changes within a defined portfolio are always conditioned linearly above the returns of all risk factors. JPMorgan presented the delta normal model in an understandable form in the early 1990s. The assumption that the portfolio return is normally distributed implies that there is a composition of assets within the portfolio having a linear delta, which delineates the change in the portfolio value, which, in turn, is dependent directly on every alteration in the asset's value, further signifying the direct dependency of the portfolio return on the entire asset returns and that the asset returns are jointly normally distributed. Further assuming that the value of the portfolio itself is just the risk factor associated with a portfolio, at 95% confidence level, VaR for N assets over a holding period is given by

$$\text{VaR} = -V_p(\mu_p - 1.645\sigma_p) \qquad (2.12)$$

where the mean μ_p is given as

$$\mu_p = \sum_{i=1}^{N} \varpi_i \mu_i \qquad (2.13)$$

and the standard deviation σ_p is given as

$$\sigma_p = \sqrt{\Omega^T \Sigma \Omega} \qquad (2.14a)$$

$$\Omega = \begin{bmatrix} \varpi_1 \\ \varpi_2 \\ \varpi_3 \\ . \\ . \\ \varpi_N \end{bmatrix} \qquad (2.14b)$$

$$\Omega^T = \begin{bmatrix} \varpi_1 & \varpi_2 & \varpi_3 & . . & \varpi_N \end{bmatrix} \qquad (2.14c)$$

Here, i refers to the return on assets i, and p refers to the return on the portfolio for standard deviation (σ_p) and means (μ_p). V_p is the initial value of the portfolio (in currency units). ϖ_i is the ratio of V_i and V_p. Σ is the covariance matrix between all the N asset returns.

The VCV model thus uses a more compact and maintainable data set, which, in turn, can often be purchased from third parties having the speed of computation by the usage of optimized linear algebra libraries. The assumption of the portfolio having a composition of assets with linear-based delta along with normal distribution of market price returns or asset returns is the major deficiency within the model.

The historical simulation (HistSim) model has emerged as the industry standard for computing VaR. This model is based on the assumption of having an equal distribution of the return on assets in the past records to be repeated in the future. HistSim, being uncomplicated and the most transparent calculation approach, associates the prevailing portfolio over an assortment of historical changes in the price structure for cropping out the changes in the worth of the portfolio along with the estimation of a percentile (VaR). Simplicity of implementation stands to be one of its benefits. Added to this, it does not assume a normal distribution of asset returns like the VCV model. The main drawbacks are the requirement for a large market database and the computationally intensive calculation.

In HistSim, VaR is evaluated as

$$\text{VaR} = 2.33 M \sigma_p \sqrt{10} \tag{2.15}$$

where M is considered to be the worth of the portfolio in the market, and σ_p is considered to be the factual excitability of the portfolio. The constant 2.33 stands for the unit of the mathematical system of σ_p required for a certainty level of 99%, and the constant $\sqrt{10}$ assigns the number of days in the holding period.

Basically, the HistSim method computes VaR in two simple steps. First, a series of pseudohistorical portfolio returns are constructed, using today's portfolio weights and historical asset returns. Second, the quantile of the pseudohistorical portfolio returns is computed to yield VaR and the current asset returns.

The Monte Carlo simulation randomly simulates future asset returns. For computation of VaR for portfolios holding securities or bonds with returns that, in turn, are nonlinear in nature, the method of Monte Carlo simulation is applied because of the nontrivial requirement of the computational effort. Having a conceptually elementary characteristic, Monte Carlo simulation proves rather to be computationally more comprehensive and demanding than both the VCV and HistSim models. The generic Monte Carlo VaR calculation comprises the following steps.

1. Predefine N, denoting the frequency of the performance of the iterations.
2. For every iteration in N,
   - Create an arbitrary sequence of movement events within the market by the usage of some existing market structure.
   - Reevaluate the portfolio based on the imitated market volatility situations.
3. Estimate the profit or loss (PnL) in the portfolio structure under the imitated scenario. For doing so, the prevailing worth within the market of the portfolio is to be deducted from the portfolio's market worth, which has been estimated in the previous step.
4. Allocate the PnL obtained henceforth to obtain the imitated PnL dissemination for the portfolio.
5. Finally, at a specific level of confidence, compute VaR with the usage of the percentile function.

2.10 Proposed Methodology

The proposed approach is centered around the optimization of the CVaR measures of a portfolio composed of several financial instruments within a market condition based on several objectives and constraints. Application of PSO, ACO, and DE for CVaR optimization is demonstrated with reference to the minimization of the risks involved in the portfolios under consideration, thereby minimizing the portfolio losses incurred. The flow diagram of the proposed methodology is shown in Figure 2.1.

The procedure of portfolio asset allocation optimization is demonstrated on a collection of portfolios with several asset variations. Here, in this process of optimization, the PSO, ACO, and DE algorithms have been run with two different numbers of generation—that is, 500 and 1000 with the constants specified in Table 2.2.

The optimization of the portfolio asset allocation is achieved with PSO (Chatfield, 2001; Ying et al., 2006). In order to faithfully allocate assets at a given level of confidence, the CVaR of the portfolio is minimized using the following function as the fitness function.

$$CVaR = \frac{e^{-\left(\frac{VaR^2}{2}\right)}}{a\sqrt{2\pi}} \tag{2.16}$$

where $a = 0.01$ considering a confidence level of 99%, and VaR is the VaR measures of the portfolios under consideration.

Tables 2.3, 2.4, and 2.5 list the different archived average optimized portfolios over two different numbers of generations along with their costs for a confidence level of 99%.

In addition, as a comparative study, the HistSim model has been used for computing VaR of the portfolios under consideration. The PSO, ACO, and DE algorithms are then used to obtain

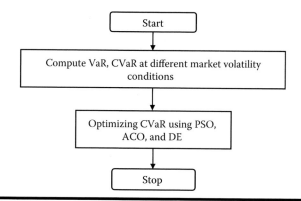

Figure 2.1   Flow diagram of the proposed methodology.

Table 2.2   Optimization Parameters Employed

Sl. No.	PSO, ACO, & DE Parameters	Values Used
1	Number of generations	(500, 1000)
2	Inertia weight	0.8
3	Acceleration coeffient (ϕ_1)	1.5
4	Acceleration coeffient (ϕ_2)	1.5

Table 2.3   Comparative Results of Optimized Portfolios of Tata Steel Ltd. with Their Costs, CVaRs, and VaRs at a Confidence Level of 99% by the Usage of PSO

Date	Symbol	Opening Price	High Price	Low Price	Last Traded Price	Closing Price	Total Traded Quantity	Turnover (in Lakhs)	Difference in Closing Prices on Consecutive Days	CVaR	VaR
2/9/15	TATA STEEL	218.9	225.9	210.3	220.9	219.5	8909770	19476.16	3.200000	0.070347	0.199387
1/9/15	TATA STEEL	222	226.25	213.05	216.4	216.3	6475249	14253.2	−9.100000	0.061473	0.200462
31/8/15	TATA STEEL	225.3	228.7	223.65	225.3	225.4	5782337	13047.13	−3.550000	0.053436	0.205600
30/8/15	TATA STEEL	232.6	234.6	223.2	229.5	228.95	9387248	21607.97	2.550000	0.061694	0.205542
29/8/15	TATA STEEL	220	229.8	215.1	227.2	226.4	14227129	31569.67	10.750000	0.054159	0.204653
28/8/15	TATA STEEL	213	219.7	208.95	214.8	215.65	8336683	17819.13	2.200000	0.077069	0.194805
27/8/15	TATA STEEL	210	217.9	200.1	215	213.45	14206932	29799.94	7.350000	0.054156	0.203642
26/8/15	TATA STEEL	229.3	229.3	202.65	204.45	206.1	117111489	25572.86	−31.150000	0.068291	0.201481

(Continued)

Table 2.3 (Continued)   Comparative Results of Optimized Portfolios of Tata Steel Ltd. with Their Costs, CVaRs, and VaRs at a Confidence Level of 99% by the Usage of PSO

Date	Symbol	Opening Price	High Price	Low Price	Last Traded Price	Closing Price	Total Traded Quantity	Turnover (in Lakhs)	Difference in Closing Prices on Consecutive Days	CVaR	VaR
25/8/15	TATA STEEL	238.5	238.5	231.5	236.3	237.25	5247042	12325.35	−4.300000	0.060858	0.203103
23/8/15	TATA STEEL	247.7	248.4	240.5	242	241.55	4626334	11255.37	−8.250000	0.068447	0.200799
22/8/15	TATA STEEL	250.1	253.35	246.75	249.55	249.8	4304085	10772.08	−2.550000	0.052530	0.205786
21/8/15	TATA STEEL	248.1	254.9	246.6	252.4	252.35	9805064	24641.63	5.600000	0.061528	0.200201
20/8/15	TATA STEEL	238.5	248.5	234.2	247.5	246.75	8524452	20665.62	9.150000	0.073113	0.200397
19/8/15	TATA STEEL	234.25	239.2	229	237.5	237.6	9065329	21282.27	4.000000	0.060508	0.200104
18/8/15	TATA STEEL	253.35	253.9	232.3	234	233.6	13764560	32979.36	−15.450000	0.050674	0.201994

(Continued)

Table 2.3 (Continued) Comparative Results of Optimized Portfolios of Tata Steel Ltd. with Their Costs, CVaRs, and VaRs at a Confidence Level of 99% by the Usage of PSO

Date	Symbol	Opening Price	High Price	Low Price	Last Traded Price	Closing Price	Total Traded Quantity	Turnover (in Lakhs)	Difference in Closing Prices on Consecutive Days	CVaR	VaR
17/8/15	TATA STEEL	254.4	257.9	246.1	249.45	249.05	15172684	38227.01	2.250000	0.066088	0.199147
16/8/15	TATA STEEL	259.95	260	245.7	247.3	246.8	8827248	22200.72	−14.350000	0.067079	0.201798
15/8/15	TATA STEEL	262.9	265	260	260.25	261.15	3401136	8929.59	−0.900000	0.061850	0.201672
14/8/15	TATA STEEL	261	264.55	260.15	262.05	262.05	3791638	9948.04	1.050000	0.069911	0.199146
13/8/15	TATA STEEL	262.35	265.4	256.25	260.25	261	6376740	16691.22	−1.300000	0.051213	0.206873
12/8/15	TATA STEEL	260	268.5	259.95	262.3	262.3	7979075	21145.9	6.000000	0.067111	0.199241
11/8/15	TATA STEEL	249.7	259.75	246.05	258.8	256.3	9723318	24527.2	–	–	–

Table 2.4 Comparative Results of Optimized Portfolios of Tata Steel Ltd. with Their Costs, CVaRs, and VaRs at a Confidence Level of 99% by the Usage of ACO

Date	Symbol	Opening Price	High Price	Low Price	Last Traded Price	Closing Price	Total Traded Quantity	Turnover (in Lakhs)	Difference in Closing Prices on Consecutive Days	CVaR	VaR
2/9/15	TATA STEEL	218.9	225.9	210.3	220.9	219.5	8909770	19476.16	3.200000	0.063405	0.200530
1/9/15	TATA STEEL	222	226.25	213.05	216.4	216.3	6475249	14253.2	−9.100000	0.055507	0.202098
31/8/15	TATA STEEL	225.3	228.7	223.65	225.3	225.4	5782337	13047.13	−3.550000	0.063312	0.200600
30/8/15	TATA STEEL	232.6	234.6	223.2	229.5	228.95	9387248	21607.97	2.550000	0.057788	0.201397
29/8/15	TATA STEEL	220	229.8	215.1	227.2	226.4	14227129	31569.67	10.750000	0.059370	0.201831
28/8/15	TATA STEEL	213	219.7	208.95	214.8	215.65	8336683	17819.13	2.200000	0.051036	0.201310
27/8/15	TATA STEEL	210	217.9	200.1	215	213.45	14206932	29799.94	7.350000	0.056202	0.207461

(Continued)

Table 2.4 (Continued) Comparative Results of Optimized Portfolios of Tata Steel Ltd. with Their Costs, CVaRs, and VaRs at a Confidence Level of 99% by the Usage of ACO

Date	Symbol	Opening Price	High Price	Low Price	Last Traded Price	Closing Price	Total Traded Quantity	Turnover (in Lakhs)	Difference in Closing Prices on Consecutive Days	CVaR	VaR
26/8/15	TATA STEEL	229.3	229.3	202.65	204.45	206.1	11711489	25572.86	−31.150000	0.061982	0.199182
25/8/15	TATA STEEL	238.5	238.5	231.5	236.3	237.25	5247042	12325.35	−4.300000	0.053047	0.207824
23/8/15	TATA STEEL	247.7	248.4	240.5	242	241.55	4626334	11255.37	−8.250000	0.068857	0.200007
22/8/15	TATA STEEL	250.1	253.35	246.75	249.55	249.8	4304085	10772.08	−2.550000	0.056428	0.201295
21/8/15	TATA STEEL	248.1	254.9	246.6	252.4	252.35	9805064	24641.63	5.600000	0.053580	0.205028
20/8/15	TATA STEEL	238.5	248.5	234.2	247.5	246.75	8524452	20665.62	9.150000	0.064736	0.202478
19/8/15	TATA STEEL	234.25	239.2	229	237.5	237.6	9065329	21282.27	4.000000	0.061239	0.202971

(Continued)

Table 2.4 (Continued)   Comparative Results of Optimized Portfolios of Tata Steel Ltd. with Their Costs, CVaRs, and VaRs at a Confidence Level of 99% by the Usage of ACO

Date	Symbol	Opening Price	High Price	Low Price	Last Traded Price	Closing Price	Total Traded Quantity	Turnover (in Lakhs)	Difference in Closing Prices on Consecutive Days	CVaR	VaR
18/8/15	TATA STEEL	253.35	253.9	232.3	234	233.6	13764560	32979.36	−15.450000	0.052852	0.206802
17/8/15	TATA STEEL	254.4	257.9	246.1	249.45	249.05	15172684	38227.01	2.250000	0.054439	0.204902
16/8/15	TATA STEEL	259.95	260	245.7	247.3	246.8	8827248	22200.72	−14.350000	0.048024	0.204045
15/8/15	TATA STEEL	262.9	265	260	260.25	261.15	3401136	8929.59	−0.900000	0.059495	0.200862
14/8/15	TATA STEEL	261	264.55	260.15	262.05	262.05	3791638	9948.04	1.050000	0.074268	0.201326
13/8/15	TATA STEEL	262.35	265.4	256.25	260.25	261	6376740	16691.22	−1.300000	0.054476	0.205098
12/8/15	TATA STEEL	260	268.5	259.95	262.3	262.3	7979075	21145.9	6.000000	0.057288	0.202807
11/8/15	TATA STEEL	249.7	259.75	246.05	258.8	256.3	9723318	24527.2	–	–	–

Table 2.5 Comparative Results of Optimized Portfolios of Tata Steel Ltd. with Their Costs, CVaRs, and VaRs at a Confidence Level of 99% by the Usage of DE

Date	Symbol	Opening Price	High Price	Low Price	Last Traded Price	Closing Price	Total Traded Quantity	Turnover (in Lakhs)	Difference in Closing Prices on Consecutive Days	CVaR	VaR
2/9/15	TATA STEEL	218.9	225.9	210.3	220.9	219.5	8909770	19476.16	3.200000	0.059405	0.20221
1/9/15	TATA STEEL	222	226.25	213.05	216.4	216.3	6475249	14253.2	–9.100000	0.06121	0.204386
31/8/15	TATA STEEL	225.3	228.7	223.65	225.3	225.4	5782337	13047.13	–3.550000	0.066086	0.202631
30/8/15	TATA STEEL	232.6	234.6	223.2	229.5	228.95	9387248	21607.97	2.550000	0.073732	0.19691
29/8/15	TATA STEEL	220	229.8	215.1	227.2	226.4	14227129	31569.67	10.750000	0.062086	0.200904
28/8/15	TATA STEEL	213	219.7	208.95	214.8	215.65	8336683	17819.13	2.200000	0.052013	0.205983
27/8/15	TATA STEEL	210	217.9	200.1	215	213.45	14206932	29799.94	7.350000	0.0577	0.200203

(Continued)

Table 2.5 (Continued)   Comparative Results of Optimized Portfolios of Tata Steel Ltd. with Their Costs, CVaRs, and VaRs at a Confidence Level of 99% by the Usage of DE

Date	Symbol	Opening Price	High Price	Low Price	Last Traded Price	Closing Price	Total Traded Quantity	Turnover (in Lakhs)	Difference in Closing Prices on Consecutive Days	CVaR	VaR
26/8/15	TATA STEEL	229.3	229.3	202.65	204.45	206.1	11711489	25572.86	−31.150000	0.065303	0.200147
25/8/15	TATA STEEL	238.5	238.5	231.5	236.3	237.25	5247042	12325.35	−4.300000	0.065598	0.200207
23/8/15	TATA STEEL	247.7	248.4	240.5	242	241.55	4626334	11255.37	−8.250000	0.069523	0.200375
22/8/15	TATA STEEL	250.1	253.35	246.75	249.55	249.8	4304085	10772.08	−2.550000	0.054056	0.203308
21/8/15	TATA STEEL	248.1	254.9	246.6	252.4	252.35	9805064	24641.63	5.600000	0.05474	0.199868
20/8/15	TATA STEEL	238.5	248.5	234.2	247.5	246.75	8524452	20665.62	9.150000	0.045669	0.205911
19/8/15	TATA STEEL	234.25	239.2	229	237.5	237.6	9065329	21282.27	4.000000	0.057716	0.201346
18/8/15	TATA STEEL	253.35	253.9	232.3	234	233.6	13764560	32979.36	−15.450000	0.055091	0.201501

(Continued)

Table 2.5 (Continued)   Comparative Results of Optimized Portfolios of Tata Steel Ltd. with Their Costs, CVaRs, and VaRs at a Confidence Level of 99% by the Usage of DE

Date	Symbol	Opening Price	High Price	Low Price	Last Traded Price	Closing Price	Total Traded Quantity	Turnover (in Lakhs)	Difference in Closing Prices on Consecutive Days	CVaR	VaR
17/8/15	TATA STEEL	254.4	257.9	246.1	249.45	249.05	15172684	38227.01	2.250000	0.056603	0.201435
16/8/15	TATA STEEL	259.95	260	245.7	247.3	246.8	8827248	22200.72	−14.350000	0.082274	0.199765
15/8/15	TATA STEEL	262.9	265	260	260.25	261.15	3401136	8929.59	−0.900000	0.056725	0.204559
14/8/15	TATA STEEL	261	264.55	260.15	262.05	262.05	3791638	9948.04	1.050000	0.052125	0.199422
13/8/15	TATA STEEL	262.35	265.4	256.25	260.25	261	6376740	16691.22	−1.300000	0.069921	0.20092
12/8/15	TATA STEEL	260	268.5	259.95	262.3	262.3	7979075	21145.9	6.000000	0.07692	0.197919
11/8/15	TATA STEEL	249.7	259.75	246.05	258.8	256.3	9723318	24527.2	–	–	–

Table 2.6 Comparative Results of Optimized Portfolios of Tata Steel Ltd. with Their Costs, CVaRs, and VaRs at a Confidence Level of 99% by the Usage of PSO, ACO, and DE

	Values Obtained			DE		ACO		PSO	
Date	Symbol	Opening Price	Closing Price	CVaR	VaR	CVaR	VaR	CVaR	VaR
2/9/15	TATA STEEL	218.9	219.5	0.059405	0.20221	0.063405	0.200530	0.070347	0.199387
1/9/15	TATA STEEL	222	216.3	0.06121	0.204386	0.055507	0.202098	0.061473	0.200462
31/8/15	TATA STEEL	225.3	225.4	0.066086	0.202631	0.063312	0.200600	0.053436	0.205600
30/8/15	TATA STEEL	232.6	228.95	0.073732	0.19691	0.057788	0.201397	0.061694	0.205542
29/8/15	TATA STEEL	220	226.4	0.062086	0.200904	0.059370	0.201831	0.054159	0.204653
28/8/15	TATA STEEL	213	215.65	0.052013	0.205983	0.051036	0.201310	0.077069	0.194805
27/8/15	TATA STEEL	210	213.45	0.0577	0.200203	0.056202	0.207461	0.054156	0.203642
26/8/15	TATA STEEL	229.3	206.1	0.065303	0.200147	0.061982	0.199182	0.068291	0.201481

(Continued)

Table 2.6 (Continued) Comparative Results of Optimized Portfolios of Tata Steel Ltd. with Their Costs, CVaRs, and VaRs at a Confidence Level of 99% by the Usage of PSO, ACO, and DE

Values Obtained				DE		ACO		PSO	
Date	Symbol	Opening Price	Closing Price	CVaR	VaR	CVaR	VaR	CVaR	VaR
25/8/15	TATA STEEL	238.5	237.25	0.065598	0.200207	0.053047	0.207824	0.060858	0.203103
23/8/15	TATA STEEL	247.7	241.55	0.069523	0.200375	0.068857	0.200007	0.068447	0.200799
22/8/15	TATA STEEL	250.1	249.8	0.054056	0.203308	0.056428	0.201295	0.052530	0.205786
21/8/15	TATA STEEL	248.1	252.35	0.05474	0.199868	0.053580	0.205028	0.061528	0.200201
20/8/15	TATA STEEL	238.5	246.75	0.045669	0.205911	0.064736	0.202478	0.073113	0.200397
19/8/15	TATA STEEL	234.25	237.6	0.057716	0.201346	0.061239	0.202971	0.060508	0.200104
18/8/15	TATA STEEL	253.35	233.6	0.055091	0.201501	0.052852	0.206802	0.050674	0.201994
17/8/15	TATA STEEL	254.4	249.05	0.056603	0.201435	0.054439	0.204902	0.066088	0.199147

(Continued)

Table 2.6 (Continued) Comparative Results of Optimized Portfolios of Tata Steel Ltd. with Their Costs, CVaRs, and VaRs at a Confidence Level of 99% by the Usage of PSO, ACO, and DE

Values Obtained				DE		ACO		PSO	
Date	Symbol	Opening Price	Closing Price	CVaR	VaR	CVaR	VaR	CVaR	VaR
16/8/15	TATA STEEL	259.95	246.8	0.082274	0.199765	0.048024	0.204045	0.067079	0.201798
15/8/15	TATA STEEL	262.9	261.15	0.056725	0.204559	0.059495	0.200862	0.061850	0.201672
14/8/15	TATA STEEL	261	262.05	0.052125	0.199422	0.074268	0.201326	0.069911	0.199146
13/8/15	TATA STEEL	262.35	261	0.069921	0.20092	0.054476	0.205098	0.051213	0.206873
12/8/15	TATA STEEL	260	262.3	0.07692	0.197919	0.057288	0.202807	0.067111	0.199241
11/8/15	TATA STEEL	249.7	256.3	–	–	–	–	–	–

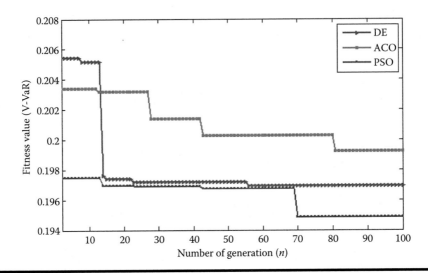

Figure 2.2   Convergence curve for VaR.

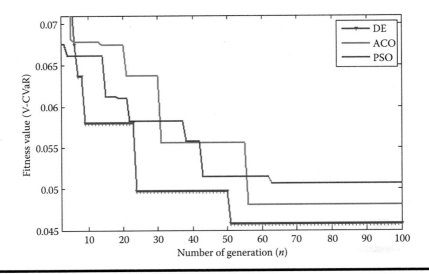

Figure 2.3   Convergence curve for CVaR.

optimum VaR measures of the portfolios using Equation 2.15 as the fitness function. The optimized VaR values obtained using the PSO, ACO, and DE algorithms are listed in Tables 2.3, 2.4, and 2.5 for the sake of comparison, along with a comparative result statement of optimized portfolios in Table 2.6.

Graphical representations of the comparative results of VaR and CVaR that are depicted by the convergence curves of VaR and CVaR are presented in Figures 2.2 and 2.3. The number of generations is stated as n, and the fitness values V-VaR and V-CVaR are the values of VaR and CVaR accordingly within the graphical representation for the convergence curve for VaR, although PSO provides better fitness value but DE proves to be converging earlier than the other techniques.

However, in the graphical representation for the convergence curve for CVaR, DE proves to be fastest in converging as well as showing the best fitness value.

2.11 Discussion and Conclusions

The implications of portfolio management, as it is applicable to larger organizations, are presented in this chapter focusing on the selection and allocation of portfolios under volatile market conditions by means of the optimization of the CVaR measures of the portfolios under consideration. The PSO, ACO, and DE algorithms-based optimization procedures are adopted on the portfolio of Tata Steel Ltd. for this purpose, centering on optimizing the CVaR (Rockafellar & Uryasev, 2002) measure under different market conditions based on several objectives and constraints, in turn, comparing the results with those obtained with the optimization of VaR measures of the portfolios under consideration. A comparative application of the proposed approach along with the VaR approach is demonstrated on a collection of several financial instruments enabling a distributional assumption for employing the particular type of financial assets for developing a much more generalized framework.

It may be noted that the proposed approach is aimed at minimizing the CVaR measures of the portfolios under consideration, and the methods, however, remain to be investigated to incorporate the aspect of return maximization in the presented scenarios through heuristic optimization approaches.

Moreover, the limitations of CVaR in quantifying market risks in non-normal loss distributions and heuristic optimization approach-based optimization techniques used to evolve an optimum portfolio selection strategy are reported. The strategy is applied to minimize the CVaR measures of a portfolio collection for a given portfolio return.

Methods, however, remain to be investigated for evolving optimum portfolio selection strategies, which would lead to maximization of portfolio returns along with minimization of portfolio risks simultaneously. The authors are currently engaged toward this direction.

References

Barricelli, N. A. 1954. "Esempinumerici di processi di evoluzione." *Methodos*, 45–68.

Bhattacharya, P., Bhattacharyya, S., & Dutta, P. 2010. "Portfolio selection based on multiobjective optimization of the risk-return paradigm." *Proceedings of National Conference on Global Management—Cultural Changes.*

Bhattacharyya, S., & Maulik, U. 2013. *Soft computing for image and multimedia data processing*, Heidelberg: Springer Verlag.

Bianchi, L., Dorigo, M., Gambardella, L. M., & Gutjahr, W. J. 2009. "A survey on metaheuristics for stochastic combinatorial optimization." *Natural Computing: An International Journal*, 8 (2): 239–287.

Black, F., Jensen, M. C., & Scholes, M. 1972. "The capital asset pricing model: Some empirical tests." In Jensen, M. C. (Ed.), *Studies of the theory of capital markets*, New York: Praeger.

Blum, C., & Roli, A. 2003. "Metaheuristics in combinatorial optimization: Overview and conceptual comparison." *ACM Computing Surveys*, 35 (3): 268–308.

Boyle, P. P., Broadie, M., & Glasserman, P. 1997. "Monte Carlo methods for security pricing." *Journal of Economic Dynamics & Control*, 21 (8–9): 1267–1321.

Brown, A. 2004. "The Unbearable Lightness of Cross-Market Risk." *Wilmott Magazine*, pp. 20–23.

Camp, C. V., Bichon, B. J., & Stovall, S. P. 2005. "Design of steel frames using ant colony optimization." *Journal of Structural Engineering*, 131 (3).

Chatfield, C. 2001. *Time series forecasting.* Boca Raton, FL: Chapman & Hall/CRC.

Crouhy, M., Galai, D., & Mark, R. 2001. *Risk management.* New York: McGraw-Hill.

Deng, L., Ma, C., & Yang, W. 2011. *Portfolio optimization via pair Copula-GARCH-EVT-CVaR model.* Systems Engineering Procedia.

Dorigo, M. 1992. Optimization, learning and natural algorithms. PhD thesis, Politecnico di Milano, Italy.

Dorigo, M., & Stützle, T. 2004. *Ant colony optimization.* Cambridge, MA: The MIT Press.

Dowd, K. 2005. *Measuring Market Risk*, 2nd edition. Hoboken, NJ: John Wiley & Sons.

Eberhart, R. C., & Kennedy, J. 1995. "A new optimizer using particle swarm theory." Proceedings Sixth International Symposium on Micro Machine and Human Science (pp. 39–43). IEEE Service Center, Piscataway, NJ.

Eberhart, R. C., & Shi, Y. 1998. "Comparison between genetic algorithms and particle swarm optimization." Proc. IEEE International Conference on Evolutionary Computing (pp. 611–616).

Elton, E. J., & Gruber, M. J. 1997. "Modern portfolio theory: 1950 to date." *Journal of Banking & Finance,* 21, 1743–1759.

Engle, R. F., & Ng, V. K. 1982. "Measuring and testing the impact of news on volatility." *Journal of Finance,* 48 (5): 1749–1778.

Filho, V. A. D. 2006. "Portfolio management using value at risk: A comparison between genetic algorithms and particle swarm optimization." Master Thesis Informatics & Economics.

Gaing, Z. L. 2003. "Particle swarm optimization to solving the economic dispatch considering the generator constraints." *IEEE Trans. on Power Systems,* 18 (3): 1187–1195.

Gambrah, P. S. N., & Pirvu, T. A. 2014. "Risk measures and portfolio optimization." *Journal of Risk and Financial Management,* 7 (3): 113–129.

Glover, F. 1977. "Heuristics for integer programming using surrogate constraints." *Decision Sciences,* 8 (1): 156–166.

Glover, F. 1986. "Future paths for integer programming and links to artificial intelligence." *Computers and Operations Research,* 13 (5): 533–549.

Haqiqi, K. F., & Kazemi, T. 2012. "Ant colony optimization approach to portfolio optimization—A lingo companion." *International Journal of Trade, Economics and Finance,* 3 (2): 148–153.

Holland, J. H. 1975. *Adaptation in natural and artificial systems.* Ann Arbor, MI: University of Michigan Press.

Holton, G. A. 2003. *Value-at-risk: Theory and practice.* San Diego, CA: Academic Press.

Jacobs, B. I., Levy, K. N., & Markowitz, H. M. 2005. "Portfolio optimization with factor, scenarios and realistic short positions." *Operations Research,* 53 (4): 586–599.

Jorion, P. 2001. *Value at risk: The new benchmark for managing financial risk,* 2nd edition. New York: McGraw-Hil.

Karaboga, D. 2010. "Artificial bee colony algorithm." *Scholarpedia,* 5 (3).

Kennedy, J., & Eberhart, R. C. 1995. "Particle swarm optimization." Proc. of IEEE Neural Networks IV. Pisctway, NJ, 1942–1948.

Krokhmal, P., Palquist, J., & Uryasev, S. 2001. "Portfolio optimization with conditional value at risk objective and constraints." *Journal of Risk,* 4 (2): 43–68.

Lim, A. E. B., George, J. K., & Vahn, G.-Y. 2011. "Conditional value-at-risk in portfolio optimization: Coherent but fragile." *Journal of Operations Research,* 39 (3): 163–171.

Markowitz, H. M. 1952. "Portfolio selection." *The Journal of Finance,* 7 (1): 77–91.

Matyas, J. 1965. "Random optimization." *Automation and Remote Control,* 26 (2): 246–253.

McNeil, A., Frey, R., & Embrechts, P. 2005. *Quantitative risk management: Concepts, techniques and tools.* Princeton, NJ: Princeton University Press.

Nelder, J. A., & Mead, R. 1965. "A simplex method for function minimization." *Computer Journal,* 7: 308–313.

Price, K., Storn, R. M., & Lampinen, J. A. 2005. *Differential evolution: A practical approach to global optimization.* Heidelberg: Springer. Natural Computing Series, Leiden Center for Natural Computing.

Rastrigin, L. A. 1963. "The convergence of the random search method in the extremal control of a many parameter system." *Automation and Remote Control,* 24 (10): 1337–1342.

Ray, J., & Bhattacharyya, S. 2015. "Value-at-risk based portfolio allocation using particle swarm optimization." *International Journal of Computer Sciences and Engineering*, 3, (special issue 1): 1–9.

Robbins, H., & Monro, S. 1951. "A stochastic approximation method." *Annals of Mathematical Statistics*, 22 (3): 400–407.

Rockafellar, R. T., & Uryasev, S. 2002. "Conditional value-at-risk for general loss distributions." *Journal of Banking & Finance*, 26 (7): 1443–1471.

Specht, K., & Winker, P. 2008. "Portfolio optimization under VaR constraints based on dynamic estimates of the variance-covariance matrix." In E. J. Kontoghiorghes, B. Rustem, & P. Winker (Eds.), *Computational Methods in Financial Engineering*. Heidelberg: Springer, pp. 73–94.

Talbi, E.-G. 2009. *Metaheuristics: From design to implementation*. Hoboken, NJ: Wiley.

Yang, X. S. 2011. "Metaheuristic optimization." *Scholarpedia*, 6 (8): 11472.

Ying, F. 2001. "EWMA method for estimating VaR of stock market and its application." *Forecasting*, 3: 34–37.

Ying, F., Yi-ming, W., & Shang-jun, Y. 2006. *Complexity in financial system: Model and analysis*. Beijing: Science Press.

Zenios, S. A. (Ed.) 1996. *Financial optimization*. Cambridge: Cambridge University Press.

Chapter 3

Big Data Analysis and Application for Video Surveillance Systems

Zheng Xu,[1] Zhiguo Yan,[1] Lin Mei,[1]
Chuanping Hu,[1,2] and Yunhuai Liu[1]

[1]Third Research Institute of the Ministry of Public Security, Beijing, China
[2]Shanghai Jiao Tong University, Shanghai, China

Contents

Abstract

Video surveillance is an integrated system with strong prevention capabilities, and it is widely used by the military, customs, police, firefighting, airports, railways, urban transport, and many other public places. It is an important part of any security system because of its visualized, accurate, timely, and rich information content. With the high-speed development of accessing and producing data, a new research area named Big Data is emerging. The existing computing infrastructure, software systems design, and application cases cannot manage and process Big Data. With the pervasiveness of the definition of the smart city, the public security surveillance system composed of a huge number of video surveillance devices, such as surveillance cameras (some statistics suggest that the number of public security surveillance cameras in Shanghai* is 500,000), boomed rapidly and produced a huge amount of data. The data volume of all video surveillance devices in Shanghai is up to the TB scale every day. In this chapter, three aspects are introduced, including (a) the intelligent analysis of video surveillance systems, (b) Big Data analysis of video surveillance systems, and (c) the application of video surveillance systems.

3.1 Intelligent Analysis of Video Surveillance Systems

3.1.1 Video Surveillance Systems in the Big Data Era

Big Data is an emerging paradigm applied to data sets whose size is beyond the ability of commonly used software tools to capture, manage, and process within a tolerable elapsed time [1]. Such data sets are often from various sources (variety), yet they may be unstructured, such as social media, sensors, scientific applications, surveillance, video and image archives, Internet texts and documents, Internet search indexing, medical records, business transactions, and web logs, and they are of large size (volume) with fast data in or out (velocity). More importantly, Big Data has to be of high value (value). Various technologies are being discussed to support the handling of Big Data, such as massive parallel processing databases [2], scalable storage systems [3], cloud computing platforms [4], and MapReduce [5]. Distributed systems is a classical research discipline

---

* The largest city in China with about 23 million people.

investigating various distributed computing technologies and applications, such as cloud computing and MapReduce. With new paradigms and technologies, distributed systems research keeps going with new innovative outcomes from both industry and academy.

Recent research shows that videos "in the wild" are growing at a staggering rate [6,7]—for example, with the rapid growth of video resources on the World Wide Web. On YouTube* alone, 35 h of video are uploaded every minute, and more than 700 billion videos were watched in 2010. Vast amount of videos with no metadata have emerged. Thus, automatically understanding raw videos solely based on their visual appearance becomes an important yet challenging problem. The rapid increase in the number of video resources has brought an urgent need to develop intelligent methods to represent and annotate the video events. Typical applications requiring representing and annotating video events include criminal investigation systems [8], video surveillance [9], intrusion detection systems [10], video resources browsing and indexing systems [11], sport events detection [12], and many others. These urgent needs have posed challenges for video resources management and have attracted research in multimedia analysis and understanding. Overall, the goal is to enable users to search the related events from the huge number of video resources. The ultimate goal of extracting video events brings the challenge to build an intelligent method to automatically detect and retrieve video events.

In fact, the huge number of new emerging video surveillance data becomes a new application field of Big Data. The processing and analyzing of video surveillance data follow the 4V feature of Big Data:

1. *Variety.* Video surveillance data come from different devices, such as traffic cameras, hotel cameras, and so on. In addition to the different surveillance devices, these devices also come from different regions. The distributed feature of video surveillance data augments the variety of the resources. For example, in criminal investigation systems, different video surveillance data from different surveillance devices are processed and analyzed to detect related people, cars, or things. The variety of video surveillance devices brings big challenges for the storage and management of distributed video surveillance data.

2. *Volume.* With the rapid development of surveillance devices, for example, the number of surveillance devices in Shanghai is up to 200,000, the volume of video surveillance data becomes Big Data. The data volume of all video surveillance data in Shanghai is up to 1 TB every day. The whole volume of all video surveillance data in Shanghai Pudong is up to 25 PB. The huge volume of video surveillance data brings big challenges for processing and analyzing distributed video surveillance data.

3. *Velocity.* Video surveillance devices have fast data in or out. They usually work 24 h per day and collect real-time videos. The real-time collected videos usually upload to a storage server or data center. The velocity of collecting video surveillance data is faster than that of processing and analyzing them. The high velocity of video surveillance devices brings big challenges for processing and analyzing video surveillance data because of this.

4. *Value.* Video surveillance data usually have high value. For example, in criminal investigation systems, video surveillance can help the police to find a suspect. In traffic surveillance systems, the video data can detect illegal vehicles or people. On the other hand, the huge volume brings challenges for mining the value from the video surveillance data. The phenomenon of "high volume, low value" also exists with video surveillance Big Data.

---

* www.youtube.com

3.1.2 Overview of Video Structural Description

Surveillance video data have grown tremendously in recent years, but traffic violations still cause a lot of accidents and personal injury every year. The increasing need for video-based applications raises the importance of parsing and organizing the content in videos. However, the accurate understanding and managing of video content at the semantic level is still insufficient. These features are at a higher-level description of the video content, but because of the lack of means of unified representation and modeling of human eye domain knowledge, a gap is formed between low-level grammar features and high-level semantic features, which is a difficult problem of semantic understanding faced in surveillance video analysis. The semantic gap between low-level features and high-level semantics cannot be bridged by manual or semiautomatic methods.

Video structural description (VSD) aims at parsing video content into text information, which uses spatiotemporal segmentation, feature selection, object recognition, and semantic web technology. The parsed text information preserves the semantics of the video content, which can be understood by humans and machines. Generally speaking, the definition of VSD includes two aspects. First, VSD aims at extracting the semantic content from the video. Relying on the standard video content description mechanism, the objects and their features in the video are recognized and expressed in the form of text. Second, VSD aims at organizing the video resources with their semantic relationships. With the semantic links across multiple cameras, it is possible to use data-mining methods for effective analysis and semantic retrieval of videos. Moreover, the semantic linking between the video resources and other information systems becomes possible. VSD is the foundation of building the next generation of intelligent and semantic video surveillance networks. It also makes the systematic, interconnected, and diverse applications of video surveillance systems possible. With the help of VSD, the simple data acquisition mode of video surveillance systems can be transferred to the integration mode of data acquisition, content processing, and semantic information services. The key issue and main innovation of VSD is the integration of video understanding and semantic web technologies. The semantic web technologies are used for representing and organizing the huge number of video resources.

3.1.3 Supporting Technologies of VSD

In this section, the supporting technologies of VSD are introduced. These technologies are used in the different layers of VSD, which can achieve the ultimate goal of VSD. The supporting technologies are listed as follows:

1. *Computer vision.* Computer vision is a field that includes methods for acquiring, processing, analyzing, and understanding images. A theme in the development of this field has been to duplicate the abilities of human vision by electronically perceiving and understanding an image. This image understanding can be seen as the disentangling of symbolic information from image data using models constructed with the aid of geometry, physics, statistics, and learning theory. Computer vision technologies can be used in the pattern recognition layer. For example, the car and people in a traffic video can be detected by the object detection technologies from the computer vision field.

2. *Semantic web.* The semantic web [13–15] is a collaborative movement led by the international standards body, the World Wide Web Consortium (W3C). The standard promotes common data formats on the World Wide Web. By encouraging the inclusion of semantic content in web pages, the semantic web aims at converting the current web dominated by

unstructured and semistructured documents into a "web of data." The semantic web technology can be used in the pattern recognition layer. For example, with the help of specific domain ontologies, the objects and relationships of videos can be detected accurately.

3. *Semantic link network.* A semantic link network (SLN) is a relational network consisting of the following main parts: a set of semantic nodes, a set of semantic links between the nodes, and a semantic space. Semantic nodes can be anything. The semantic link between nodes is regulated by the attributes of the nodes or generated by interactions between nodes. The semantic space includes a classification hierarchy of concepts and a set of rules for reasoning and inferring semantic links for influence nodes and links, for networking, and for evolving the network. The semantic link network can be used in the video resources layer. For example, with the help of the semantic link network model, the videos can be organized with their semantic relationships.

4. *Cloud computing.* Cloud computing is a colloquial expression used to describe a variety of different computing concepts that involve a large number of computers that are connected through a real-time communication network. In science, cloud computing is a synonym for distributed computing over a network and means the ability to run a program on many connected computers at the same time. The cloud computing technologies can be used in the video application layer. For example, with the help of cloud computing technologies, the huge number of videos can be managed and indexed efficiently and robustly.

3.1.4 Framework of VSD

The basic framework of VSD is given. The starting point of the VSD is a set of videos. The output of the VSD is a set of organized videos based on their semantics.

1. *Semantic content extraction module.* The input data of this module is a single video. The input video is parsed in this module. The parsing procedure is done with the help of the defined domain ontology. For example, the domain ontology about traffic rules can be used for parsing the traffic videos. The output of this module are objects, spatial and temporal relationships between objects, and events with the related objects and relationships. The output results of this module are conversed as the resources description framework (RDF). This conversion process facilitates the semantic representation of parsed videos. Thus, the parsing result of this module is represented as a graph. The nodes of the graph are the parsed objects; the links between the nodes are their spatial and temporal relationships.

2. *Semantic linking module.* The input data of this module are a set of parsed videos from the semantic content extraction module. The videos are linked in this module with the help of the semantic link network framework. For example, one video is about a car crossing a red traffic light, and another video is about the same car crashing into a pedestrian. These two videos can be linked because the same car appears. The output of this module is a network. The nodes of this network are the single videos, and the links of this network are the existing semantic relationships between videos. Because the parsed videos are represented as an RDF, the parsed videos can be enriched with other open sources with the same semantic web-based format. For example, one video is about the concept "Big Ben." With the help of an open GIS source, such as Open Street Map, the geolocation of the object in this video can be found.

3. *Video resources storage module.* This module aims at managing the video resources and builds the related index of these video resources. In particular, the number of video resources

has become a Big Data feature. For example, the data volume of all video surveillance devices in Shanghai is up to 1 TB every day. Thus, it is impossible to store these videos in a database. In this module, the Hadoop distributed file system (HDFS) is used to store the video resources. Meanwhile, the cloud computing-based infrastructure is used for uploading and downloading video resources.

4. *Video resources application module.* This module aims at using the organized video resources in real applications. For example, the related videos of the same car or person can be used for trajectory tracking. The organized videos can support a content-based image search (CBIR) with their extracted semantic contents. In simple terms, the content of the videos can be described by a set of regulated semantic keywords using the VSD resolving technique and produce the corresponding logic link. As a result, we can utilize these semantic keywords to retrieve the set of related video clips directly or locate the relevant frames.

3.2 Big Data Analysis of Video Surveillance Systems

3.2.1 Hierarchical Structure of VSD

VSD is set as a hierarchical semantic data model including three different layers. The different layers of VSD are illustrated in Figure 3.1.

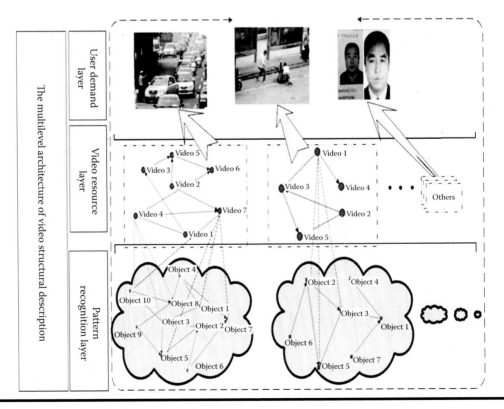

Figure 3.1 Hierarchical structure of VSD.

1. *Pattern recognition layer.* In this layer, VSD technology wants to extract and represent the content of the videos. For example, the people, vehicles, and traffic signs of the traffic video are extracted in this layer. Different from the existing video content extraction and representation method, VSD uses domain ontology, including basic objects, events, and relationships. These domain ontologies can be used by users for annotating and representing video events unambiguously. In addition, the spatial and temporal relationships are defined, which can be used by users for annotating and representing the semantic relationships between objects in video events.
2. *Video resources layer.* In the pattern recognition layer, VSD extracts and represents the content of a single video. In the video resources layer, VSD technology aims at linking the video resources with their semantic relationships. Similar to the World Wide Web, which uses hyperlinks to link resources, VSD uses semantic links instead of hyperlinks to link video resources.
3. *Video application layer.* The pattern recognition layer and video resources layer focus on processing video resources using their semantics. The video application layer focuses on using the organized video resources in real application tasks.

From Figure 3.1, the bottom layer consists of different objects. These objects, recognized from related pattern recognition methods, are composed of single videos. The middle layer consists of different videos. These videos consist of the different objects from the bottom layer. The semantic relationships also exist between video resources. In the top layer, users can search, annotate, and browse the related video resources. For example, if a user wants to know which vehicles cross the red traffic light in a video, the video resources layer can return the related videos.

3.2.2 Basic Procedures of the Pattern Recognition Layer

In this section, the bottom layer of the VSD is introduced. Because the computer vision and semantic web are the supporting technologies of this layer, the method for building domain ontology is given in this section. In this section, the basic procedures in the pattern recognition layer are given. The basic procedures of this layer are as follows:

Figure 3.2　Object detection results for traffic surveillance devices.

1. *Object detection.* Taking an unannotated video as input, related object detection methods [16–18] are employed. These methods use mixtures of deformable part models to represent objects and localize objects in images. These models are trained using a discriminative method that only requires bounding boxes for the objects in an image. In the surveillance video, we usually pay more attention to people and cars. For example, if the input videos are from traffic surveillance devices, the related detectors, such as person detection and car detection, are used. In Figure 3.2, detection results, including people, cars, and a motorbike are localized by red boxes. In this procedure, the domain ontology provides useful background knowledge and gives the hierarchies and constraints related to the object detectors.

2. *Object relation mining.* In this procedure, the relationships between the detected objects are mined. The spatial, temporal, and semantic relationships are detected through the object relation network [19], contextual information [20,21], etc. For example, if the detected objects from a video are a car and a person, the relationship of these two objects is mined. Similar to the above procedure, the domain ontology gives the relationship constraints related to the objects.

3. *RDF generation.* In this procedure, the detected objects and their relationships are transferred into RDF format. For example, if the detected objects are a car and a person and the detected relationship is a crash, then the generated RDF format can be seen as subject: car, object: person, predicate: crash.

3.2.3 VSD Pattern Recognition Layer

The ontology provides standard and accurate concepts and relationships for representing and annotating the content in videos. However, the existing ontology-based representation and annotation methods rely on the domain ontology. In other words, different domains study different ontology, and the different videos are limited to the use of their specific domain. For example, sports videos use a sport-based domain ontology, and traffic videos use a traffic-based domain ontology. In the VSD model, a wide-domain applicable video representation and annotation framework is proposed in order to model the semantic content. The proposed framework is a defined model for building domain ontology. It is an alternative to the rule-based and domain-dependent extraction methods. Building rules for extraction is a tedious task and is not scalable. Without any standard on rule construction, different domains can have different rules with different syntax. In addition to the complexity of handling such differences, each rule structure can have weaknesses. In addition, the proposed framework provides a standard rule construction ability with the help of its ontology. It eases the rule construction process and makes its use on larger video data possible. The rules that can be constructed via domain ontology can cover most of the event definitions for a wide variety of domains.

The proposed framework consists of three layers. The root layer contains three general classes, Object, Relation, and Attribute. Object means the class of the extracted objects from the video. Relation means the class of relations between the extracted objects from the video. Attribute means the visual feature such as shape and color of the extracted objects from the video. The visual layer contains the objects that can be extracted by the existing object extracting method. For example, a person detector and a ball detector use Hough Circle Transform in OpenCV. Of course, the extracted object is a subclass of Object. The semantic layer contains domain knowledge about the semantic hierarchies of object and relation classes. Obviously, ontology with hierarchical information is preferred since it carries more semantic information.

3.2.4 Semantic-Enhanced Intermediate Layer of the Cloud Environment

Recently, cloud computing has been proposed as one of the promising next-generation computing paradigms because it promises consumers they will be able to access applications and data from a "cloud" anywhere on demand. The definition of cloud computing can be considered as a type of parallel and distributed system consisting of a collection of interconnected and virtualized computers that are dynamically provisioned and presented as one datum or more unified computing data. The feature of cloud computing depends on the large-scale aggregation of homogeneous and orderly resources.

In this section, in addition to the semantic-based representation of distributed video data, a semantic-enhanced intermediate layer, which has a global view of data with different classifications, is proposed. The proposed semantic layer clusters the video data with similar or associated relationships. The technologies from the SLN are used to organize data and form semantic clouds, that is, similarity-enhanced clouds and associated enhanced clouds. The SLN is the bridge over different kinds of data, which can link cross-domain data.

The current cloud computing layer is shown in the left part of Figure 3.3. At the bottom of the cloud computing layer, the cloud provider provides the related computing or storage service.

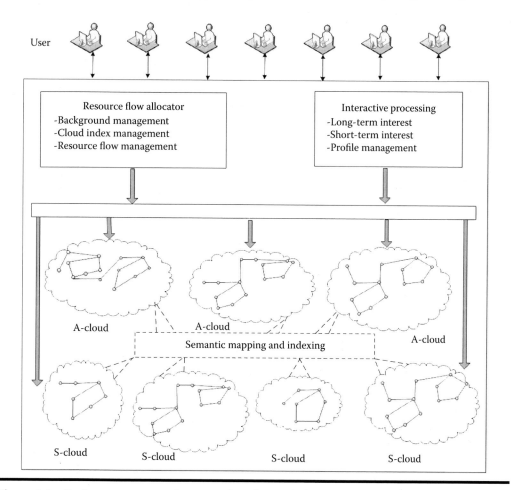

Figure 3.3   Basic components of a semantic-enhanced cloud.

At the middle of the cloud computing layer, through utility computing, the cloud user or SaaS provider can provide a web-based application. At the top of the cloud layer, the SaaS user can use the related web-based service. Different from the users, cloud providers have their own powerful computing capability, which can provide high-speed computing ability or large volume storage space. Direct exposure to the cloud's user or service provider may lead to the problem that the final services to users are also uniform. The absence of connections between cloud providers is not helpful to improve that case either.

Thus, we add an additional semantic layer for cloud computing shown in the right part of Figure 3.3. The added semantic-enhanced layer builds a global virtual semantic structure, which clusters the related data into the same class. This new vision for the cloud users or service providers can make them offer much better service to end users. Unlike the classical technique of the semantic web, our method is based on computation, which makes it much easier to build the semantic layer and, at the same time, hold as much semantic information as possible.

3.2.5 SLN-Based Intermediate Layer

The main concerning issues of a cloud environment include hardware systems, software systems, data centers, and quality of services. The SLN model concerns the two latter factors. As a data management model, an SLN can be a semantic-enhanced data center model, which organizes the data with their semantic relationships. Because the video data are represented as defined objects and their relationships, the SLN model can be easily applied. For the quality of services, the SLN model is easily provided to users just in the form of services. When a large amount of data are gathered together in the SLN model, similarity-enhanced clouds and association-enhanced clouds are naturally formed.

Similarity-enhanced clouds (S-clouds) and associated-enhanced clouds (A-clouds) organize the video data based on their similarity and associated relationships. Because each video is represented by defined objects, the similarity and associated relationships between these objects can be mined easily. S-clouds and A-clouds offer the foundation of a semantic-enhanced cloud. Apart from them, to make the cloud scalable and to be able to identify the global optimal resource clusters to users, hierarchical resource clusters and an interactive process are needed.

1. *Hierarchical resource clusters.* In order to improve the robustness and link as much data as possible, S-clouds and A-clouds are constructed as illustrated in Figure 3.3. The components of S-clouds and A-clouds have two different grains. Because the number of clouds is small, the number of this kind of S-clouds and A-clouds is fewer also. Their role is also important because their range is much wider than the fine-grained S-clouds and A-clouds.
2. *Interactive process.* S-clouds and A-clouds should meet the different needs of each individual user. Traditional search engines just return the result of the query and do not provide an interactive process for users to make deeper and wider browses or searches. Hierarchical resource clusters rely on interactive processing to identify a user's search objectively, which continuously corrects returned data with the feedback from users.

The basic components of a semantic-enhanced cloud are shown in Figure 3.3.

1. The resource cluster allocator performs as the interactive interface between the cloud and users. When a user submits a search or browse request, the resource cluster allocator analyzes the profile of the user and returns the related video data.

2. The user interactive component is started by a user's requirements upon the data allocated by the resource cluster allocator. When a user's feedback shows his or her interests, the interactive process chooses the next potential datum dynamically according to the long-term or short-term profile.

3. S-clouds and A-clouds are created offline and would be incremented with the increase in data. S-clouds and A-clouds could evolve and be reorganized with the change of the content of data. That is also the "floating" of clouds.

When different parts of a recourse flow-oriented cloud are combined as a complete architecture, the resource flow-oriented clouds have their own characteristics:

1. *Scalability.* The creation of a semantic cloud is efficient, and the update of SLN clouds and ALN clouds has low cost. This would pave the way for the floating and evolving of clouds.

2. *Global optimization.* Although lower SLN clouds provide locally optimized results, the upper ALN clouds link data from different organizations, domains, and fields that have global vision.

3. *Robustness.* Our architecture owns the robustness in two ways. In SLN clouds, data abundance can be obtained easily by gathering data with the same kind of ability. Second, in ALN clouds, robustness is supported by the structure of the networks. ALN clouds can keep working if the core parts of the ALN are not broken.

3.3 Application of Video Surveillance Systems

3.3.1 VSD Technology of Mobile Terminal Systems

In this section, we introduce the application of a mobile device to video data acquisition and intelligent content-wise analysis. To be specific, aiming at the solution of deepening video application to intelligent transportation and public security, the VSD technique on the Android platform is utilized to execute the scene description task and implement the recognition tasks, such as face recognition and vehicle recognition. The schema of VSD on mobile computing architecture is figured out, and the synthesis searching framework is introduced by utilizing the semantic web search engine. As our experiments show, the OpenCV for Android-based video analysis and event detection is eligible for the present ARM-based hardware configuration. Furthermore, the offline training and online recognition mechanism can adequately utilize the advantage of the mobile computing environment in the WLAN and can guarantee real-time VSD on the Android platform. The extensive application in video portals shows the inspiring prospect of the proposed video analysis technology. The present deficiency of the lightweight VSD is also discussed.

3.3.2 Introduction to VSD

VSD [22] is widely utilized in many fields of city management. As a powerful anticrime tool, it has gained popularity in public security since 9/11. Nowadays, video surveillance systems play an irreplaceable role in city management and city safety.

In a city video surveillance system, due to the large number of cameras and the enormity of storing video records, it is a tedious and painful task to search for a specific object or person in the surveillance system. In most cases, it is an almost impossible mission to find and track a criminal across multiple cameras in vast video records, not to mention real-time finding and tracking.

VSD was first proposed for a visual surveillance system by the Third Research Institute of the Ministry of Public Security (TRIMPS) in 2009 in China.

The radical deficiency of the traditional surveillance system lies in that it was designed as a data collecting center rather than an information processing system. Different from other content-based intelligent video analysis techniques, by mining the prior field knowledge and scenario characteristics, according to the predefined rules for specific events, the VSD technique can use the standard metadata to describe the occurrence; the related people, vehicles, and objects; and the corresponding scenario overview. In other words, the VSD can translate the video information to structured text information composed of the elements related to the event itself. By utilizing the VSD technique, the surveillance video information can be extracted and processed automatically online, and a prompt warning message can be produced shown in Figure 3.4.

We have built several VSD systems on general servers for practical applications in transportation management, jail management, and service area surveillance on the highway. The built VSD

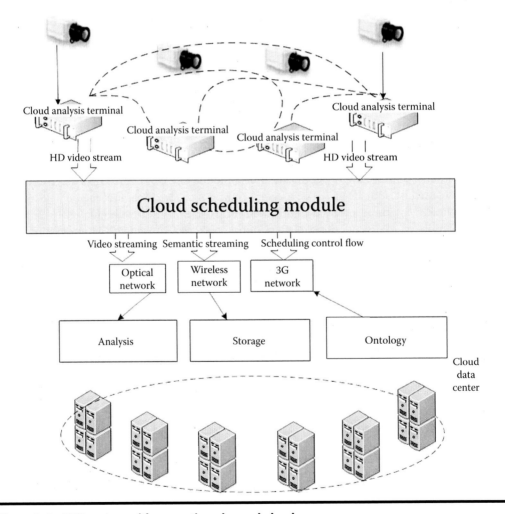

Figure 3.4 VSD system with semantic-enhanced cloud.

systems have greatly improved management efficiency and enhanced the ability of information acquisition.

Now we give an exact and comprehensive specification about the VSD as follows: VSD is a technique that extracts and refines information from video data and structures it into both human- and machine-readable text according to the information's intrinsic semantic relationships.

To extract knowledge from video, typical methods could be employed, such as spatial–temporal segmentation, feature extraction, object recognition, and so on. The basic idea of VSD is illustrated in Figure 3.5. Before the original video data are pushed to a storage unit, they are inputted into a processor for analysis. We call this processor the structured description unit. Information on video contents is extracted here and organized for storage with the assistance of a certain semantic model. There are two outputs of the description unit: video and its knowledge description. The text channel is parallel to the transportation channel of the duplicated video.

That is to say, the VSD bypasses the existing video analysis system, and we can keep the system compatibility to the farthest extent. Correspondence between video and description data is also kept by the system for further applications. Video system users could use a description to locate the wanted clips efficiently and to retrieve the exact content without tedious video review. Then, the exact video clips could be delivered by the Internet or business network once they are located by a search engine. At this time, video transportation is purposeful, and bandwidth consumption is highly reduced by removing irrelevant video data. It makes video data sharing operable between different networks, and on-site data acquisition could be replaced by the popular network sharing. Furthermore, a content-related storage policy could be used, and content information could be kept as much as possible.

Real-world information that video recorded can be classified into three levels: visual features, objects, and concepts. Visual features include low-level information including color, shape, texture, and spatial relationships. Object information is at the middle level; they are people, vehicles, characters, etc., in surveillance scenarios. The top-level information is semantic concept; this is the rational understanding or explanation of the video by different people, such as "whether a control point in a railway station was running soundly." VSD was designed for surveillance systems to achieve video knowledge extraction, representation, and sharing over a wide range of networks.

As an application-oriented surveillance solution, there are three fundamental techniques that are involved in the VSD framework: (a) visual knowledge modeling, (b) feature extraction and video understanding, and (c) video knowledge representation.

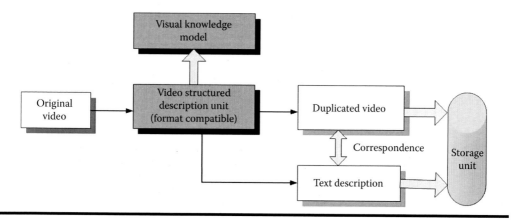

Figure 3.5   Schematic diagram of VSD technique.

Now we discuss the role and hierarchy of the component techniques in VSD.

1. *Visual knowledge modeling*: Visual knowledge modeling defines which kind of information should be used to describe and refine both low-level features and semantic information. Moreover, it defines the structure of this knowledge and the logical relationships between different parts of a certain structure. The most important of all is the visual knowledge model we argued must be a semantic one, which could be supported by domain knowledge modeling.

2. *Feature extraction and video understanding*: Low-level features were well-researched information and various extracting methods proposed by different researchers. Video understanding aims to extract middle- and high-level semantic information. In recent decades, different researchers have focused their interests on image understanding, and some important theories were proposed [23]. Identifying objects from a scenario image and understanding the scenario are two main tasks of image understanding [24]. Object identification is the preparatory step that aims to describe the scenario–scenario understanding, and description supplies prior knowledge for object identification. Traditional object identifications are face detection, face recognition, human detection, and so on. In VSD, we stress that video understanding is relevant to a specific surveillance task and constrained by a semantic knowledge model.

3. *Video knowledge representation*: There are two missions of representation. The first one is how to instance a video knowledge model, which is composed of metadata sets and syntax. Metadata is the basic elements of visual knowledge, and metadata syntax reflects the structures of visual knowledge. Once metadata and its corresponding syntax are determined, a definition language, such as XML, RDF(S), or OWL, must be chosen. Considering the computation consumption and feasibility on the Android platform, RDF is adopted as the description language. Ontology is a powerful knowledge modeling technique and widely uses information or knowledge cataloguing and representation. It was recommended for semantic web by W3C [25]. For VSD, ontology and OWL were highly recommended. The other mission is to organize video information distilled from video clips. It needs to optimize and trim a full-function model for a special description task.

Moreover, the semantic search engine is an intrinsic component of the VSD. With the help of the semantic analysis tool, we can execute an efficient and effective search on the online and offline video data. For example, we can use keywords such as "red," "small vehicle," "Volkswagen," etc., to locate the exactly wanted images and video clips. In addition to this kind of text-to-video search, we also can implement an image-to-image search by measuring the similarity of the image and the video frame.

3.3.3 Data Acquisition by Android Terminals

Mobile computing [26] involves mobile communication, mobile hardware, and mobile software. Mobile computing is able to use a computing device even when being mobile and therefore changing location. Portability is one aspect of mobile computing.

Communication issues include ad hoc and infrastructure networks as well as communication properties, protocols, data formats, and concrete technologies. Hardware includes mobile devices or device components, such as tablet PCs and powerful smartphones. Following the development of Android OS and ARM CPU, the prevalent smartphones all have large screens and powerful

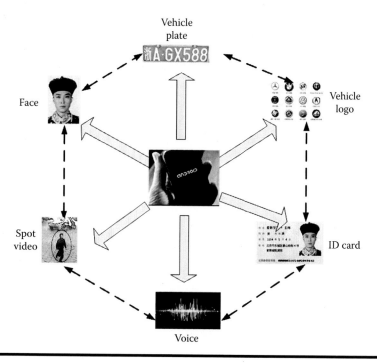

Figure 3.6   Data acquisition illustration of Android terminal.

computation ability; the boundary between the tablet PC and mobile handheld device becomes blurry. Mobile software deals with the characteristics and requirements of mobile applications.

The Android-based terminal can be competent for mobile data acquisition and the mobile computing node [27]. As for the data acquisition, we can use the built-in camera to capture the spot evidence, such as photos of related people, voices, the number plate of a specific vehicle, the vehicle logo, the video on the spot, etc. Furthermore, with the near field communication (NFC) technique, the handheld terminal can read the ID card information and the correlation across the various pieces of information can be acquired in terms of the uniqueness of the ID card number.

As Figure 3.6 shows, the Android handset can not only act as a portable data acquisition center to acquire the spot video, voice data, and the related vehicle information, but can also be the mobile computing node to process the information in the wireless environment, such as WLAN or 3G.

As Figure 3.6 shows, through the built-in image sensor and NFC unit, the Android handset can execute prompt data acquisition, such as image, video, voice, and RFID card information. To some extent, with the imbedded camera and mobility, the Android terminal can be regarded as an effective supplement to the fixed surveillance cameras.

Through the flexible deployment of Android terminals, the dead zone of the existing video can be compensated for rapidly and cheaply.

3.3.4 Realization of VSD on the Android Platform

As mentioned, Android terminals can be used for data acquisition on the spot, but their more meaningful role is their mobile computing performance. As the portable data acquisition center to acquire the spot video, voice data, and the related vehicle information is just the traditional data collecting function of the Android terminals, their major importance lies in their mobile computing node role, processing the spot information in the wireless environment, such as WLAN or 3G.

In other words, mobile computing is the ability to use computing capability without a predefined location and/or connection to a network to publish and/or subscribe to information. As to the Android terminal in the movable operation manner, if the OS version is 4.0 or above, the direct WiFi connection is very convenient to execute the B/S, C/S server and other lightweight distributed computing tasks within a limited range.

In Figure 3.7, we can not only observe the data acquisition function but also figure out the mobile computing function. With the help of specific field knowledge and a rule database, the VSD technique on the Android platform (we call it Android VSD) can deal not only with the surveillance but also the network video and local private entertainment video. For example, to those video portal websites, such as YouTube, the video maker can tag his or her video products by VSD and upload the corresponding text description document while uploading the local video files. To those subscribers to the video portal website, before they browse the downloaded video on their Android terminals, the VSD on Android will automatically analyze the video content and give out the coarse brief introduction in a text file.

The example of an extensive application of Android VSD shows the inspiring prospect in many fields. Figure 3.8 shows the detailed implementation of lightweight realization of VSD on Android. This block diagram illustrates two important aspects of Android VSD: One is object recognition, and the other is event detection. As to the object recognition, the classic application case is face recognition and vehicle plate recognition. Considering the relatively weak computation performance and the time consumption during the training phase, we adopt the offline training and online recognition mechanism. That is to say, we transport the extracted features to the PC for training, and the PC returns the coefficients of the classifier after finishing the training. Then, the classification algorithm running on the Android platform executes the object recognition task. Through this strategy, we can avoid the tedious and time-consuming training phase. This mode can guarantee the real-time object recognition with the present hardware configuration.

In addition, the design of the lightweight algorithm on object recognition plays an important role in the realization of Android VSD. For example, as far as the face recognition is concerned, it is a time-consuming task in the Android environment if we adopt those mature algorithms on the desktop computer platform, such as the PCA and neural network.

Experimental results from physiology and psychophysics have shown that the edges of an object contain important information about its shape and structure and can be used in face recognition. It is suggested that the edge maps of faces are useful and efficient in face identification in terms of light computation. In another aspect, the edge map contains less data and is convenient to process and store.

Moreover, comparing with the classifiers, the template-matching method is more rapid and has been shown to have better performance than the feature-based techniques. As an image feature, edges have the advantages of simplicity of presentation and robustness to illumination change.

In our experiment, we acquire the edge maps of the training set offline and store them to the Android terminal. Relatively, online computing the edge map of the object face is a light computation load. Then, the template-matching method using Hausdorff distance is also a less time-consuming task. This strategy on face recognition in a simple scenario is a

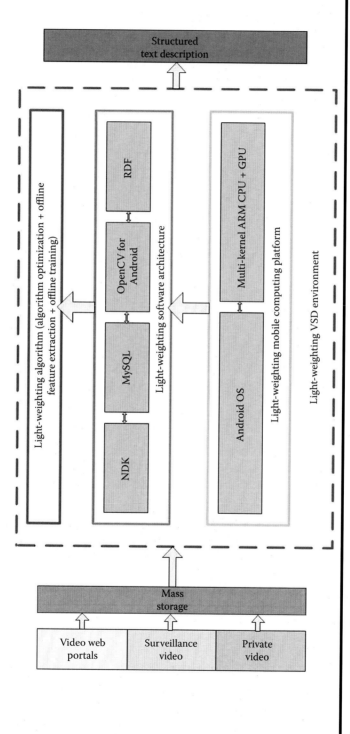

Figure 3.7 VSD realization in the mobile computing environment.

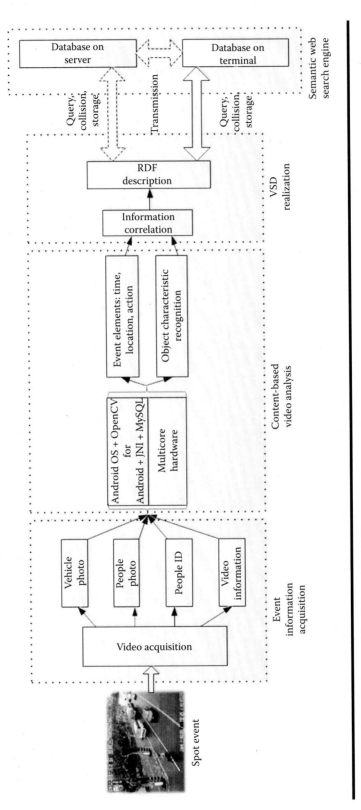

Figure 3.8 Flow diagram of the lightweight VSD.

kind of effective and efficient algorithm, which can enable the real-time face recognition on the Android platform. The proposed lightweight algorithm of online face recognition is just one kind of suitable real application. There is still a lot of work to be done considering the tremendous differences of algorithms implemented between the X86 family and ARM family architecture.

Similar to the abovementioned depiction, the algorithms for the vehicle number plate also should be lightweight and adjusted to run on the Android platform.

As for the event detection, we adopt the mature development package OpenCV for Android. For those simple scenarios, we can use the less time-consuming background segmentation algorithm, such as the background subtraction algorithm. For complicated scenarios, the Gause mixed modeling (GMM) is a prevalent algorithm. By utilizing the OpenCV for Android development package, we can exploit different event detection programs for various scenarios.

In summary, the lightweight algorithm scheme involves two kinds of methodology for reducing the computational load. One is about the reduction of feature set and the effort of exploiting the effective and efficient task-dependent classifier. The other is about the training strategy, such as the offline training and online recognition.

3.3.5 Application Instance

Figure 3.9 shows the Android VSD execution process under traffic surveillance circumstances. In the video, a car is across the intersection. By analyzing the characteristics, such as car color, number plate, car logo, and other additional spot information, the Android VSD produces the

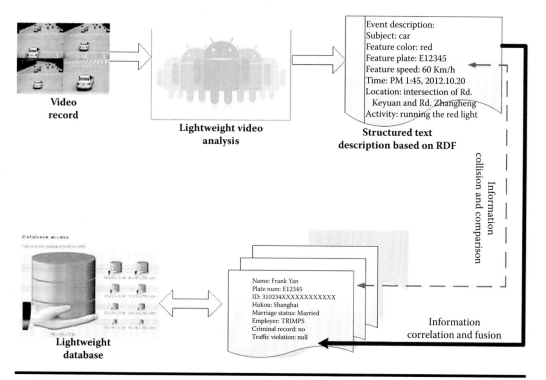

Figure 3.9   Lightweight VSD in transportation surveillance video.

text description file about the related events the car is involved in. Then, through the information collision in the appropriate time span and location, we can get more correlation about this vehicle such as the owner and the records of traffic offences.

3.4 Vehicle and Pedestrian Detection and Description

After the histograms of oriented gradients (HoG) feature was proposed, a lot of detectors were developed based on the feature. The HoG feature has its defects, such high dimensional data leading to inefficiency, complex scenes leading to poor performances, and so on. In this chapter, we propose a vehicle detector based on the deformable part model (DPM). This detector uses a DPM to classify the front and the rear of the vehicles.

3.4.1 Introduction

Object detection, such as vehicle detection, pedestrian detection, and so on, is one of the most popular research fields in computer vision. Normally, the common detecting solutions are using HoG, Sift, or Haar to extract features and using SVM or Adaboost as classifiers. In this section, we propose a solution by using DPM to detect vehicles. In consideration of the variety of appearances of vehicles, they are affected by many factors, such as changes in illumination or angle of view. The traditional detecting algorithms have difficulty overcoming the rigid deformations. DPM uses a mixture of multiscale deformable part models to describe an object detection system, which represents highly variable objects [28] and which has better robustness against deformation.

DPM, as one of the most successful detection algorithms, was proposed by Pedro Felzenswalb in 2008 and he was awarded the PASCAL VOC Lifetime Achievement Prize in 2010. Due to Felzenswalb's paper, the resulting system is both efficient and accurate, achieving state-of-the-art results on PASCAL VOC benchmarks and the INRIA Person data set in 2007 [29]. The strong, low-level features of DPM are based on the HoG features. So the DPM can be considered to be an upgrade of HoG in some ways [30].

As shown in Figure 3.10, the upgraded HoG feature in DPM kept the "cell" concept of the HoG feature but altered the normalization process. The result shared similarity with the result of the HoG feature as the upgraded HoG feature normalized the region that consisted of the target cell and the four surrounding cells. In order to reduce the feature dimension, Felzenswalb used principal component analysis (PCA) [31] to analyze the unsigned gradients. As illustrated in Figure 3.10, there are 31 dimensional features.

In his work, Felzenswalb showed a pedestrian detection model, as shown in Figure 3.11. Panel a of the figure shows the pedestrian, panel b is a root filter, panel c shows several part models with high resolution, and panel d shows the spatial relationships of the part filters.

DPM uses a root filter, several part filters, and the corresponding deformable model; the construction of the whole model is based on the pictorial structures. Normally, the part models use higher resolution than the root filter—about two times. Figure 3.11b and c illustrates the visual structure of the root and part models, and shows the weighted sum of SVM coefficients, oriented in the gradient direction, and the brightness is proportional to the value. In order to reduce the complexity of the whole model, the part models are symmetric. Figure 3.11d shows the deviation cost of the part model. The cost is zero in the ideal case; the further the part model deviates, the greater the cost is. Then the target object can be represented by a collection of parts and the relative deformable position

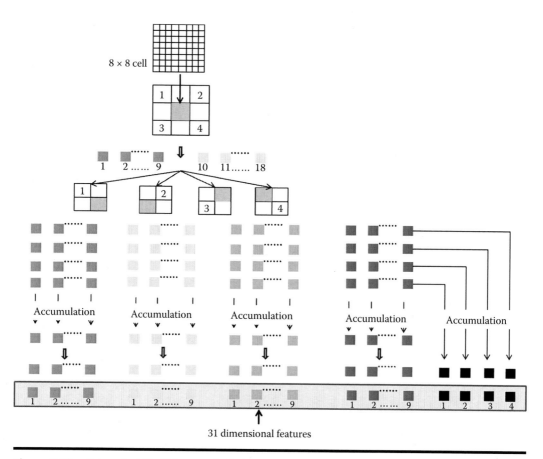

Figure 3.10   Upgraded HoG feature in DPM.

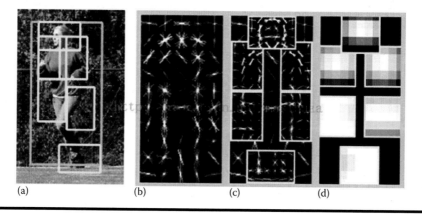

Figure 3.11   DPM pedestrian detection model.

of the parts; the parts are connected in certain ways. Each part describes local properties, and the spring-like connections are used to represent the relationship between the deformable models. As a single deformable model is not capable of describing an object, usually multiple deformable models are in accordance with the request. In this chapter, the variations among different vehicle types are quite significant, so the mixture of deformable models is required.

3.4.2 DPM Detection Model

In the detection process, a scale pyramid is constructed, and a scan window approach is used to scan different layers of the pyramid. Figure 3.12 shows the detection process of DPM. In Figure 3.12, the score of layer l_0 coordinates (x_0, y_0) can be calculated as follows:

$$score(x_0, y_0, l_0) = R_{0,i_0}(x_0, y_0) + \sum_{i=1}^{n} D_{i,l_0-\lambda}(2(x_0, y_0) + v_i) + b. \tag{3.1}$$

where $R_{0,i_0}(x_0, y_0)$ is the score of the root filter; in other words, it expresses the matching degree between model and target; $\sum_{i=1}^{n} D_{i,l_0-\lambda}(2(x_0, y_0) + v_i)$ is the scores of n part filters; b is the root of

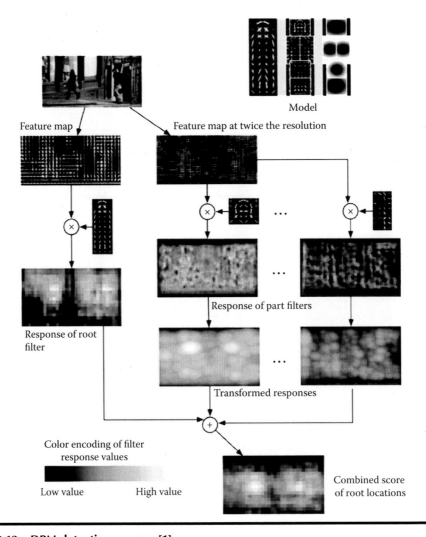

Figure 3.12 DPM detection process [1].

set that is used to align the components; (x_0, y_0) is the coordinate of the root filter's left top in the root feature map; and $(2(x_0, y_0) + v_i)$ is the coordinate of the ith part filter in the root feature map. The score of part filters can be calculated as follows [7]:

$$D_{i,l}(x, y) = \max_{dx, dy}(R_{i,l}(x + dx, y + dy) - d_i \cdot \Phi_d(dx, dy)). \tag{3.2}$$

where $D_{i,l}(x, y)$ is the optimal solution of the part filter; namely, it searches the anchor position and within a certain range for a proper location that has combined matching and optimal deformation; (x, y) is the ideal position of the ith part filter in layer l; (dx, dy) illustrates the relative offset from (x, y); $R_{i,l}(x + dx, y + dy)$ is the matching score in coordinate $(x + dx, y + dy)$; $d_i \cdot \Phi_d(dx, dy)$ expresses the offset loss caused by the offset (dx, dy); $\Phi_d(dx, dy) = (dx, dy, dx^2, dy^2)$; and d_i is the coefficient of offset loss; it is to be calculated in the training process. To initialize the model, $d_i = (0, 0, 1, 1)$ is the Euclidean distance between offset location and ideal location, namely, the offset loss.

3.4.3 Experiment and Conclusion

The original image data are captured from a traffic surveillance system somewhere in JiangSu province. The training data that are used in DPM are illustrated as in Figure 3.13.

In the training process, positive samples must be labeled with bounding boxes, which are illustrated in Figure 3.13. In this experiment, 1700 images of vehicle fronts and 1900 images of vehicle rears are positive samples, which are labeled with bounding boxes, and the property files are generated.

The training procedure is completed by initializing the structure of a mixture model and learning parameters. The parameters are learned by training a latent support vector machine (LSVM). The LSVM is trained by a gradient descent algorithm and the data-mining approach with a cache of feature vectors.

Figure 3.13   DPM training data: vehicle front.

In this experiment, three models are designed by DPM: the vehicle front model is used to recognize the frontal side of a vehicle, the vehicle rear model is used to recognize the back side of a vehicle, and the vehicle mixture model is used to capture either the frontal or back side of a vehicle. There are two testing sets in this experiment: 100 vehicle front images and 100 vehicle rear images. The testing results of the vehicle front model are illustrated in Tables 3.1 through 3.4. In Table 3.1, the number of correctly recognized objects is 96—this means in some sample images, there exist several vehicles. In other words, there are 96 vehicles in the 93 sample images.

The testing results of the vehicle rear model are illustrated in Table 3.2. This case is the same as the abovementioned case. There are 112 vehicles in the 96 sample images.

Table 3.1 Performance of the Front Model on Front Testing Samples

DPM Vehicle Front Model Recognizing Testing Images of Vehicle Front			
Total Image Samples	*Correctly Recognized Samples*	*Accuracy*	*Correctly Recognized Objects*
100	93	93%	96

Table 3.2 Performance of the Rear Model on Front Testing Samples

DPM Vehicle Rear Model Recognizing Testing Images of Vehicle Front			
Total Image Samples	*Correctly Recognized Samples*	*Accuracy*	*Correctly Recognized Objects*
100	96	96%	112

Table 3.3 Comparison Experiment

DPM Vehicle Front and Rear Models Recognizing Testing Images of Vehicle Front					
DPM Vehicle Front Model			DPM Vehicle Rear Model		
Total Image Samples	*Correctly Recognized Samples*	*Accuracy*	*Total Image Samples*	*Correctly Recognized Samples*	*Accuracy*
100	39	39%	100	69	69%
DPM Vehicle Front and Rear Models Recognizing Testing Images of Vehicle Rear					
DPM Vehicle Front Model			DPM Vehicle Rear Model		
Total Image Samples	*Correctly Recognized Samples*	*Accuracy*	*Total Image Samples*	*Correctly Recognized Samples*	*Accuracy*
100	47	47%	100	76	76%

Table 3.4 Performance of the Mixed Model

DPM Mixture Model Recognizing Testing Images of Vehicle Front			
Total Image Samples	Correctly Recognized Samples	Accuracy	Correctly Recognized Objects
100	70	70%	70
DPM Mixture Model Recognizing Testing Images of Vehicle Rear			
Total Image Samples	Correctly Recognized Samples	Accuracy	Correctly Recognized Objects
100	90	90%	203

It sounds odd that the rear model surpasses the front model on the front testing samples. In order to know which model performs better under the same conditions, we used the two models to recognize the same image objects and then outputted the results with the higher confidence degree in Table 3.3.

As the front and rear sides of the same vehicle always share certain similarities, we conjecture the probability of using one model to recognize the two sides of a vehicle. So we used DPM to design a mixture model to capture the vehicles in two-way lanes. The testing results are shown in Table 3.4.

By comparing the results from three DPM vehicle models, the non-mixed models acquired higher accuracy. But they did not perform satisfactorily in the mixture test. In order to capture the vehicles in a two-way lane, we proposed the third mixture DPM vehicle model. It is more efficient to capture vehicle vision and shows high versatility.

3.5 Face Detection and Description

Most face recognition and tracking techniques employed in surveillance and human–computer interaction (HCI) systems rely on the assumption of a frontal view of the human face. In alternative approaches, knowledge of the orientation angle of the face in captured images can improve the performance of techniques based on nonfrontal face views.

Facial orientation detection plays an important role in city surveillance video for specific applications, such as face identification, face recognition, and screening face snapshot images for saving the storage volume. In this section, we propose a kind of method of facial orientation by combining Haar-feature and LVQ technique. First, we execute the eye location based on the Haar-like feature. Then, we divide the face image into several subimages and statistical information of the binary subimage at the eye location. After acquiring the statistical pixel distribution, we exploit the LVQ classifier to execute the classification on facial orientation. According to the result, the algorithm we propose can achieve a 95% correct detection rate. By executing the facial orientation classification, we can get the upright frontal face image with the best recognizable and most distinctive quality for further application.

3.5.1 Introduction

In the past two decades, automatic human face image analysis and recognition has become one of the most important research topics in computer vision and pattern recognition. Because of the tremendous potential application, topics such as face detection, face identification and recognition, and facial expression analysis have attracted more and more attention. Among these research topics, one fundamental but very important problem to be solved is face orientation detection. Face orientation detection is the premise of face recognition.

Face detection refers to determining the presence and location of faces in an image. Human face detection is very important in a face recognition system and quite useful in multimedia retrieval [32]. Numerous face detection methods have been proposed for frontal face detection, such as region-based face detection [33], the triangle-based approach [34], the feature-based method [35], and the template matching method [36]. The aforementioned methods limit themselves to dealing with human faces in frontal view. So knowing how to detect the facial orientation and store the upright frontal face image for further face recognition is of significance in civil video surveillance.

Orientation is one of the basic characteristics in image understanding and pattern analysis. Many approaches have been proposed to solve the above problem. Jie Zhou [37] proposed an orientation histogram for orientation analysis. Chia-Feng Juang found that a self-organizing fuzzy network with SVM [38] worked well in color image detection. R. Brunelli [39] developed a good method to estimate the pose of a face, limited to in-depth rotations.

However, these novel approaches are limited to special situations. Rotated faces can only be detected within the image plane when using the orientation histogram; the self-organizing fuzzy network with SVM method uses color as an eigenvalue, so it's hard to work with in gray images; the algorithm in [39] needs an appropriate template because the algorithm he presented requires the location of one of the eyes be approximately known, together with the direction of the axis; the stimuli that is used in Martini's experiments is hard to obtain.

Facial detection and recognition is based on the operation of eye localization. To some extent, the performance is determined by the correctness of the eye detection. Much research has been conducted on human eye detection, and several algorithms have been proposed, such as region segmentation, template matching, the AdaBoost algorithm, and so on.

Region segmentation is a simple but rewarding algorithm, which has attracted numerous researchers. The threshold is not easy to decide appropriately, although it is the key to correct eye detection. The template matching method costs expensive computation when normalizing the scale and orientation of a face image. Inho Choi used the AdaBoost algorithm in eye detection and eye blink detection almost successfully, but the size of the subregions is hard to predict when dividing them to build an image pyramid. As far as eye localization is concerned, making use of the distinct characteristic of the eyeball is the key step no matter what method is used. Document developed a fast eye localization method based on a new Haar-like (ref) feature, which proved impressive in eye detection. However, it still needs further research to find a more adequate threshold segmentation method in order to make the algorithm more robust.

Most face recognition and tracking techniques employed in surveillance and HCI systems rely on the assumption of a frontal view of the human face. In alternative approaches, knowledge of the orientation angle of the face in captured images can improve the performance of techniques based on nonfrontal face views.

Our approach is partly motivated by the work of Chen and Liu [40] and Kasinski and Schmidt [41], in which they use the Haar-like feature and the boosting classification strategy to locate the eyes. On the basis of their achievement, we go a step further by using the learning vector quantization (LVQ) classifier to detect the face orientation.

3.5.2 Face Detection Methods

Haar-like features are digital image features used in object recognition. They owe their name to their intuitive similarity with Haar wavelets and were used in the first real-time face detector.

Historically, working with only image intensities (i.e., the RGB pixel values at each and every pixel of image) made the task of feature calculation computationally expensive. A publication by Papageorgiou and Poggio [42] discussed working with an alternate feature set based on Haar wavelets instead of the usual image intensities.

Viola and Jones [43] adapted the idea of using Haar wavelets and developed the so-called Haar-like features. A Haar-like feature considers adjacent rectangular regions at a specific location in a detection window, sums up the pixel intensities in each region, and calculates the difference between these sums. This difference is then used to categorize subsections of an image. For example, let us say we have an image database with human faces. It is a common observation that among all faces the region of the eyes is darker than the region of the cheeks. Therefore, a common Haar feature for face detection is a set of two adjacent rectangles that lie above the eye and the cheek region. The position of these rectangles is defined relative to a detection window that acts like a bounding box to the target object (the face in this case).

In the detection phase of the Viola–Jones object detection framework, a window of the target size is moved over the input image, and for each subsection of the image, the Haar-like feature is calculated. This difference is then compared to a learned threshold that separates nonobjects from objects. Because such a Haar-like feature is only a weak learner or classifier (its detection quality is slightly better than random guessing), a large number of Haar-like features is necessary to describe an object with sufficient accuracy. In the Viola–Jones object detection framework, the Haar-like features are therefore organized into something called a classifier cascade to form a strong learner or classifier.

The key advantage of a Haar-like feature over most other features is its calculation speed. Due to the use of integral images, a Haar-like feature of any size can be calculated in constant time.

A simple rectangular Haar-like feature can be defined as the difference of the sum of pixels of areas inside the rectangle, which can be at any position and scale within the original image. This modified feature set is called the two-rectangle feature. Viola and Jones also defined three-rectangle features and four-rectangle features. The values indicate certain characteristics of a particular area of the image. Each feature type can indicate the existence (or absence) of certain characteristics in the image, such as edges or changes in texture. For example, a two-rectangle feature can indicate where the border lies between a dark region and a light region.

One of the contributions of Viola and Jones was to use summed area tables, which they called integral images. Integral images can be defined as two-dimensional lookup tables in the form of a matrix with the same size as the original image. Each element of the integral image contains the sum of all pixels located on the upper left region of the original image (in relation to the element's position). This allows computing the sum of rectangular areas in the image at any position or scale, using only four lookups (see Figure 3.14).

Equation 3.3 calculates the sum of the shaded rectangular area:

$$sum = I(C) + I(A) - I(B) - I(D) \tag{3.3}$$

where points *A*, *B*, *C*, and *D* belong to the integral image *I*, as shown in Figure 3.14.

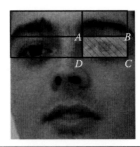

Figure 3.14 Sketch of computation of an integral image.

Each Haar-like feature may need more than four lookups, depending on how it was defined. Viola and Jones' two-rectangle features need six lookups, three-rectangle features need eight lookups, and four-rectangle features need nine lookups.

Lienhart and Maydt [44] introduced the concept of a tilted (45°) Haar-like feature. This was used to increase the dimensionality of the set of features in an attempt to improve the detection of objects in images. This was successful as some of these features are able to describe the object in a better way. For example, a two-rectangle, tilted Haar-like feature can indicate the existence of an edge at 45°.

Messom and Barczak [45] extended the idea to a generic, rotated Haar-like feature. Although the idea sounds mathematically sound, practical problems prevented the use of Haar-like features at any angle. In order to be fast, detection algorithms use low-resolution images, causing rounding errors. For this reason, rotated Haar-like features are not commonly used.

The LVQ network model is shown in Figure 3.15. An LVQ neuron network consists of three layers, that is, input, competition, and linear output. The network input layer is completely connected to the competition layer, and the competition layer is partially connected to the linear output layer. A different connection exists between each output neuron group, competition neuron group, and their fixed value is one.

The connection reference value of input and competitive neuron vector is established (a reference vector is appointed to each competitive neuron). In the training process, the network weights will be modified.

Both competition neurons and linear output neurons are of binary output value. When an input mode was sent to a network, when the reference vector is closest to input mode, the competitive neurons are started and win the competition.

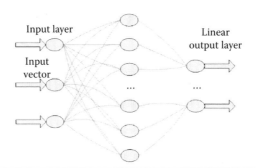

Figure 3.15 LVQ network model.

Thus, the generation of "1" is allowed, and other competitive neurons are forced to generate "0." Competition neurons, including the winning neuron group, connected to output neurons also generate "1," and other neurons generate "0." The output that generated "1" issues the input mode to the output neurons, and each output neuron produces different classes.

LVQ can be understood as a special case of an artificial neural network; more precisely, it applies a winner-take-all Hebbian learning-based approach. It is a precursor to self-organizing maps (SOM). LVQ was invented by Teuvo Kohonen.

An LVQ system is represented by prototypes, which are defined in the feature space of observed data. In winner-take-all training algorithms, one determines, for each data point, the prototype that is closest to the input according to a given distance measure. The position of this so-called winner prototype is then adapted, that is, the winner is moved closer if it correctly classifies the data point or moved away if it classifies the data point incorrectly.

An advantage of LVQ is that it creates prototypes that are easy to interpret for experts in the respective application domain. LVQ systems can be applied to multiclass classification problems in a natural way. It is used in a variety of practical applications.

A key issue in LVQ is the choice of an appropriate measure of distance or similarity for training and classification.

There exist two classic approaches to train the LVQ, named LVQ1 and LVQ2, respectively. LVQ can be a source of great help in various classification tasks.

3.5.3 Experiments and Conclusion

To verify the effectiveness of the proposed method for facial orientation detection, we utilized it on a real-time video stream and face image database, respectively. For simplicity, we mounted a USB camera on a laptop to test the effectiveness of the Haar-like feature on eye detection. Further study shows the proposed technique also has good performance on the IP camera and other types of surveillance cameras.

Figure 3.16 shows the result of eye detection in a range of head rotation. We can infer coarsely that the Haar-like feature is an advisable method to locate the eyes. In addition to the photos acquired by the USB camera, photos of 10 people (5 male and 5 female) were obtained from the

Figure 3.16 Eye location by using the Haar-like feature in a real-time video stream.

Figure 3.17 Illustration of five face orientations.

Figure 3.18 Illustration of eye location and the grid of subimages.

PIE Face Database of CMU from the online website posted for scientific use. Each subject has five different head postures: left, slight left, frontal, slight right, and right.

As Figure 3.17 shows explicitly, when people face different orientations, the eye location and the distance between the two eyes on the images vary dramatically following head rotation. Considering this fact, we adopt the statistical information about eye location as the input to the LVQ classifier. We denote the five orientations as 1, 2, 3, 4, and 5, respectively, as the output of the LVQ classifier.

As Figure 3.18 shows, we divide the face image into 6 × 8 subimages and execute the edge detection by Canny operator, then accord the eye horizontal location denoted by the rectangle; we calculate the sum of orientation 1 pixels in the corresponding horizontal eight subimages. The sum is adopted as the feature feed to the LVQ classifier.

As mentioned above, the total face images we got is 50 (10 persons, each person with 5 images). We randomly selected 30 images for training from the images. The remaining 20 images are used as test samples to verify the performance of the proposed technique on face orientation detection.

3.6 Identity Verification Based on Face Verification

Nowadays, passing through self-service security checkpoints under high throughput is an emerging application challenge. The identity verification technique is the key factor to solving this dilemma, especially in the railway station, bus station, airport, etc. The essence of this question is the one versus one face verification. It involves two crucial application knots: the real-time, super-resolution image reconstruction and the real-time face detection and recognition in the video stream under the surveillance scene. To improve the performance of the identity verifications system based on face similarity assessment, we exploited the deep learning mechanism to train the face detection module and to realize the super-resolution construction. The experiment proves its effectiveness.

3.6.1 Introduction

In recent years, with the boosting demand for security checks in railway stations, bus stations, and airports, the self-service passenger pass as an important precheck mechanism has attracted wide attention. The general application mode lies in the identity verification between the passenger onsite face image and the electronic identification photo. When the passenger approaches the security check gate, he or she swipes the RFID ID card, and the RFID reader captures the stored electronic photo. At the same time, the face images are captured and stored by the on-the-spot surveillance camera mounted on the security gate. The identity verification system will automatically judge whether the passenger is identical to his or her carried ID card based on the face similarity measurement. Those passengers whose score meets the threshold condition are allowed to pass the security check gate. Otherwise, they will be blocked.

This procedure involves two key techniques: the identification photo enhancement and the dynamic face verification based on the real-time video stream. It is well known that the size of the electronic photo stored in the RFID ID card is 126 × 102 pixels. This image quality is too weak and unsuitable to execute face verification. As a premise, the enhancement is a necessary preprocessing. The advisable preprocessing for image enhancement will effectively reduce the false alarm dramatically. Considering that low resolution is the key difficulty that impedes practical application, we focus our attention on super-resolution (SR) reconstruction [21] during the image enhancement stage. Different from the work in [21], we adopt the online SR reconstruction for the captured electronic photos. The reason lies in that we can't get the electronic photos prior to the identity verification. Furthermore, with respect to the online SR construction for the electronic identification photos, what we can utilize is just themselves. In other words, no redundant information derived from other photos will be introduced into the superconstruction process.

As far as the real-time video stream is concerned, the content analysis focuses on the pedestrian detection and face region segmentation. The frontal face capture is the crucial step during the dynamic face verification. As to the frontal face image capture, our previous work [41] has addressed one kind of promising method.

Pedestrian detection in complex scenes is a tough problem. In the general surveillance scene, the unsuitable illumination intensity, the body occlusion, and the backlight and shadow exist frequently and have a severe adverse impact on face region segmentation. To speed up pedestrian detection, we execute the downsampling for those raw frames with 1920 × 1080 pixels, and the DPM algorithm is utilized to identify the pedestrian. In some cases, there exist several pedestrians in one frame image, which gives rise to multiface detection. To avoid this phenomenon, we tune the focus and the Tele-Wide button to select the advisable view coverage. Moreover, the narrow passageway will limit the occurrence of multiple faces in one frame. In the worst case, there still exist multiple faces in one frame; we adopt the face with maximum face region as the analyzed target.

3.6.2 Identity Verification System

As shown in Figure 3.19, the identity verification system is composed of four parts: the onsite surveillance camera module, the RFID card reader module, the online face verification module, and the automatic security gate control module.

In Figure 3.19, the onsite surveillance camera module is designed to capture the corresponding onsite face image when the passenger is swiping his or her ID card. The RFID reader module provides the electronic ID photo for the online face verification module. From Figure 3.20, we can figure out that the opening of the security gate is trigged by the positive verification result.

Figure 3.21 shows the configuration of the identity verification system integrated with the luggage x-ray security check device. While passengers approach the security check system, their luggage bags will be transmitted by the transmission belt in the x-ray scanner, and they will pass through the security check gate with self-service. The security system will determine whether to allow the passenger to pass the gate according to the joint judgment of the luggage security check and the identity verification.

In the identity verification system, the threshold value setting for the image similarity is vital. If the threshold value is too high, many eligible people could not pass the identity verification, and false alarms would occur too frequently. Conversely, if the threshold value is too low, those ineligible people will pass the identity verification. In this case, the system is invalid. So the setting

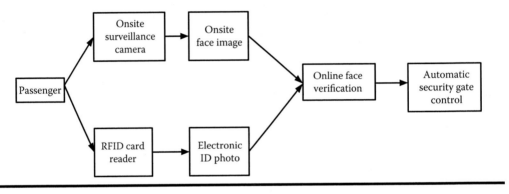

Figure 3.19   Schematic drawing of identity verification.

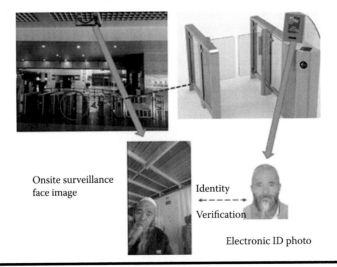

Figure 3.20   On-the-spot deployment of identity verification.

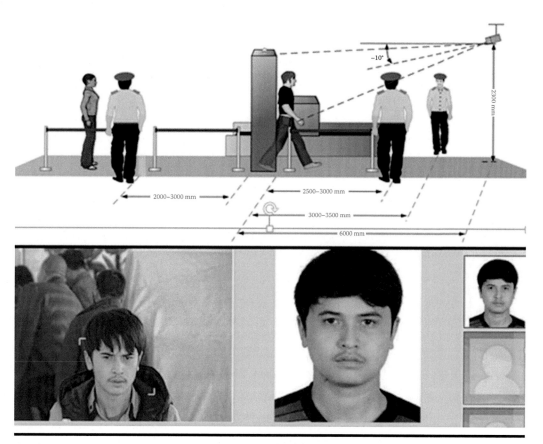

Figure 3.21 Identity verification security check gate.

of threshold value should keep the balance between the rapidness and the false alarm rate. The trade-off acquisition is handcrafted and time-consuming. There are no specific rules or principles to guide the setting; it just depends on the practical experiments in particular cases. In our further work, we will study the technique for setting the optimum threshold value.

In the following paragraphs, we introduce the two core techniques in the image similarity-based identity verification system. One is the SR reconstruction; the other is the deep learning-based face detection.

Generally speaking, SR construction is a kind of restoration technique, which consists of a frequency domain algorithm and a time domain algorithm for the original high-resolution image based on multiframe low-resolution images [46]. All the low-resolution images are captured in the same scene with the original high-resolution image, and there just exist slight changes. If there only exists one low-resolution image, the ordinary method to get the high-resolution image is interpolation.

In the case of only one low-resolution image, different from the traditional interpolation method, in [40] the authors proposed the deep learning-based strategy for single image SR. With lightweight structure deep convolution neural network (CNN), this method as directed learns an end-to-end mapping between the low- and high-resolution images. They also proved that the sparse coding-based SR can be viewed as a CNN. This work claimed state-of-the-art performance and to be suitable for online usage.

In this abovementioned work, the authors took the low-resolution (LR) image as the input and output the high-resolution (HR) one. To execute the image quality enhancement using this deep learning-based method, the training stage should be carried out prior to the output stage. Referring to this method, we utilize more than 5000 pairs of LR images and HR images, with 126 × 102 pixels and 441 × 358 pixels, respectively, as a training data set.

Face detection in the complex scenes is an essential but rarely rough task. To the fixed surveillance camera, the field of view (FOV) is constant. In this scene, the face region in the frame image is enough to execute the face detection. But in the ordinary surveillance scenes, to those people far away from the fixed-focus camera, the face region may be too small to be detected. In this case, pedestrian detection should be utilized to detect the concerned people and track these people until their approach makes the face region big enough to be detected. This strategy was proposed in our previous work [47] and proved to be effective and efficient.

Considering the complexity of face detection in ordinary surveillance scenes, the researchers present a new state-of-the art approach in [48]. They observed that the aligned face shapes provide better features for face classification. To combine the face alignment and detection more effectively, they learned these two tasks in the same cascade. By exploiting the joint learning, the capability of cascade detection and real-time performance can both achieve the satisfied status.

As shown in Figure 3.22, we use 38 key points to describe the face shape, 10 points for face contour, 6 points for eyebrows, 10 points for eyes, 7 points for the nose, and 5 points for the lip, respectively.

We bought a face image data set consisting of about 20,000 face images and 20,000 natural scene images without faces from the web. All the face images are transferred into grayscale images.

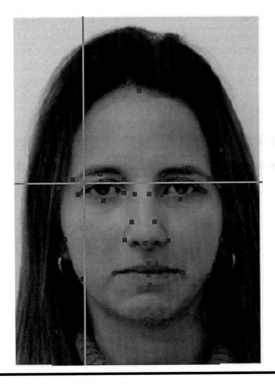

Figure 3.22   Key point annotation on face shape.

After all the face images are labeled, the data set is utilized to train the classification/regression tree.

3.6.3 Experiment and Conclusion

We utilized the combination of the onsite surveillance camera and RFID reader to realize the self-service passenger pass. The key techniques focus on the effectiveness of the onsite face detection and the online SR reconstruction for the LR ID electronic photos. As a comparison, we also directly adopted the electronic ID photos without the SR construction.

The subject consists of 131 people. In the experiments, five people's faces couldn't be detected successfully. Of the other 126 people, 102 people could pass the security check with the online SR construction—nearly an 80.9% hit rate. At the same scene, without the SR construction, only 46 people among the 126 people could pass the security check gate with self-service, nearly a 36.5% hit rate. The interface of the identity verification system is shown in Figure 3.23.

As mentioned before, some face images can't be successfully detected in the surveillance vision. This is partly due to the limited FOV of the focus-fixed camera. In our future work, we will adopt a dual-camera configuration consisting of a static camera and an active camera to replace the single focus-fixed camera (see Figure 3.24).

The static camera is a fixed-focus camera with wide view range, and it is in charge of the pedestrian detection and transmitting the corresponding position information to the active camera, which has the variable focus. The active camera tracks the pedestrian and grabs the clear HR face image for the identity verification system.

The proposed identity verification system is based on the image similarity measurement, and practical experiments show that it is effective in practice. On the other hand, frankly speaking, the performance without the SR construction is inferior to expectations, that is, the electronic ID photo is unsuitable to be used directly for identity verification.

3.7 Conclusions

The VSD framework consists of three layers. The root layer contains three general classes: object, relationship, and attribute. Object means the class of the extracted objects from the video. Relationship means the class of relationships between the extracted objects from the video. Attribute means the visual feature, such as shape or color, of the extracted objects from the video. The visual layer contains the objects that can be extracted by the existing object extraction method. The semantic layer contains domain knowledge about the semantic hierarchies of object and relationship classes. The increasing need for video-based applications raises the importance of parsing and organizing the content in videos. However, the accurate understanding and managing of video content at the semantic level is still insufficient. In this chapter, a semantic-based model, VSD, for representing and organizing the content in videos is proposed. It is safely concluded that VSD used in Android terminals makes video data application much easier, for example, evidence collection in spot events. Moreover, visual information or content knowledge distilled by a VSD system can be shared conveniently in the mobile computing framework, so more general information mining and social trend forecasting could be further developed. By comparing the results from three DPM vehicle models, the nonmixed models acquired higher accuracy. But they did not perform satisfactorily in the mixture test. In order to capture the vehicles in a two-way lane,

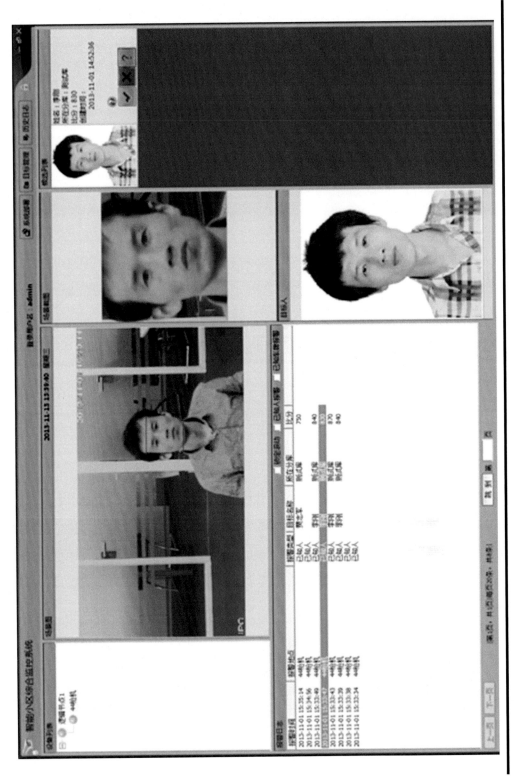

Figure 3.23 Interface of the identity verification system.

Figure 3.24 Dual-camera configuration in identity verification system.

we proposed the third mixture DPM vehicle model. It is more efficient to capture vehicle vision and shows high versatility.

On the basis of the Haar-like feature and the boosting classification strategy to locate the eyes, we use the LVQ classifier to detect face orientation. We mounted a USB camera on a laptop to test the effectiveness of the Haar-like feature on eye detection. Further study shows the proposed technique also has good performance on the IP camera and other types of surveillance cameras. We utilized the combination of the onsite surveillance camera and RFID reader to address the self-service passenger pass. The key techniques focus on the effectiveness of the onsite face detection and the online SR reconstruction for the LR ID electronic photos.

References

1. Xu Z, Liu Y, Mei L, Hu C, and Chen L. Semantic based representing and organizing surveillance big data using video structural description technology. *Journal of Systems and Software*, 2015, 102:217–225.
2. Hu C, Xu Z, Liu Y, Mei L, Chen L, and Luo X. Semantic link network-based model for organizing multimedia big data. *IEEE Transactions Emerging Topics in Computing*, 2014, 2(3):376–387.
3. Wu L, and Wang Y. The process of criminal investigation based on grey hazy set. In: Proceedings of 2010 IEEE International Conference on System Man and Cybernetics, 2010, 26–28.
4. Liu L, Li Z, and Delp E. Efficient and low-complexity surveillance video compression using backward-channel aware wyner-ziv video coding. *IEEE Transactions on Circuits and Systems for Video Technology*, 2009, 19(4):452–465.
5. Zhang J, Zulkernine M, and Haque A. Random-forests-based network intrusion detection systems. *IEEE Transactions on Systems, Man, and Cybernetics, Part C: Applications and Reviews*, 2008, 38(5):649–659.
6. Yu H, Pedrinaci C, Dietze S, and Domingue J. Using linked data to annotate and search educational video resources for supporting distance learning. *IEEE Transactions on Learning Technologies*, 2012, 5(2):130–142.
7. Xu C, Zhang Y, Zhu G, Rui Y, Lu H, and Huang Q. Using webcast text for semantic event detection in broadcast sports video. *IEEE Transactions on Multimedia*, 2008, 10(7):1342–1355.
8. Berners-Lee T, Hendler J, and Lassila O. The Semantic Web. *Scientific American*, 2001, 284(5):34–43.
9. Ma H, Zhu J, Lyu M, and King I. Bridging the semantic gap between image contents and tags. *IEEE Transactions on Multimedia*, 2010, 12(5):462–473.
10. Chen H, and Ahuja N. Exploiting nonlocal spatiotemporal structure for video segmentation. In: Proceedings of 2012 IEEE Conference on Computer Vision and Pattern Recognition, 2012, 741–748.
11. Javed K, Babri H, and Saeed M. Feature selection based on class-dependent densities for high-dimensional binary data. *IEEE Transactions on Knowledge and Data Engineering*, 2012, 24(3):465–477.

12. Choi M, Torralba A, and Willsky A. A tree-based context model for object recognition. *IEEE Transactions on Pattern Analysis and Machine Intelligence*, 2012, 34(2):240–252.

13. Luo X, Xu Z, Yu J, and Chen X. Building association link network for semantic link on web resources. *IEEE Transactions on Automation Science and Engineering*, 2011, 8(3):482–494.

14. Xu Z, Luo X, and Wang L. Incremental building association link network. *Computer Systems Science and Engineering*, 2011, 26(3):153–162.

15. Liu Y, Zhu Y, Ni M, and Xue G. A reliability-oriented transmission service in wireless sensor networks. *IEEE Transactions on Parallel and Distributed Systems*, 2011, 22(12):2100–2107.

16. Felzenszwalb P, McAllester D, and Ramanan D. A discriminatively trained, multiscale, deformable part model. In: Proceedings of 2008 IEEE Computer Society Conference on Computer Vision and Pattern Recognition, 2008.

17. Felzenszwalb P, Girshick R, McAllester D, and Ramanan D. Object detection with discriminatively trained part based models. *IEEE Transactions on Pattern Analysis and Machine Intelligence*, 2010, 32(9):1627–1645.

18. Felzenszwalb P, Girshick R, and McAllester D. Cascade object detection with deformable part models. In: Proceedings of 2010 IEEE Computer Society Conference on Computer Vision and Pattern Recognition, 2010.

19. Chen N, Zhou Q, and Prasanna V. Understanding web image by object relation network. In: Proceedings of International World Wide Web Conferences, 2012, 291–300.

20. Kulkarni G, Premraj V, Dhar S, Li S, Choi Y, Berg A, and Berg T. Baby talk: Understanding and generating image descriptions. In: Proceedings of 2011 IEEE Computer Society Conference on Computer Vision and Pattern Recognition, 2011.

21. Qi G, Aggarwal C, and Huang T. Towards semantic knowledge propagation from text corpus to web images. In: Proceedings of International World Wide Web Conferences, 2011, 297–306.

22. Zhang H, Mei L, and Liang C. *Video Structured Description: A Novel Solution for Visual Surveillance*, 2010: pp. 629–636.

23. Davies E R, *Machine Vision, Theory, Algorithms, Practicalities*. 2009: Posts & Telecom Press.

24. Szeliski R, *Computer vision: Algorithm and application*. Tsinghua Univiersity Press.

25. OWL 2 Web Ontology Language Document Overview http://www.w3.org/TR/owl2-overview/

26. Park J H, Au O C, Wiberg Mik et al. Recent advances and future directions in multimedia and mobile computing. *Multimed Tools Appl* 2012, 57: 237–242.

27. Vidas T, Z C, Christin N et al. Toward a general collection methodology for Android devices. *Digital Investigation*, 2011(8):14–24.

28. Felzenswalb P F, Girshick R B, McAllester D, and Ramanan D. Object detection with discriminatively trained part based models. *IEEE Trans. PAMI*, 2010, 32(9):1627–1645.

29. Everingham M, van Gool L, Williams C K I, Winn J, and Zisserman A. The PASCAL Visual Object Classes Challenge 2007 (VOC 2007) Results. [Online]. Available from http://www.pascalnetwork.org/challenges/VOC/voc2007/

30. Dalal N, and Triggs B. Histograms of oriented gradients for human detection, in IEEE Conference on Computer Vision and Pattern Recognition, 2005.

31. Ke Y, and Sukthankar R. PCA-SIFT: A more distinctive representation for local image descriptors, in IEEE Conference on Computer Vision and Pattern Recognition, 2004.

32. Chellappa R, Wilson C L, and Sirohey S. Human and machine recognition of faces: A survey. *Proceedings of the IEEE*, 1995, 83(5):705–741.

33. Ayinde O, and Yang Y-H. Region-based face detection. *Pattern Recognition*, 2002, 35(10):2095–2107.

34. Lin C, and Fan K-C. Triangle-based approach to the detection of human face. *Pattern Recognition*, 2001, 34(6):1271–1284.

35. Yow K C, and Cipolla R. Feature-based human face detection. *Image and Vision Computing*, 1997, 15(9):713–735.

36. Jin Z, Lou Z, Yang J et al. Face detection using template matching and skin-color information. *Neurocomputing*, 2007, 70(4–6):794–800.

37. Zhou J, Lu X G, Zhang D et al. Orientation analysis for rotated human face detection. *Image and Vision Computing*, 2002, 20(4):257–264.

38. Juang C-F, and Shiu S-J. Using self-organizing fuzzy network with support vector learning for face detection in color images. *Neurocomputing*, 2008, 71(16–18):3409–3420.

39. Brunelli R. Estimation of pose and illuminant direction for face processing. *Image and Vision Computing*, 1997, 15(10):741–748.

40. Chen S, and Liu C. Discriminant analysis of Haar features for accurate eye detection. 15th International Conference on Image Processing, Computer Vision, and Pattern, 2011.

41. Kasinski A, and Schmidt A. The architecture of the face and eyes detection system based on cascade classifiers. *Computer Recognition Systems 2: Advances in Soft Computing*, 2007, 45:124–131.

42. Papageorgiou C, and Poggio T A. Trainable pedestrian detection, Image Processing, 1999. ICIP 99. Proceedings. 1999 International Conference on, Volume: 4.

43. Viola P, and Jones M. Rapid object detection using a boosted cascade of simple features. Proceedings of the 2001 IEEE Computer Society Conference on Computer Vision and Pattern Recognition. CVPR 2001.

44. Lienhart R, and Maydt J. An extended set of Haar-like features for rapid object detection[C]. Proceedings of the 2002 International Conference on Image Processing. Rochester: IEEE Press, 2002, 1: 900–903.

45. Messom C, and Barczak A. Stream processing of geometric and central moments using high precision summed area tables. Advances in Neuro-Information Processing, Volume 5506 of the series Lecture Notes in Computer Science, pp. 1095–1102.

46. Dong C et al. Image super-resolution using deep convolution networks. arXiv preprint arXiv:1501.00092, 2014:12.

47. Yan Z, Yang F, and Wang J. Face orientation detection in video stream based on Haar-like feature and LQV classifier for civil video surveillance. In 2013 IET Second International Conference on Smart and Sustainable City 2013: Zhangjiajie, Hunan, p. 5.

48. Zhang L, Zhang H, and Shen H. A super-resolution reconstruction algorithm for surveillance images. *Signal Processing*, 2010, (90):12.

Chapter 4

Trends in Mining Biological Big Data

Deepthi P. S.[1] and Sabu M. Thampi[2]

[1]LBS College of Engineering, Kasaragod, India

[2]Indian Institute of Information Technology and Management–Kerala (IIITM-K), Trivandrum, India

Contents

Abstract

Research in clinical and medical data has proliferated with the advent of Big Data technologies like Apache Hadoop. While traditional analytics were carried out in stand-alone machines, Big Data requires parallel processing capabilities due to the ever-increasing data volume. These parallel processing tools facilitate information aggregation and analytics of varieties of data, thereby enabling the market of health care industries and medical informatics. Big Data analytics in the health care domain enables many useful tasks like clinical outcome prediction, decision support systems for assisting physicians, and disease surveillance, thus enhancing health care systems. This chapter introduces the potential of Big Data in the field of health care and bioinformatics. We also give an overview of how structured and unstructured data in the form of electronic health records, patient reports, clinical images, genomic data, etc., are managed and analyzed. The general architecture and capabilities of Big Data in health care will also be outlined. This chapter will also discuss the application of the MapReduce framework in the health care domain and case studies that utilize data mining techniques for various clinical predictions using different types of data. We also present the security and privacy issues that have loomed large with the increase in opportunities for Big Data analytics in health care.

4.1 Introduction

The tremendous increase in the volume of data has led to the emergence of Big Data platforms in the Internet industry. Big Data refers to a "vast amount of data, which cannot be effectively processed, captured and analyzed by traditional database and search tools in a reasonable amount of time" (Shivakumar 2013). The range of data has increased from kilobytes to megabytes, gigabytes, terabytes (10^{12}), petabytes (10^{15}), exabytes (10^{18}), zettabytes (10^{21}), and so on, thus becoming a fast-moving target. This chapter introduces the realm of Big Data in the field of health care and bioinformatics. Health care data include electronic health records (EHRs), medical images, doctor's prescriptions, laboratory results, gene expression data from microarray experiments, machine- and sensor-generated data, data from social media, etc. The advent of Big Data technologies, such as Apache Hadoop, facilitates information aggregation and analytics of varieties of data, thereby enabling the market of health care industries and medical informatics. Big Data analytics in the health care domain provides many useful functions, such as clinical outcome prediction, decision support systems for assisting physicians, and disease surveillance, thus enhancing health care systems. This chapter gives an overview of how structured and unstructured data in the form of EHRs, patient reports, clinical images, genomic data, etc., are managed and analyzed. The general architecture of Big Data in health care is also outlined. With the increase in opportunities for Big Data analytics in health care, security and privacy concerns have also loomed large. This chapter also discusses the state of the art of Big Data analytics and data mining in health informatics and the related privacy and security issues.

4.2 Place of 5 Vs in Health Informatics

Data sets of size above 10^{15} (petabytes) are generally agreed upon as Big Data. However, this size is quite rare in the health informatics domain, and hence a more general definition would be the one given by Demchenko et al. (2012), which defines Big Data using 5 Vs Volume, velocity, and variety are the commonly accepted 3 Vs, and veracity and value are the two more that have been added over time. Data from biological and health care domains exhibit most of these properties.

4.2.1 Volume

In health informatics, the large amount of records related to a patient contributes to the volume. For example, gene expression data, which measure thousands of genes in parallel for each patient, EHRs, MRI images, etc., require huge storage space.

4.2.2 Velocity

Big velocity occurs when new data evolve over time at enormous speed. Consider, for example, data generated by sensors used to monitor a patient's condition or the large number of tweets to be analyzed to predict the spread of an epidemic.

4.2.3 Variety

Big variety attributes to data sets gathered from different sources with a large amount of several types of independent attributes, for instance, search query data from different age groups that use a search engine or complex data sets that need to be tackled at many levels.

4.2.4 Veracity

Veracity in the case of health data arises when dealing with incomplete, noisy, or erroneous data. Such discrepancies can happen as part of faulty sensors, devices, microarray experiments, or errors in information stored in databases.

4.2.5 Value

The health care data gathered from different sources are of high value as they provide insight to clinicians and enable them to make decisions, thus providing quality health care to patients.

4.3 Sources and Types of Biological Big Data

This section discusses the sources and types of Big Data arising in the biological and health care domain including genomic data, EHRs, machine-generated data, and behavior data.

4.3.1 Genomic Data

There are five main categories of data that arise in bioinformatics research: (a) microarray data; (b) DNA, RNA, and protein sequence data; (c) protein–protein interaction data; (d) pathway data; and (e) gene ontology (GO).

4.3.1.1 Microarray Data

Microarray technologies, such as oligonucleotide arrays and cDNA microarrays, help to monitor thousands of genes in parallel. Data arising from these experiments, also called gene expression data, have been used by the research community to gain insight into gene functions and related diseases. A gene expression data set can be represented by a real-valued *expression matrix* as shown in Figure 4.1 in which rows form the expression profiles of samples, columns represent the expression patterns of genes, and each cell is the measured expression level of gene in sample. The original data obtained from microarray experiments contain noise, missing values, and systematic variations arising from the experimental procedure. Data preprocessing is applied on these data, and data mining tasks, such as clustering and classification, help to unveil hidden structures within these data sets (Jiang et al. 2004). Predicting the subtype of disease, such as cancer, and understanding the cellular processes are typical tasks performed on gene expression data.

4.3.1.2 DNA, RNA, and Protein Sequence Data

DNA sequencing is used to discover the structure of DNA, RNA, and protein. It helps to understand genomes and proteins and how they are associated with diseases and phenotypes. It can also

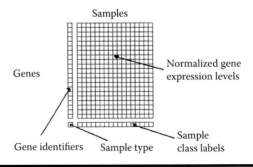

Figure 4.1   Gene expression data

be used for drug target identification, mutation identification, detection of viruses, etc. Sequence alignment and database search are the associated analytics tasks used to analyze these sequence data. Owing to the massive amount of data that are being generated, next-generation sequencing or high-throughput sequencing technologies have evolved and remain the interest of biomedical researchers.

4.3.1.3 Protein–Protein Interaction Data

Protein–protein interactions convey significant information about biological processes by determining the physical contacts between proteins. Several fields, such as biochemistry, quantum chemistry, molecular dynamics, and signal transduction, exploit these data to study about the interactions occurring between proteins.

4.3.1.4 Pathway Data

Pathway analysis helps to extract differentially expressed genes associated with a disease.

4.3.1.5 Gene Ontology

GO represents gene products based on associated biological processes, cellular components, and molecular functions in a species-independent manner. The GO database consists of GO terms, a name associated with it, and the domain to which it belongs. The GO is represented as a directed acyclic graph, and the terms in a domain will have relationships with those within the domain and to other domains.

The major sources of all the five types of genomic data discussed above are listed in Table 4.1.

Table 4.1 Types and Publicly Available Sources of Genomic Data

Type of Data	Sources
Microarray data	ArrayExpress Gene Expression Omnibus (GEO) Stanford Microarray Database (SMD) Cancer Genome Anatomy Project (CGAP)
DNA, RNA, and protein sequence data	DNA Data Bank of Japan Ribosomal Database Project (RDP) microRNA database (miRBase) European Molecular Biology Laboratory (EMBL)
Protein–protein interaction data	Database of Interacting Proteins (DIP) Search Tool for the Retrieval of Interacting Genes/Proteins (STRING) Biological General Repository for Interaction Datasets (BioGRID) Biomolecular Interaction Network Database (BIND)
Pathway data	Kyoto Encyclopedia of Genes and Genomes (KEGG) Reactome Pathway Commons
Gene ontology	AmiGO, DAG-Edit, OBO-Edit

4.3.2 Clinical Data

4.3.2.1 Structured Electronic Health Record

The International Organization for Standardization (ISO) defines EHR as a "repository of patient data in digital form, stored and exchanged securely, and accessible by multiple authorized users" (ISO/TR 20514:2005). These data are essential for clinical decision making to improve health care systems. The main types of EHR include the electronic medical record (EMR), departmental EMR, interdepartmental EMR, electronic patient record, electronic hospital record, electronic health care record, clinical data repository, and many others (Häyrinen et al. 2008). Some publicly available EHR data sets are listed in Table 4.2.

4.3.2.2 Unstructured EHR

Apart from structured EHR, floods of unstructured data arise in the health domain, and they require human intervention to interpret properly. These include machine-written and handwritten information on unstructured paper forms, scanned medical reports, diagnostic images, invoices and purchase orders, medical claims, audio voice dictations, email messages and attachments, typed transcriptions, etc. Unstructured data account for more than 80% of the data in health informatics. It has also been estimated that about 60% of information among 1.2 billion clinical documents produced in the United States is in unstructured form (Data Mark Incorporated 2013). Table 4.3 lists two publicly available data sets comprising clinical texts, which can be analyzed using natural language processing.

4.3.2.3 Medical Images, Biometric Data, and Other Machine-Generated Data

Medical images, such as magnetic resonance imaging, x-ray, and radiographic images, and biometric data, such as fingerprints, retinal scans, genetics, and handwriting, also contribute to

Table 4.2 Publicly Available EHR Data Sets

Data Set	Link
Texas hospital inpatient discharge	http://www.dshs.state.tx.us/thcic/hospitals/Inpatientpudf.shtm
Framingham health care data set	http://www.framinghamheartstudy.org/researchers/description-data/index.php
Medicare basic stand alone claim public use files	http://resdac.advantagelabs.com/cms-data/files/bsa-puf
VHA medical SAS data sets	http://ecp.acponline.org/mayjun02/murphy.htm
CA patient discharge data	http://www.oshpd.ca.gov/HID/Products/PatDischargeData/PublicDataSet/index.html
Nationwide inpatient sample	https://www.hcup-us.ahrq.gov/nisoverview.jsp
MIMIC II clinical database	https://physionet.org/mimic2/index.shtml

Table 4.3 Unstructured EHR Data Sources

Data Set	Link
i2b2 Informatics for integrating biology & the bedside	https://www.i2b2.org/NLP/DataSets/Main.php
Computational medicine center	http://computationalmedicine.org/challenge/previous

Table 4.4 Publicly Available Medical Image Databases

Image Database	Link
Cancer imaging archive database	https://public.cancerimagingarchive.net/ncia/dataBasket Display.jsf
Digital mammography database	http://marathon.csee.usf.edu/Mammography/Database.html
Public lung image database	https://veet.via.cornell.edu/lungdb.html
Image CLEF database	http://www.imageclef.org/2013/medical
MS lesion segmentation	http://www.ia.unc.edu/MSseg/download.php
ADNI database	http://adni.loni.usc.edu/data-samples/access-data/

clinical Big Data. Researchers have been automating the processing of medical images to identify abnormalities so as to aid radiologists and doctors in disease diagnosis. Readings from remote sensors and other devices that are used to monitor patients also form significant clinical data sources. Table 4.4 lists the publicly available MRI and mammogram image databases.

4.3.3 Behavior Data

Behavior data include web and social media data, for instance, clickstream and interaction data from social networking sites, such as Twitter. Several studies show that the posts generated over these sites play a significant role in detection of epidemics and flus, etc. Hence, analyzing health-related data from these sources is of potential value.

4.4 Big Data Capabilities in Health Care

Big Data offers tremendous opportunities and capabilities that can assist the health care industry to leverage effective Big Data-based strategies.

4.4.1 Data Analytics

Data analytical capability refers to the analytical techniques used to process huge volumes of data arising from a variety of sources with high velocity. The analytics starts by collecting data in the health care domain, storing them in distributed databases outside the health care sectors, filtering them, and analyzing them to integrate meaningful outcomes for the data warehouse. The unstructured data collected from multiple sources can be stored in Hadoop distributed file system (HDFS) and NoSQL databases and retrieved upon user queries. NoSQL databases help in storage and retrieval of both unstructured and semistructured data from different sources in multiple formats in real time. The HDFS and MapReduce framework provides analytical capabilities, which are discussed in detail in Section 4.5.1. The results of analytics can be stored in a data warehouse, making it accessible for decision making.

4.4.2 Decision Support

Decision support capability emphasizes the ability to produce reports about daily health care services to take appropriate actions and help in the decision-making process. Sharable information in the form of reports and summaries, statistical analysis, and comparison of time series data facilitate decision making. This information can be utilized to devise personalized health care services, disease surveillance, and giving warning about the outbreak of flu, etc.

4.4.3 Predictive Capability

Predictive capability is "the ability to apply diverse methods from statistical analysis, modeling, machine learning, and data mining to both structured and unstructured data to determine future outcomes" (Zikopoulos 2012, cited in Wang et al. 2016). Wessler (2013, cited in Wang et al. 2016) defines predictive capability as "the process of using a set of sophisticated tools to develop models and estimations of what the environment will do in the future." Both these definitions portray the relevance of predicting future trends, hence making recommendations. Predictions are made possible through analytical engines incorporating machine learning and data warehousing. Predictive analysis helps to alleviate uncertainty and enables clinicians to develop preventive care.

4.5 Big Data Architecture in Health Care

The architecture for traditional health care analytics is modified to accommodate huge volumes of data coming from heterogeneous sources. Although traditional analytics were carried out in standalone machines, Big Data urges the need for parallel processing capabilities due to the ever-increasing data volume. Figure 4.2 shows the general architecture of Big Data analytics. Among the Big Data platforms and tools, MapReduce framework on top of HDFS is the most popular one. Hadoop is a software platform that provides distributed storage and computational requirements. It follows a distributed master–slave architecture comprising a HDFS for storing data and MapReduce for performing computations on data distributed over HDFS. MapReduce is a programming framework that allows a programmer to define two functions, namely, map and reduce, for processing huge volumes of distributed data. It follows functional programming paradigms and permits a high degree of parallelism. The workload is divided across a number of machines called nodes, which together form a cluster. Taylor et al. (2010) give an overview of the applications of Hadoop in bioinformatics applications, such as next-generation sequencing, gene set enrichment analysis, and multiple sequence alignment.

Wang et al. (2016) give a conceptual architecture of Big Data analytics in health care, consisting of five layers: data, data aggregation, analytics, information exploration, and Big Data

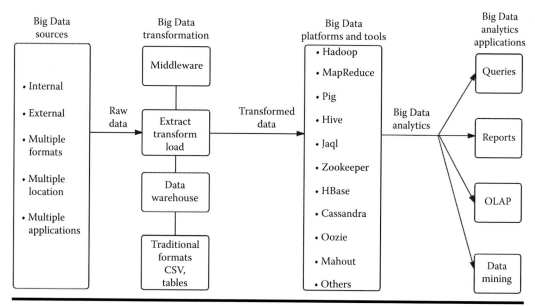

Figure 4.2 Architecture of Big Data analytics. (Reprinted from Raghupathi, W., and Raghupathi, V., "Big data analytics in healthcare: promise and potential," *Health Information Science and Systems*, 1, 2014.)

governance. The components at these levels perform functions that can turn health care data into meaningful information through analytical capabilities, which is depicted in Figure 4.3.

1. *Data layer.* This layer comprises all data sources, including structured and unstructured EHR, data from health monitoring devices, clinical images, etc., collected from different locations inside or outside the hospital and stored in databases or distributed systems.

2. *Data aggregation layer.* This layer handles data from various sources by performing data acquisition, transformation, and storage. These data are then loaded into HDFS or in Hadoop cloud for processing.

3. *Analytics layer.* This layer processes the variety of data stored in HDFS and carries out analytics. Data analysis can be divided into three major components: Hadoop MapReduce, stream computing, and in-database analytics. *MapReduce* is the popular programming model used for Big Data analytics, and it provides parallel processing capabilities. *Stream Computing* caters stream data processing in real time. *In-database analytics* deals with processing data within the data warehouse and provides secure analysis for confidential information.

4. *Information exploration layer.* This layer generates outputs of various analytics tasks in the form of reports and summaries. These outputs and predictions help clinicians to do real-time monitoring of health and disease.

5. *Big Data governance layer.* The Big Data governance layer affects all of the logical layers. This layer is composed of master data management (MDM), data life cycle management, and data security and privacy management. *MDM* involves processes, governance, policies, standards, and tools for managing data. *Data life cycle management* is the process of managing information throughout its life cycle, including archiving data, maintaining the data

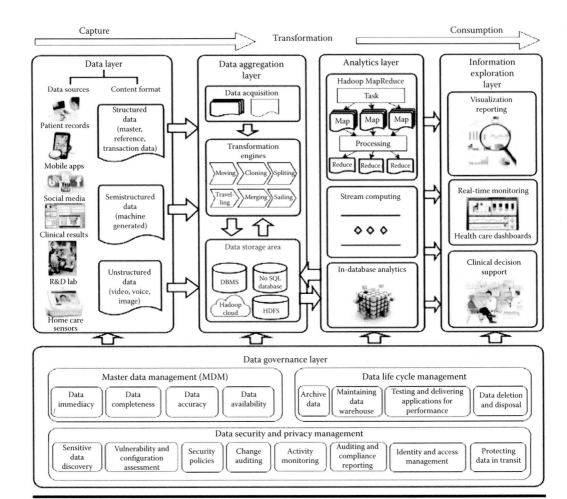

Figure 4.3 Architecture of Big Data analytics in health care. (Reprinted from Wang et al., "Big data analytics: Understanding its capabilities and potential benefits for healthcare organizations," *Technological Forecasting and Social Change,* **2016, doi: 10.1016/j.techfore.2015.12.019, with permission from Elsevier.)**

warehouse, testing and delivering different application systems, and deleting and disposing of data. *Data security and privacy management* provides security to data stored by controlling access and providing authentication.

4.5.1 Application of MapReduce Framework

The MapReduce framework on top of HDFS has been widely used in processing health care domains as it provides a high degree of parallelism. Parallelism is achieved by breaking processing into small tasks across a number of nodes in the cluster. Mohammed et al. (2014) present a review of the applications of the MapReduce framework for health care data.

Aphinyanaphongs et al. (2013) used the MapReduce algorithm to identify unproven cancer treatments from the Internet. Identifying unproven treatments is important as people rely on the Internet for browsing information about their diseases. The authors collected web page corpus related to unproven treatments and stored them in HDFS. For feature selection, generalized local learning—Markov blanket that implements Markov blanket and Markov boundary—to find the optimal feature subset is used. A support vector machine (SVM) and logistic regression are used for classification.

Meng et al. (2011) proposed an ultrafast and scalable cone–beam computed tomography reconstruction algorithm using MapReduce in a cloud computing environment. The authors reported using the Feldcamp–Davis–Kress algorithm to a MapReduce implementation to achieve speedup. The *map* functions are used to filter and back-project subsets of projections and *reduce* functions to aggregate that partial back-projection into the whole volume. The speedup of reconstruction time was found to be roughly linear with the number of nodes employed. Faster reconstruction was made possible by allocating a higher number of nodes.

Markonis et al. (2012) proposed two approaches for content-based image indexing using the MapReduce framework: component-based versus monolithic indexing. A cluster of heterogeneous computing nodes is set to run a maximum of 42 concurrent map tasks. The authors implemented MapReduce algorithms for three medical image processing scenarios: (a) parameter optimization for lung texture classification using support vector machines, (b) content-based medical image indexing, and (c) three-dimensional directional wavelet analysis for solid texture classification.

The MapReduce programming framework has also been used to perform face matching, iris recognition, and fingerprint recognition. Kohlwey et al. (2011) built a prototype system for searching biometric data in the cloud and find matches with synthetic human iris images. The authors used Apache MapReduce with HDFS, HBase, and Zookeeper for facilitating distributed computing. The Iris ID SDK, which is an implementation of the well-known Daugman's algorithm, is used to segment images and produce iris codes. Blocks of iris biometric templates are scanned in parallel, and matching is performed using the simple hamming distance. Omri et al. (2012) developed an application in which a mobile phone is used to capture biometrics to safely access the cloud. The authors used JQuery, which is used for building web pages, and biometric capture and recognition are performed. The Hadoop platform is used to establish connection between a mobile user and the server in the cloud.

Zhang et al. (2015) proposed a task-level MapReduce framework for processing streaming data in health care applications. The generic MapReduce framework is extended by making each map and reduce task a consistent running loop daemon. In this approach, instead of fetching static data from HDFS, stream data cached in HDFS are fetched repeatedly by the map task, and intermediate key value pairs are given to the corresponding reduce tasks. The authors also present a case study of streaming data from wearable devices used to monitor patients' health.

Wang et al. (2013) developed a parallel version of the random forest algorithm using MapReduce on top of Hadoop for large-scale population genetic association studies involving multivariate traits. The algorithm is applied to a genome-wide association study on Alzheimer's disease consisting of a high-dimensional neuroimaging phenotype describing longitudinal changes in human brain structure. The parallel algorithm achieved significant speedup for processing these large-scale data.

4.6 Data Mining for Big Data Analytics

The increasing health care Big Data offers tremendous capabilities in assisting clinicians and building decision support systems. Data mining techniques are found to be useful to make predictions from the clinical and health-related data. The following sections present case studies that utilize data mining techniques for various clinical predictions using different types of data discussed so far.

4.6.1 Prediction of Clinical Outcome from Microarray Data

Case Study 1

A gene expression profiler is proposed by Haferlach et al. (2010) to classify patients into 18 different subclasses of either myeloid or lymphoid leukemia. A total of 3334 patient samples were considered in which 2143 were used for training and 1191 for testing, and 54,630 gene probe set samples from each patient were considered (3334 × 54,630 ≈ 182,000,000). An all-pairwise approach using the trimmed mean of differences between perfect match and mismatch intensities with quantile normalization signals was used for multiclass classification. There were 153 distinct class pairs for 18 classes and a linear binary SVM was used for every class pair. The method was tested by 30-fold cross-validation in which the top 100 probe sets with the highest t statistic for each pair were chosen for each of the 30 runs. The method attained a specificity of 99.7% and an accuracy of 92.2%. In another experiment with test sets, specificity was found to be 99.8% and 95.6% for classifying acute leukemia into six lymphoid and eight myeloid subclasses.

Case Study 2

In a study by Salazar et al. (2010), the gene expression signature associated with the risk of recurrence in patients with stage II or III colorectal cancer was considered. Training data were collected over a 19-year period (1983–2002) from three different institutions from different counties and the validation set over 8 years (1996–2004) from another institution from a different country. A total of 33,834 gene probes were considered initially, and feature selection was used to find probes strongly correlated with the 5-year distant metastasis-free survival by performing a t test. Finally, a set of 18 gene probes were chosen. The authors used a nearest centroid-base classifier for classification. The aim was to classify patients as low risk or high risk of disease recurrence. It was found that two thirds of patients with stage II colon cancer are at low risk of recurrence, and hence, they don't require adjuvant chemotherapy, and 25% to 35% of patients will experience recurrence of cancer within 5 years after surgery.

4.6.2 Clinical Prediction from MRI Images

Magnetic resonance imaging (MRI) data can be used to make predictions by processing images of suspected areas.

Case Study 1

Estella et al. (2012) suggested a method to place patients into three classes: completely healthy, mild cognitive impairment, and already has Alzheimer's. The study used 240 GB of brain image data for 1200 patients stored by the Alzheimer's Disease Neuroimaging Initiative. The method involves spatial normalization, extraction of features, feature selection, and patient classification. Two subgroups of features—332 morphological and 108 mathematical features—were extracted initially. Morphological features include area centroid, major axis length, whole matter volumes, etc., and mathematical features include mean, cosine transform coefficients, Euclidean distance, etc. Another group that consists of features from both these subgroups is termed a mixed group. Mutual information (MI) along with the minimal redundancy–maximal relevance criterion (mRMR) is used for feature selection. MI determines the dependence between two given variables, and the mRMR selects features correlated to the final prediction by removing redundant features. A fuzzy decision tree, an extension to the traditional decisions to handle fuzzy data, is used for classification. Results indicate that, using a minimal number of morphological and mathematical features, the proposed method could efficiently classify patients into three classes of Alzheimer's disease.

Case Study 2

Yoshida et al. (2013) proposed a method to combine clinical features of patients and MRI images consisting of millions of voxels. A voxel is a point on a grid in 3-D space. The authors used radial basis function–sparse partial least squares (RBF-sPLS) to select clinical features as well as brain regions. Feature selection and dimensionality reduction were performed simultaneously. The method was tested on a dataset of 102 patients having chronic kidney disease, and 73 clinical features and around 2.1 million voxels from the MRI data were gathered. RBF-sPLS could extract two regions from the brain: the temporal lobe, which is associated with aging, and the occipital lobe associated with anemia. It was also found that clinical variables related to chronic kidney disease and the bilateral temporal lobe of the brain are strongly correlated. Hence, this research proved to be useful for physicians to determine if a patient has kidney disease or is likely to have kidney disease, etc. It will also be promising if correlations between MRI and other diseases could be found so that diagnosis and treatment can be made at an early stage.

4.6.3 Prediction of Intensive Care Unit Readmission and Mortality Rate

The following sections present prediction of intensive care unit (ICU) readmission, mortality rate, and 5-year life expectancy rate after discharge from ICU. Life expectancy rate predicts the likelihood of a patient's survival within a period of 5 years. These studies allow physicians to determine whether to extend the ICU stay of patients and whether they need more treatment after discharge.

Case Study 1

Fialho et al. (2012) present a method to predict ICU readmission of patients after discharge. The authors used the Multiparameter Intelligent Monitoring for Intensive Care (MIMIC II) database, which consists of ICU patients admitted to the Beth Israel Deaconess Medical Center, collected from 2001 to 2006. The database is anonymized by removing protected information. The MIMIC II database has 26,655 patients, of which 19,075 are adults (>15 years old at the time of admission). The database consists of high-frequency sampled data from bedside monitors, clinical data (laboratory tests, physicians' and nurses' notes, imaging reports, medications, and other patient-related data), and demographic data. From the data set of 25,549 patients, a reduced set of 1267 patients was chosen based on the criteria shown in Figure 4.4. The final prediction of these patients after discharge is also depicted.

Two feature selection methods—sequential forward selection (SFS) and sequential backwards elimination (SBE) feature selection—are used. SFS starts with a single feature and keeps on adding features in each iteration until the best set is found, following a bottom-up approach. SBE, on the other hand, starts with the entire set of features and removes one feature in each iteration until the best set is found, which is a top-down approach. SFS gave better results in terms of area under the curve than SBE. Six physiological features from 24 original features were chosen by SFS: mean heart rate, mean temperature, mean platelets, mean blood pressure, mean SpO_2, and mean lactic acid. Takagi-Sugeno (TS) fuzzy modeling is used for classification. If-then rules and logical connectives are formulated using this model to make the connection between selected features and final prediction.

Case Study 2

In another study, Mathias et al. (2013) tried to predict whether a patient dies within 5 years of discharge from the ICU using an ensemble index. The data set consisted of 7463 patients taken from an

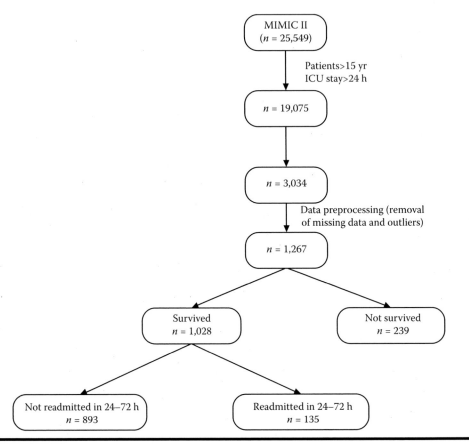

Figure 4.4 Patient Selection Scheme. (Reprinted from Fialho, A. S. et al., "Data mining using clinical physiology at discharge to predict ICU readmissions," *Expert Systems with Applications,* **39, 18, 2012: 13158–1316, 3907560873345[2016] with permission from Elsevier.)**

EHR with 980 attributes for each patient. Only patients older than 50 years were considered because increasing age was a significant prediction factor for this study. Another requirement was that the patient should have had at least one hospital visit during the year 2003. Correlation feature selection (CFS) along with greedy stepwise search was used to select features from the original set. This method yielded a subset of 52 features, which was further reduced manually, followed by another application of CFS resulting in a subset of 23. Another attribute, gender, was added to make a final subset of 24 variables. After ranking using information gain, six attributes were considered, namely, age, comorbidity count, amount of hospitalization a year prior to admission, high blood urea nitrogen levels, low calcium, and mean albumin. For classification, rotation forest ensembling with an alternating decision tree (ADT) was used with tenfold cross-validation. The RFE algorithm is an ensemble of decision trees in which each tree is assigned a subset of features randomly chosen, and principle component analysis is applied to each subset. The ADT is a decision tree that has a "probability of class membership" prior to each terminal node, and all these values along an instance's path are summed up to predict its class. The authors also present the results of two other life expectancy indices, namely, the modified Walter life expectancy index and Charlson comorbidity index, and the proposed method achieved better precision and recall.

4.6.4 Mining Data from Social Media

Apart from traditional data generated from clinicians, hospitals, and laboratories, data generated from social media platforms such as Twitter, discussion forums, etc., also serve as a potential source of Big Data. Mining these data adds value to the modern health care domain and poses several challenges, such as text mining, handling noisy and missing data, etc. The case studies given below describe how data from discussion forums can be mined for personalized health care and how an outbreak of an epidemic can be predicted from Twitter posts. Mining social media data helps to get spatiotemporal information about disease outbreaks, real-time tracking of harmful and infectious diseases, increasing the knowledge of various diseases, and providing a platform for people to get information about their health-related questions.

4.6.4.1 Use of Data from Discussion Forums

Case Study 1

Social media and the Internet have been used for searching and sharing medical data. An online forum to maintain the health state of patients and to share information on patients having a similar state is suggested by Rolia et al. (2013). The system is tested with the case of Type II diabetes. The authors generated synthetic EMR with the aid of medical professionals to determine the clinical state of patients and find similar patient information while browsing and rank similar topics in the discussion forum. The authors also created possible clinical pathways related to patients having diabetes and simulated the model with 1000 synthetic patient data. Further, a set of clinical states, such as healthy or undiagnosed, newly diagnosed diabetes, uncontrolled diabetes, controlled diabetes, controlled diabetes with complications, and poorly controlled diabetes, are defined, and patients are classified into one of these states through a rule-based system. Posts from two forums, namely, Diabetes Forum (www.diabetesforum.com) and Diabetes Daily (www.diabetesdaily.com), are collected and assigned a score by medical experts. This score indicates the percentage of views of a particular post by patients in a state defined above. The cosine similarity between each state using the weights determined by each of the selected posts was calculated, and topics were ranked based on correlation to current user's state. The patients can also give a score of 1–5 or like/dislike a post so that ranks change over time. The prototype was tested with synthetic data and appears to be helpful to engage patients in their own health care.

Case Study 2

Another platform for sharing patient experience is suggested by Ashish et al. (2012). The Abzooba Smart Health Informatics Platform (SHIP) described in this work abstracts and mines patient experiences and provides retrieval capabilities. This study uses 400,000 posts collected from discussion forums, such as Inspire and Medcare. A distillation pipeline that combines natural language processing, machine learning, and ontologies is at the core of SHIP (Figure 4.5).

Fifty facts and experiences are abstracted after applying machine learning techniques to the posts collected from the forums. Elementary extraction, the first step of this system, parses using HTML and extracts information such as how many replies are received, etc., and assigns a unique ID to each of the posts in the forum. The next step is the entity extraction step in which elements related to health, such as drugs, side effects, treatments and procedures, adverse events, etc., are extracted using ontology, such as the unified medical language system. In the next stage, the system classifies whether each post is related to one of the five categories: personal experience, advice, information, support, and outcome. Five classifiers are built, and a J48 decision tree algorithm is employed for classification. Finally, the data from all the previous steps are aggregated. As a case study, the authors chose the scenario of a patient having a severe cough after using a drug called Tarceva. The patient searches to see if coughing is a side effect of that drug, but does not find any such information on the Traceva website or any related sites. But coughing has been given as a side effect of the drug on the authors' site, and suggestions on how to deal with it could also be extracted. The precision and recall of all the five classifiers reported are found to be promising. These studies throw light into how data across discussion forums could be used, but it is difficult to see if this could be applied in real-world scenarios.

4.6.4.2 Analyzing Tweets to Predict the Spread of Diseases

Twitter is a popular social networking site on which users can post messages of up to 140 characters. These messages are called Tweets and, as per Statistic Brain (2015), currently has about 645 hundred million members worldwide with around 58 million Tweets per day.

Case Study 1

Signorini et al. (2011) present a study in which they analyze Twitter data to predict the spread of influenza disease. They collected Tweets from April 29, 2009, based on some search keywords related to influenza, such as swine, flu, vaccine, influenza, etc., using Twitter's new streaming application programmer's interface (API). The intention is to monitor influenza-related traffic within the United States, and hence, Tweets arising outside the United States are excluded. Tweets having fewer than five characters and comprising non-ASCII characters are also excluded. A dictionary of English words is created by excluding commonly used informal words. To reduce the dictionary size, inflected words are converted to root words, using Porter's stemming algorithm

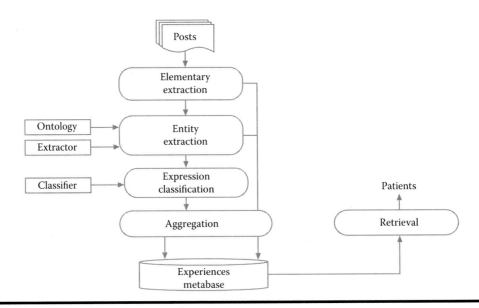

Figure 4.5 Distillation pipeline. (Reprinted from Ashish, N. et al., "The Abzooba Smart Health Informatics Platform (SHIP) TM-From Patient Experiences to Big Data to Insights," *arXiv preprint arXiv:1203.3764[2012].)*

(e.g., "knowing" becomes "know"). The usage statistics for dictionary words are then compiled from data across all valid Center for Disease Control and Prevention (CDC) influenza reporting region levels.

In order to estimate the weekly influenza-like illness (ILI) epidemic status, support vector regression is used, which is a generalized version of SVM. When data are not linearly separable, a kernel function is used to map data into high-dimensional space. In this work, authors used a polynomial kernel function. In this model, a Tweet is considered as a data point. Dictionary words that occur more than 10 times per week represent features. The fraction of each Tweet that contains the corresponding dictionary word denotes the value of that feature.

Case Study 2

Achrekar et al. (2012) developed a data collection framework—Social Network-Enabled Flu Trends (SNEFT)—to monitor Tweets related to influenza, thereby predicting the spread of the disease. Tweets related to flu and the profile of users who tweeted on the disease collected from October 18, 2009, were the data set used. An Online Social Network (OSN) crawler is used to retrieve Tweets using keywords such as flu and swine flu and to store information about the Tweets, including location and relative keyword frequency.

The CDC is a body that monitors ILI on a weekly basis using reports prepared by doctors manually. These reports are also collected from the Internet. In 2009–2010, the analysis of Tweets gave a correlation coefficient of 0.98 showing that influenza is a larger issue, but in the 2010–2011 period, it dropped to 0.47 due to the presence of spurious messages. Hence, authors applied text mining to eliminate spurious Tweets. Decision tree, SVM, and naïve Bayes are the classification methods chosen among which SVM outperformed the other two in terms of precision and recall. Some additional configurations are set up for improved learning. Data cleaning is also done to remove re-Tweets—that is, a Tweet initially posted by someone and forwarded by others. Logistic auto regression moving average is the prediction model used to predict CDC statistics by analyzing Tweets and CDC reports. Current ILI activity is predicted from past weeks using the auto regression model. A logit link function is also used for CDC reports, and logarithmic transformation is applied to Twitter posts. The authors also studied the prediction of flu in specific regions of the United States and among different age groups of people. It is also found that Twitter data and ILI reports are strongly correlated. The model could give timely updates about the percentage of visits by physicians. The model is found to be effective to create public awareness about influenza by processing Tweets.

4.7 Challenges and Issues

As data in the health care domain arise from multiple sources, such as medications, laboratories, and medical procedures, the main concern is to address the issue of integrating data from these sources. Data from devices may also contain noisy and missing data, which necessitates data cleaning and normalization. Other issues include the violation of privacy and security of patient information, which are discussed in the following sections.

4.7.1 Security and Privacy in Health Care Data Analytics

With the data deluge in health care, several security and privacy issues have also emerged, which put sensitive data at risk. Several security breaches of EHR that violate patient privacy and the

Health Insurance Portability and Accountability Act (HIPAA) and the Health Information Technology for Economic and Clinical Health (HITECH) Act in the United States have been reported over the years. According to recent research (Ponemon Institute 2015), more than 90% of health care organizations chosen for the study had a data breach, and 40% had more than five data breaches over the past 2 years. The average cost of a data breach was reported to be more than $2.1 million.

In another incident (McCann 2013) Kaiser Permanente (an integrated managed care consortium in the United States) notified 49,000 patients that their health information was compromised due to the missing unencrypted USB drive at Anaheim Medical Center. The USB drive contained sensitive information, such as patient names, dates of birth, medication data, and medical record details. They also notified 670 patients of a HIPAA breach that protected medical information, such as names, medical record numbers, email addresses, employers, phone numbers, department names, and appointment dates, which was sent as an email to a recipient outside Kaiser.

4.7.2 Privacy Preserving Analytics

4.7.2.1 Threat to Health Records

Collection of medical and health care data is essential for monitoring the adverse effects of medicines, ensuring safety of new drugs, tracking the spread of new diseases, and various other research purposes. Kupwade and Seshadri (2014) discuss security and privacy-related issues. Patient information needs to be disclosed in order to ensure quality health care, which, in turn, poses a privacy threat. People have no other choice than to disclose sensitive information as it is legally mandatory to collect and store it. Personal health records are being used by insurance companies and employers, thereby putting patient privacy at risk. Including genomic data in the EHR also raises privacy concerns. Gymrek et al. (2013) point out that genomic data together with some other information can help to identify surnames. Hence, there is a need to protect sensitive data by controlling the ways data are stored, accessed, and analyzed. One commonly used method is de-identification by which attributes that help to identify a patient are removed. But this approach has several problems. First of all, some of the research purposes mentioned above cannot be accomplished with these de-identified data due to missing information. Also, it is not clear whether removing some attributes will provide privacy and whether de-identification makes the health records unidentifiable. In addition, there are situations in which patient data need to be identified, such as when combining data about patients treated in different locations. It is an arduous task to meet all these requirements and simultaneously provide patient privacy. This paves the way for research on developing new methods for secure storage and retrieval of health care data. These include developing new authorization mechanisms, control access, and better encryption techniques for safe transmission of data.

Shin et al. (2013) discuss the need for keeping medical records safe while storing them before processing. Three environments for storing medical records ready for retrieval are considered: a plain text environment in which data are not encrypted; Microsoft encryption, which uses encryption using the built-in tools of Microsoft; and advanced encryption standard (AES) combined with the bucket index in Data as a Service (DaaS). The AES–DaaS mechanism was found to be better and more scalable than Microsoft encryption.

4.7.2.2 Threat to Data from Health Care Devices

The electronic era has resulted in the deployment of health care gadgets, such as sensors, to provide better care for patients. Implantable devices, such as pacemakers and wearable sensors, transmit information, which opens up privacy threats. Other vulnerabilities include hacking, surveillance, and malware attacks. The proliferation of wireless communication devices has also resulted in interfacing medical equipment with mobile devices for providing better health care. Zawoad and Hasan (2012) discuss the threats posed by mobile devices to medical devices and how to mitigate these attacks. They suggest usage of strong defense against malware and denial of service attack, strong authentication and encryption techniques, and intrusion detection based on anomaly.

All these threats necessitate the need for data anonymization prior to data analytics. Prediction algorithms should be able to run and produce accurate results on encrypted data. Hence, accuracy and privacy preserving data analytics is gaining popularity these days. The rise of IoT devices allows health records to be stored in the cloud, and hence, data analytics should be performed in a distributed manner. But preserving privacy in such environments is a challenging task. Laws should be enforced to protect privacy to patients; for example, consent should be obtained from patients before disclosing their data for analytical or research purposes. Devising new encryption and authentication mechanisms for providing security in data stored in the cloud is also worth investigating.

4.8 Summary

This chapter gives an overview of health care and biological Big Data, the conceptual architecture of Big Data analytics, and case studies that showcase the capabilities and applications of data mining in health informatics and issues, such as threats to privacy and security. It is evident that Big Data analytics is able to transform the way huge volumes of data are analyzed by leveraging sophisticated technologies. The health industry has witnessed a rapid increase in the deployment of Big Data technologies and tools over the last few years. Traditional machine learning techniques have been integrated into the MapReduce framework for dealing with heterogeneous biological data. Big Data analytics and data mining on health care data provide opportunities for better patient care, diagnosis, and prediction. The studies discussed in this chapter highlight the potential of health care data analytics in this regard. The techniques presented so far can be extended and tested on a variety of other biological data sets arising from different sources. However, the ever-increasing volume of data poses several issues and challenges. Ensuring privacy and security of patient information and controlling access is an additional concern, which has also been discussed in detail. Improving the technologies and tools for analytics, parallelization of existing algorithms and ensuring the safety and privacy of information will gain the focus of researchers in the future.

References

Achrekar, H., Gandhe, A., Lazarus, R., Yu, S. H. and Liu, B., 2012. "Twitter Improves Seasonal Influenza Prediction." In *HEALTHINF* (pp. 61–70).

Aphinyanaphongs, Y., Fu, L. D. and Aliferis, C. F., 2013. "Identifying unproven cancer treatments on the health web: Addressing accuracy, generalizability and scalability." *Studies in Health Technology and Informatics*, 192, p. 667.

Ashish, N. et al. 2012. "The Abzooba Smart Health Informatics Platform (SHIP) TM-From Patient Experiences to Big Data to Insights." arXiv preprint arXiv:1203.3764.

Data Mark Incorporated, 2013. "Unstructured Data in Electronic Health Record (EHR) Systems: Challenges and Solutions." White paper.

Demchenko, Y. et al. 2012, December. "Addressing big data challenges for scientific data infrastructure." In Cloud Computing Technology and Science (CloudCom), 2012 IEEE 4th International Conference on (pp. 614–617). IEEE.

Estella, F. et al. 2012, May. "Advanced system for autonomously classify brain MRI in neurodegenerative disease." In Multimedia Computing and Systems (ICMCS), 2012 International Conference on (pp. 250–255). IEEE.

Fialho, A. S. et al. 2012. "Data mining using clinical physiology at discharge to predict ICU readmissions." *Expert Systems with Applications*, 39(18), pp. 13158–13165.

Gymrek, M., McGuire, A. L., Golan, D., Halperin, E. and Erlich, Y., 2013. "Identifying personal genomes by surname inference." *Science*, 339(6117), pp. 321–324.

Haferlach, T. et al. 2010. "Clinical utility of microarray-based gene expression profiling in the diagnosis and subclassification of leukemia," report from the International Microarray Innovations in Leukemia Study Group. *Journal of Clinical Oncology*, 28(15), pp. 2529–2537.

Häyrinen, K., Saranto, K. and Nykänen, P., 2008. "Definition, structure, content, use and impacts of electronic health records: A review of the research literature." *International Journal of Medical Informatics*, 77(5), pp. 291–304.

Jiang, D., Tang, C. and Zhang, A., 2004. "Cluster analysis for gene expression data: A survey." *Knowledge and Data Engineering, IEEE Transactions on*, 16(11), pp. 1370–1386.

Kohlwey, E. et al. 2011, July. "Leveraging the cloud for big data biometrics: Meeting the performance requirements of the next generation biometric systems." In Services (SERVICES), 2011 IEEE World Congress on (pp. 597–601). IEEE.

Kupwade, P. H. and Seshadri, R. 2014, June. "Big data security and privacy issues in healthcare." In Big Data (BigData Congress), 2014 IEEE International Congress on (pp. 762–765). IEEE.

Markonis, D. et al. 2012, September. "Using MapReduce for large-scale medical image analysis." In 2012 IEEE Second International Conference on Healthcare Informatics, Imaging and Systems Biology (p. 1). IEEE.

Mathias, J. S. et al. 2013. "Development of a 5 year life expectancy index in older adults using predictive mining of electronic health record data." *Journal of the American Medical Informatics Association*, 20(e1), pp. e118–e124.

McCann, E., 2013. Kaiser reports second fall data breach. *Healthcare IT News*.

Meng, B., Pratx, G. and Xing, L. 2011. "Ultrafast and scalable cone-beam CT reconstruction using MapReduce in a cloud computing environment." *Medical Physics*, 38(12), pp. 6603–6609.

Mohammed, E. A., Far, B. H. and Naugler, C., 2014. "Applications of the MapReduce programming framework to clinical big data analysis: Current landscape and future trends." *BioData Mining*, 7(1), p. 22.

Omri, F. et al. 2012. "Cloud-ready biometric system for mobile security access." In *Networked Digital Technologies* (pp. 192–200). Springer: Berlin Heidelberg.

Ponemon Institute, 2015. "Fifth Annual Benchmark Study on Patient Privacy and Data Security," Ponemon Institute LLC.

Raghupathi, W. and Raghupathi, V., 2014. "Big data analytics in healthcare: Promise and potential." *Health Information Science and Systems*, 2(1), p. 3.

Rolia, J. et al. 2013, September. "Tell me what I don't know—Making the most of social health forums." In Healthcare Informatics (ICHI), 2013 IEEE International Conference on (pp. 447–454). IEEE.

Salazar, R. et al. 2010. "Gene expression signature to improve prognosis prediction of stage II and III colorectal cancer." *Journal of Clinical Oncology*, pp. JCO-2010.

Shin, D., Sahama, T. and Gajanayake, R., 2013, October. "Secured e-health data retrieval in DaaS and Big Data." In e-Health Networking, Applications & Services (Healthcom), 2013 IEEE 15th International Conference on (pp. 255–259). IEEE.

Shivakumar, S. K., 2013. "Big Data–A big game changer." *CSI Communications*, p. 9.

Signorini, A., Segre, A. M. and Polgreen, P. M., 2011. "The use of Twitter to track levels of disease activity and public concern in the US during the influenza A H1N1 pandemic." *PloS One*, 6(5), p. e19467.

Statistic Brain Research Institute publishing as Statistic Brain. 2015. Twitter statistics—Statistic brain. [http://www.statisticbrain.com/twitter-statistics/] [Accessed: 2016-1-20].

Taylor, R. C., 2010. "An overview of the Hadoop/MapReduce/HBase framework and its current applications in bioinformatics." *BMC Bioinformatics*, 11(Suppl. 12), p. S1.

Wang, Y. et al. 2013. "Random forests on Hadoop for genome-wide association studies of multivariate neuroimaging phenotypes." *BMC Bioinformatics*, 14(Suppl. 16), p. S6.

Wang, Y. et al. 2016. "Big data analytics: Understanding its capabilities and potential benefits for healthcare organizations." *Technological Forecasting and Social Change*, doi: 10.1016/j.techfore.2015.12.019.

Yoshida, H., Kawaguchi, A. and Tsuruya, K. 2013. "Radial basis function-sparse partial least squares for application to brain imaging data." *Computational and Mathematical Methods in Medicine*, 2013, Article ID 591032.

Zawoad, S. and Hasan, R. 2012. "The enemy within: The emerging threats to healthcare from malicious mobile devices." arXiv preprint arXiv:1210.2149.

Zhang, F. et al. 2015. "A task-level adaptive MapReduce framework for real-time streaming data in healthcare applications." *Future Generation Computer Systems*, 43, pp. 149–160.

Chapter 5

Computational Challenges in Group Membership Prediction of Highly Imbalanced Big Data Sets

William A. Rivera and Amit Goel

Institute for Simulation and Training, University of Central Florida, Orlando, Florida, USA

Contents

Abstract

Predicting group membership in highly skewed data is a common problem found in observational studies. Highly skewed data are also called class imbalanced data. Classifiers using class imbalance data will typically create rules that are biased toward the overrepresented group. Imbalance is thought to only affect classification when the data set is highly imbalanced and relatively small, although no formal definition or study has been proposed to indicate what level of imbalance matters, especially with respect to Big Data. Large imbalanced data sets present computational issues beyond that of just imbalance, and not all classifiers react the same. We present a formal definition of imbalance along with an understanding of at what levels researchers should consider alternative approaches when faced with large imbalanced data.

5.1 Introduction

One of the more common supervised learning tasks includes prediction of group membership, which is also called classification. In two-group or binary classification, the predicted outcome of interest is limited to two classes, namely, $y \in \{G_0, G_1\}$. The task of accurately predicting group membership is often difficult when dealing with large data sets that have a disparity between the two groups. This imbalance is considered a class imbalance problem, and it is common for real-world data to have a degree of imbalance. Class imbalance is usually associated with extremely skewed data, although technically any disparity can be considered imbalance.

The most noticeable issue with class imbalance is that the classifier or learner tends to be biased toward the overrepresented or majority group. Because the performance for prediction is based on the number of correctly identified samples, the performance metric may remain high, although the target of interest is group membership in the underrepresented or minority group.

There are four basic ranges of classification problems, which range from identifying one group or one-group classification to full-balance group classification as depicted in Figure 5.1. In a dichotomous setting, each group has a class with members sharing similar characteristics and that they belong to regardless of class skew. When samples do not share a characteristic in one of the groups, the problem becomes an anomaly detection problem, which is different from class imbalance.

Class imbalance is common in all data sets, although it is generally applicable in scenarios involving high imbalance. Most noticeably, the learning rules generated by the sample data set favor the overrepresented group and will perform poorly when new cases belonging to the underrepresented groups are classified. The inherent bias produced is increased when larger levels of imbalance exist. Domains impacted by this problem include loan default, fraud detection, and observational studies in health care, to name a few. Extreme imbalance ratios, such as 100,000 to 1, are quite common in these domains (D'Agostino 1998; Chawla et al. 2002; Tian et al. 2010; Mendes-Moreira and Soares 2012; Longadge and Dongre 2013).

To further illustrate the problem, we consider a real-world scenario involving loan default. Let's consider the case that observing past data provides evidence that the disparity between groups has been observed to be as much as 100 to 1 when loan default is rare with people who have good credit. Constructing a classifier for prediction with a 99% accuracy is trivial if we simply classify all cases as nondefault regardless of the population size. However, doing so does not aid in identifying members of the default group, which impacts the amount of money we stand to lose.

One class	Anomaly detection	Imbalance	Full balance
0%	Each–unique	(0–50%)	50%

Figure 5.1 Spectrum of the imbalance problem space.

We can construct a cost–benefit matrix outlining the different scenarios as shown in Table 5.1. Predicting an actual loan default can help save x dollars, and predicting default will occur when it will not result in money that could have been gained, so we lose some amount that we believe to be much lower than money lost, which we call x/y. Correctly identifying loan default gives us no benefit or cost, and predicting nondefault when default does occur results in x; potentially the cost may be higher because we need to spend more time managing assets and employee salaries in handling cases.

The optimal scenario would be if we could correctly identify each case, but that may not be feasible, so an alternative scenario is to increase the ability to identify cases that are actually in default and reduce those that will not default but are predicted to be. In a similar fashion to the cost–benefit matrix, a confusion matrix can be constructed to provide the results of classification in which each cell corresponds to the amount that fell into that category. For example, the cell with a benefit of $+x$ would correspond to the true positives, the cell with a cost of $-x$ corresponds to false negatives, the cells with a cost of x/y are false positives, and the cells with no benefit or cost associated are true negatives. The expected values can be calculated in the discrete case as follows:

$$E(X,Y) = \sum_i \sum_j p\{x_i, y_j\} \cdot x_i y_j = \sum_i \sum_j p\{y_j\} \cdot p\{x_i | y_j\} \cdot x_i y_j \tag{5.1}$$

where i and j correspond to the ith row and the jth cell, respectively, in the cost–benefit matrix. In this case, we can produce the following expected value:

$$
\begin{aligned}
E(\text{prediction, fraud}) = &\ (p\{\text{fraud} = \text{yes}\} \cdot p\{\text{predicted} = \text{yes}|\text{fraud} = \text{yes}\} \cdot x) \\
&+ (p\{\text{fraud} = \text{yes}\} \cdot p\{\text{predicted} = \text{no}|\text{fraud} = \text{yes}\} \cdot -x) \\
&+ (p\{\text{fraud} = \text{no}\} \cdot p\{\text{predicted} = \text{yes}|\text{fraud} = \text{no}\} \cdot -x/y) \\
&+ (p\{\text{fraud} = \text{no}\} \cdot p\{\text{predicted} = \text{no}|\text{fraud} = \text{no}\} \cdot 0)
\end{aligned}
\tag{5.2}
$$

Using the 99% accuracy scenario in which we automatically classify all examples as not fraud, we incur a cost of xn where n is the number of fraudulent transactions that do actually occur. In general, the underrepresented examples ($p\{fraud = yes\}$) provide the most benefit or cost. Identifying just half correctly reduces the benefit/cost to 0 because $x\dfrac{n}{2} - x\dfrac{n}{2} = 0$. In general, increasing the benefit x depends on the accuracy of the classifier for detecting fraud cases; if $p\{predicted = yes|fraud = yes\} > p\{predicted = no|fraud = yes\}$, then the ability to predict the target group correctly minimizes the cost spent and maximizes the costs saved.

To combat class imbalance, the machine learning community has relied upon three broad approaches: embedded (Domingos 1999; Zadrozny and Elkan 2001; Liu and Zhou 2006;

Table 5.1 Cost–Benefit Matrix

		Prediction	
		Yes	No
Default	Yes	+x	-x
	No	-x/y	0

Haro-Garcia and Garcia-Perajas 2011), data preprocessing (Chawla et al. 2002; Estabrooks et al. 2004; Guo and Viktor 2004; Stefanowski and Wilk 2008; He and Garcia 2009; Zhang et al. 2010; García et al. 2012; Thanathamathee and Lursinsap 2013; Şeref et al. 2017), and ensemble learning (Sun et al. 2006; Junfei et al. 2010; Tian et al. 2010; Seiffert et al. 2010; Thanathamathee and Lursinsap 2013) approaches. All of these techniques are useful when collecting data is expensive or difficult.

Embedded approaches attempt to change the internal properties of the learner to compensate for the class imbalance. This includes the addition of loss or cost functions that attempt to reweight both majority and minority group observations; kernel-based methods, which apply kernel adjustment techniques; or the use of active learning.

Data preprocessing approaches attempt to preprocess the data before using a learner in order to divide the problem space in two. These are also considered external because they occur externally from the learner, and embedded approaches occur internally. Typical preprocessing steps include feature selection and resampling strategies composed of both oversampling and undersampling.

The last group of approaches are ensemble learning techniques, which implement a collection of models and choose the best approach, which may include an aggregation of the best approaches. Techniques, such as bagging, random forest, and boosting, allow for ensembles to be individually generated and weighted against other ensembles based on performance. Ensembles have become exceedingly popular for dealing with class imbalance partly because they offer the ability for both data preprocessing and embedded modification combinations.

Big Data has computational challenges beyond that of a heavy skewed distribution. Oversampling techniques become increasingly difficult if not impossible to implement because the main goal is to create more samples for the underrepresented group.

In this chapter, we present the computational challenges and solutions to oversampling imbalanced data sets. In Section 5.2, we discuss the related oversampling techniques that have been proposed to deal with imbalanced data. In Section 5.3, we present the parallel noise reduction a priori oversampling technique, which combats class imbalance while dealing with computational challenges in class imbalance data. Section 5.4 outlines the experiments to validate improvement using this technique followed by the conclusion in Section 5.5.

5.2 Related Work

Resampling techniques offer simple alternatives to dealing with class imbalance that are easy to implement and understand. Resampling consists of both oversampling and undersampling data. Undersampling will reduce samples from the majority group to reduce the size. In oversampling, new data are created from the minority group in order to match the majority group size. In the remainder of this section, we discuss oversampling methods that have been proposed to combat class imbalance.

In 2002, Chawla et al. proposed the synthetic minority oversampling technique (SMOTE). SMOTE is an oversampling technique that creates synthetic samples in the minority group by applying an iterative search and selection approach (Chawla et al. 2002). Each observation from the minority group will be iterated through until the needed amount is reached. To generate new samples, k nearest neighbors are selected based on a user-defined threshold. One of the k nearest neighbors is then selected at random and synthesized, and then the process continues until all necessary synthesized samples have been created.

For example, if a ratio of 300% is specified, then for each observation in the minority group 3 *knn* will be selected. One will be chosen at random, and a new instance x_{n+1} is generated from the features of the random sample x_j and the original x_i observation used to generate it. New features are generated by the feature difference of x_i and x_j multiplied by a random number r between 0 and 1 as shown in Equation 5.3:

$$x_{n+1} = x_i + r \cdot (x_j - x_i), 0 \leq r \leq 1 \tag{5.3}$$

Drawbacks to this approach include generating samples that are noisy or found within class-overlapping regions. Using this technique on larger data sets has complications, including degradation of performance (Rivera et al. 2014). The Borderline–SMOTE method was introduced in 2005 as a way to selectively sample what it deems as samples in danger of misclassification (Han et al. 2005).

In general, there exist three regions for a given example: safe, borderline, or noise. Given a number of negative examples g having k nearest neighbors, we can define these regions using Table 5.2.

Given training set X where $X = (x_i, y_i)$, $y_i \in \{0, 1\}$ and $x_i \in R^n$ composed of minority group Y having $y_i = 1$ and majority group M having $y_i = 0$, thus $Y \cup M \subseteq X$.

The borderline–SMOTE method selects only those samples in Y that fall into the borderline as determined by Table 5.2. These members that contain more neighbors from the majority group are then selected as members of the danger group, $Danger \subseteq Y$ (Han et al. 2005).

The danger group includes minority members in danger of misclassification and therefore used as candidates to oversample as a way to strengthen those examples that lie closest to the decision boundary. This approach was originally introduced as two versions; in the first version, new synthetic samples are created from the nearest neighbors found only in minority group Y, and in the second version, we use the entire set X to create new samples for each member in the danger group.

If using the entire training set X for creating the new samples and its nearest neighbor is in M, then the random value r shown in Equation 5.3 is then constrained to $0 \leq r \leq 0.5$; otherwise r remains as $0 \leq r \leq 1$.

The safe-level SMOTE method extends the borderline-based approach by considering the "safe" examples found in minority group Y. The "safe" level (sl) is considered the number of minority group Y examples found in k nearest neighbors, traditionally using Euclidean distance. Examples that do not have similar membership are considered noise. In order to consider examples for candidates to be synthesized, the "safe" level ratio (slr) is used (Bunkhumpornpat et al. 2009).

The "safe" level ratio is defined as $slr = \dfrac{slp}{sln}$ where slp is the "safe" level for a given example x_i, and

Table 5.2 Region Definitions

Region	Definition
Noise	$G = k$
Borderline	$\frac{1}{2}k \leq g < k$
Safe	$0 \leq g < \frac{1}{2}k$

sln is the "safe" level for the selected neighbor of x_i, which we call x_j. In general, we consider only candidates that have minority group observations for both x_i and x_j. Those examples chosen to generate new samples are done according to Equation 5.3 but with r is calculated in one of the three following ways:

1. If *slr* = 1, then $r \in (0,1)$.
2. If *slr* > 1, then $r \in (0,(1/slr))$.
3. If *slr* < 1, then $r \in ((1-slr),1)$.

A ratio of 1 means that both x_i and x_j are equally "safe"; thus, the new example can be chosen at random. When the ratio is greater than 1, the newly synthesized data will be weighted in the positive direction, which makes the newer set lie closer to example x_i. When the ratio is less than 1, it is weighted in the negative direction, which makes the newer sample lie closer to example x_j.

The local neighborhood extension to the SMOTE (LN-SMOTE) method extends safe-level SMOTE by redefining the eligible members in the safe level under special conditions. For example, when the safe-level method is determining its safe-level ratio *slr*, it will choose a random *knn* of x_i, which we previously refereed to as x_j. If x_i is actually an outlier and x_j is from the majority group M and also has no *knn* from minority group Y, then the safe-level ratio under the safe-level method is *slr* = 0, resulting in a new sample generated closest to x_j, which is highly undesirable (MacIejewski and Stefanowski 2011).

LN-SMOTE combats these scenarios by replacing x_i with the next neighbor of x_j that is not a neighbor of x_i, which we refer to as *knn* + 1 if $x_j \in M$ and x_i is a *knn* of x_j. Another modification offered through LN-SMOTE is that the range of the random value r is changed to $r < 1$.

Oversampling using propensity scores (OUPS) attempts to provide an alternative to using the Euclidean distance measure that SMOTE introduced. The propensity score is defined as the conditional probability of group membership of the minority group (Y) based on its covariates, formally:

$$e(x) = p(Y|X) \tag{5.4}$$

The OUPS method will calculate and assign propensity scores for each observation and then orders the entire data set by the propensity score in descending order so that observations with the highest propensity score appear first. The needed amount to oversample is calculated using the imbalance ratio, which is defined as $f = \dfrac{|M|}{|Y|}$ (Rivera et al. 2014). The imbalance ratio defines the amount of majority members per minority member.

For each observation belonging to the minority group Y, f closest samples based on propensity scores are then used to generate f new samples by applying Equation 5.3.

Safe-level OUPS uses local regions to produce new samples based on the safe levels described in Table 5.2. This procedure will oversample observations that do not appear as noise based on probability of minority group membership $p(Y|X)$ (Rivera and Asparouhov 2015).

The main distinction between safe-level OUPS and OUPS is twofold. First, OUPS performs oversampling on all minority examples until the needed amount is reached, and safe-level OUPS only synthesizes selected samples, thus reducing the overhead and increased time complexity needed to produce so many samples. This makes the learning phase more computationally efficient.

The main concerns for SMOTE and OUPS are that they replicate all members of the minority group, which will cause outliers to be synthesized. The region-based approaches (safe level, borderline, local neighborhood) do not consider how to handle the examples that appear as outliers; moreover, the variation of choosing the random variable r in Equation 5.3 does not seem to aid if the sample chosen for replication is noise.

5.2.1 Computation Complexity

Aside from the briefly described shortcomings of these approaches, we must also mention that implementing these algorithms becomes increasingly difficult in larger data sets. The OUPS-based approaches calculate the probability of group membership using a nonparametric approach requiring the use of a numerical method to solve an optimization problem. One such method often uses the iterative reweighted least squares (IRLS) approach, which is based upon the Newton–Raphson method for finding the roots of squares. This approach will iteratively update the weights for each variable in the feature space until it reaches a defined error threshold or the maximum number of iterations are reached. The update step is in the form

$$\beta^{(t+1)} = \beta^t + (XWX^T)^{-1}XWz \tag{5.5}$$

where X represents the data, W represents the diagonal matrix of weights, and z is the response vector. Since our focus is not on numerical algorithms but computational complexity, we will not be discussing the details of this approach.

If the Newton–Ralphson method is used, the usual running time is $O(logt)f(t)$, where t is the amount of steps it will iterate, and $f(t)$ is the cost of calculating $\dfrac{f(x)}{f'(x)}$. Usually $f'(x)$ will represent the Hessian matrix, which is a matrix of second-order partial derivatives for each of the k features found in the given data set x, and $f(x)$ will be represented by the Jacobian matrix, a first-order matrix of partial derivatives.

We must also sort by propensity score $O(nlogn)$ and finally create new samples $O(mk)$, where n represents the amount of examples in the data set, k represents the features, and m represents the amount of minority members needed to resample for each minority member. Of course, this is just the upper bound, but the amount of total operation leaves room for improvement.

The SMOTE-based approach must also resample $O(mk)$, but before doing so, it will calculate *knn* using some distance metric. This will require comparing each member of the minority group and each k feature for a running time of $O(gk)$ to compute the distance, where g represents the amount of minority members. We must also perform some comparison, which could be handled by a hash table once the score is calculated, which is bound by some constant.

The safe-level approaches each require similar complexity with a little less computation to generate new members since it only creates a small amount of copies. This would result in a run time complexity $\propto O(gk)$ as an upper bound.

The concern with the OUPS-based approaches is the needed time to calculate the propensity score. For each of the remaining techniques, there is concern for resampling the needed amount. Focusing on marginal improvement of the upper bound is not enough in big data sets. The parallel noise reduction a priori oversampling (PNRAP) is geared at improving prediction while reducing the amount of computation needed. In Big Data, this is especially useful.

5.3 Parallel Noise Reduction A Priori Oversampling

PNRAP performs oversampling using a priori information on data projected into a lower dimension to help remove noise from the minority group. The proposed technique will then perform parallel resampling to reach the needed amount. This section outlines the steps and theoretical rationale in detail.

In general, we can view the entire process in two main steps. First is data reduction; we reduce the overall size of the feature space. The next step will selectively produce synthetic samples to help improve classification performance.

At first, we reduce the size of our features by performing orthogonal linear transformation using a technique called principal component analysis (PCA). By applying this technique, we are able to transform our data into a smaller dimensional space while preserving the structure. Before performing this operation, we perform some scaling so that computation can potentially be easier. Consider the data set in matrix form as $X \in R^{n \times k}$ where each of the rows represents a sample with k features. First, we normalize X to have zero mean by subtracting the column means from each entry in the corresponding column $X^{(i)} - \frac{1}{n} \sum_{j}^{n} X_{j}^{(i)}$.

Next, the covariance matrix $\Sigma = X^T X$ is computed. We then perform eigenvalue decomposition on Σ. Eigenvalue decomposition will factor out a scalar value and a vector that will make up a matrix; for example, $\Sigma = Av = \lambda v$ where $A \in R^{n \times n}$ represents a square matrix, λ represents a scalar, and v represents a vector. Having n equations, there are $1 \le n$ possible solutions with different eigenvectors λ and eigenvalues v.

The solution with the highest eigenvalue represents the most information, so we then construct a feature matrix by placing the eigenvectors into a matrix F. This new matrix is called the feature matrix. For calculation simplification, the matrix is transformed to a unit vector and unit variance. The most important features are then retained. The reduced data set R is then calculated by using the feature matrix reduced with the desired features and the original adjusted data $R = F^T X^T$.

Next, the probability of minority group membership is calculated. The probability of group membership is based on Bayes' theorem:

$$p(y|x) = \frac{p(x|y) \cdot p(y)}{p(x)} \tag{5.6}$$

where $p(y)$ is the prior probability of group y, and $p(x|y)$ is the probability of x given group y. We then assign x to the group, which satisfies $p(y = 1|x) > p(y = 1 \cdots n|x)$. Since the denominator is the same for each group and does not affect the outcome, it can be omitted to make the calculation simpler.

$$p(y|x) = p(x|y) \cdot p(y) \tag{5.7}$$

The multivariate normal distribution is used:

$$f(y|x) = p(y) \frac{1}{\sqrt{(2\pi)^k |S|}} e^{\frac{-1}{2}(x-\mu)^T S^{-1}(x-\mu)} \tag{5.8}$$

where S^{-1} is the pooled covariance matrix and is the same for all groups, and μ is the group mean. In the two-group case, we look at the log odds ratio:

$$\log\left(\frac{f(y=1|x)}{f(y=0|x)}\right) = \log\left(\frac{p(y=1)}{p(y=0)}\right) - \frac{1}{2}(x-\mu_1)^T S^{-1}(x-\mu_1) + \frac{1}{2}(x-\mu_2)^T S^{-1}(x-\mu_2) = \quad (5.9)$$

$$\log\left(\frac{p(y=1)}{p(y=0)}\right) + 2S^{-1}\left(\left(-x^T x + 2x^T\mu_1 - \mu_1^T\mu_1\right) + \left(x^T x - 2x^T\mu_2 + \mu_2^T\mu_2\right)\right) = \quad (5.10)$$

$$\log\left(\frac{p(y=1)}{p(y=0)}\right) + 2S^{-1}\left(-x^T x + 2x^T\mu_1 - \mu_1^T\mu_1 + x^T x - 2x^T\mu_2 + \mu_2^T\mu_2\right) = \quad (5.11)$$

$$\log\left(\frac{p(y=1)}{p(y=0)}\right) + 2S^{-1}\left(\left(2x^T\mu_1 - 2x^T\mu_2\right) + \left(-\mu_1^T\mu_1 + -\mu_2^T\mu_2\right)\right) = \quad (5.12)$$

$$\log\left(\frac{p(y=1)}{p(y=0)}\right) + x^T S^{-1}(\mu_1 - \mu_2) - \frac{1}{2}(\mu_1 + \mu_2)^2 + S^{-1}(\mu_1 - \mu_2) \quad (5.13)$$

In the two-group case, the log likelihood ratio gives the estimated weights as a linear function of x; visually this can be seen as

$$\beta x + a = \log\left(\frac{p(y=1)}{p(y=0)}\right) + x^T S^{-1}(\mu_1 - \mu_2) - \frac{1}{2}(\mu_1 + \mu_2)^2 + S^{-1}(\mu_1 - \mu_2) \quad (5.14)$$

where

$$\begin{cases} a = \log\left(\frac{p(y=1)}{p(y=0)}\right) - \frac{1}{2}(\mu_1 + \mu_2)^2 + S^{-1}(\mu_1 - \mu_2) \\ \beta = S^{-1}(\mu_1 - \mu_2) \end{cases} \quad (5.15)$$

This is nice because we can easily classify groups using a closed-form solution that is simple to derive.

For each item in X that is a minority member, we examine each of the knn neighbors. If the amount of neighbors has $<k/3$ minority group membership, we remove it from the data set. The amount of new samples to create is then calculated from the imbalance ratio $f = \dfrac{|MajorityMembers|}{|MinorityMembers|}$ of the remaining members. Each of the remaining members of the minority group is then used

to create f new members using Equation 5.3. The f new samples are generated from the chosen observation and random choice of one of the knn each f times. This approach is done in a parallel manner. Last, the data are then projected back to the original feature space for testing. The algorithm is presented as Algorithm 5.1.

Algorithm 5.1 PNRAP

1: **procedure** PNRAP(k)
2:     **Input :** $t \leftarrow$ **desired** knn **to choose**
3:     **Output : resampled data set**
4:     $X = \{(x_i; y_i)|1 \leq i \leq n\}, y_i \in \{0, 1\}$ The data Set
5:     $X' \leftarrow X - \bar{X}$, subtract mean
6:     $\Sigma \leftarrow Covariance(X')$
7:     $F \leftarrow$ resulting feature vector after Eigen decomposition on Σ
8:     $F' \leftarrow \dfrac{F}{StandardDeviation\,(F)}$ transform to unit vector
9:     order F' by highest eigenvalue and retain the most valuable features
10:     $R \leftarrow F'^T X^T$
11:     $R' \leftarrow$ calculate propensity score and assign to R
12:     $f = \dfrac{|MajorityMembers|}{|MinorityMembers|}$
13:     $NewData \leftarrow \emptyset$;
14:     $Removals \leftarrow \emptyset$;
15:     **parallel for** i to $|R'|$ **do**
16:         **if** R'_i is a member of the minority group **then**
17:             $KNN \leftarrow findKnn(k, R')$ return all knn
18:             **if** $|KNN \in MajorityGroup| > \dfrac{f}{3}$ **then**
19:                 $Removals \leftarrow R'_i \cup Removals$
20:             **else**
21:                 $j \leftarrow 0$
22:                 **parallel for** $j \in f$ exists **do**
23:                     $knn \leftarrow ChooseRandomKnn(KNN)$
24:                     $r \leftarrow Random(0, 1)$
25:                     $new \leftarrow R'_i + r \cdot \left(knn - R'_i\right)$
26:                     $NewData \cup new$
27:                 **end parallel for**
28:             **end if**
29:         **end if**
30:     **end parallel for**
31:     $NewData \leftarrow NewData - Removals$
32:     **return** $NewData$
33: **end procedure**

The process to transform the original feature space into a subset of dimensions is similar to matrix multiplication, which is usually considered to have an $O(n^3)$ asymptotic running time where n is the number of existing observations in the data set before any resampling occurs. The resampling procedure is now reduced by the number of processors that can run in parallel, which is bounded by the hardware of your system.

The major advantage of this approach is that we can reduce the amount of computation by leveraging the most important features and reducing the overall size. The parallelization of the code is an effective approach to dealing with Big Data. The secondary concern is on improving the performance measures of the data set. The researcher needs to consider the trade-off when making the decision to select both the amount of *knn* and the number of features to retain.

Generated synthetic samples on closely matched propensity scores allow for similar observations to be created with the same likelihood, thus effectively increasing the group amount and reducing the bias. This can be seen as a way of applying costs to the minority observations that does not rely on any previous knowledge or distributional assumptions.

For example, let us assume that we are given an observation $x_i \in X = \{x_1,\dots,x_n\}$ where X represents examples in the minority group. When we apply Equation 5.3, we see that the synthesized data are weighted approximately $n\left[x_i + \left(\dfrac{x_i - \Delta x}{2}\right)\right]$ where n is the number of synthesized samples to generate per ith iteration, and $\Delta x = \dfrac{1}{n}\sum_{j=i+1}^{n} x_j$. This weight applies to all original x_i members of X. Again, we provide this rationale to support the concept that OUPS shares similar properties to embedded approaches at a local level.

5.4 Experiments

Experiments were performed to compare PNRAP against the traditional approaches with different degrees of imbalanced data using feed-forward neural networks comprised of 5, 10, and 20 nodes and support vector machine (SVM) classifiers with a linear and a radial basis kernel. The following techniques were used: SMOTE (Chawla et al. 2002), LN-SMOTE (MacIejewski and Stefanowski 2011), safe-level SMOTE (SLSMOTE; Bunkhumpornpat et al. 2009), both versions of borderline SMOTE (SMOTEBL1, SMOTEBL2; Han et al. 2005), safe-level OUPS (SLOUPS), and OUPS.

Due to the complexity issues imposed by the other techniques, we restricted the size of our data sets to show the improvements proposed by the PNRAP approach; we later show the results of increased time improvements as outlined further in the results section. Forty-five data sets were obtained from online repositories, including UCI Machine Learning Repository* and the Keel Data Repository† with varying degrees of class imbalance. More information regarding the data is publicly accessible online. Table 5.3 summarizes the data sets used.

SMOTE and the SMOTE-based sampling techniques require a *knn* for performing local searches during sampling. We limited our choice of *k* to be 5 in these cases as these produced the most consistent results. After applying the sampling techniques, we then performed stratified sampling to generate the training set (López et al. 2013). The test sets were generated from the original

---

* http://archive.ics.uci.edu/ml
† http://www.keel.es/

Table 5.3 Data Summary

Data	Instances	Features	Imbalance Ratio (f)
cleveland-0_vs_4	177	13	12.62
ecoli-0-1-3-7_vs_2-6	281	7	39.15
ecoli-0-1-4-6_vs_5	280	6	13
ecoli-0-1-4-7_vs_2-3-5-6	336	7	10.59
ecoli-0-1-4-7_vs_5-6	332	6	12.28
ecoli-0-1_vs_2-3-5	244	7	9.17
ecoli-0-1_vs_5	240	6	11
ecoli-0-2-3-4_vs_5	202	7	9.1
ecoli-0-2-6-7_vs_3-5	224	7	9.18
ecoli-0-3-4-6_vs_5	205	7	9.25
ecoli-0-3-4-7_vs_5-6	257	7	9.28
ecoli-0-3-4_vs_5	200	7	9
ecoli-0-4-6_vs_5	203	6	9.15
ecoli-0-6-7_vs_3-5	222	7	9.09
ecoli-0-6-7_vs_5	220	6	10
glass-0-1-4-6_vs_2	205	9	11.06
glass-0-1-5_vs_2	172	9	9.12
glass-0-1-6_vs_2	192	9	10.29
glass-0-1-6_vs_5	184	9	19.44
glass-0-4_vs_5	92	9	9.22
glass-0-6_vs_5	108	9	11
glass2	214	9	10.39
glass4	214	9	15.47
glass5	214	9	22.81
led7digit-0-2-4-5-6-7-8-9_vs_1	443	7	10.97
page-blocks-1-3_vs_4	472	10	15.85
shuttle-c0-vs-c4	1829	9	13.87
shuttle-c2-vs-c4	129	9	20.5

(Continued)

Table 5.3 (Continued) Data Summary

Data	Instances	Features	Imbalance Ratio (f)
vowel	988	13	10.1
yeast-0-2-5-6_vs_3-7-8-9	1004	8	9.10
yeast-0-2-5-7-9_vs_3-6-8	1004	8	9.14
yeast-0-3-5-9_vs_7-8	506	8	9.12
yeast-0-5-6-7-9_vs_4	528	8	9.35
yeast-1-2-8-9_vs_7	947	8	30.56
yeast-1-4-5-8_vs_7	693	8	22.10
yeast-1_vs_7	459	7	13.87
yeast-2_vs_4	514	8	9.08
yeast-2_vs_8	482	8	23.10
yeast4	1484	8	28.41
yeast5	1484	8	32.78
yeast6	1484	8	39.15

data sets before any resampling was used. These test sets were used against all the resampled versions, including the non-resampled ones as well. This procedure was applied 30 times per data set, resulting in 30 test sets per data set. This method was chosen over the k-fold cross-validation approach because it may be the case that there is not enough represented samples in some of the folds, thus increasing the variance.

5.4.1 Evaluation Criteria

A confusion matrix similar to Table 5.4 was used to produce metrics of classification accuracy, sensitivity, specificity, and F-measure. True positives (TPs) are results that were correctly classified as belonging to the minority group, and true negatives (TNs) represent all the results correctly classified as belonging to the majority group. False positives (FPs) are results that belong to the majority group but were incorrectly classified as belonging to the minority group, and false negatives (FNs)

Table 5.4 Confusion Matrix

		Prediction	
		Positive	Negative
Truth	Positive	TP	FN
	Negative	FP	TN

are results that belonged to the minority group but were incorrectly classified as belonging to the majority group (Baldi et al. 2000; Batista et al. 2004).

For imbalanced data sets, the traditional accuracy metric $\left(\dfrac{TP + TN}{TP + TN + FP + FN} \right)$ can seem misleading since the majority group may be accurately classified, and the minority group, being small, will not impact the performance metric. For example, assume there are 190 observations that belong to the majority group and only 10 to the minority group. If the classifier is able to identify 185 observations accurately from the majority group and zero from the minority group, you have a classifier with 93% accuracy and with no ability to identify the target concept correctly. Therefore, the sensitivity metric is preferred. Sensitivity, sometimes referred to as the hit rate or recall rate, is the ability to identify a condition correctly $TP/(FN + TP)$. If the desire is to exclude a condition correctly instead of including it, then the specificity or TN rate can be used as an evaluation metric $TN/(FP + TN)$. In a patient level setting, specificity is the probability of a well patient testing negative, and sensitivity is the probability of an ill patient testing positive.

The G-mean was also used as an evaluation metric. The G-mean represents the geometric mean for both specificity and sensitivity and provides a balanced representation of specificity and sensitivity simultaneously.

$$G = \sqrt{\frac{TP}{FN + TP} \cdot \frac{TN}{FP + TN}} \qquad (5.16)$$

5.4.2 Results

5.4.2.1 Performance Metric

In most experimental designs, the use of analysis of varance (ANOVA) along with a parametric post hoc test is typically employed. However, the ANOVA-based assumptions (independence, normality, and homoscedasticity) are most probably violated when analyzing machine learning algorithm performance when comparing across different data sets and using different learners (Demšar and Demšar 2006; García et al. 2010; Raeder et al. 2012). Therefore, nonparametric tests are most appropriate, and thus, the use of the Friedman test followed by the Holm post hoc procedure was employed in some of the comparisons when it was deemed appropriate. The Friedman test is a nonparametric test with a null hypothesis that the ranks are equal. If they are not equal, then the Holm post hoc procedure will test each of the n techniques pairwise for significance. These tests are outlined in the results section when used along with the average ranking (Tables 5.5 through 5.16).

A rank of 1 is higher than a rank of 2 and so on. If a tie occurs, then the average is computed and used; thus, the smaller the number, the better it performed.

Our results show that the PNRAP approach was the most effective technique when compared against the other oversampling methods. Using neural networks resulted in statistically significant improvement for G-mean and sensitivity. Specificity will always trade off with sensitivity, so if a technique performs well in one measure, the opposite will happen in the other.

Using SVM classifiers resulted in similar measures. While the difference in ranks was statistically significant compared against most techniques, the SMOTE-based method was not although

Table 5.5   Neural Networks with Five Nodes Average Mean Rank over All Data Sets

Technique	Sensitivity	G Mean	Specificity
LN-SMOTE	5.6829	5.3902	2.7561
SMOTEBL1	5.1829	4.7439	2.0122
SMOTEBL2	4.7317	4.5122	3.5000
SLSMOTE	5.2805	5.0000	2.5976
SMOTE	2.2439	2.8293	5.8049
OUPS	3.4756	4.0366	5.6951
PNRAP	1.4024	1.4878	5.6341

Table 5.6   Holm Post Hoc Method Using Neural Networks with Five Nodes *p* Values Compared against PNRAP; Values in Bold Indicate Statistical Significance of PNRAP over Comparison

	LN-SMOTE	SMOTEBL1	SMOTEBL2	SLSMOTE	SMOTE	OUPS
Sensitivity	**0.0000**	**0.0000**	**0.0000**	**0.0000**	**0.0006**	**0.0000**
Specificity	0.0001	0.0000	0.0001	0.0001	0.8477	0.9275
G Mean	**0.0000**	**0.0002**	**0.0002**	**0.0001**	**0.0113**	**0.0000**

Friedman tests: sensitivity chi-squared = 105.38, $df = 6$, p value < 2.2E-16. Specificity chi-squared = 154.05, $df = 6$, p value < 2.2E-16. G mean chi-squared = 103.18, $df = 6$, p value < 2.2E-16.

Table 5.7   Neural Networks with 10 Nodes Average Mean Rank over All Data Sets

Technique	Sensitivity	G Mean	Specificity
LN-SMOTE	5.7073	5.6341	3.0122
SMOTEBL1	5.4146	5.1951	2.0244
SMOTEBL2	4.8293	4.6341	3.6098
SLSMOTE	5.3537	5.0732	2.4024
SMOTE	1.9756	2.4268	6.1585
OUPS	3.3049	3.7195	5.8171
PNRAP	1.4146	1.3171	4.9756

Table 5.8 Holm Post Hoc Method Using Neural Networks with 10 Nodes *p* Values Compared against PNRAP; Values in Bold Indicate Statistical Significance of PNRAP over Comparison

	LN-SMOTE	SMOTEBL1	SMOTEBL2	SLSMOTE	SMOTE	OUPS
Sensitivity	**0.0000**	**0.0000**	**0.0000**	**0.0000**	**0.0041**	**0.0000**
Specificity	0.0002	0.0001	0.0002	0.0001	0.0096	0.0184
G Mean	**0.0002**	**0.0003**	**0.0003**	**0.0003**	**0.0000**	**0.0000**

Friedman tests: sensitivity chi-squared = 171.17, df = 6, p value < 2.2E-16. Specificity chi-squared = 155.57, df = 6, p value < 2.2E-16. G mean chi-squared = 139.16, df = 6, p value < 2.2E-16.

Table 5.9 Neural Networks with 20 Nodes Average Mean Rank over All Data Sets

Technique	Sensitivity	G Mean	Specificity
LN-SMOTE	5.7195	5.6585	2.9756
SMOTEBL1	5.3902	5.1585	2.1829
SMOTEBL2	4.6463	4.5488	3.4878
SLSMOTE	5.4024	5.2683	2.4756
SMOTE	2.0000	2.5732	6.3780
OUPS	3.3537	3.5976	5.6098
PNRAP	1.4878	1.1951	4.8902

Table 5.10 Holm Post Hoc Method Using Neural Networks with 20 Nodes *p* Values Compared against PNRAP; Values in Bold Indicate Statistical Significance of PNRAP over Comparison

	LN-SMOTE	SMOTEBL1	SMOTEBL2	SLSMOTE	SMOTE	OUPS
Sensitivity	**0.0000**	**0.0000**	**0.0000**	**0.0000**	**0.0088**	**0.0000**
Specificity	0.0001	0.0000	0.0001	0.0000	0.0001	0.0122
G Mean	**0.0002**	**0.0003**	**0.0003**	**0.0003**	**0.0000**	**0.0000**

Friedman tests: sensitivity chi-squared = 166.89, df = 6, p value < 2.2E-16. Specificity chi-squared = 151.8, df = 6, p value < 2.2E-16. G mean chi-squared = 145.15, df = 6, p value < 2.2E-16.

Table 5.11 SVM with Radial Basis Function Average Mean Rank over All Data Sets

Technique	Sensitivity	G Mean	Specificity
LN-SMOTE	5.8415	5.7683	2.4878
SMOTEBL1	5.4512	5.3780	2.2927
SMOTEBL2	4.5732	4.4512	3.4634
SLSMOTE	5.4390	5.4024	2.6585
SMOTE	1.9878	1.8049	5.8293
OUPS	3.3049	3.5854	5.0854
PNRAP	1.4024	1.6098	6.1829

Table 5.12 Holm Post Hoc Method Using SVM with RBF Kernel *p* Values Compared against PNRAP; Values in Bold Indicate Statistical Significance of PNRAP over Comparison

	LN-SMOTE	SMOTEBL1	SMOTEBL2	SLSMOTE	SMOTE	OUPS
Sensitivity	**0.0000**	**0.0000**	**0.0000**	**0.0000**	0.0333	**0.0011**
Specificity	0.0000	0.0000	0.0000	0.0000	0.2038	1.0000
G Mean	**0.0004**	**0.0005**	**0.0000**	**0.0004**	0.2516	**0.0080**

Friedman tests: sensitivity chi-squared = 173.46, *df* = 6, *p* value < 2.2E-16. Specificity chi-squared = 161.95, *df* = 6, *p* value < 2.2E-16. G mean chi-squared = 158.65, *df* = 6, *p* value < 2.2E-16.

Table 5.13 SVM C = 1 Average Mean Rank over All Data Sets

Technique	Sensitivity	G Mean	Specificity
LN-SMOTE	5.6220	5.4268	2.2073
SMOTEBL1	5.8780	5.8049	2.0854
SMOTEBL2	4.7683	4.5854	3.5366
SLSMOTE	5.1829	5.0732	2.7805
SMOTE	1.9024	1.8902	5.9390
OUPS	2.9512	2.8293	5.1585
PNRAP	1.6951	2.3902	6.2927

Table 5.14 Holm Post Hoc Method Using SVM C = 1 *p* Values Compared against PNRAP; Values in Bold Indicate Statistical Significance of PNRAP over Comparison

	LN-SMOTE	*SMOTEBL1*	*SMOTEBL2*	*SLSMOTE*	*SMOTE*	*OUPS*
Sensitivity	**0.0000**	**0.0000**	**0.0000**	**0.0000**	0.8083	**0.0075**
Specificity	0.0000	0.0000	0.0000	0.0000	0.0499	0.0000
G Mean	**0.0007**	**0.0006**	**0.0021**	**0.0008**	1.000	0.2549

Friedman tests: sensitivity chi-squared = 175.6, *df* = 6, *p* value < 2.2E-16. Specificity chi-squared = 177.78, *df* = 6, *p* value < 2.2E-16. G mean chi-squared = 177.78, *df* = 6, *p* value < 2.2E-16.

Table 5.15 SVM C = 100 Average Mean Rank over All Data Sets

Technique	Sensitivity	G Mean	Specificity
LN-SMOTE	5.5244	5.3780	2.2927
SMOTEBL1	5.7561	5.6829	2.1585
SMOTEBL2	4.8780	4.8293	3.5732
SLSMOTE	5.2317	5.0488	2.7439
SMOTE	1.9634	1.9878	5.8415
OUPS	2.9268	2.7927	5.1951
PNRAP	1.7195	2.2805	6.1951

Table 5.16 Holm Post Hoc Method Using SVM C = 100 *p* Values Compared against PNRAP; Values in Bold Indicate Statistical Significance of PNRAP over Comparison

	LN-SMOTE	*SMOTEBL1*	*SMOTEBL2*	*SLSMOTE*	*SMOTE*	*OUPS*
Sensitivity	**0.0000**	**0.0000**	**0.0000**	**0.0000**	0.2762	**0.0032**
Specificity	0.0000	0.0000	0.0000	0.0000	0.1066	0.0000
G Mean	**0.0018**	**0.0010**	**0.0111**	**0.0025**	0.7399	0.3422

Friedman tests: sensitivity chi-squared = 169.22, *df* = 6, *p* value < 2.2E-16. Specificity chi-squared = 165.64, *df* = 6, *p* value < 2.2E-16. G mean chi-squared = 135.59, *df* = 6, *p* value < 2.2E-16.

the rank was lower. These results highlight the improved performance of this technique among the importance of computational concerns with Big Data.

5.5 Conclusion and Future Work

Computational issues are prevalent with Big Data because of the amount of computation needed to process all the samples. In this chapter, we discussed the computational issues with Big Data in imbalanced data sets. We presented the PNRAP method to combat these issues and highlighted the performance of this technique compared to competing approaches.

The PNRAP method indicated statistically significant improvement compared to popular oversampling methods SMOTE, LN-SMOTE, borderline SMOTE, SLSMOTE, SLOUPS, and OUPS, using neural network classifiers. Similar results were seen when using SVM classifiers, although in some cases, it was not statistically significant over the SMOTE method.

Large data sets are difficult to process, and leveraging multiprocessing and multithreaded techniques may aid in producing results in a reasonable amount of time. Future work should consider performing weighted-based approaches that can be processed in a parallel fashion. Cost-based methods are similar to resampling methods without the need to produce more samples. Although the computation may not be improved, running further experiments would be conducted on a smaller data set.

References

Baldi, P., S. R. Brunak, and Y. Chauvin (2000). Assessing the accuracy of prediction algorithms for classification: An overview. *Bioinformatics 16*(5), 412–424.

Batista, G. E., R. C. Prati, and M. C. Monard (2004). A study of the behavior of several methods for balancing machine learning training data. *ACM SIGKDD Explorations Newsletter 6*(1), 20.

Bunkhumpornpat, C., K. Sinapiromsaran, and C. Lursinsap (2009). Safe-Level-SMOTE: Safe-Level-Synthetic Minority Over-Sampling TEchnique for Handling the Class Imbalanced Problem. In T. Theeramunkong, B. Kijsirikul, N. Cercone and T.-B. Ho (Eds.) *Advances in Knowledge Discovery and Data Mining*, pp. 475–482.

Chawla, N. V., K. W. Bowyer, L. O. Hall, and W. Philip (2002). SMOTE: Synthetic minority oversampling technique. *Journal of Artificial Intelligence Research 16*, 321–357.

D'Agostino, R. B. (1998). Tutorial in biostatistics: Propensity score methods for bias reduction in the comparison of a treatment to a non-randomized control group. *Stat Med 2281*, 2265–2281.

Demšar, J. and J. Demšar (2006). Statistical comparisons of classifiers over multiple data sets. *Journal of Machine Learning Research 7*, 1–30.

Domingos, P. (1999). Metacost: A general method for making classifiers cost-sensitive. *In Proceedings of the fifth ACM SIGKDD international conference on Knowledge discovery and data mining.*

Estabrooks, A., T. Jo, and N. Japkowicz (2004). A multiple resampling method for learning from imbalanced data sets. *Computational Intelligence 20*(1), 18–36.

García, S., A. Fernández, J. Luengo, and F. Herrera (2010). Advanced nonparametric tests for multiple comparisons in the design of experiments in computational intelligence and data mining: Experimental analysis of power. *Information Sciences 180*(10), 2044–2064.

García, V., J. Sánchez, and R. A. Mollineda (2012). On the effectiveness of preprocessing methods when dealing with different levels of class imbalance. *Knowledge-Based Systems 25*(1), 13–21.

Guo, H. and H. L. Viktor (2004). Learning from imbalanced data sets with boosting and data generation: The DataBoost-IM approach. *ACM SIGKDD Explorations Newsletter 6*(1), 30–39.

Han, H., W.-Y. Wang, and B.-H. Mao (2005). Borderline-SMOTE: A new over-sampling method. *Advances in Intelligent Computing*. In *LNCS 2644*, pp. 878–887.

Haro-Garcia, A. D. and N. Garcia-Perajas (2011). A scalable method for instance selection for class-imbalance datasets. *Intelligent Systems Design and Applications (ISDA)*, 1383–1390.

He, H. and E. A. Garcia (2009). Learning from imbalanced data. *IEEE Transactions on Knowledge and Data Engineering 21*(9), 1263–1284.

Junfei, C., W. Qingfeng, and D. Huailin (2010). An empirical study on ensemble selection for class-imbalance data sets. *2010 5th International Conference on Computer Science & Education*, 477–480.

Liu, X.-Y. and Z.-H. Zhou (2006). The influence of class imbalance on cost-sensitive learning: An empirical study. *Sixth International Conference on Data Mining (ICDM'06)*, 970–974.

Longadge, R. and S. Dongre (2013). Class imbalance problem in data mining review. arXiv preprint arXiv:1305.1707 2(1).

López, V., A. Fernández, S. García, V. Palade, and F. Herrera (2013). An insight into classification with imbalanced data: Empirical results and current trends on using data intrinsic characteristics. *Information Sciences 250*, 113–141.

MacIejewski, T. and J. Stefanowski (2011). Local neighbourhood extension of SMOTE for mining imbalanced data. *IEEE SSCI 2011: Symposium Series on Computational Intelligence—CIDM 2011: 2011 IEEE Symposium on Computational Intelligence and Data Mining*, 104–111.

Mendes-Moreira, J. and C. Soares (2012). Ensemble approaches for regression: A survey. *ACM Computing Surveys (CSUR) 45*(1).

Raeder, T., G. Forman, and N. V. Chawla (2012). Learning from imbalanced data: Evaluation matters. In *Data Mining: Foundations and intelligent paradigms*. Springer, Berlin Heidelberg, pp. 315–331.

Rivera, W. A. and O. Asparouhov (2015). Safe level OUPS for improving target concept learning in imbalanced data sets. *IEEE SoutheastCon 2015*.

Rivera, W. A., A. Goel, and J. P. Kincaid (2014). OUPS: A combined approach using SMOTE and propensity score matching. *Proceedings of the 2014 13th International Conference on Machine Learning and Applications 1*(2), 424–427.

Seiffert, C., T. M. Khoshgoftaar, J. Van Hulse, and A. Napolitano (2010). RUSBoost: A hybrid approach to alleviating class imbalance. *IEEE Transactions on Systems, Man, and Cybernetics—Part A: Systems and Humans 40*(1), 185–197.

Şeref, O., T. Razzaghi, and P. Xanthopoulos (2017). Weighted relaxed support vector machines. *Annals of Operations Research 249*(1), 235–271.

Stefanowski, J. and S. Wilk (2008). Selective pre-processing of imbalanced data for improving classification performance. In I.-Y. Song, J. Eder, and T. M. Nguyen (Eds.) *Data Warehousing and Knowledge Discovery*. Springer, Berlin Heidelberg, pp. 283–292.

Sun, Y., M. S. Kamel, and Y. Wang (2006). Boosting for learning multiple classes with imbalances class distribution. *Proceedings—IEEE International Conference on Data Mining, ICDM*, 592–602.

Thanathamathee, P. and C. Lursinsap (2013). Handling imbalanced data sets with synthetic boundary data generation using bootstrap re-sampling and AdaBoost techniques. *Pattern Recognition Letters 34*(12), 1339–1347.

Tian, J., H. Gu, and W. Liu (2010). Imbalanced classification using support vector machine ensemble. *Neural Computing and Applications 20*(2), 203–209.

Zadrozny, B. and C. Elkan (2001). Learning and making decisions when costs and probabilities are both unknown. *Proceedings of the seventh ACM SIGKDD international conference on Knowledge discovery and data mining—KDD '01*, 204–213.

Zhang, Y.-P., L.-N. Zhang, and Y.-C. Wang (2010). Cluster-based majority under-sampling approaches for class imbalance learning. *2010 2nd IEEE International Conference on Information and Financial Engineering*, 400–404.

DATA ANALYTICS AND PREDICTION MODELS

Chapter 6

A New Paradigm in Fraud Detection Modeling Using Predictive Models, Fuzzy Expert Systems, Social Network Analysis, and Unstructured Data

Goran Klepac,[1] Robert Kopal,[2] and Leo Mršić[2]

[1]Raiffeisenbank Austria d.d., Zagreb, Croatia
[2]University College Algebra, Zagreb, Croatia

Contents

Abstract

Fraud detection systems are a hot topic in the area of business intelligence. Traditionally, this field has been focused mostly on predictive analytics based on neural networks, Bayesian networks, logistic regression, and similar methods. Predictive analytics as a key driver for fraud detection modeling rarely delivers sufficient accuracy and can be significantly improved. Fortunately, fraud is not a frequent event, and it is always a problem to isolate a reliable data sample for a predictive analytical model. On the other hand, after conducting the attribute relevance analysis, predictive models recognize only a few important predictors regarding aim variable (fraud "yes" or "no"), which can be an insufficient tool for reaching adequate accuracy in fraud detection because fraudsters are very inventive. The predictive model is often based on a few integrated variables and is often a weak tool for fraud detection. Also, predictive model development depends on reliable history data samples. Reliability in fraud detection means a significant number of cases with common characteristics. Moreover, fraud demands quick recognition at an early stage, and pattern recognition in a late phase often becomes too slow and unusable for fraud prevention purposes. The authors do not neglect the importance of predictive models in fraud detection but emphasize that a more sophisticated approach should be used with significant improvement in accuracy. The main hypothesis is that qualitative fraud detection solutions should contain expert rules based on expert experience and should take into consideration other approaches, such as social network analysis, as well as Big Data sources for building efficient fraud detection models. The proposed approach integrates predictive models, fuzzy expert systems, social network analysis, and unstructured data, taking into account structured data from databases and data warehouses, social network data, and unstructured data from Internet resources within one solution. The chapter describes case studies in the area of fraud detection, based on proposed methodology. The case studies confirm the efficiency of the proposed methodology as a complex business intelligence system, which includes a traditional approach toward data sources as well as features of Big Data sources.

6.1 Introduction

Fraud detection systems have been an emerging tool of the modern age for detecting anomalies, red flags, and patterns within voluminous amounts of data that are often challenging to analyze. The use of fraud analytic models does not have to be complex to be effective. The techniques of parties involved in fraud are becoming more and more sophisticated due to available technology and its usage in hiding fraudulent activities. Although technology significantly increases the opportunities to commit fraud, it can also play a key role in developing new methods to detect and prevent fraud. New ideas, methodologies, strategies, and techniques with powerful software are constantly evolving.

The term "fraud" is commonly used for many forms of misconduct, even though the legal definition of fraud is very specific. In the broadest sense, fraud can encompass any crime for gain that uses deception as a principal way of behavior. More specifically, "fraud" is defined as "a knowing representation of truth or concealment of a material fact to induce another to act to his or her detriment." Consequently, fraud includes any intentional or deliberate act to deprive another of property or money by guile, deception, or other unfair means (Spann, 2014; Baesens et al., 2015; Ward and Peppard, 2016). Fraud modeling starts when analysis relies on "critical thinking" skills to integrate the output of diverse methodologies into a cohesive actionable analysis product (Spann, 2014; Baesens et al., 2015; Krambia, 2016). Fraud models are used for various purposes, depending on data or information types that are available and the type of analysis that is being performed. The analysis process requires the development and correlation of knowledge. Nowadays, more and more organizations are depending upon the most effective and efficient tools that can get the job done, while new paradigms are introduced to increase the efficiency of traditional approaches in fraud detection and management.

6.2 Fraud Model Development and Early Warning Systems

An optimal fraud model is multidimensional, involving strategic, organizational, process, and technology and data components.* In terms of strategy, it has to successfully reduce the financial and operational impacts of fraud; senior leadership must set the right tone from the top. That, furthermore, means conveying the seriousness of fraud as a business issue that needs to be on the minds of top managers. As antifraud strategies and plans take shape, organizations need to change boundaries to ensure the key functions are working collaboratively to address the problem. In terms of organizational resources, there is a clear need for skilled resources and adequately defined roles, responsibilities, and accountability. Multiple layers are to be considered in the model, such as underwriters, claims adjusters, screeners, and investigators, all working toward common fraud detection and prevention goals. Implementing a fraud model may necessitate some adjustments inside the organization or at least better coordination across functional lines with possible special investigative units, which are optimally integrated with their counterparts in claims or other areas. In terms of processes, the detection stream is the key component of an antifraud model. There are plenty of inputs for a company to consider while preparing the model. Product development, actuarial, and underwriting processes can all prevent likely fraudulent parties from their opportunity, and automation of fraud scoring for all claims leads to efficient workflows ready to detect, triage, investigate, and manage fraud events. Systematic tracking of fraud trends and metrics should be incorporated into a comprehensive set of feedback loops and tactics to drive prevention and deterrence. In terms of technology and data, it is obvious that better data quality leads to better analytics prediction. Different

---

* EY. (2015). Rethinking the business case for antifraud programs in insurance.

tools and new techniques help leverage new claims and underwriting platforms and can automate initial detection steps and focus skilled resources on the cases that need further scrutiny (for example, analysis of unstructured text can be used for a more comprehensive review of available information, social media scanning, network link analysis, known fraudulent party databases, and other relevant industry data). For many companies, advanced analytics tools have become new, improved, and daily used approaches in fighting fraud. However, it is essential for companies to know and understand the quality of their data, analytics, and operational maturity curves to know where to focus. An agile control framework will leverage quality data, integrated systems, and robust and repeatable processes along with enhanced investigative skills and capabilities.

As fraud grows more sophisticated, to fight it, a company must step up efforts to protect good clients, uncover organized fraud, and improve the effectiveness of analytics tools and specialized investigative units. But the most powerful approach in the fight against fraud may be a broad-based and strategic rethink of the overall business process with a focus not just on "what" is being done but also on the "why" and the "how." Although a typical organization loses 5% of its annual revenues to occupational fraud,* some industries are considerably more susceptible than others. Fraud obviously affects individual industries in different ways. For example, the retail industry may experience a greater number of individual fraud occurrences, but the average loss tends to be smaller than in other industries. The common denominator is that everyone is susceptible to fraud, and although almost 40% of the most recent fraud cases took place in private companies, almost 28% occurred in public offices, 17% in government agencies, and 10% in nonprofit organizations.

Industries that can be selected as ones in which the highest percentage of fraud occurs are the following:

- The banking and financial services industry (fraud affecting this sector ranges from simple cash larceny to sophisticated check tampering, kiting, and billing schemes to identity theft and credit cards)
- Government (extremely susceptible to fraud because of its sheer size and number of employees, government agencies have fallen victim to nearly every type of fraud that exists, including billing fraud, the purchase of substandard or low-quality products, asset misappropriation, and payroll or expense reimbursement fraud)
- The manufacturing sector (carries a higher risk for fraud; the nature of this industry makes it susceptible to noncash fraud, including the stealing of goods and materials by employees as well as intellectual property, such as trade secrets or technology)
- Health care practices (particularly vulnerable to billing schemes with a high ratio of some sort of billing scam or insurance fraud perpetrated by providers)
- Educational institutions (particularly susceptible to billing and expense reimbursement schemes including corruption, skimming, and payroll fraud)
- Retail sector (including inventory theft and cash larceny leading the way)
- Insurance (different types of fraud related to a different industry for insurers)
- Telecommunications (mostly related to payment and tariff issues)

Each industry adopts internal controls that offer the best protection against fraud and abuse. These safeguards may overlap throughout industries or be totally unique for the sector itself. The financial services industry has been monitoring its controls by incorporating security measures and analytic methods. Government uses internal auditors along with retaining outsourced assistance

---

* Maxwell, Locke, & Ritter; http://www.mlrpc.com/articles/which-industries-are-hardest-hit-by-fraud.

to audit its various departments and implement controls. As manufacturers have become more automated, types of controls include inventory management programs, installation of surveillance equipment in plants and loading docks, GPS tracking on delivery trucks, and corporate charge card monitoring for business expenses. Retailers use surveillance, inventory security tags, perpetual inventory systems, and sophisticated point-of-sale systems to track purchases and returns to thwart perpetrators. Insurance companies have updated their claims auditing systems to spot suspected instances of fraud.

Even with these controls, fraudulent activity still becomes more and more complex and hard to track.

The fraud analysis process is not a series of steps that are processed in a strict order; rather the processes represent a methodology for accurate and concise analysis and information sharing that will change according to the red flags that are detected such as those shown in Figure 6.1 (Spann, 2014).

As explained by Spann (2014), the direction process involves establishing the boundaries of the analysis and what will be discovered during the process. This is also a step in which analytical gaps and the effectiveness of the analysis are determined, and the significance of the analysis is established. The collection process involves the gathering of raw data from which a finished analysis is produced. The collection process seeks to establish a criminal or fraudulent scope with a person or organization. The analysis process also seeks to collect information on trends, patterns, and methods of anomalies that help describe the phenomena of a fraud event. The evaluation process involves the conversion of large amounts of data into a final analytical product. The process is done through a variety of methods to ascertain the most effective analysis, including decryption and data reduction. Evaluation includes entering raw data into databases (fraud analysis) where

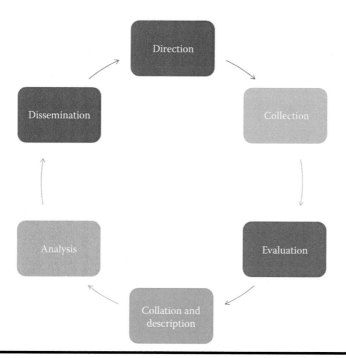

Figure 6.1 The six-step analysis process. (Source: Central Intelligence Agency; D. D. Spann, *Fraud analytics: Strategies and methods for detection and prevention,* **Wiley, 2014.)**

the data will be used in the analysis process. It includes recommendations, findings, and interpretation of information stored in the fraud summary reports, investigative reports, and similar reports. Finally, the collation and description process has four distinct stages in the fraud analytical process, which include evaluating raw data from the information gathered to detect its utility for analysis, examining the validity of raw data for cleanliness, clearly defining the analysis process in order to collect additional resources that will assist in gaining the most accurate raw information for robust analysis, and utilizing other activities in the collation and description process. The analysis process is the heart of the methodology. It is essentially the approach to problem solving. It uses established methodologies that are qualitative and quantitative and that seek to integrate correlated variables in a section of raw data in order to understand their meaning. Finally, the dissemination process is essentially an analytical product that has virtually no value unless the system is able to get the right information.

The results of any analysis process should be the following:

- Easy to understand
- Clear and concise
- Easily transferrable to others involved in the fraud examination and/or financial investigation
- Accurate

Two components that are essential parts of almost any effective strategy to fight fraud are fraud detection and fraud prevention (Baesens et al., 2015). Fraud detection refers to the ability to recognize or discover fraudulent activities, whereas fraud prevention refers to measures that can be taken to avoid or reduce fraud. The difference between both is clear: the former is an ex post approach, whereas the latter is an ex ante approach. Both tools may and likely should be used in a complementary manner to pursue the shared objective: fraud reduction.

Following this approach, two types of measures are typically taken to correct fraud (corrective) or prevent fraud (preventive).

6.3 New Paradigms in Fraud Analytics

There are several important characteristics of fraud explained by Van Vlasselaer et al. (2015):

- Fraud is uncommon.
- It is imperceptibly concealed because fraudsters succeed in hiding by well considering and planning how to precisely commit fraud.
- Techniques and tricks fraudsters adopt evolve in time along with or, better, ahead of fraud detection mechanisms.
- Fraud is often as well a carefully organized crime.
- It comes in different forms (credit card fraud, insurance fraud, corruption, counterfeiting, product warranty fraud, health care fraud, telecommunications fraud, money laundering, click fraud, identity theft, tax evasion, plagiarism).

The so-called fraud triangle (Figure 6.2) provides a more elaborate explanation for the underlying motives or drivers for committing occupational fraud (Baesens et al., 2015).

This basic conceptual model explains the factors that together cause or explain the drivers for an individual to commit occupational fraud, yet it provides a useful insight into the fraud

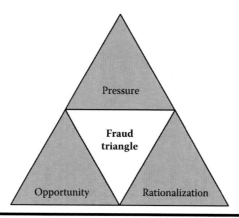

Figure 6.2   Fraud triangle.

phenomenon from a broader point of view as well. The model has three parts that together constitute fraudulent behavior:

1. Pressure is the first leg and concerns the main motivation for committing fraud. An individual will commit fraud because pressure or a problem is experienced of a financial, social, or any other nature, and it cannot be resolved or relieved in an authorized manner.
2. Opportunity is the second leg of the model, and it concerns the precondition for an individual to be able to commit fraud. Fraudulent activities can only be committed when the opportunity exists for the individual to resolve or relieve the experienced pressure or problem in an unauthorized but concealed or hidden manner.
3. Rationalization is the psychological mechanism that explains why fraudsters do not refrain from committing fraud and think of their conduct as acceptable.

All those drivers lead to fraudulent activity, which can be explained like the fraud cycle as shown in Figure 6.3.

The fraud cycle introduces several cycle phases or essential activities (Baesens et al., 2015) as follows:

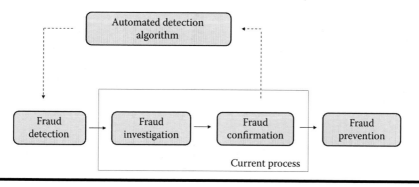

Figure 6.3   The fraud cycle. (From B. Baesens, V. van Vlasselaer, & W. Verbeke, *Fraud analytics using descriptive, predictive, and social network techniques*, Wiley, 2015.)

- *Fraud detection*: Applying detection models on new, unseen observations and assigning a fraud risk to every observation.
- *Fraud investigation*: A human expert is often required to investigate suspicious, flagged cases given the involved subtlety and complexity.
- *Fraud confirmation*: Determining the true fraud label, possibly involving field research.
- *Fraud prevention*: Preventing fraud to be committed in the future.

A conceptual overview of the analytics process model (Hand, Mannila, and Smyth, 2001; Tan, Steinbach, and Kumar, 2005; Han and Kamber, 2011) is shown in Figure 6.4. As a first step, a thorough definition of the business problem is needed to be solved with analytics. Next, all source data must be identified that could be of potential interest. This is a very important step as data are the key ingredient to any analytical exercise, and the selection of data will have a deterministic impact on the analytical models that will be built in a subsequent step. All data will then be gathered in a staging area that could be a data mart or data warehouse. Some basic exploratory analysis can be considered here using, for instance, online analytical processing (OLAP) facilities for multidimensional data analysis (e.g., roll-up, drill down, slicing, and dicing). This will be followed by a data cleaning step to get rid of all inconsistencies, such as missing values and duplicate data. Additional transformations may also be considered, such as binning, alphanumeric to numeric coding, geographical aggregation, and so on. In the analytics step, an analytical model will be estimated on the preprocessed and transformed data. In this stage, the actual fraud detection model is built. Finally, once the model has been built, it will be interpreted and evaluated by the fraud experts.

Trivial patterns that may be detected by the model, for instance, similar to expert rules, are interesting as they provide some validation of the model. But, of course, the key issue is to find the unknown yet interesting and actionable patterns (sometimes also referred to as knowledge diamonds) that can provide added insight and detection power. Once the analytical model has been appropriately validated and approved, it can be put into production as an analytics application (e.g., decision support system, scoring engine). Important to consider here is how to represent the model output in a user-friendly way, how to integrate it with other applications (e.g., detection and

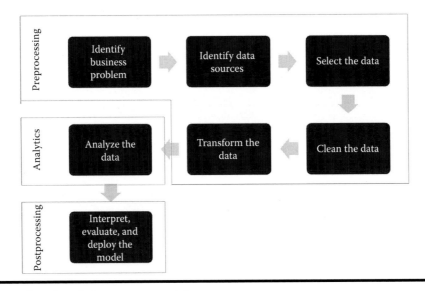

Figure 6.4 Fraud analytics process model.

prevention system, risk engines), and how to make sure the analytical model can be appropriately monitored and back-tested on an ongoing basis (Baesens et al., 2015).

As game changers, new paradigms include improvement in the analytics process by introducing the following:

- Large-volume data sets (Big Data, graph data, and NoSql)
- Fuzzy logic
- Social network analysis (SNA) metrics
- Unstructured data

6.4 Social Network Analysis Metrics in Fraud Management (Insurance Industry Example)

The insurance industry is based on the principle of mutual benefit. It is basically designed to protect against unsafe but significant losses. Insurance fraud undermines that because of false applications and requirements; amounts are paid to the insured to minimize the effects of actual damage. Fraud affects not only the insurers and the insured, but also the entire society because it can be used to finance other illegal activities. Consequently, insurance frauds are significant fraud offenses with many consequences. Most honest customers eventually pay for this dishonesty through higher premiums. In addition to false claims and the costs of their discovery, it inevitably leads to higher premiums for honest policyholders, while they adversely affect the ability of insurers to deal with legitimate claims for damages.

The European Association of Insurers and Reinsurers, in the publication called *Impact of Fraud in Insurance*, notes that most common forms of fraud are false or incomplete information by the client when applying for insurance, and this has implications for damages based on mistaken or untrue circumstances by insurers misled in the process of risk calculation based on the insurance contract. Fraud can also be committed by contractors or others who emphasize the claim from the insurer. Requirements in real life cover a wide range of areas, such as claims for compensation for opportunity costs, compensation claims for fake travelers, fake injuries in traffic accidents, or organized criminal activity.

The fight against fraud is a constant process for insurance companies. Its complexity includes science and technology with large financial roles played by all involved parties. It affects all kinds of insurance regardless of whether it is life insurance, property, health, or a combination. Threats arising from fraud and concrete initiatives aimed at its detection and prevention vary considerably between different countries. In some countries, insurers even exchange relevant information for the purpose of efficient identification of fraudulent behavior. In Europe, such exchanges exist in Croatia, Estonia, Finland, Germany, Ireland, Malta, the Netherlands, Norway, Portugal, Slovenia, Spain, Sweden, and the United Kingdom. In the exchange of information, parties involved also include state institutions and departments. In some countries, including France, Sweden, and the United Kingdom, insurance companies have even established a formal group to explore insurance fraud at different levels. Important roles in the prevention of fraud also include training and education of staff with the intention to raise awareness about the dimension of fraud and practical skills acquisition for discovery of constantly changing methods used by fraudsters.

Fraud detection efficiency can be significantly increased using methods based on advanced technology and information collected from open sources. It includes electronic devices for detecting the authenticity of documents submitted in damage claims and use of publicly available information gathered from various websites. Particularly interesting is the growing trend toward use of advanced computer-aided analytical techniques for the detection and prevention of fraud. Detecting insurance fraud is mostly studied as a problem of supervised and unsupervised machine learning. As a basis for machine learning, analysts were using data from previous cases manually entered into models in order to create learning cases from proven cases of fraud. Because insurance companies analyze a relatively large number of claims, business process automation based on the results of machine learning can dramatically increase the efficiency of the evaluation process. A prerequisite automation information system is arranged to systematically record all business events and store the data in a database. Such a system offers the potential application of a wide range of analytical techniques to improve business performance and reduce damage caused by fraud. Although the internal structure and purity of the stored information is a necessary prerequisite for effective fraud detection in insurance, those data samples are not always sufficient and have to be enriched by other data collected from open sources with special emphasis on various social networks. Here come into play the analysis methodology of social networks described in this case by which the benefits of machine learning are improved around the image of the association and behavior patterns of a potential claim but based on fraudulent claims. If a (potential) client is not paying attention to your own behavior on the Internet, the insurance company can assemble a mosaic and a profile of him or her on the basis of fragments of data scattered throughout various social media and estimate its value according to different criteria. One of these values is the social media score* based on the analysis of activities on social media. Tools for analyzing social media can follow the conversations that are, on the one hand, related to the brand, industry, and competitors and, on the other side, related to personality and behavior of the customer. Therefore, insurers are all actively involved in the virtual community to build even stronger relationships and more easily studied data from, for example, Twitter, Facebook, and other available sources. As for the risk assessment of the client, insurers commonly use credit scores, so it is expected that the security conditions are increasingly affected by the social media score as well. It opens up new opportunities in the classification of clients: what they are watching, what and where they buy, and what they comment on as being particularly interesting, with whom they associate, and with whom and how they communicate. This approach opens up new possibilities for the classification of clients. Insurers then, among other things, are guided to complete an individualization approach toward customers, starting from the decision about whether the client does offer an insurance policy to a flexible individual, calculating the premium payable for each client individually.

The popularization of social networks in recent years offers social network client data to insurers available almost at a click, allowing the formation of detailed dossiers and encouraging trend adjustment of premiums and conditions with "digital" estimated client risk. In addition to the assessment of risk and business value of the customer before the conclusion of the insurance policy, the analysis of social networks can be invaluable in the evaluation of claims,† revealing patterns of suspicious behavior that involve a larger number of people or companies, and relatively easily discover ingenious attempts at fraud and the individual level. If the client for instance, submits a claim for the sake of a knee injury while social publishing a photograph shows him passing through the end of the marathon, this photo can mean the difference between acceptance and rejection of the claim. Of course, posts to social networks can also confirm an honest story of the claim.

---

* Sheryl Nance-Nash. What Insurers Could Do with Your "Social Media Score." Available at http://www.dailyfinance.com/2011/12/12/what-insurers-could-do-with-your-social-media-score.

† Reda Alhajj, Jon Rokne. *Encyclopedia of Social Network Analysis and Mining*, chapter: *Dark Sides of Social Networking.*

An insurer that intends to understand cause of claim related to, for example, health or injury is very interested in learning about whether the client engages in risky sports and activities or whether the customer travels to countries affected by war. This does not mean that the insurer is curious in terms of indiscretion, but the insurer needs to use the available material in order to verify the information. The aim is rational risk assessment and determination of the fair value of insurance or justification of the claim. Although some clients, especially honest policyholders, at first glance, may not like the idea of such control, fraud systems are indirect and are a part of the honest policyholder's problem because fraud increases the average price of insurance products or services. If insurers were more likely to discover scammers, it would consequently lead to lower insurance rates, which are certainly a positive step in the context of broader social interests.

It should be noted that indicators, such as recent social media or various metrics of social networks, which are available to insurance companies, must be approached with caution and understanding to avoid violating regulatory rules and legal restrictions, especially in the area of privacy protection. The line between access to information and its legal use in some cases can be very thin.

6.4.1 Role of Social Networks in Detecting Insurance Fraud

When an automobile accident occurs, drivers and passengers usually exchange addresses and phone numbers and then submit them to the insurer. However, one address or one of the vehicles may already be included in one or more reported adverse events. The ability to obtain this information may save the insurer a lot of time and may provide the insurer with new information about the case and/or indicate potential fraud. SNA allows the insurer to create a proactive view of the links between participants and previously identified patterns of dishonorable conduct. For this purpose, traditional methods and SNA are combined with other tools and methods. Such a hybrid approach involves organizational business rules, statistical methods, the analysis of links, the analysis of behavior patterns, and SNA over large data sets to gain more obvious recognized forms of connectivity. Typical examples of publicly available data that may be included in the production of hybrid models are judgments of the courts, enforcement, criminal records, and the frequency of address change. A hybrid insurance model can comprehensively rank the claims based on the assigned rating. If the assessment of the claim shows, for example, an address that is in the records of previous fraud or a vehicle that is already involved in more accidents and that exceeds a specified limit, automated detection of such cases may focus investigators on a specific suspicious claim.

A typical hybrid case study includes six components:

1. Structured and unstructured data from different sources using extract, transform, load (ETL) tools loaded in the analytical data warehouse.
2. An analytical team formed on the basis of information from various sources in order to estimate the likelihood of fraud. Relevant information can be based on a wide range of data sources, such as final judgments, any link with previous proven cases of fraud, multiple refused requests for damages, unusual combinations of data, or suspicious modification of personal information.
3. Technologies and methods, such as text mining, sentiment analysis, categorization of content, process modeling, and predictive SNA to identify suspicious cases, which are then assigned a rating or score.
4. Depending on the score of each part of the network, alarms or alerts are generated.
5. Investigators can then focus on the deeper study of the potential cases of fraud.
6. Finally, identifiers of fraud are implemented in a business system that is part of a hybrid network.

6.4.2 Fraud Detection Model Described in 10 Steps

Many tools for detecting insurance fraud target specific verticals of business (such as receivables management), and then build a framework system around it. To make the system more robust, methodology requires a broader view that includes integration of all potential areas related to fraud (claims, premiums, employees, vendors, suppliers) in the big picture.

In order to create robust and efficient system for fraud detection, a 10-step approach was created by R. Verma and S. R. Mani (2013). The authors proposed a complete analytical system that provides quick organization and analysis of unstructured data from claims, notes, and investigators' reports as a third source. The system analyzes the sentiment requests and directs in-depth analysis on specific items for risky clients. Synthesized complex fraudulent patterns learned from historical cases can lead to early warning before small problems become big. The proposed analytical system for fraud detection with an integrated analysis of social networks is shown in Figure 6.5.

6.5 Fraud Model Development Using Unstructured Data, SNA Metrics, and Fuzzy Logic (Finance Industry Example)

The case of the bankrupt U.S. company Enron is known to the general public; however, the question remains: Do we know the whole truth? The reason for this is the fact that the collapse of Enron was happening simultaneously with the September 11th attacks in 2001, which was also a complex case of economic crime (i.e., white collar crime) more interesting to the general public than the corporate general fraud.

In 1985, the Enron Corporation was established by a group of Texan entrepreneurs led by Kenneth Lay, who, taking advantage of the policy of deregulation of the energy market, introduced Enron among the giants of American corporations. Enron lasted until 2001 when it collapsed. The case of Enron is not special because bankruptcy can happen even with the largest companies, but it is because of the greed and unfairness of upper management who managed to sell their shares prior to the bankruptcy while assuring the middle management and employees until the last moment that buying shares was okay, telling them the company was in good standing and was not facing bankruptcy. What is specific to the Enron case was also the participation of fraudulent workers and shareholders and a number of institutions such as banks and audit firms. For example, employees of the Arthur Andersen audit company have been accused of destroying documents that would help prove the illegal conduct of Enron's upper management. In the destroyed business documents, along with paper documents, there were emails containing the correspondence important for the course of the investigation.

Recognizing the value of electronic communication for future investigations, the U.S. Federal Energy Regulatory Commission (FERC), which was responsible for investigating the Enron case, published the electronic communications of Enron workers on the Internet. The published data set contained about half a million messages with a large amount of data that were incomplete with a clear question about the data integrity issue. Several data set versions prepared and cleaned using the FERC data base became available. For the purposes of this example, a data set was used* that was taken from an address containing 252,759 messages sent by 151 employees. The data set was created in the form of a MySQL database, which consists of four tables. The first table contains data on 151 employees (name, email address). Table 6.1 provides information on electronic messages (sender, date, subject, message, and file in which the message was located). The third table

---

* http://www.isi.edu/~adibi/Enron/Enron.htm

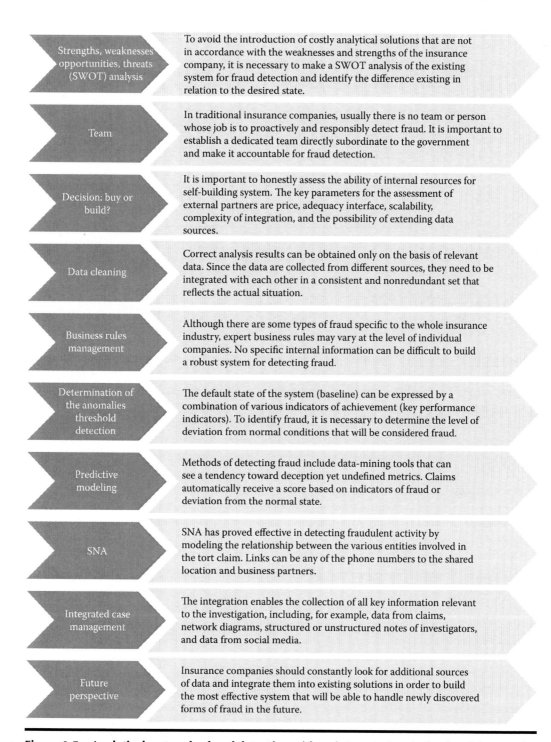

Figure 6.5 Analytical system for fraud detection with an integrated analysis of social networks.

Table 6.1 Number of Employees according to Position in the Company

Position	Number of Employees
CEO	4
Director	13
Employee	83
In-House Lawyer	3
Manager	10
Managing Director	3
President	4
Trader	12
Vice President	19
Total	151

contains information about the recipient (email address, type of message: to, cc, bcc), and the last table shows information on the forwarded and answered messages.

The Enron case study prevents incomplete and inconsistent data—in particular the lack of full email correspondence, incomplete data on the position of employees in the company, the use of multiple email addresses of employees, and interviews with former employees and those indirectly related to the company. However, more analysis and a partial data set can help gain insight into the problem and develop a methodology for future cases, which were not lacking after the Enron case (e.g., WorldCom).

According to open source information, positions of 151 Enron employees were arranged in several groups, which was used for analysis, as shown in Table 6.1.*

Using frequency of communication by email analysis (as shown in Figure 6.6), it is clear that intense communication took place during 2001, especially in May, after which communication decreases. After that, we can see an increasing trend in October again, just before the bankruptcy publication.

Following the significant increase in communication in October 2001, further analysis was focused on comparison of communication during October 2000 and 2001 with a focus on the position of employees in the company. Comparison of the received and sent email analysis in October 2000 and 2001 indicates a significant change in the type of communication among employees at a certain position: executive director, manager, or trader. More messages were sent in 2000 and received during 2001, and employees in the position of general manager received more and sent fewer emails during 2000 compared to 2001. Comparison also recorded a significant increase in the sent email by employees in the position of vice president in October 2001. Email frequency divided per position and incoming/outgoing emails is shown in Table 6.2.

Analysis of network communication in October 2000 and 2001 indicates a significant density of the network in October 2001 (0.036) as opposed to October 2000 (0.141). It also analyzes the consistency of the network, in which greater consistency is perceived in 2001 (eight components) than in

---

* Available at http://www.isi.edu/~adibi/Enron/Enron_Employee_Status.xls

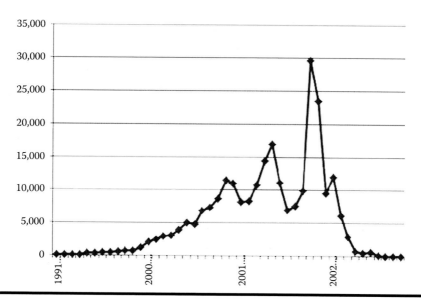

Figure 6.6 **Displaying the frequency of communication by email from 1999 to October 2002.**

Table 6.2 **Analysis Comparing Received and Sent Emails**

Position	October 2000		October 2001	
	Emails Sent	*Emails Received*	*Emails Sent*	*Emails Received*
CEO	70%	30%	25%	75%
Director	8%	92%	41%	59%
Employee	53%	47%	55%	45%
In-House Lawyer	26%	74%	43%	67%
Manager	52%	47%	42%	58%
Managing Director	43%	57%	56%	44%
President	57%	43%	52%	48%
Trader	61%	39%	32%	68%
Vice President	37%	63%	45%	55%

2000 (26 components). Greater consistency of the network in October 2001 points to the fact that, during the crisis, a group of people (not otherwise communicated) established a joint communication with higher density of the network in October 2001, which, in turn, indicates the intense and widespread communication within the entire network in contrast to the same period before the crisis.

Further analysis is aimed at determining the individual employees who were "important" in the network of Enron's electronic communication. Table 6.3 shows the five most important employees in the communication network (their positions) throughout the analyzed period and October 2001, according to centrality measures.

Table 6.3 Five Most Important Employees in the Communication Network

Closeness			
All Years		October 2001	
liz.taylor@enron.com	Employee	sally.beck@enron.com	Employee
sally.beck@enron.com	Employee	louise.kitchen@enron.com	President
lavorato@enron.com	CEO	john.arnold@enron.com	VP
louise.kitchen@enron.com	President	jay.reitmeyer@enron.com	Employee
kenneth.lay@enron.com	CEO	j.kean@enron.com	VP
Betweenness			
All Years		October 2001	
liz.taylor@enron.com	Employee	sally.beck@enron.com	Employee
lavorato@enron.com	CEO	robert.badeer@enron.com	Director
sally.beck@enron.com	Employee	sean.crandall@enron.com	Director
susan.scott@enron.com	Employee	jeff.dasovich@enron.com	Employee
louise.kitchen@enron.com	President	bill.williams@enron.com	Employee
Eigenvector			
All Years		October 2001	
sally.beck@enron.com	Employee	sally.beck@enron.com	Employee
liz.taylor@enron.com	Employee	louise.kitchen@enron.com	President
louise.kitchen@enron.com	President	john.arnold@enron.com	VP
kenneth.lay@enron.com	CEO	mike.grigsby@enron.com	Manager
lavorato@enron.com	CEO	j.kean@enron.com	VP
In-Degree			
All Years		October 2001	
louise.kitchen@enron.com	President	mike.grigsby@enron.com	Manager
mike.grigsby@enron.com	Manager	louise.kitchen@enron.com	President
scott.neal@enron.com	VP	jason.williams@enron.com	Employee
greg.whalley@enron.com	President	steven.harris@enron.com	Employee
m..presto@enron.com	VP	john.arnold@enron.com	VP

(Continued)

Table 6.3 (Continued) Five Most Important Employees in the Communication Network

Out-Degree			
All Years		*October 2001*	
liz.taylor@enron.com	Employee	sally.beck@enron.com	Employee
sally.beck@enron.com	Employee	mike.grigsby@enron.com	Manager
lavorato@enron.com	CEO	monique.sanchez@enron.com	Employee
louise.kitchen@enron.com	President	louise.kitchen@enron.com	President
kenneth.lay@enron.com	CEO	john.arnold@enron.com	VP

Twenty different people appear in the table: 10 people in network communications during all years (5 persons in one degree of centrality, 1 person in three steps, 3 in four steps, and 1 person in five measures) and 13 people in the network communications in October 2001 (8 persons in one measure, 1 person in two steps, 1 person in three steps, and 3 people in four measures), and 3 people appear in both networks. Looking at the structure of the network according to the position, three employees that appear in both networks are in position of employee (two) and manager (one) (low-ranking persons).

At the same time, people who appear in the entire network but did not appear in 2001 belong to the same group of employees as the CEO, and the network of 2001 people appear, at the position of vice president (VP). Calculation of measures of centrality and statistical analysis of sending email messages to the position suggest that during the period before the crisis, dominant corporate culture was sending directives from the top management (CEO, president), who during the crisis withdrew from direct leadership (perhaps in order to conceal), and in times of crisis management was sending information down on a slightly lower level management (HR and other executives), and the lowest part of the management and employees have retained their position due to the fact that it could have been used for spreading false information and increase the cohesion of the network, which, in turn, helps greatly in supporting fraud in the Enron case. A view of the entire social network with positions/indication of significant persons is shown in Figure 6.7.

For further analysis and identification of key people, we have used the ability to filter email messages according to their content. As FERC had a key role in the operation and control of Enron, the communication of October 2001 was singled out, and the condition was that the messages contained the commission acronym (FERC). The filtered data set consisted of 27,606 messages and 3038 connections with the participation of 94 employees who were identified as having a position in Enron. SNA association maps showed the participation of four employees at the VP position (Richard Shapiro, James Steffes, Steven Kean, and Kevin Presto) and one at the position of employee (Jeff Dasovich) with extra high communication in the network. As persons with very good authority measure, Steven Kean (68% of received messages in his communication) and Kevin Presto (98% of received messages in his communication) stand out among employees at the VP position, and as opposed to them, Richard Shapiro stands out as a node with high closeness (30% of received messages in his communication, 70% of sent messages).

Figure 6.8 shows a map of integration of the filtered data set provided that nodes shown on the map have multiple input connections of 10 (the size of the node also determines the number of input connections: the more the connections, the bigger the node), and the color of fixtures shows

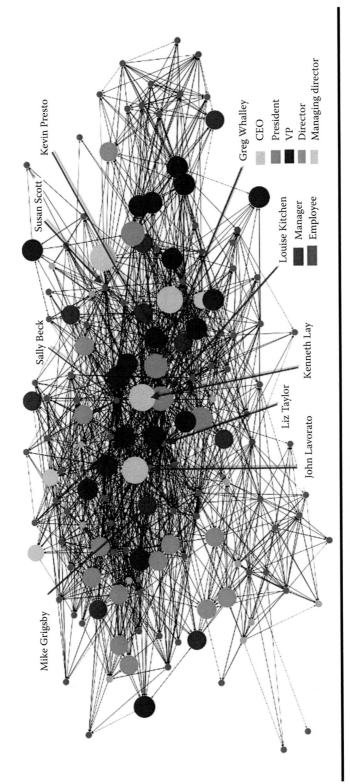

Figure 6.7 View of the entire network with positions of significant persons.

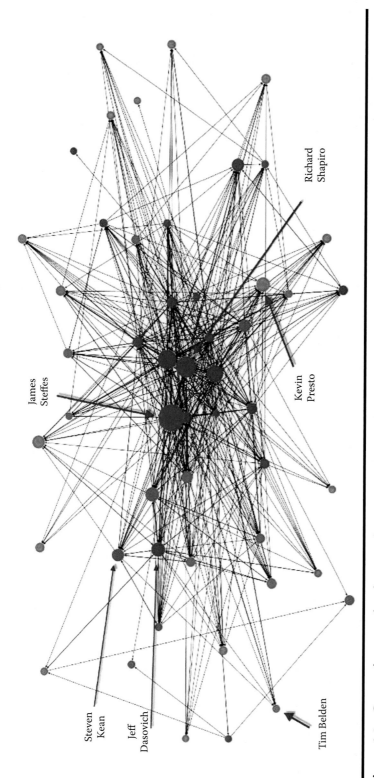

Richard
Shapiro

James
Steffes

Kevin
Presto

Steven
Kean

Jeff
Dasovich

Tim Belden

Figure 6.8 Connection map for the most important persons of October 2001 communication (email messages including the acronym "FERC").

a certain percentage of received messages in the total number of messages (red indicates a lower percentage of received messages, and green indicates a person whose communication consists entirely of incoming communications). The map identified the Tim Belden connection as a key figure in the trade part of Enron Energy Services, the person who many consider to be the "brains" of the operation of raising energy prices in California (Hansen et al., 2010, p. 123). Tim Belden belongs to the group of people for whom outgoing messages were not observed, which may point to a cover-up in communication.

Analysis of communication by email in the case of Enron shows how even with partial data sets an analyst can create interesting and significant results. The density of the October 2001 network changed and became more centralized, and significant changes in the structure of the position of significant persons point to the possibility of illegal activities. Results indicate that communication between employees at respectable formal positions, at which high-ranking executives formed a group among themselves, was densely interwoven and supported by low-ranking managers and employees in the execution of illegal activities.

6.6 Car Insurance Claims Evaluation Using SNA and Fuzzy Logic (Insurance Industry Example)

This case study, described in Pinheiro and McNeill (2014), describes the methodology for the detection of problematic claims analyzing social networks based on the transaction data on reported adverse events. The goal of network analysis is to find unusual patterns of behavior of actors listed in the compensation claim: insurance holders, suppliers, services, witnesses, etc. based on their mutual links.

The first step in the definition of the network is to identify the participants (network nodes) and their roles. All the participants considered within one claim are interrelated. The network is composed on the basis of 22,815 requests. All claims are made on the aggregate level of unique requirements with multiple participants. They identified 41,885 unique participants associated with 74,503 links.

Network metrics are calculated for the entire network, including all links and all nodes, regardless of their role. They then identified all metrics assigned to individuals and companies. Analysis is made according to various roles, for example, insured person, driver, repairman, etc. Metrics of a service unit can show extreme deviations (outliers) when they are viewed in relation to other servicemen but not when compared to category of service recommended by the insurance company.

To create a network and calculate network metrics, we used graph analysis and identification of unusual behavior and extreme deviation exploratory analysis. Extremes have been detected by various methods, including univariate analysis, principal component analysis (PCA), and clustering. We analyzed the level of network metrics for the whole network and categorized network subsets. The incidence of extreme values, as in traditional exploratory analysis, can be used to define the set of rules and thresholds for describing suspicious events and unusual behavior. However, in this analysis, extremes and unusual behavior are not defined by specific attributes but by links between nodes, taking into account claims labeled as suspicious. A large number of similar addresses or the same persons involved in various adverse events can highlight a person and related requirements. It is possible to create a set of rules from online metrics using different analytical methods, which should be combined in practice. In cases in which several claims have the average value of the attribute (e.g., total amount, number of participants, number of different roles, etc.), any one of them will be identified as suspicious. However, if someone, for example, the supplier or the insured, is involved in all of them, this level of connectivity becomes the trigger for labeling requirements as suspicious and is subject to further investigation. Because network metrics describes the relationship between nodes, frequency of occurrence and importance in the network analysis can signal suspicious links and use them to identify problematic actors. This is the reason why analysis should be focused not only on the claim but also on related persons and other associated claims.

In the present network, 41,885 nodes are analyzed, 30,428 of which relate to people and 4423 to a company. To highlight the unusual activity resulting from the grouping of participants in terms of nodes and links, further analysis of the personal and organizational role of the participants is conducted. Analyzed nodes help describe participants and their relationship to claims, and the analysis of links displays their network reach. The study is also made as a kind of joint analysis at the community level with clusters and connected components. These groups actually represent clusters of actors associated to specific categories of claims extracted in the form of subsets of the entire network, isolated network as extreme. In this way, a group of actors is discovered who behave differently from the rest of the network but would remain unnoticed if they were observed only at the individual level. Specifically, the present study observes 6236 related components. Given that some of the removed entities are mentioned in almost every claim, it is important to note that during the cleaning data process, part of the data entities, such as government agencies and other insurers, have been removed because their presence would result in total connections within the network. Furthermore, the network consists of a total of 15,734 double-related components (biconnected components) whose articulation is 2307 points highlighted for further investigation. Of these 2307 articulation points, 984 of the people are referred to as suspicious. Finally, taking into account all the nodes, there have been 13,279 communities revealed regardless of whether they are classified as a person or company.

At the following stage, the individual metrics are compared with the total, and each node and edge is assigned to a measure that shows the relationship, which has contributed to the identification of the most relevant structural aspects of social networks. Metrics of individual nodes or edges are then compared with averages for the entire network and in relation to individual categories, such as person, company, insured, etc. Both have discovered unusual or unexpected behavior, and further analysis also shows extreme values among average and individual values of individual measures. The methods used are univariate analysis, PCA, clustering, analysis of bond-related and double-related components, and community analysis. The process of identifying extreme values resulted in rule sets. The idea of access was not that different rules are used in a variety of analyses but that they have already created all the rules included in the common assessment framework based on which all the claims made are processed. Table 6.4 provides a list of the techniques used and the resulting number of suspects for each technique.

Analysis of related components is neglected for the sake of the excessive number of identified persons. Other techniques are allocated from 2 to 24 persons. If the aggregate persons identified all the techniques, there can be a total of 33 different people involved in a total of 706 instances of reported damage.

The individual attributes of the claims contain useful information about the transaction adverse event. They, however, individually correlate poorly with fraud or excessive demands, and the connection between the different claims may indicate the strangeness with which fraud and excessive demands are becoming more visible. Analysis of social networks has the potential of discovery of different roles and group participants in adverse events that may be in collusion; a graphical representation can help to highlight the visual samples obtained by civil analysis.

Table 6.4 Number of Unique Suspects Detected Using Different Analysis Techniques

Techniques	Number of Suspects
Univariate analysis	21
Principal component analysis (PCA)	23
Clustering	2
Relationship analysis	18
Analysis of double-related components	15
Analysis of related components	555
Analysis of communities	24

Figure 6.9 visualizes the connection between one medical specialist whose name is (too) often placed in a series of requests from the unjustifiably high amounts sought in damages. It is connected with a large number of different people, probably patients. Further analysis indicated the unexpectedly wide geographical area of the addresses associated with this person as a qualified doctor, which warranted further investigation.

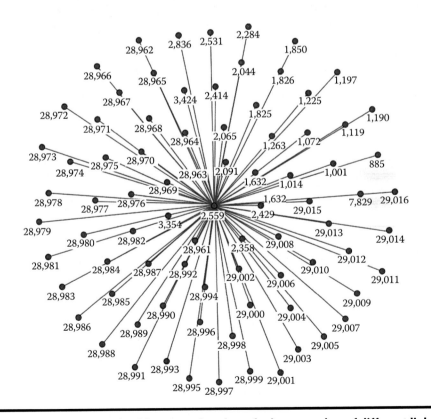

Figure 6.9 Star-view network with a central node and a large number of different links.

To highlight the peculiarities when it comes to related components and community benefits to the group view, some groups are rare or fall into extremes because their network metrics or structure is beyond the expected when it is compared with the rest of the network. Other groups may be separated by comparing business attributes associated with the metrics of such groups (e.g., amount of the claim, the involved cars, address, etc.) and the average data for the entire structure of the network. In addition to fraud, the business may be affected by excessive compensation requests. Excessive claims are a special problem for most insurance companies. Sometimes they encourage clients and sometimes suppliers. It is not always clear which side is responsible for loss of profits in such cases in which financial damage can take on significant proportions but all the actors involved in claims that are identified as unjustified should be closely monitored to avoid possible unexpected payments.

Like other industries, the market for car insurance is very dynamic. Changes in the market are reflected in source data used in the model. Therefore, an analytical model uses this information to analyze social networks to be monitored and periodically evaluated to ensure adjustment of the network, and uses metrics for new business situations, different scenarios, regulatory changes, and other variable factors. An example of unusual groups of related components based on network metrics and business attributes in relation to the rest of the network is shown in Figure 6.10.

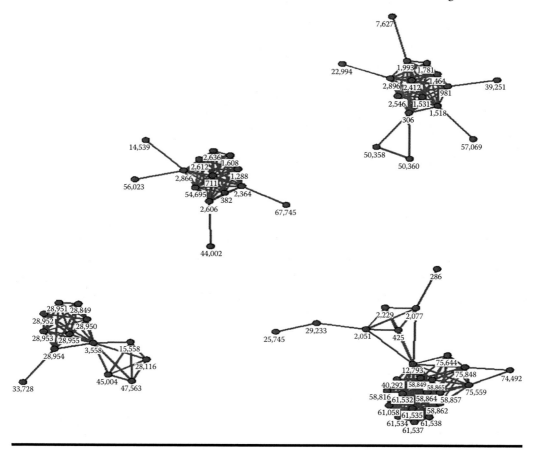

Figure 6.10 Unusual groups of related components and related components extracted twice because of differing values of network metrics and business attributes in relation to the rest of the network.

Application to insurance comes with some general limitations: SNA-related data and their preparation and specific constraints may be affected by regulatory barriers (Kirchner and Gade, 2011). Generally, the source data must be well documented so that the effectiveness of the SNA would not be jeopardized with increasing amounts of data. While query languages of structured data, such as SQL, can be quite effective with relatively small data sets, it should be remembered that in the processing of large quantities of normalized data, efficiency can significantly decrease due to latency of operations using large number of data table joins. It, first of all, relates to the transaction base that is typically needed to consolidate and aggregate (Goldberg and Wong, 1998). Specific restrictions are generally different regulations in different countries. Laws that protect data privacy and other regulatory requirements can seriously jeopardize analytical efforts and are, in some cases, even impossible. Therefore, before the implementation of the screening process, it is recommended to check compliance of the foreseen SNA analysis steps with regulations.

6.6.1 Early Warning System Enriched with Fuzzy Logic Model

The main task of early warning systems is to warn about potential business problems at an early stage in order to create a time frame for analysis and prevention of unwanted trends. Business entities from various industries expressed interest in early warning system implementation. Insurance companies use this type of system for diagnosis and finding the causes of interruption of contractual relations. Early warning systems in certain economic sectors are gaining in prominence in periods of crisis, when adverse trends in business are expected, but no one can accurately predict which segment will be most affected or what the adverse trend for the company might be.

An early warning system is a systematic process of early assessment and measurement of risk with the aim of taking certain steps for preventing and minimizing its negative impact on business.

Although some crises occur unexpectedly, many can be predicted. In such cases, early warning systems are extremely important because they allow the prediction of problems and taking the necessary steps to avoid or respond on time to the impending crisis. For the establishment of early warning systems, it is necessary to identify potential crisis triggers and risk areas and enable their continuous monitoring and control.

For an early warning system to be effective, it is necessary to meet the following criteria:

- Ability to signal danger with reasonable margin errors
- Supervising and monitoring the internal and external environment
- Systematic coordination of information from different sources
- Consideration of current events in the relevant sector
- Due process review and updating of existing information

The ideal competitive early warning process consists of three phases or steps (also shown in Figure 6.11):

- The first phase involves potential risk identification, which is achieved through exhaustive analysis of trends and problems and consideration of the quintessence of the problem as well as different contexts in which the phenomenon occurs. Because of the limited resources that companies have at their disposal, we need to focus only on trends and issues that are relevant. This is the analytical phase and requires the application of analytical techniques,

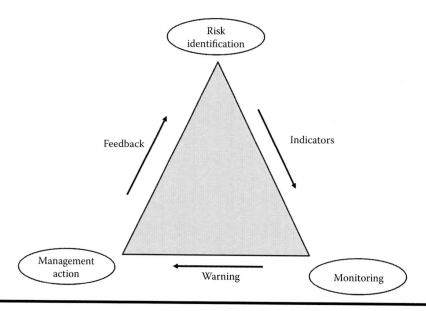

Figure 6.11 Phases of competitive early warning systems. (From Gilad, B., Early Warning: Using Competitive Intelligence to Anticipate Market Shifts, Control Risk, and Create Powerful Strategies, AMACOM, p. 69, 2003.)

such as the development of a hypothesis or elaborate scenarios in order to raise the efficiency of the whole process.

■ The second stage is the risk monitoring "intelligence." Individuals or teams responsible for monitoring must act as intelligence agents in their area and regularly report; teams are made up of experts from various fields in charge of the analysis, assessment, and business problem identification together with operational risks estimation. Areas of possible risk differ from company to company, and what is the same for all is the fact that there is no substitute for doing a good job of collecting data and information that will enable the accurate and timely identification of potential risk triggers (Ansof, 1975). Spotting "weak" or "bad" signals is achieved by scanning the organizational environment, the process of systematically searching relevant information for the purpose of early risk signal identification, and how possible changes in the environment affect these risks (Aguilar, 1967).

■ In the third phase, adequate strategy is determined for dealing with trends and issues that are identified as relevant.

When a risk is identified, it is necessary to establish a system of indicators that will include key components of risk as shown in Figure 6.12. Reactive and proactive data flow scheme related to risk components is shown in Figure 6.13, while risk components are shown in Figure 6.12.

Indicators must be visible, valid, reliable, stable, and unique. In the present model, structured analytical techniques can be of invaluable benefit for analysts in various stages of early warning, especially in the first phase of forecasting and identification of potential risks. Problem-solving analytical techniques allow us to organize and structure the analysis of certain problems or challenges or problem areas. The term "analysis" means the decomposition

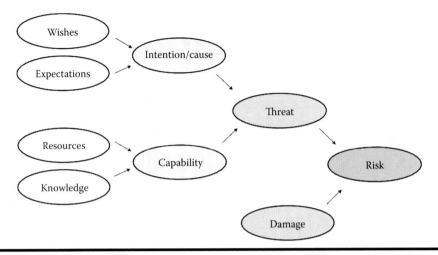

Figure 6.12 Risk components. (EUROPOL: Strategic Intelligence Analysis Course, Reading Material. File No: 2520-47 Rev. 1, October 2002.)

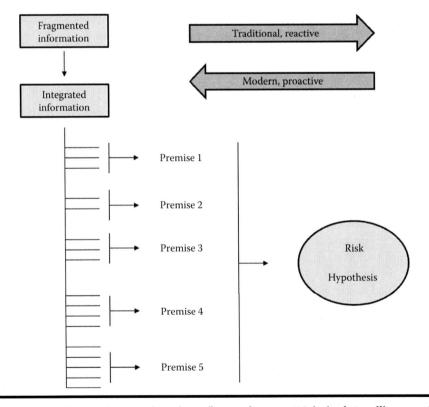

Figure 6.13 Reactive and proactive data flow scheme. ("Criminal Intelligence Analysis: Development of Inferences" (1982–2003) Anacapa Sciences, Inc., USA. pp. 1–23.)

of specific problems, which helps reduce the complexity of the problem and enables us to deal with each component at a time.

Useful analytical techniques for decomposition and visualization of problems or risks are issue redefinition (problem restatement), network analysis, mental maps, etc. For the idea generation phase (identifying the risk), analytical techniques used are structured brainstorming, Delphi method, morphological analysis, De Bono's six hats, quadrant crunching, and others. For scenarios analysis and indicator system management, it is best to use techniques such as scenario analysis, indicators, indicator validator, and others.

6.6.2 Case Conclusion

Insurers will, undoubtedly, use SNA more and more in assessing customers based on their behavior in the social media space because it opens the door to a completely new world in relation to the recently dominant hand evaluation rating and damage. From an optimistic point of view, such an approach could result in a breakthrough that will discourage most unfair clients in the implementation of unscrupulous practices and thereby improve the position of honest customers who use insurance as it is initially meant to be, according to the principle of solidarity. New technologies and methods help us more effectively in detection of false information statements when concluding insurance policies. One of them is the SNA, which shows growing potential in the context of identifying discrepancies between actual events and the events described in damage claims. The message to customers who want to stay out of the limelight is as follows: Thanks to new technologies and methodologies, such as SNA, we can now find and tackle scammers more accurately.

6.7 Putting It All Together: Fraud Detection Model Development (Insurance Industry Example)

6.7.1 Problem Description

A Croatian company is faced with an increasing problem of fraudulent cases within its portfolio. Since its start on the Croatian market, in the last 2 years, they noticed an increasing trend of suspicious insurance claims. The fraudulent cases did not have a common denominator or pattern that would be useful for fraud prevention. It proved the hypothesis that fraudsters are very inventive and use potential omissions within insurance companies for fraudulent activities. This demanded a creative approach for finding an adequate solution, which was not based on developing a predictive model only. Predictive models are sample based, which means that the model will recognize some patterns only if there are enough existing cases within a population. Fraud solutions are much more different as a concept than, for example, churn models, because in churn modeling, we can expect a significant concentration of cases for predictive modeling, which can be relevant for predictive churn modeling.

Fraud has a different nature, and almost every fraudster tries to find his or her own way to commit a fraud. That leads us to the conclusion that fraud detection models should be developed with a focus on seeking suspicious details.

6.7.2 Proposed Solution

The traditional approach, which is focused on predictive modeling by using, for example, logistic regression, neural networks, or Bayesian networks, could be useful, but it is not sufficient. Taking into consideration that the Internet can be a valuable source of information, especially when we have developed fraud models, social network resources and other Internet resources can also be used as a base for fraud detection model development.

The basic idea was developing a solution that will unite four basic parts:

■ Predictive fraud model
■ Expert fraud model
■ Social network analysis
■ Text mining

The expected benefit from developing a predictive fraud model was not only a probabilistic calculator for the probability of fraud for each potential contracted insurance policy, but also understanding and discovering some potential hidden patterns within the data, which could be useful as a base for further investigation. The most important stage in predictive model development is attribute relevance analysis, and at this stage, depending on aim variable, some interesting patterns could be revealed. Each predictive modeling project demands that almost 80% of time be spent on data preparation. Contrary to the rooted belief that a data preparation process consists of ETL processes, data quality improvement, or data extraction from different data sources only, it is a much broader process.

Data preparation starts with data sample construction planning. Experience shows that behavioral attributes are the most important variables for fraud predictive model construction, and sociodemographic attributes are like a spice that gives flavor to the fraud models.

6.7.3 Expert Fraud Model Improved with Fuzzy Logic

The main purpose of the expert fraud models was recognition of suspicious activities on an individual client level. The traditional approach, which leans on predictive models as a base for fraud detection models, was not sufficient. The main reason for that is that the predictive model contains a few more predictive attributes as an integral part. Because they make a predictive model implies that those attributes have the highest impact on the aim variable. That impact by traditional methodology is measured using attribute relevance analysis. The criterion with the highest impact on the aim variable is statistical significance, and that fact hides pitfalls because if some trend became so obvious that it has statistical significance, it is doubtful that it is appropriate for an early warning sign. That means that some deviant trend has happened during the longest period of time, and it makes a statistically significant data pattern recognizable through attribute relevance analysis. If some trend or event happens on an individual level, and it is fraudulent activity, it is impossible to recognize it with traditional statistical predictive models. For basic trend recognition and fraudulent pattern recognition, which have mass characteristics, the methodology is good enough, but for an early complete fraud detection solution, it is not sufficient. It does not mean that predictive models should not be used for fraud modeling; it only means that predictive models should not be the only element or base for fraud detection systems. Fuzzy expert systems give power to fraud detection models to recognize potential suspicious activities based on human expert knowledge, which is integrated within an automatic solution.

SNA is of valuable help for finding hidden connections between previously detected suspicious subjects, objects with newly contracted subjects, and objects. SNA also was used as a proactive tool for finding potential concentrations, which have some links with suspicious activities.

Text mining was used as a tool for finding interesting textual patterns on social networks, forums, and other Internet sources, which contain text and are somehow interesting for the insurance company or the insurance company was mentioned within the text.

The main power of a planned system was the synergy effect realized in the way that the fuzzy expert model contains an integrated predictive model as well as social network metrics. That approach assured integration of different concepts, which provides a powerful tool for fraud detection.

6.7.4 Developing a Predictive Fraud Model

The first important thing before model development is a data quality check. In our case, it consolidates the following:

■ Basic statistical measures and distribution checking for continuous variables
■ Missing value analysis
■ Data gap analysis for each attribute
■ Logical attribute check
■ Business data check and business review of constructed sample

Basic statistical measures were useful for attribute auditing. Mean, standard deviation, quartiles, and percentiles applied on continuous variables gave an insight into existing attribute characteristics. Standard deviation was useful in finding outliers and extremes within attributes. Extreme values in variables are often milestones for further investigation regarding fraud. Another important thing in the data quality check was missing value analysis. Attributes that have a significant percentage of missing values are not suitable for model development. Missing value analysis gives information about missing values within attributes. It is not the universal rule that attributes with a significant percentage of missing values are not usable for model development. An example for that is the situation in which the client, buyer, or contractor does not want to provide some piece of information, and that information has great impact on the aim variable, like providing a residential phone number in fraud detection models. A useful technique in the data quality check is an attribute logical check. This technique controls attribute values by using simple logic checks. An example could be to check if work experience is higher than the current year minus the year of first employment. Another example could be checking how many people within the data sample are older than 120 years or if phone number attributes contain illegal characters. A business data check and business review of the constructed sample are an often unduly neglected step during the model development process. It implies that the model development process should include people from the business (model users). Model development is under the jurisdiction of modelers, who do not necessarily have expert business knowledge in some specific domains, such as telecommunication or insurance. It is important to achieve cooperation between them during model development, as it was during this project.

At this stage, as a result of cooperation between modelers and business users, a bunch of virtual variables were created. Virtual variables, also known as derived variables in the literature, are a powerful tool for customer behavior exploration. A virtual variable mainly does not exist within the database relation model, and it is constructed based on expert knowledge. Virtual variable construction has a lot in common with the methodology of expert system planning because expert knowledge should be expressed in variables, and experts in the process of knowledge elicitation should provide knowledge. In this case, virtual variables were created for predictive modeling purposes as well as for developing expert models. Virtual variables as behavioral variables finally showed high importance for solution building. The attribute relevance analysis process, as its task, had to find the best predictors, which goes into the following fraud prediction model-building stage. Most of the attributes were removed from the sample as predictors because of poor predictive power in relation with the fraud flag. Before attribute relevance analysis starts, the data sample was divided into two parts: a development sample and test sample on an 80%:20% ratio. In the case of attribute relevance analysis, information value and weight of evidence measure were used.

Formulas for weight of evidence calculation and information value calculation are shown below:

$$WoE = \ln\left(\frac{D_{nf}}{D_f}\right)$$

$$IV = \left(D_{nf_i} - D_{f_i}\right) * \ln\left(\frac{D_{nf_i}}{D_{f_i}}\right)$$

Weight of evidence is calculated as a natural logarithm of the ratio between distribution of nonfraudsters (D_{nf}) and fraudsters (D_f) in distribution spans. Information value is calculated as the sum of differences between distribution of nonfraudsters and fraudsters in distribution spans and product of corresponding weight of evidence. Data samples for fraud detection models have one common characteristic, a low fraud rate within the sample, which could be a serious problem for predictive model development. To solve that problem, a strategy could be extension of the data sample observation period. The problem is that this strategy can cause dilution of the data sample, which can result in an inadequate model.

In our case, attribute relevance analysis was done on a two-and-a-half-year observation period. Attribute relevance analysis covered 78 variables, and most of them have behavioral characteristics. Only 15 of them had sociodemographic characteristics. Attribute relevance analysis was done by insurance type, and for collision damage, waiver analysis showed the highest importance for some variables. The collision damage waiver had a fraud rate of 0.23%, which was the highest fraud rate in comparison to other products. This confirmed the hypothesis about the highest fraudulent activities within that segment.

As the most important variables for the collision damage waiver, the following variables were discovered:

■ Time from contract to damage report
■ Period of the day when accident has occurred
■ Type of injuries

- Presence of children in car accidents
- Time of the day when damage was entered into the company information system

After deeper analysis, it was apparent that fraudulent cases had occurred within a short period of time after the contract was signed; mostly at the end of the day (later it was discovered that it has a correlation with the dark period of the day); injuries were whiplash and soft tissue injuries; there were no children in the vehicle at the time of the accidents; and for a significant number of fraudulent contracts, data were entered into the company information system after work time. Attribute relevance analysis gave a pretty clear description of suspicious fraud regarding the collision damage waiver. The last mentioned attribute, time of the day when damage was entered into the company information system, was the base for the hypothesis about inside fraud, and it was motivation to investigate external data resources (Big Data analytics) and to use social network analysis as a tool for proactive fraud detection on internal and external data sources.

6.7.5 Developing the Expert Fraud Model

The fuzzy expert system was built based on expert knowledge and discovered relationships in the process of attribute relevance analysis and SNA. The fuzzy expert system contained rules that point to suspicious activities, such as a short time period from contracting to damage report, time of the day when damage was entered into the company information system, number of accidents in a certain period of time, insurance or damage ratio, etc.

Knowledge extracted in the process of attribute relevance analysis was also integrated into the expert model as well as social network metrics. As an illustration, Table 6.5 shows selected (partial) results on the portfolio level based on the fuzzy expert system.

The expert fraud model was developed as a result of classifying each contract into the following categories:

1. Unsuspicious
2. Low suspicious
3. Suspicious
4. Very suspicious

First processing from the expert fraud model recognized 0.15% very suspicious cases, 0.23% suspicious cases, and 2% low suspicious cases. Some of the dominant mutual characteristics of all suspicious cases were in a short time period from contracting to damage report, high number of accidents in the last 2 years, significant concentration between some of the lawyers, and suspicious accidents. All suspicious cases were investigated individually, and the model proved efficient after investigation.

6.7.6 Social Network Analysis as Part of the Fraud Detection Solution

SNA had the task to investigate and discover potential concentrations among participants in the contracting process for cases that were discovered to be fraudulent. Also, SNA had the task to investigate potential links between elements within cases that were discovered as fraudulent with other participants who are not directly (obviously) connected with those cases. For that purpose, a meta-model with all participants internal and external, as well as with objects of insurance, was created.

Table 6.5 Results on Portfolio Level Based on Fuzzy Expert System

Highest Abstraction Level	Abstraction Level 1 Signals/Key Indicators	Abstraction Level 2 Signals/Key Indicators	Abstraction Level 3 Signals/Key Indicators	Abstraction Level 4 Signals/Key Indicators
				Number of accidents in last 2 years Low 85% Medium 10% High 5%
				Damage amount Low 60% Medium 30% High 10%
			Fraud indicator related to customer High 2% Medium 8% Low 90%	Injury type A 35% B 45% C 20%
				…
			…	…
		Fraud indicator related to participants High 2% Medium 10% Low 88%		…
	Riskiness High 3% Medium 5% High 92%		…	…
				…

(Continued)

Table 6.5 (Continued) Results on Portfolio Level Based on Fuzzy Expert System

Highest Abstraction Level	*Abstraction Level 1 Signals/Key Indicators*	*Abstraction Level 2 Signals/Key Indicators*	*Abstraction Level 3 Signals/Key Indicators*	*Abstraction Level 4 Signals/Key Indicators*
		Fraud probability related to time markers Certain 1% Possible 2% No 97%	⋮	⋮
				⋮
				⋮
			⋮	⋮
				⋮
				⋮
			⋮	⋮
Portfolio level Unsuspicious 97.62% Low suspicious 2% Suspicious 0.23% Very suspicious 0.15%		Fraud indicator related to other factors High 18% Medium 2% Low 80%	⋮	⋮
				⋮
				⋮
			⋮	⋮
				⋮
				⋮
			⋮	⋮
				⋮
				⋮

Note: This sample structure extends accordingly.

As a toll for analysis, Python library NetworkX was used, by using the following code:

```
import networkx as nx
from operator import itemgetter

G=nx.Graph()
G=nx.read_pajek("Fraud.net")

print "Info:"
print nx.info(G)

print "Degree histogram:"
print nx.degree_histogram(G)

print "Density:"
print nx.density(G)

print "Number of nodes:"
print G.number_of_nodes()

print "Number of edges:"
print G.number_of_edges()

dc= nx.degree_centrality(G)
Sorted_degree = sorted(dc.items(), key=itemgetter(1), reverse=True)
print "Sorted degree:"
print Sorted_degree [0:5]

bc= nx.betweenness_centrality(G)
Sorted_betweenness = sorted(bc.items(), key=itemgetter(1), reverse=True)
print "Sorted betweenness:"
print Sorted_betweenness [0:5]

cc= nx.closeness_centrality(G)
Sorted_closeness = sorted(cc.items(), key=itemgetter(1), reverse=True)
print "Sorted closeness:"
print Sorted_closeness [0:5]
```

As a result of SNA, it was apparent that there was a significant concentration between some of the contractors and suspicious accidents and a significant concentration between some of the lawyers, and suspicious accidents were discovered. That leads to the conclusion that there is potential doubt about fraudulent activities if a request for paid compensation is connected with a specific lawyer. Regarding contractors and a significant concentration between some of the contractors and suspicious accidents, it was discovered that there are only three unique contractor IDs within a system for contracting in the company, and that was the reason why SNA discovered a significant concentration between contractors and suspicious accidents.

6.7.7 Role of Text Mining as Part of the Fraud Detection Solution

The final stage of fraud solution development was text mining on external data sources, such as social networks, blogs, forums, etc., which are significant for the Croatian population. In theory, social network data, by their complexity, can be interpreted as a Big Data source even if collected mainly from internal sources for fraud modeling purposes. The reason for that lies in its combinatory tendency, which rises with the number of included nodes. The reading scalability and complexity of textual data from external sources depends on a Big Data environment. The aim of analysis was to discover potential patterns within textual data, which is in relation to the insurance company for which we are making the fraud detection solution. For that purpose, Python programming language was used with the NLTK library. Data capturing from targeted sources was done with Python scripts united within several text containers dependent on the data source. The process of data cleansing, tokenization, and removing stop words was done by NLTK library usage. As a result of the analysis, one interesting fact from the perspective of fraud was discovered. For one district, there was a discussion group related to car glass insurance for the company for which the fraud detection model was developed, in which the participants of the discussion group gave advice on how to avoid inspection of car glass by an officer from the insurance companies. They noticed that if someone parked the car or mentioned to an officer from the insurance companies that he or she parked the car far away from the insurance office that the officer would not inspect the condition of the car glass and create the contract without inspection. The discussion group saw that as an opportunity to mend broken car glass very cheaply and to motivate other readers to do the same. Results from text mining were motivation for further analysis regarding paid compensation for car glass insurance in a specific district. Analysis showed a significantly higher paid compensation rate for car glass insurance in comparison with other districts within a short time period from contracting to damage report, especially in the last 7 months. As a result of that analysis, the officer was warned that she must inspect every car's glass before making a car glass insurance contract.

6.7.8 Predictive Power of the Model and Implementation Notes

Measuring the predictive power of the proposed solution should be observed partially for each part of the proposed solution. The predictive model should be evaluated partially, the expert model should be evaluated partially, and for text mining and SNA, it is hard to evaluate predictive power in the classical way.

An integrated predictive model has relatively weak predictive power, and has an area under the curve (AUC) of 65%. Predictive power became much higher when it was incorporated within the fuzzy expert model, when AUC increased to 78%. Text mining helped in revealing some suspicious activities, which helped in fraud prevention, as well as SNA.

The solution was implemented in one Croatian insurance company. The fuzzy model along with social analysis metrics exist as a permanent solution, which evaluates riskiness on a client level. Text mining is used frequently for seeking suspicious activities related to fraud.

With this system, the company prevented and revealed a few situations with car glass insurance. The system showed through SNA a high concentration in connection with officers in one district in Croatia where there was an increasing number of requests for damage payment. Additional analysis showed through text mining that customers wrote instructions through social networks, through Facebook and similar services, how to avoid car glass inspection. They recognize that a specific officer was sometimes too lazy to inspect the car glass before contracting this kind of insurance. They also noticed that it was not too hard to demotivate her to go do the car glass inspection before contracting. Instructions were written by clients on social networks to encourage other potential clients to do the same, which caused great expense to the insurance company.

The presented solution was valuable for fraud recognition, and the model showed efficiency in the way it combined different analytical methodologies.

6.8 Conclusion

The presented case studies show the importance of integrating different analysis concepts based on traditional data sources and Big Data sources for a successful fraud detection solution. Each methodology or concept does not have answers for all questions, but integrated, it can create a synergy effect, which can contribute much more efficient solution than in the situation in which we are using only one methodology or concept. The case study shows the importance of the result of chaining through different systems, and that can result in some new pattern or knowledge revelation. The traditional approach to fraud detection, which leans on reporting and predictive modeling, is not sufficient, especially in a Big Data environment and new techniques suitable for pattern recognition from Big Data sets. Business intelligence concepts tend to integrate new methods and concepts to be as efficient as possible in business decisions in a complex business environment. The presented case study shows one possible solution for fraud detection in insurance, which can be applicable in complex business environments and which uses the advantages of advanced analytical models, internal data sources, and Big Data sources.

The solution unites different concepts instead of a single concept and model usage. The advantage of this approach is a model that can detect fraud with much more efficiency. Fraud, by nature, is infrequent in appearance, which complicates predictive statistical model development. Another issue is that even in a case in which fraud hypothetically is frequent in a way that for modeling purposes we have a significant data sample, it is unrealistic to expect uniform pattern recognition, which would be a base for predictive modeling. However, we should not neglect the potential of fraud predictive modeling, but we also should not lean only on that concept as a universal solution for fraud detection.

The solution is fraud system development that unites different paradigms, such as predictive modeling, expert knowledge integration via fuzzy expert systems, text mining, and SNA. The presented approach is a good tool for discovering fraudster's creativity.

Leaning on one concept or method can cause inadequate results because, as has already been mentioned, fraudsters are very creative, and in the case in which some pattern becomes obvious, it is often too late to apply data science for finding solutions because a company can be in deep trouble. Text mining, SNA, and a Big Data approach can be helpful for sniffing out potential omissions in working processes, which allows fraudsters some opportunities to act. On the other hand, if a company does not analyze internal data with the intention of fraud prevention, it is also bad strategy.

If internal fraud prevention is based on a predictive model only, then a significant part of the potential fraudulent behavior remains uncovered because predictive models operate on 6 to 12 variables only, which is insufficient for covering all possible fraudulent situations. To be much more efficient, fuzzy expert systems are introduced to cover as many potential gaps and indicators as possible, which are not frequent but significant for fraud detection.

Bibliography

Aguilar, F. J. (1967). *Scanning the Business Environment*. New York: Macmillan.

Alvarez, R. M. (2016). *Computational social science: Discovery and prediction*. Cambridge: Cambridge University Press.

Ansof, H. I. (1975) "Managing strategic surprise by response to weak signals," *California Management Review*, 18 (2): 21–33.

Armstrong, J. S. (2001). "Selecting forecasting methods." In J. S. Armstrong, ed. *Principles of forecasting: A handbook for researchers and practitioners.* New York: Springer Science + Business Media, pp. 365–386.

Baesens, B. (2014). *Analytics in a Big Data world: The essential guide to data science and its applications.* Hoboken, NJ: John Wiley & Sons.

Baesens, B., van Vlasselaer, V., & Verbeke, W. (2015). *Fraud analytics using descriptive, predictive, and social network techniques.* Hoboken, NJ: Wiley.

Bolton, R. J., & Hand, D. J. (2002). "Statistical fraud detection: A review." *Statistical Science,* 17 (3): 235–249.

Caron, F., Vanden Broucke, S., Vanthienen, J., & Baesens, B. (2013). "Advanced rule-based process analytics: Applications for risk response decisions and management control activities." *Expert Systems with Applications,* Submitted.

Chakraborty, G., Murali, P., & Satish, G. (2013). *Text mining and analysis: Practical methods, examples, and case studies using SAS.* Cary, NC: SAS Institute.

Cressey, D. R. (1953). *Other people's money; A study of the social psychology of embezzlement.* New York: Free Press.

DeSanto, D., & Pirc, J. (2016). *Threat forecasting: Leveraging big data for predictive analysis.* Cambridge, MA: Syngress.

Duffield, G., & Grabosky, P. (2001). "The psychology of fraud." In *Trends and Issues in Crime and Criminal Justice.* Canberra: Australian Institute of Criminology.

Elder, J., IV, & Thomas, H. (2012). *Practical text mining and statistical analysis for non-structured text data applications.* New York: Academic Press.

Fawcett, T., & Provost, F. (1997). "Adaptive fraud detection." *Data Mining and Knowledge Discovery,* 1–3 (3): 291–316.

Gilad, B. (2003) *Early Warning: Using Competitive Intelligence to Anticipate Market Shifts, Control Risk, and Create Powerful Strategies.* AMACOM, pp. 67–168.

Goldberg, H. & Wong, R. (1998). Restructuring Transactional Data for Link Analysis in the FinCEN AI System. AAAI Technical Report FS-98-01.

Grabosky, P., & Duffield, G. (2001). *Red flags of fraud. Trends and issues in crime and criminal justice.* Canberra: Australian Institute of Criminology.

Han, J., & Kamber, M. (2011). *Data mining: Concepts and techniques,* Third Edition. Waltham, MA: Morgan Kaufmann.

Hand, D. (2007). "Statistical techniques for fraud detection, prevention, and evaluation." Paper presented at the NATO ASI: Mining Massive Data Sets for Security, London.

Hand, D. J., Mannila, H., & Smyth, P. (2001). *Principles of data mining.* Cambridge, MA: MIT Press.

Hansen, D., Shneiderman, B. I., & Smith, M. A. (2010). *Analyzing Social Media Networks with NodeXL: Insights from a Connected World.* Burlington, MA: Morgan Kaufmann.

Jamain, A. (2001). *Benford's law.* London: Imperial College.

Jennings, C. R., & Poston, R. J. (2016). *Global business fraud and the law: Preventing and remedying fraud and corruption.* New York: Practising Law Institute (PLI).

Junqué de Fortuny, E., Martens, D., & Provost, F. (2013). "Predictive modeling with Big Data: Is bigger really better?" *Big Data* 1 (4): 215–226.

Kirchner, C. and Gade, J. (2011). Implementing social network analysis for fraud prevention. Düsseldorf: CGI Group Inc.

Klepac, G. (2010). "Preparing for new competition in the retail industry." In A. Syvajarvi, & J. Stenvall (Eds.), *Data mining in public and private sectors: Organizational and government applications* (pp. 245–266). Hershey, PA: IGI Global.

Klepac, G. (2014a). "Data mining models as a tool for churn reduction and custom product development in telecommunication industries." In P. Vasant (Ed.), *Handbook of research on novel soft computing intelligent algorithms: Theory and practical applications* (pp. 511–537). Hershey, PA: IGI Global.

Klepac, G. (2014b). "Particle swarm optimization algorithm as a tool for profiling from predictive data mining models." In *Handbook of research on swarm intelligence in engineering,* Hershey, PA: IGI Global.

Klepac, G., Kopal, R., & Korkut, D. (2011). "Sustavi ranog upozorenja temeljeni na metodama poslovne inteligencije." Zbornik radova Međunarodne konferencije Dani kriznog upravljanja, 25./26.05.2011, Velika Gorica, Croatia, pp. 567–582.

Klepac, G., Kopal, R., & Mršić, L. (2014a). "Artificial intelligent algorithms and techniques for handling uncertainties: Theory and practice." In *Early warning system framework proposal based on structured analytical techniques, SNA and fuzzy expert system for different industries.* Hershey, PA: IGI Global.

Klepac, G., Kopal, R., & Mršić, L. (2014b). *Developing churn models using data mining techniques and social network analysis.* Hershey, PA: IGI Global.

Klepac, G., Kopal, R., & Mršić, L. (2015). "Efficient risk profiling using Bayesian networks and particle swarm optimization algorithm." In *Analyzing risk through probabilistic modeling in operations research.* Hershey, PA: IGI Global.

Klepac, G., & Mršić, L. (2006). *Business intelligence through business cases.* Zagreb: Tim Press/Liderpress.

Kopal, R., Bereček, B., & Krnjašić, S. (2009). "Application of intelligence analysis software in competitive intelligence." Central European Conference on Information and Intelligent Systems, CECIIS 2009, Varaždin 2009, pp. 243–251.

Kopal, R., & Korkut, D. (2014). "Tehnike kompetitivne analize." Visoko učilište Effectus—Visoka škola za financije i pravo, Zagreb, IN2DATA, Zagreb.

Krambia, K. M. (2016). *Corporate fraud and corruption: A holistic approach to preventing financial crises.* New York: Palgrave Macmillan.

Little, R. J. A., & Rubin, D. B. (2002). *Statistical analysis with missing data (2nd ed.).* Hoboken, NJ: Wiley.

Maydanchik, A. (2007). *Data quality assessment.* Bradley Beach, NC: Technics Publications.

Navarette, E. (2006). "Practical calculation of expected and unexpected losses in operational risk by simulation methods." *Banca & Finanzas: Documentos de Trabajo*, 1 (1): 1–12.

Petropoulos, F., Makridakis, S., Assimakopoulos, V., & Nikolopoulos, K. (2014). "Horses for courses in demand forecasting." *European Journal of Operational Research*, 237 (1): 152–163.

Pinheiro, C. A. R., & McNeill, F. (2014). Heuristics in Analytics: A Practical Perspective of What Influences Our Analytical World. Hoboken, NJ: Wiley.

Roselle, B. E. (2016). *The fraud factor: Recognize it. Overcome it*, Leader Press.

Schneider, F. (2002). "Size and measurement of the informal economy in 110 countries around the world." In *Workshop of Australian National Tax Centre*, ANU, Canberra, Australia.

Spann, D. D. (2014). *Fraud analytics: Strategies and methods for detection and prevention.* Hoboken, NJ: Wiley.

Tan, P.-N. N., Steinbach, M., & Kumar, V. (2005). *Introduction to data mining.* Boston, MA: Addison Wesley.

Van Gestel, T., & Baesens, B. (2009). *Credit risk management: Basic concepts: Financial risk components, rating analysis, models, economic and regulatory capital.* Oxford: Oxford University Press.

Van Vlasselaer, V., Eliassi-Rad, T., Akoglu, L., Snoeck, M., & Baesens, B. (2015). "Gotcha! Network-based fraud detection for social security fraud." *Management Science*, doi: 10.1287/mnsc.2016.2489.

Van Vlasselear, V., Meskens, J., Van Dromme, D., & Baesens, B. (2013). "Using social network knowledge for detecting spider constructions in social security fraud." *Advances in Social Networks Analysis and Mining (ASONAM)*, 2013 IEEE/ACM International Conference.

Verbeke, W., Dejaeger, K., Martens, D., Hur, J., & Baesens, B. (2012). "New insights into churn prediction in the telecommunication sector: A profit driven data mining approach." *European Journal of Operational Research*, 218: 211–229.

Verma, R., & Mani, S. R. (2013). "Using analytics for insurance fraud detection." Digital Transformation White-Paper, FINsights.

Ward, J., & Peppard, J. (2016). *The Strategic Management of Information Systems: Building a Digital Strategy.* Hoboken, NJ: Wiley.

Chapter 7

Speedy Data Analytics through Automatic Balancing of Big Data in MongoDB Sharded Clusters

R. Sasikala

School of Computer Science and Engineering, VIT University, Vellore, Tamil Nadu, India

Contents

Abstract

IT industries, government, and nongovernment organizations have initiated more investments toward handling Big Data, specifically infrastructure-based projects on Big Data. Managing past and present data supports the industries to carry out market analysis, auditing, and investment decisions and to future business growth prediction. The variety of technologies are leading for infrastructural approaches to managing Big Data, such as sharding, Hadoop, Spark, massive parallel processing, and the cloud. Sharding is one such technology for partitioning, replicating, and distributing a database over multiple remote servers, which show the way to speedy data processing, support global access, limit a single point of failure, and a lot more. MongoDB, a NoSQL document-oriented database technology, has built-in processing stages for configuring sharding and balancing the data over multiple servers. A sharding key and schemes are the cornerstones of sharding technology performance. Moreover, sharding can come together with MapReduce, parallel processing, and the cloud. The implementation and result analysis in this chapter have been done on MongoDB standard built-in sharding schemes and range-based, hashed, and tag-aware sharding schemes for speedy data analytics. The results analysis is performed on three parameters in MongoDB auto balancing: query execution time, number of keys, and documents examined. The results showed that the range-based sharding technique is good for key-based and relevant search, and the hashed sharding technique is a good option for random and key-based search. Application and predetermined searching always require tag-aware sharding. Tag-aware sharding is also superior to the other two techniques for data analytics operations on more than one key field.

7.1 Introduction

Over the past 20 years, the storage and handling of digital information have increased by a large volume in all fields. When a database keeps on growing, handling it in a single machine and operations, such as analytics and mining, is critical. Also, the Gartner group [1] says that not only twentieth-century data are increasing in size, but also the database is totally unstructured and complex in nature. A variety of new technologies are being developed to handle large data volumes with the characteristics variety, velocity, and volume [2].

NoSQL: Not only SQL (NoSQL) database technology handles a database in its unstructured format and drops the complex relational data model structure. The variety of NoSQL databases gives market software the opportunity to go with specific open source NoSQL for specific applications [3]. The data model of storage column-oriented, graph databases; key value data stores; and document data stores allow people to provide quality solutions for different uses. Several NoSQL databases are being developed with different features, including MongoDB, Cassandra, HBase, Riak, PostgreSQL, and CouchDB.

Cloud data centers: Handling Big Data in a centralized server and also in a single data center is not only tedious; it also leads to a single point of failure, requires costly servers, increases latency while accessing database online and social networks, and is not scalable. Big Data management over a cloud data center provides the solutions for the above issues through virtualization, backup and recovery, replication, and dynamic migration, and also it requires less maintenance.

MapReduce: This is a technique well suited to perform parallel processing on distributed large data. It divides the entire parallel processing operation into two sections: map and reduce. Map is an initial level parallel processing technique performed on a number of distributed data nodes. The second level reduce operation is to forward the results into more focused output through the function called reduce. Before the operation starts, data are distributed into multiple nodes, and the same set of operations is applied in a parallel manner on the distributed nodes. Sharding is one such technique to distribute data on multiple servers either locally or globally. It improves the performance of database management techniques, data mining, and data analytics operations. Hadoop, Dryad, MangoDB, and Hadoop–MongoDB connector are the better options for MapReduce implementation [3].

Database sharding: Database sharding is a suitable solution for scalability, performance, and fault tolerance challenges for database-centric applications. It follows shared nothing architecture—that is, divides the large database into small databases and distributes it into servers. Each partitioned database is called a shard. The shards are replicated and stored in different servers in the same location or remote places. The smaller databases are faster, have quicker disaster recovery, and are easier to manage with minimum cost. The problems of sharding are balancing and failover. Balancing is necessary when the load grows larger. Hence, it is necessary to equalize the load among all the servers. The shards can also be replicated to solve failover issues. A replica set (shards) is a set of *n* servers to copy the partitioned database. At least one copy should be online. MongoDB has the facility of auto-sharding. Automatic balancing or sharding is the process of distributing the database evenly into multiple servers [4].

Automatic balancing of sharded clusters: Choosing the best hardware with a high power processor, memory, and storage is not the only solution to handle Big Data. Scalability and reliability are the major issues when we go for an individual server. The data mining and analytics on a single server is not only expensive; it also increases computational complexities. MongoDB supports sharding with the additional features of replication and an auto-balancer. The replication and balancer are fully transparent to the user. The user can choose the replication factor and requirement of auto-balancing while configuring sharded clusters.

This chapter proposes to take advantage of the database sharding concept with auto-balancing of chunks on multiple servers for increasing the speed of the data analytics process. The chapter takes advantage of built-in functions available in MongoDB and sharding techniques. This chapter also deals with performance analysis on database sharding with failover issues, dynamic balancing, and the latency factor of complex data analytics operations. Moreover, the flow of the proposed work is to help readers to understand sharding with data analytics in a practical way. The NoSQL database MongoDB supports three different sharding techniques: range-based sharding, hashed sharding, and tag-aware sharding. This chapter illustrates these three techniques with case studies, implementation commands, and detailed results analysis. Moreover, the step-by-step practical implementation of sharding with different shard key algorithms gives great insight into Big Data research in a distributed environment.

The rest of the chapter is organized as follows: Section 7.2 presents the related works of sharding and data analytics with MongoDB and sharding. Sections 7.3 and 7.4 describe sharding architecture and MongoDB sharding techniques. Section 7.4 also presents the basics of NoSQL DB, MongoDB, and sharding configuration steps. Section 7.5 deals with implementation of sharding and results analysis. Finally, Section 7.6 concludes with the results of data analytics performance on sharding with auto-balancing and future scope. The list of references to build the work is furnished at the end.

7.2 Related Work

Having a database grow bigger and bigger consequently requires more architectures, algorithms, and tools to handle and find the solutions. The term Big Data not only refers to size; it also indicates data that are semistructured or unstructured in nature, data generated from different resources, and complexity in the nature of data. Traditional techniques, such as relational database management systems (RDBMS) and SQL, are not suitable for all the cases of processing Big Data. Hence, software industries and researchers are focusing on developing specific tools for handling Big Data and finding solutions for Big Data issues [5]. The following are a few sample technologies and tools used by Big Data developers and researchers:

- Processing Tools for Big Data Analytics
  - R, Apache Spark
- NoSQL DBs
  - MongoDB, HBase, Cassandra, CouchDB
- Storage
  - Storage as a Service, S3, Hadoop Distributed File Systems
- MapReduce
  - Hadoop, Pig, MapR, Hive

Large database systems on a single server make the data retrieval process slow, lead to a single point of failure, and challenge the applications that require high throughput. To address these issues, NoSQL DBs propose two approaches: vertical scaling and horizontal scaling.

Vertical scaling: Adding more CPUs and storage in a single server to match the growing database. Throwing hardware at issues is not the right solution because the cost of the high-capacity single server is higher than smaller systems, and cloud centers also offer small instances only. Hence, vertical scaling is not the best option for processing Big Data.

Horizontal scaling: Distributed computing is a better option than a centralized server for performance and reliability reasons because a larger database scales into a number of small servers and has been proven to be the best option to handle Big Data. This technique is called sharding. Sharding distributes the database into a number of servers called shards. Each shard handles only a small amount of data (chunks) and makes it quicker to read and write data operations. This chapter provides an introduction to sharding and its architecture, MongoDB sharding programming examples, the significance of the sharding key, and various sharding techniques and also proves how far auto-balanced sharding increases the performance of search (query execution time) and data analytics operations. Various NoSQL DBs support sharding, including HBase, MongoDB from version 1.6, Oracle NoSQL database, and MonetDB. In addition, dbShards is the product specifically designed for sharding and allows the existing applications to use shards without any modification to the existing application code. dbShards supports database applications as an external product.

7.2.1 Advantages of Sharding

The following are the reasons to go for partitioning, replication, and distribution of Big Data over distributed servers:

- The partition and distribution of database over remote servers supports customers who access the data globally, for example, Amazon, Facebook, Google, etc.
- Keeping the data on replicated servers results in lower recovery time.
- The costs of simple configuration servers are less than higher configuration single servers.
- Accessing the database for read, write, and query execution performance is faster than a centralized server in terms of speed and reliability.
- Deploying shards on cloud servers is easy because most of the cloud instances are small.

7.2.2 Survey on Sharding Techniques

The performance of sharding depends on the number of sharded clusters, the sharding key, and the distribution of related information among shards. Above all, the sharding key is the deciding factor for other performance characteristics. Various sharding key techniques are developed for focusing on specific applications. Krasuski and Szczuka proposed a technique to show how far sharding assists the performance of data analytics on large databases. Here, the sharding technique is used for partitioning the query instead of the database for speedy data analytics [6]. BIMCloud is a cloud-based Big Data management tool proposed by Das et al. The technique integrates the splitting and merging of data, social interaction with BIM, and sharding of BIM data [7]. Quamar et al. proposed a partitioning technique for online transactions for dynamic load balances [8].

Ahirrao and Ingle proposed a not fully dynamic or static partitioning algorithm for online transaction data. Initially, a transactions log file is used for partitioning data, and later, at regular intervals, the partitioning is reconfigured [9]. Duong et al. proposed zero replication partitioning for minimizing the sharding cost [10]. The existing techniques are developed and proven for specific applications and on specific databases, such as online transactions, social networks, BIM information, etc. This chapter performs implementation on standard techniques that are applicable for any database application and performs detailed comparison analysis. The following is a list of various sharding techniques proposed for various Big Data applications:

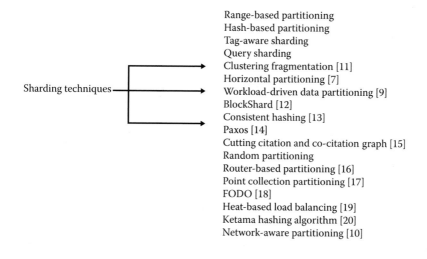

Sharding techniques

Range-based partitioning
Hash-based partitioning
Tag-aware sharding
Query sharding
Clustering fragmentation [11]
Horizontal partitioning [7]
Workload-driven data partitioning [9]
BlockShard [12]
Consistent hashing [13]
Paxos [14]
Cutting citation and co-citation graph [15]
Random partitioning
Router-based partitioning [16]
Point collection partitioning [17]
FODO [18]
Heat-based load balancing [19]
Ketama hashing algorithm [20]
Network-aware partitioning [10]

7.2.3 Survey on Data Analytics over Sharded Data

Lin et al. proposed data analytics on health care data with a sharding procedure. The author concluded that MapReduce shards enhanced the performance of data analytics and data mining operations, particularly when analyzing interactive effects and temporal events [21]. Raj et al. proposed the significance of high-performance integrated systems to the optimization of simplifying and streaming Big Data for fast analytics operation [22]. Dwivedi and Dubey concluded that data analytics tools play a vital role in analyzing the database in a complex environment. MongoDB does not provide a trigger built-in feature for data analytics operation. But they proposed a trigger-based feature in MongoDB to improve the performance of data analytics operations [23]. Araújo et al. proposed an architecture that combines the MongoDB feature replication and the data pipeline task through an aggregate command for providing real-time data analytics on behavioral biometrics [24]. Social networking sites create a substantial amount of data every day. Bhat et al. suggested that the data must be partitioned and shards must be distributed into a number of servers. They proposed making use of topological details for creating shards. And the results concluded that it provides lower network utilization, better query performance, and load balancing [25].

7.2.4 Analysis of Sharding Techniques

The findings of implementation of various sharding schemes and the results analysis are given as follows:

- In addition to partitioning the database, sharding techniques can also be applied on queries to provide better analytics.
- The knowledge of query and data structure are important factors to find new sharding keys, and tag-aware sharding is one such key.
- Implementation of sharding schemes on various databases helps to identify the better sharding key, which is applicable to all data analytics operations.
- MongoDB autosharding, repartitioning, and load balancing support dynamic sharding techniques for load balancing online.
- Sharding the data with the same category increases the speed of data analytics.
- The survey also identified that random and range-based partitioning are not well suited for load balancing.
- The results of range-based sharding key implementation show that the relevant information will be stored in a single chunk to further help to speed up data analytics operations.
- The existing survey concluded that MongoDB and Cassandra have built-in auto-sharding facilities.
- Microsoft web application stress tool, iSearch test collection, VbLabelProp, Hadoop-MongoDB connector, and Graclus are the tools used by sharding schemes.
- Research work can be further advanced on the following:
  - Dynamic online sharding.
  - Minimum migration steps for auto-balancing.
  - Hybrid solutions, such as the MongoDB-Hadoop connector.
  - In-memory computing, such as Spark, improves data analytics speed.
  - Query sharding.

The objective of the proposed work in this chapter is to help readers to realize the significance of sharding and sharding keys with an auto-balancing feature to speed up the analytics process.

7.3 Sharding

Shards: The large database is partitioned into a collection of data called chunks. One or more chunks are stored in a single server with a condition that the same data are not presented on more than one server. At the same time, shards have a replica set. A backup of a single shard is also presented on a different server in the same cluster or in a different cluster. As chunk size grows, split operation can be applied to repartition and migrate the chunks to other shards for balancing servers. The shard status of the MongoDB command key value pair *{balancing: true}* indicates whether balancing is enabled in the MongoDB shard or not.

Sharding key: Sharding is a complex procedure, which requires shards (database servers), an application server, a configuration server, and a sharding algorithm. The complexity and efficiency of the algorithm highly depend on the sharding key. The sharding key is an index field or a combination of more than one field to assist in partitioning the database into a number of chunks. The effectiveness of sharding depends on the shard key. The key is immutable. MongoDB uses range-based partitioning, hash-based partitioning, and tag-aware sharding.

7.3.1 MongoDB Built-In Sharding Techniques

7.3.1.1 Range-Based Partitioning

Range-based partitioning divides the database based on the key range from low to high. For example, employee name starting with the letters "A" to "K" are grouped in one shard and "L" to "Z" in another shard. The technique is easy for the query router to route the client request to matching shards. However, it creates unbalanced shards; that is, shards will be of different sizes.

Case Study 1

Create a student database for the academic details, and partition and distribute the database across multiple machines. Select a shard key to assist Admin to identify the students based on their joining year. Which sharding algorithm can be applied? How many shards?

Answer

Sharding algorithm: Range-based partitioning
Number of shards: Three
Partition the student database into three shards with those joining in 2013 in Shard 1, in 2014 in Shard 2, and in 2015 in Shard 3 (Figure 7.1). For this case study, the student database might be more or less equal in all the batches. Hence, the shards are balanced, but this is not the case for all applications if range-based partitioning is followed.

7.3.1.2 Hash-Based Partitioning

A sharding key with a hashing algorithm is used to create chunks. Hash function is applied to a maximum of one field to identify the location of a record on a shard. The field is called a sharding key. The system will get balanced shards, but the related records will not be stored in a single shard, and the algorithm is more complicated than range-based partitioning.

Case Study 2

With the same example in Case Study 1, Admin wanted to identify the students based on their CGPA. In the following example, shown in Figure 7.2, hashing function CGPA%10 is applied,

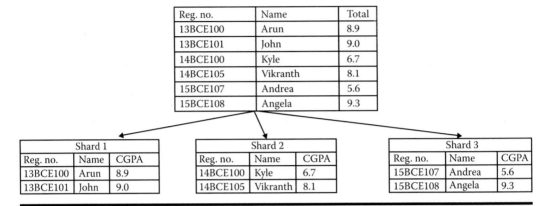

Figure 7.1   Range-based partitioning.

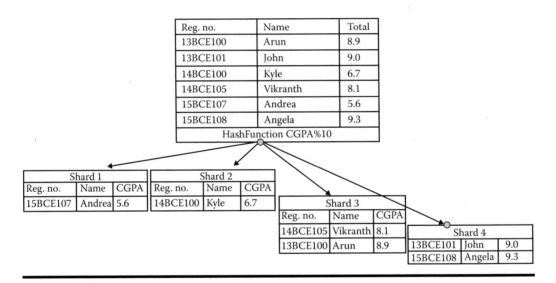

Figure 7.2   Hash-based partitioning.

and records are distributed to four shards. Here again, shards are imbalanced because of the hashing function. Hence it depends on the hashing function; shards can be set as balanced or imbalanced.

7.3.1.3 Tag-Aware Sharding

This is a technique to shard the data based on the tags assigned, which balance to organize the shards in terms of geographical location of the accessing user, data center, size of the shard, how often the data are required, and many other characteristics. The database is divided into a number of shards based on the unique tags assigned. It assists the query router to access the relevant data quickly. Here the restriction is that the programmer should predict the nature of access before the shards are configured.

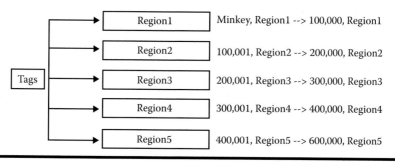

Figure 7.3   Tag-aware sharding.

Case Study 3

Create shards for a social network website database. Consider that the world map is divided into five regions, and each region has 100,000 records except Region5, which consists of 200,000 records. Five shards are fixed in five regions. Here the assumption is that the users of the social network often access their details and their friends' details, and it is less frequent to access the users in social networks across the region. Which sharding can be applied? How many shards are required?

Answer

The most appropriate sharding technique is tag-aware sharding. Initially, create five shards for five regions and create the tags as Region1, Region2, Region3, Region4, and Region5. Assign the country names of each region to the corresponding tag from Region1 to Region5. Set the shard key as country name for tag award sharding technique as shown in Figure 7.3. Now, to balance the shards, the fifth shard can be split into two chunks, and one chunk can be moved into a new shard.

In addition to range-based, hash-based, and tag-aware partitioning schemes, several sharding strategies are evaluated for various applications, such as social networks, genome analysis, biological data, U.S. Census data, health insurance, the scientific literature, etc. The following is the case study to show how to choose the suitable sharding key based on the application.

Case Study 4

Fix temperature sensors in five different countries: India, China, Brazil, Canada, and Australia. The sensors will generate 1 TB of data every day. You want to store the data for the next 20 years. The database will be used by five research groups from five countries. They want to access their country data for read, write, and update operations. But they want access to other countries' data for read-only operation to compare their country's data with others. They access the last 5 years of data frequently and from the last 6 to 20 years of data on the odd occasion. They maintain more tables with different formats. Queries access the data from more than one table at a time. For example, check the temperature of a particular month for the last 5 years and compare the results with other countries' data, and final decisions are again updated in the table. Here, the IT solutions group need to answer the following questions and design the architecture for the database.

   Is sharding necessary? Why?
      Yes. Because data size is big and the research group is spread all over the world, sharding is very much needed.

Which is the most suitable sharding algorithm?

Tag-aware sharding

How many shards? What field is chosen for the shard key?

Access is based on research group, so five shards and a shard key of country.

What is the replication architecture? Locations of replicas?

One primary and four secondary servers (replica set) because the research group will access other countries' details for read operation. Replicas can be kept in other countries.

Which server needs to be accessed for read, write, and update operations?

Primary server for write and update, replicas for read operation.

The above case studies (Figures 7.1 through 7.3) point out the features of the most common sharding techniques available in MongoDB. The next section gives the MongoDB sharding configuration steps and overall flow of the chapter from data retrieval to data analytics.

7.4 MongoDB

MongoDB is an open-source, document-oriented NoSQL data store, which is a popular choice for web applications development and Big Data management applications. Basically, MongoDB scales well horizontally through sharding techniques. The implementation of sharding and distributing the data across multiple machines is easy through MongoDB built-in methods. To support reliability, MongoDB shards are replicated internally using a replication factor [26]. The shards can also be placed on the cloud as cloud databases [27]. Also MongoDB has the facility of auto-sharding, which is a technique to balance the shards automatically. Many recent projects with the growing database opt for MongoDB as the best option instead of relational databases. Initially, MongoDB configures sharding clusters before the sharding process. Each cluster has three components: config servers, query routers, and shards. Out of three servers, shards and config servers are database servers, and the query router is an application server to coordinate the client and database servers. MongoDB supports JavaScript as a default scripting language. Throughout this chapters JavaScript is used to illustrate the code samples of sharding and data analytics query execution.

7.4.1 Sharding Architecture

Shard: This is a database server-stored partitioned database, and a shard also has a replica set. The client can contact the shard only through query routers. Its sharding and replication details will be stored in the config server as metadata.

Config servers: These are meta servers that store details of the shard key in its shard. The query router initially sends a query to the config server to know which shard has which database. Based on the config server response only, the query router forwards the client request to the right shard always. By default, the MongoDB cluster has more than one config server.

Query routers: An application server acts as an interface between the shards and client application. It routes the client request to the appropriate shards with the help of config servers. By default, MongoDB uses more than one query router in each cluster. But the client sends a request to only one server. The MongoDB sharded cluster can be set up in a single machine with a fewer number of services than the production environment. Figure 7.4 shows a pictorial representation

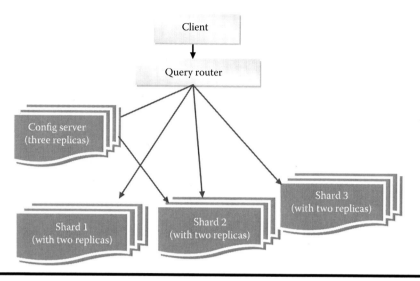

Figure 7.4   MongoDB sharding architecture.

of the MongoDB sharding architecture. MongoDB recommends that the sharding cluster must have the following components in a production environment:

- Three config servers
- Three shards
- Query router

7.4.2 Flow of Data Analytics from Data Retrieval to Analytics Report

The flow diagram shown in Figure 7.5 is the step-by-step procedure of the chapter from database retrieval to analysis of query execution on various sharding techniques:

Step 1: Retrieve the database from application.
Step 2: Convert the database from CSV to JSON format.
Step 3: Use Mongoimport to import the JSON file into MongoDB.
Step 4: Use aggregate command to extract the required database from existing db (optional).
Step 5: Apply sharding.
    i. Fix and configure cong servers.
    ii. Fix and configure shard servers.
    iii. Fix and configure applicatiion server or query routers.
    iv. Choose range or hash or tag-aware sharding key.
    v. Fix replication factor and balancer.
Step 6: Apply create, read, update, and delete (CRUD) queries and find execution time using .explain() command.
Step 7: Apply MapReduce and aggregate queries and find query execution time.
Step 8: Analyze range-based, hash-based, and tag-aware sharding keys with different queries mentioned in Steps 6 and 7.

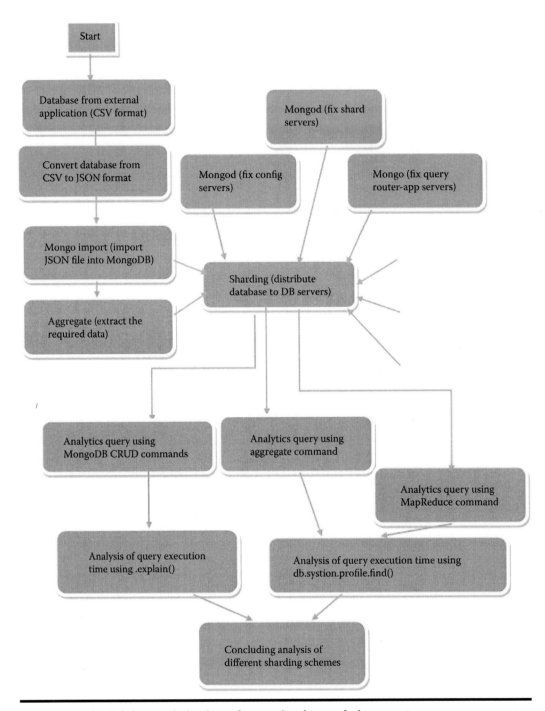

Figure 7.5 Flow of data analytics from data retrieval to analytics report.

7.4.3 *MongoDB Sharding Configuration*

MongoDB sharding configuration steps are given through Case Study 5. The configuration steps for Case Study 5 are given for a local host machine.

Case Study 5

Set up three config servers, two shard servers with replication factor 3, and one application server. Create a database collection with 50,000 documents. Distribute the documents into three shard servers with range-based partitioning and execute a query on the database with a single server and execute the same query on three sharded servers.

Installation of MongoDB in Windows, Linux-based OS is easy. After installation, we have to ensure the following:

Check any other mongod instance running in the local system. For example, check this in Ubuntu by

```
>pgrep mongo
```

This command will print, process ID of mongod, which is currently running. Ubuntu will start mongod instance automatically. Hence, to delete monogd instance, use admin account:

```
>sudo kill pid no
```

A config server and sharded servers are database servers, and *mongod* service is required to run these services. The query router is an application server, and *mongos* service is required to run the query router. The following steps are required to set up a sharded cluster in a single machine:

Step 1

Create a directory for the config server, a meta server to store metadata of shards. The directories can be created in the same drive or different.

```
sudo mkdir config_svr1
sudo mkdir config_svr2
sudo mkdir config_svr3
```

The directory path created must be mentioned in the mongod service with the parameter dbpath.

Step 2

Start the service mongod to configure the config svr in port no 27019. Execute the following service in a separate prompt (Ubuntu). Repeat the steps three times with different port numbers to create three config servers.

```
        >sudo mongod --configsvr --dbpath /var/lib/config_svr1 --port
27019 --fork --logpath /var/lib/config_svr1/log --logappend
        >sudo mongod --configsvr --dbpath /var/lib/config_svr2 --port
27020 --fork --logpath /var/lib/config_svr2/log --logappend
        >sudo mongod --configsvr --dbpath /var/lib/config_svr3 --port
27021 --fork --logpath /var/lib/config_svr3/log --logappend
```

Now the config servers will wait on three ports 27019, 27020, and 27021 to receive the request from the query router. The config server run on port 27019 is a default server and on ports 27020 and 27021 are replicas of the config server. In order to run this command on a Linux environment, add an option fork as a parameter in the above command.

Step 3
Create a directory for the shard server, database server to store the partitioned database: two shards with replication factor 3

```
sudo mkdir shard_svr11
sudo mkdir shard_svr12
sudo mkdir shard_svr13
sudo mkdir shard_svr21
sudo mkdir shard_svr22
sudo mkdir shard_svr23
```

The directories *shard_svr11* and *shard_svr21* are for shard primary servers, and *shard_svr12*, *shard_svr13*, and *shard_svr22*, *shard_svr23* are for replica servers. The directories can also be created on the same or a different drive, which is to be mentioned in the dbpath parameter of mongod service.

Step 4
Create two shards, and every shard server will have a replica set with replication factor 3 using mongod service with parameters. The following service should be executed in a separate command prompt (Ubuntu):

Shard 1 with two replicas

```
    > mongod --shardsvr --replSet shard_svr1 --dbpath /var/lib/shard_
svr11 -logpath /var/lib/shard_svr11/log --port 27000 -logappend -
smallfiles -oplogSize 50 -fork -nojournal
    > mongod --shardsvr --replSet shard_svr1 --dbpath /var/lib/shard_
svr12  -logpath /var/lib/shard_svr12/log --port 27001 -logappend -
smallfiles -oplogSize 50 -fork -nojournal
    > mongod --shardsvr --replSet shard_svr1 --dbpath /var/lib/shard_
svr13 -logpath /var/lib/shard_svr13/log --port 27002 -logappend -
smallfiles -oplogSize 50 -fork -nojournal
```

Shard 2 with two replicas

```
    > mongod --shardsvr --replSet shard_svr2 --dbpath /var/lib/shard_
svr21 -logpath /var/lib/shard_svr21/log --port 27100 -logappend -
smallfiles -oplogSize 50 -fork -nojournal
    > mongod --shardsvr --replSet shard_svr2 --dbpath /var/lib/shard_
svr22  -logpath /var/lib/shard_svr22/log --port 27101 -logappend -
smallfiles -oplogSize 50 -fork -nojournal
    > mongod --shardsvr --replSet shard_svr2 --dbpath /var/lib/shard_
svr23 -logpath /var/lib/shard_svr23/log --port 27102 -logappend -
smallfiles -oplogSize 50 -fork -nojournal
```

In a Windows environment, the service should be executed on a separate prompt. The parameter 'replSet' in above code is to mention the name of the replica set for the primary and replica servers. Here port numbers 27000 and 27100 are primary shard servers, and 27001, 27002, 27101, and 27102 are replicas. The above commands successfully created two sharded clusters with two replicas. The next two steps are to configure shard servers, initiate, and add members into the replica set.

Step 5

Create a primary shard server (query router) and members to the replica set. The following command should be executed on command prompt (Ubuntu):

```
> mongo   --port 27000
```

which will enter into the MongoDB shell. Now initiate port 27000 as primary

```
>rs.initiate()
```

which will create the following prompt. Wait for seconds to convert the mongo shell into the primary server and add port 27001 and 27002 as members into replicas

```
shard_svr1:PRIMARY> rs.add("localhost : 27001")
shard_svr1:PRIMARY> rs.add("localhost : 27002")
```

Now the shard cluster with one primary and two replicas is created. To know the status and configuration details, we can run the `rs.status()` and `rs.conf()` commands on the MongoDB shell.

Step 6

Exit from the MongoDB shell, go to the prompt, and repeat Step 5 for the second sharded cluster of port 27100 (Primary), 27101 (Replica), and 27102 (Replica). Now Steps 5 and 6 successfully created and configured two sharded clusters. The next step is to start mongos service and create a link to config servers.

Step 7

Create a query server and create a link to the config servers using mongos service with parameters. Execute this command on the command prompt:

```
>mongos --configdb  localhost:27019 –logpath /var/lib/mongos.log –fork
–logappend --chunkSize 50
>mongos --configdb  localhost:27020 –logpath /var/lib/mongos.log –fork
–logappend --chunkSize 50
>mongos --configdb  localhost:27021 –logpath /var/lib/mongos.log –fork
–logappend --chunkSize 50
```

This command successfully connected the config servers with the query router. Port 27019 is the default config server, and the remaining are config replicas. All the above steps (Steps 1 to 7) created and configured a sharded cluster with three config servers, two sharded servers with two replicas each, and one query router.

Step 8

Create a link with the MongoDB shard server to the sharded cluster by executing mongo service on command prompt:

```
>mongo
```

This will connect to the MongoDB shell with mongos service. Now create a link with the sharded cluster by using the addShard command:

```
mongos>sh.addShard("localhost:27000")
mongos>sh.addShard("localhost:27100")
```

The above steps added two sharded clusters to the query router *(mongos)* service. Now internally *mongos* is connected to the config server and the sharded cluster.

Step 9

Assume that the database "Zib" consists of the collection "Zipcode." The sharding will be applied to the collection "Zipcode" by the following command:

```
sh.enableSharding( "Zip" )
sh.shardCollection ("Zip:Zipcode" , { "_id" : 1 } )
```

The sh.shardCollection() command distributes the collections by the unique key "_id." The method applies range-based partitioning as explained in Section 7.3.1. The Zip Collection is partitioned based on _id tag and distributed into two shards. Even the database is stored in a single shard due to the size and heavy read operations; MongoDB will migrate the chunks from one shard to another automatically, which is called auto-balancing.

Step 10

To know the status of sharded collections and chunk details. Run

```
mongos> sh.status()
```

The above steps configured shard clusters, config servers, and a query router. Also the Zipcode collection of database Zip is partitioned and distributed into shards.

7.4.4 Significance of the Sharding Key

As the database is distributed on machines in a number of locations, the key requirement is to retrieve the data from shards with minimum latency. The objective of this chapter is to analyze performance of data analytics operations on various sharding techniques. In general, random sharding always exhibits poor performance even if the data are distributed on many nodes. Hence, the system requires the following techniques for partitioning the database.

Here the sharding key plays a significant role in fixing chunk and shard sizes, balancing the shards, and the nature of data distribution over the shards. Selection of the shard key not only balances the shards, that is, evens distribution of data over all the shards, but also decides the performance characteristics of the system, such as query execution time and fewer chunk migrations. The following are different sharding algorithms that played significant roles in various applications:

- *Random sharding*: Each datum is assigned to randomly different shards, leading to near worst case performance. Even the algorithm is simple to implement; neighboring data always present in different locations.
- *Network-aware sharding*: Nodes of a block are assigned to single shards, helping manager nodes to search a single node for all the neighbors in a block.
- *Tag-aware sharding*: This is a MongoDB built-in feature for sharding. It considers the global scenario and allows more than one tag for sharding. It assists in the balancing operation.
- *Sharding balancer*: After the execution of sharding, the database stored in chunks is not distributed evenly in most cases. The required solution is to manage the shards, and the balancing operation should not be manual. Hence, the data analytics will make it faster to access the data on a distributed environment. The MongoDB provides the solution through a balancer, which works as a built-in process. The balancer is a built-in process on *mongos* instance, and during sharding execution, it ensures that the chunks are balanced and distributed evenly on all shards. In most cases, the existing MongoDB configuration for the balancer is sufficient. Here, the implementation configures the balancer in three sharding schemes.

7.5 Implementation and Results Analysis

The system is implemented in MongoDB with three built-in popular sharding techniques: range-based sharding, hash-based sharding, and tag-aware sharding techniques. MongoDB version 3.2 is installed on Ubuntu 14.4. MongoDB recommends a minimum of three sharded clusters, three config servers, and one shard server for the production environment. For experimental results analysis, the same setup is configured on a local host machine as explained in Section 7.4.3. The command `sh.status()` running on mongos service prints the chunk and sharding configuration details. The partial output of `sh.status()` is

```
mongos> sh.status()
--- Sharding Status ---
  sharding version: {
       "_id" : 1,
       "minCompatibleVersion" : 5,
       "currentVersion" : 6,
       "clusterId" : ObjectId("56c891089f0db48befdc636e")
}
  shards:
{ "_id" : "Replica1",   "host" : "Replica1/sasikala:27011,sasikala:27012,s
asikala:27013" }
{ "_id" : "Replica2",   "host" : "Replica2/sasikala:27021,sasikala:27022,s
asikala:27023" }
{ "_id" : "Replica3",   "host" : "Replica3/sasikala:27031,sasikala:27032,s
asikala:27033" }
```

The above status output shows that three sharded clusters are created as Replica1, Replica2, and Replica3, and each cluster has one primary and two secondary nodes. Now the database can be added into the shards. Initially an *"employee"* database is created with two collections for storing employee and production details. The database is created randomly by using JavaScript. First and second collection, initially 1 lac records (documents) are inserted. In MongoDB, the database is called the database, the table is called the collection, and a record is called a document. The collections are *emp1* and *machine*. The *_id, name,* and *location* in the *emp* collection and *id, name,* and manufacturing date in the machine collection are inserted using JavaScript. Sharding on a range-based key, hashing key, and tag-aware sharding are implemented using the following code.

Run *mongo* command on prompt; it will enter into *mongos* instance

```
>mongo
```

i. **Collection emp (range-based partitioning):**

```
sh.enableSharding( "employee" )
sh.shardCollection( "employee.emp1" , { "_id" : 1 } )        //
Range based partitioning
```

The above range-based sharding steps obtain collection "emp1" from the "employee" database and divide the collection by the key "_id." The key value pair {"_id":1} indicates that the collection is sharded based on a key "_id."

ii. **Collection machine (hash-based partitioning):**

```
db.machine.ensureIndex({ "_id" : hashed } )
sh.shardCollection( "employee.machine" , { _id  : "hashed" },
{ numInitialChunks  : 2 } )
```

The above hash-based sharding steps assign initially "_id" as the hash key by using the key value pair {"_id":hashed}. In addition, chunks are fixed as 2 at the initial level. Hence, the hashing algorithm divides the database into two chunks initially. Moreover, the hashed index does not support the floating point value, and it truncates floating point numbers. Hence, it is better to choose a hash key as an integer field. MongoDB computes hash value for *"_id"* field, and application is not necessary to apply any algorithm for computing hash.

iii. **Collection inventory (tag-aware sharding)**

Here the tag-aware technique sharded the collection *"inventory"* based on the code and id fields by using the key value pair *{" code ": 1," _id": 1}.*

```
sh.shardCollection(" employee.inventory",{" code " : 1,"_id" : 1})
mongos> sh.addShardTag( "Rep1" , "item1" )
mongos> sh.addShardTag( "Rep2" , "item2" )
mongos sh.addTagRange( "employee.inventory" , { code:0 } , {
code:1 }, "item1" )
mongos> sh.addTagRange( "employee.inventory" , {code:1} , {code:2}
, "item2" )
mongos>for( i=0; i<50000; i++ ) { db.inventory.insert ( { iname :
"item1_" +i, count : 100 , code  :0 } ) }
mongos>for ( i=0; i<50000; i++ ) { db.inventory.insert ( { iname :
"item2_" + i , count : 200 , code : 2 } ) }
```

Output will be

```
mongs> sh.status()
— Sharding Status —
  sharding version: {
        "_id":1,
        "minCompatibleVersion":5,
        "currentVersion":6,
        "clusterId":ObjectId("56cd4dd455729a856d7658f1")
}
  shards:
```

Tag-aware sharding on shards *Rep1* and *Rep2*

```
      {"_id":"Rep1","host":"Rep1/sasikala:27011,sasikala:27012,sasikala:27013",
"tags":["item1"]}
      {"_id":"Rep2","host":"Rep2/sasikala:27021,sasikala:27022,sasikala:27023",
"tags":["item2"]}
      {"_id":"Rep3","host":"Rep3/sasikala:27031,sasikala:27032,sasikala:27033"}
```

```
After the execution of above commands, the database is sharded over
clusters as follows databases:

      {"_id":"employee","primary":"Replica2","partitioned":true}
            employee.emp1
                  shard key:{"_id":1}
                  unique:true
                  balancing:true
                  chunks:
```

Range-based Sharding on two Replicas *Rep1* and *Rep2* with 8 chunks

```
                  Replica1      1
                  Replica2      7
```

```
      {"_id":{"$minKey":1}}—>>{"_id":1}on:Replica1 Timestamp(2,0)
      {"_id":1}—>>{"_id":25760}on:Replica2 Timestamp(2,1)
      {"_id":25760}—>>{"_id":38640}on:Replica2 Timestamp(1,3)
      {"_id":38640}—>>{"_id":51520}on:Replica2 Timestamp(1,4)
      {"_id":51520}—>>{"_id":64400}on:Replica2 Timestamp(1,5)
      {"_id":64400}—>>{"_id":77280}on:Replica2 Timestamp(1,6)
      {"_id":72280}—>>{"_id":90160}on:Replica2 Timestamp(1,7)
   {"_id":90160}—>>{"_id":{"$maxKey":1}}on:Replica2 Timestamp(1,8)
            employee.machine
                  shard key:{"_id":"hashed"}
                  unique:false
                  balancing:true
                  chunks:
```

Hash-based sharding on *Rep2* with 10 chunks

```
                  Replica2      10
{"_id":{"$minKey":1}}—>>{"_id":NumberLong("-7186171677479770932")}
on:Replica2 Timestamp(1,11)

{"_id":NumberLong("-7186171677479770932")}—>>{"_id":NumberLong
(-5131248759579078970)}on:Replica2 Timestamp(1,12)
```

The above results indicated an *emp1* collection with range-based partitioning sharded into Replica 1 (one chunk) and Replica2 (seven chunks). Also the *machine* collection with hash-based partitioning sharded into only one cluster, Replica2 (10 chunks). The number of documents in *emp1* and *machine* is 100,000. Because MongoDB enables auto-balancing, the chunks are moving dynamically from shard to shard for balancing the shards.

7.5.1 Query Execution on Sharding Key

Analysis has been done on various read operations (*db.collection.find()*) and update operations (*db.collection.update()*) on three different types of sharding techniques. For analysis, the read operation using the sharding key and other criteria other than the sharding key are also implemented. The MongoDB commands *db.collection.find().explain()* and *db.collection.find().explain("executionStats")* are used to check the number of shards checked, the number of documents examined, and the query execution time. For example, the following command

```
mongos> db.emp1.find( {_id : { $gte : 100 , $lte : 120 } }
).explain("executionStats")
```

prints the results as (partial output)

```
"executionStats" : {
      "nReturned" : 21,
      "executionTimeMillis" : 0,
      "totalKeysExamined" : 21,
      "totalDocsExamined" : 21,
      "executionStages" : {
            "stage" : "SINGLE_SHARD",
            "nReturned" : 21,
            "executionTimeMillis" : 0,
            "totalKeysExamined" : 21,
            "totalDocsExamined" : 21,
```

The above command returned 21 documents by exactly checking 21 keys. Because the config server identified the exact shard and chunk, the total document examined is 21 out of 100,000 documents. The query execution time in milliseconds is zero. The above query search of the collection for the documents between *_id* is 100 and 120. Here, the key for search and sharding key are the same *_id*. Hence, the documents examined are exactly the same as documents displayed—that is, it hits what we want exactly.

7.5.2 Query Execution on Other Criteria

The same command is executed with different criteria other than shard key *"_id"*—that is, searching is based on the name of the employees.

```
mongos> db.emp1.find({name:{$gte:"emp_100",$lte:"emp_120"}}).
explain("executionStats")
```

The results are (partial):

```
        ....
  "executionStats" : {
        "nReturned" : 42,
        "executionTimeMillis" : 42,
        "totalKeysExamined" : 0,
        "totalDocsExamined" : 100000,
        "executionStages" : {
                "stage" : "SHARD_MERGE",
                "nReturned" : 42,
                "executionTimeMillis" : 42,
                "totalKeysExamined" : 0,
                "totalDocsExamined" : 100000,
```

The above results show that the query examined all `Replica Set 2` and 100,000 documents, and the execution time is 42 ms. In the previous command, it is 21 documents and 0 ms. This is the difference between a query executed on a shard key and other search criteria. As with the above, read, update, and aggregate commands are executed with different options on three sharding techniques in the following section. The results analysis has been done on four different possibilities.

  i. Sharding has been done on a range-based sharding key, and performance reports have been taken with parameters execution time, the number of keys examined, and documents examined for query execution on the sharding key and other criteria. Performance results are given in Section 7.5.3.
 ii. Sharding has been done on a hash-based sharding key, and performance reports have been taken with parameters execution time, the number of keys examined, and documents examined for query execution on the sharding key and other criteria. Performance results are given in Section 7.5.4.
iii. Sharding has been done on a tag-aware sharding key, and performance reports have been taken with parameters execution time, the number of keys examined, and documents examined for query execution on sharding key and other criteria. Performance results are given in Section 7.5.5.

7.5.3 Data Analytics Experimental Results on Range-Based Sharding Key Value

The `emp1` collection on the employee database is sharded using a range-based partitioning key, and the sharding key is `"_id"`. Now various queries are executed, and the results are given in Tables 7.1 and 7.2. Table 7.1 shows that query execution time is based on the criteria sharding key and criteria other than the sharding key. The following are the different types of queries (MongoDB built-in commands):

i. Read operation on equality condition:

```
mongos> db.emp1.find({_id:10000})
mongos>db.emp1.find({location:"loc_"=10000})
```

Table 7.1 Query Execution Time for Range-Based Sharding Key

Sl. No.	Queries	On Sharding Key	On Other Criteria
1	Read operation (find)	0	68
2	Read operation (range of documents)	0	60
3	Query execution using AND and OR operators	0	88
4	Query execution on embedded document (update)	0	54
5	Query execution on array element	0	42
6	Query execution with multiple criteria on array elements	0	64
7	Aggregation commands on sharded databases	–	82

Table 7.2 Documents and Keys Examined by Query Execution on Range-Based Sharding Key

Sl. No.	Queries	On Sharding Key		On Other Criteria	
		No. of Keys Examined	No. of Documents Examined	No. of Keys Examined	No. of Documents Examined
1	Read operation (find)	1	1	0	100,000
2	Read operation (range of documents)	9	9	0	100,000
3	Query execution using AND and OR operators	1	1	0	100,000
4	Query execution on embedded document (update)	1 1	1 1	0	100,000
5	Query execution on array element	1	1	0	100,000
6	Query execution with multiple criteria on array elements	1	1	0	100,000
7	Aggregation commands on sharded databases	–	–	0	29,353

ii. find() on range of documents

```
mongos>db.emp1.find({_id:{ $gt:10000,$lt:10009})
mongos>db.emp1.find({location :{ $gt:"loc_"+10000,$lt:""loc_"+10009})
```

iii. Query execution on $and and $or operators

```
mongos> db.emp1.find({$or:[{_id:10000},{location:"loc_"+95000}]})
```

iv. Update() on embedded documents

```
mongos> db.emp1.explain("executionStats").update({_id:1001},{mail_
id:"aaa@gmail.com"})
mongos>db.emp1.explain("executionStats").update({_id:10001},{"name":"emp
new_10001", "location":"locnew_10001",mail_id:"aaa@gmail.com","addr":{"st
rno":45,"zip":600001}})
```

v. Query execution on array elements

```
mongos> db.emp1.explain ("executionStats"). update({name: "emp_10003 "},
{$set: {"name": "empnew_10003", "location": "locnew_10001", mail_id:
"aaa@gmail.com", "addr": {"strno": 45, "zip": 600001}}}, {multi: true})
mongos> db.emp1.find({"addr.strno":  {$gte: 45,  $lte: 46}}).
explain("executionStats")
```

The collection zip is downloaded from the MongoDB website as a JSON (Javascript object notation) file and imported into mongos using

```
>mongoimport --db employee --collection zip --path /home/hostname/
Desktop/zip.json
then apply sharding command with specific sharding key algorithm
```

vi. Aggregate command on 29353 document of collection zip

```
db.zip.aggregate( [    { $group: { _id: "$state", count: { $sum: "$pop"
}} }])
mongos> db.zip.aggregate( [    { $group: { _id: "$state", tot: { $sum:
"$pop" }} },    { $match: { tot: { $gte: 10*1000*1000 } } } ] )
```

Table 7.1 and Figure 7.6 contain the results of different queries executed on sharding and based on other criteria. The results show how much time the system takes to execute a query on a single machine. Query execution using an $or operator and aggregate takes more time than another process. Query execution using $or operator is applied on two documents with different shards. Hence, it takes more time, and the aggregate command needs to retrieve the data from the entire database on a single shard. Hence, the range-based partitioning performance depends on how far the required data are distributed on the shard cluster. The read operation on a range of relevant documents retrieved from a single shard takes less time than using an $or operator. Hence, the range-based partitioning is good for performing a data analytics operation on mostly relevant documents, and search is based on the sharding key.

Query execution on the sharding key always searches the exact document, but the other criteria search the entire collection as with a single machine. Hence in Table 7.2, criteria based on the

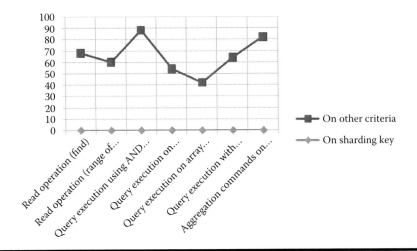

Figure 7.6 **Query execution on sharding key and other criteria using range-based sharding.**

sharding key examine exactly one document and one key. But the other criteria search all 100,000 documents every time. Hence, it is good to have a compound shard key (i.e., more than one field as a shard key), which provides the right mix of cardinality and reduces execution time further even if we go with other search criteria.

7.5.4 Data Analytics Experimental Results on Hash-Based Partitioning Key

A hash-based partitioning algorithm applies a hashing algorithm on the key, which is specified at the time of sh.ensureIndex() command execution before applying the sh.shardCollection() command. Here, the sharding key chosen is "_id." As in Section 7.5.3, the different types of queries are executed on sharded data, and the results are given in Tables 7.3 and 7.4 and Figure 7.7. Here, the query execution time is less than in range-based partitioning. This hash-based partitioning is suitable for data that is uniformly distributed. Also, the sharding algorithm distributes the data evenly

Table 7.3 **Query Execution Time for Hash-Based Sharding Key**

Sl. No.	Queries	Sharding Key	On Other Criteria
1	Read operation (find)	0	45
2	Read operation (range of documents)	0	41
3	Query execution using AND and OR operators (find)	0	59
4	Query execution on embedded document (update)	0	44
5	Query execution on array element (update)	0	65
6	Query execution with multiple criteria on array elements (find)	0	41
7	Aggregation commands on sharded databases (pipeline)	–	76

Table 7.4 Documents and Keys Examined by Query Execution on Hash-Based Sharding Key

Sl. No.	Queries	On Sharding Key		On Other Criteria	
		No. of Keys Examined	*No. of Documents Examined*	*No. of Keys Examined*	*No. of Documents Examined*
1	Read operation (find)	1	1	0	100,000
2	Read operation (range of documents)	9	9	0	100,000
3	Query execution using AND and OR operators	1	1	0	100,000
4	Query execution on embedded document	1	1	0	100,000
5	Query execution on array element	1	1	0	100,000
6	Query execution with multiple criteria on array elements	1	1	0	100,000
7	Aggregation commands on sharded databases	–	–	0	29,353

into multiple chunks. Query execution time on find command (Sl. No. 1, 2, and 6) is much less compared to the update command. The query that uses $or and $and operators takes more execution time than another find operation, but it is less than the range-based partitioning algorithm. The update command, Sl. No. 5, takes more time because it updates the entire document. The comparison results are given in Figure 7.7. The sharding algorithm is good for an application that

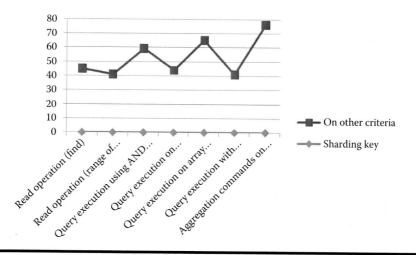

Figure 7.7   Query execution on sharding key and other criteria using hash-based sharding.

is accessing irrelevant data often. Aggregation is mostly applied for the fields other than the sharding key; hence, the sharding key-based aggregation command is not tried. The following are two examples of query execution on update command:

```
mongos> db.machine.explain ( "executionStats" ) . update( { _id : 10008 }
, { mail_id : "aaa1@gmail.com" } )
mongos>  db.machine.explain( "executionStats" ) . update( { name :
"machine_10003" } , { $set : { "name" : "machinenew_10003" , "location" :
"locnew_10001" , "addr" : { "strno" : 45, "zip" : 600001 } } } , { multi
: true } )
```

7.5.5 Data Analytics Experimental Results on Tag-Aware Sharding

The inventory collection is classified as two categories, *item1* and *item2*. The documents are created for *item1* and *item2*. Hence, the inventory detail items belonging to *item1* are directed to one shard; the *item2* documents are directed to another shard. Hence, the items that are continuously recorded are not stored in a single shard, which is followed in range-based partitioning. The results are given in Tables 7.5 and 7.6 and Figure 7.8. The relevant documents are not scattered over all the shards like hash-based key; that is, irrelevant documents will not be stored in a single shard. Hence, the programmer should know the details of documents and, at the time of sharding configuration, the documents that are under the same category (belonging to item1 and item2) are stored in a single shard. The query execution on relevant documents (Sl. No. 3) takes less time than in range-based and hash-based partitioning. In Sl. No. 1, all 50,000 documents belonging to *item1* will be examined; hence, it takes 30 ms for query execution. Tag-aware sharding is suitable for sharding the database, which is relevant to a particular category like geographical sharding.

Table 7.5 Query Execution Time for Tag-Aware Sharding Key

Sl. No.	Queries	Sharding Key	On Other Criteria
1	Read operation (find)	1	37
2	Read operation (range of documents)	0	53
3	Query execution using AND and OR operators	0	54
4	Query execution on embedded document (update)	0	35
5	Query execution on array element	0	37
6	Query execution with multiple criteria on array elements		
7	Aggregation commands on sharded databases	34	79

Table 7.6   Documents and Keys Examined by Query Execution on Tag-Aware Sharding Key

Sl. No.	Queries	No. of Keys Examined	No. of Documents Examined	No. of Keys Examined	No. of Documents Examined
1	Read operation (find) on two keys (_id) (_code)	1 1	1 50,000	0	100,000
2	Read operation (range of documents)	7	7	0	100,000
3	Query execution using AND and OR operators	1	1	0	100,000
4	Query execution on embedded document	1	1	0	100,000
5	Query execution on array element	1	1	0	100,000
6	Query execution with multiple criteria on array elements	1	1	0	100,000
7	Aggregation commands on sharded databases	29,353	29,353	0	29,353

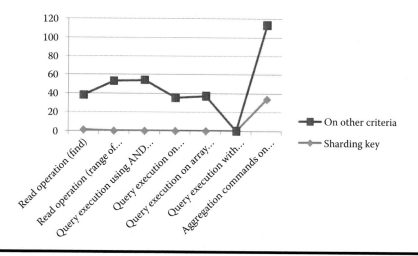

Figure 7.8   Query execution on sharding key and other criteria using tag-aware sharding.

i. Find command (on sharding key)

```
mongos> db.inventory.find ( { $or : [ { _id : ObjectId("56cd56a76dab      1
01e594e5"} , { code : 0 } ] } ) . explain ( "executionStats" )
```

ii. Find command (on other criteria)

```
mongos> db.inventory.find ( { $or : [ { _id : ObjectId("56cd56a76dabdafd0
1e594e5") } , { iname : "item1_" + 1100 } ] } ) . explain (
"executionStats" )
```

iii. Update command

```
 mongos > db.inventory.explain ( "executionStats" ) . update ( { "_id" :
ObjectId ( "56cd56a76dabdafd01e594e5" ) } , { "warehouse" : "aus" , code
: 0 } )
mongos > db.inventory.explain ( "executionStats" ) . update ( { iname :
"item1_1003" } , { $set : { "name" : "item1new_1003", "location" :
"locnew_1003" , mail_id : "aaa@gmail.com" , "addr" : { "strno":45 , "zip"
: 600001 } } } , { multi : true } )
```

iv. Aggregate command

The following command is stored as JavaScript file.js and run the command as mongo file.js use employee;

```
d = new Date;
db.zip.aggregate ( [   { $group: { _id: "$state", totalPop: { $sum:
"$pop" } } },   { $match: { totalPop: { $gte: 10*1000*1000 } } }] )
print(new Date - d + 'ms');
```

7.5.6 Comparison Results Analysis on Range-Based, Hash-Based, and Tag-Aware Sharding Keys

For comparison analysis on the above sharding keys, the zip code database in JSON format has been taken and applied to a range-based sharding key with the rule {"_id":1}, hash-based sharding key on {"_id":hashed}, and tag-aware sharding key on sh.shardCollection(" zip.zipcodes",{" state ": 1,"_id": 1}). The comparison results are given in Figure 7.9. The commands Aggregate and MapReduce executed statewise and the execution time are compared. Because the range- and hash-based keys sharded the data based on _id, and the tag-aware key sharded based on statewise, the MapReduce and Aggregate commands execution time of tag-aware is less than the other two. The opposite would be the case, if the data sharded on the _id field and the commands are executed on random data. Hence, the results indicated that tag-aware sharding is a better option for domain-specific sharding, and search should also be domain-specific.

The following conclusions are identified from the experimental results of the above sharding schemes:

- Query sharding can also be a significant area in addition to data sharding.
- Range-based sharding is a good scheme to apply for the speedy data analytics applications that need relevant data.

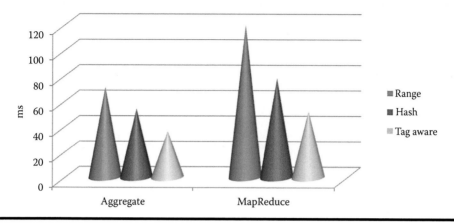

Figure 7.9 Comparison of range, hash, and tag-aware sharding.

- Range-based sharding also produces optimum results to retrieve the data in sorted order in terms of date and serial number.
- Initially, MongoDB configures the database in one shard after the series of data retrieval; the built-in auto-balancing technique creates greater effect in balancing the shards.
- Hashing algorithm with right choice of sharding key balances the shards at the initial level itself.
- Hash-based sharding is a completely better option than range-based for random searching.
- Tag-aware sharding scheme allows the administrator to choose the shard, shard size, and decision on shard balancing at the time of configuration itself.
- Even if a particular shard size is high, the split function divides the shards further.
- Auto-balancing provides an additional load to the sharding servers and requires a lot of background work to make the balanced shards. Hence, choosing the right key during partitioning reduces the risk of auto-balancing dynamically and frequently.

7.6 Conclusion

Achieving efficiency in algorithms for partitioning and sharding of a large volume database over a distributed network is a great challenge to the research and network administrator community. Dynamic balancing of shards automatically without a preprogramming decision leads to higher complexity. This chapter has taken advantage of built-in functions available in sharding schemes and demonstrated how important the sharding key is in solving scalability issues of the Big Data management technique. This chapter has taken standard sharding schemes: Range-based partitioning, hash-based partitioning, and tag-aware scheme. The results concluded that although identifying the sharding algorithm for a specific application is difficult, tag-aware sharding and predicting the right tag for the database is a standard technique for any type of application. The chapter assists readers in extending this work on different data mining, data analytics, and machine learning algorithms on Big Data in a distributed environment. The proposed work can also be extended as sharded clusters in a cloud environment; hence, the VM migration with auto-balancing improves the data analytics and data mining operations further.

References

1. Gartner Inc. http://www.gartner.com/
2. Wu, Lengdong, Liyan Yuan, and Jiahuai You. "Survey of large-scale data management systems for big data applications." *Journal of Computer Science and Technology* 30.1 (2015): 163–183.
3. Lourenço, João Ricardo et al. "Choosing the right NoSQL database for the job: A quality attribute evaluation." *Journal of Big Data* 2.1 (2015): 1–26.
4. https://docs.mongodb.org/manual/core/sharding-introduction/
5. Min Chen, Shiwen Mao, and Yunhao Liu. "Big Data: A survey" *Journal of Mobile Network Applications* 19 (2014): 171–209.
6. Krasuski, Adam, and Marcin S. Szczuka. "Knowledge driven query sharding." *CS&P*. Vol. 225. 2012.
7. Das, Moumita, Jack C. P. Cheng, and Srinath S. Kumar. "Social BIMCloud: A distributed cloud-based BIM platform for object-based lifecycle information exchange." *Visualization in Engineering* 3.1 (2015): 1–20.
8. Quamar, Abdul, K. Ashwin Kumar, and Amol Deshpande. "SWORD: Scalable workload-aware data placement for transactional workloads." *Proceedings of the 16th International Conference on Extending Database Technology*. ACM, 2013.
9. Ahirrao, Swati, and Rajesh Ingle. "Scalable transactions in cloud data stores." *Advance Computing Conference (IACC), 2013 IEEE 3rd International*, IEEE, 2013.
10. Duong, Quang et al. "Sharding social networks." *Proceedings of the sixth ACM international conference on Web search and data mining*. ACM, 2013.
11. Wiese, Lena. "Clustering-based fragmentation and data replication for flexible query answering in distributed databases." *Journal of Cloud Computing* 3.1 (2014): 1–15.
12. Sasikala. "Research based literature survey and analysis on various sharding techniques." *IIOAB Journal* 7.9 (2016): 479-494.
13. Wenbin, Jiang, Lei Zhang et al. "A novel clustered MongoDB-based storage system for unstructured data with high availability," *Journal of Computing* (2014) 96: 455–478.
14. Rao, Jun, Eugene J. Shekita, and Sandeep Tata. "Using Paxos to build a scalable, consistent, and highly available datastore." *Proceedings of the VLDB Endowment* 4.4 (2011): 243–254.
15. Zhao, Haozhen. "Sharding for literature search via cutting citation graphs." *Big Data, 2014 IEEE International Conference on*. IEEE, 2014.
16. Strauch, Steve, Vasilios Andrikopoulos, and Thomas Bachmann. "Migrating application data to the cloud using cloud data." *3rd International Conference on Cloud Computing and Service Science*, 2013.
17. Zhang, Shuai et al. "Point collection partitioning in MongoDB Cluster." Proceedings of the 12th International Conference on GeoComputation, LIESMARS, Wuhan University, Wuhan, China, (2013).
18. Liu, Yimeng, Yizhi Wang, and Yi Jin. "Research on the improvement of MongoDB Auto-Sharding in cloud environment." *Computer Science & Education (ICCSE), 2012 7th International Conference on*. IEEE, 2012.
19. Wang, Xiaolin, Haopeng Chen, and Zhenhua Wang. "Research on improvement of dynamic load balancing in MongoDB." *Dependable, Autonomic and Secure Computing (DASC), 2013 IEEE 11th International Conference on*. IEEE, 2013.
20. Wenbin, Jiang et al. "A novel clustered MongoDB-based storage system for unstructured data with high availability," *Journal of Computing* (2014) 96: 455–478.
21. Lin, Chin-Ho et al. "Temporal event tracing on big healthcare data analytics." *Big Data (BigData Congress), 2014 IEEE International Congress on*. IEEE, 2014.
22. Raj, Pethuru et al. "High-performance integrated systems, databases, and warehouses for big and fast data analytics." In *High-Performance Big-Data Analytics*, Springer (2016): 233–274.
23. Kalpana, Dwivedi, and Sanjay Kumar Dubey, "Implementation of data analytics for MongoDB using trigger utility." In *Computational Intelligence in Data Mining*, Springer (2015).
24. Araújo, Daniel et al. "Providing wellness services using real time analytics," Ambient Intelligence-Software and Applications–*7th International Symposium on Ambient Intelligence* (ISAmI 2016).

25. Bhat, Pranav Thulasiram, Rohit Varkey Thankachan, and K. Chandrasekaran. "Sharding distributed social databases using social network analysis." *Social Network Analysis and Mining* 5.1 (2015): 1–11.
26. Dede, Elif et al. "Performance evaluation of a mongodb and hadoop platform for scientific data analysis." *Proceedings of the 4th ACM workshop on Scientific cloud computing.* ACM, 2013.
27. Balamanohari, S., and R. Sasikala. "Transaction processing system for efficient maintenance of databases in cloud," *CiiT International Journal of Networking and Communication Engineering,* 2.6 (2010).

Chapter 8

Smart Metering as a Service Using Hadoop (SMAASH)

Ankur Dumka

Department of Computer Science, University of Petroleum and Energy Studies, Dehradun, India

Contents

Abstract

Smart metering as a service using Hadoop (SMAASH) is an approach to analyze the electricity consumption of a user on a real-time basis. SMAASH can be used for determining real-time analysis of electricity consumption using Hadoop technology based on customer-based segmentation, area-based segmentation, usage-based segmentation, or purpose-based segmentation based on the type of parameter analysis that needs to be done. The analysis of these said parameters can be done based on an hourly basis, weekly basis, monthly basis, or yearly basis, and based on these parameters, a suitable solution for power theft, time of use tariff options, grid failure, load distribution, and the load shedding problem can be provided. Thus, using the SMAASH approach provides faster and parameter-based real-time solutions for these problems.

8.1 Big Data

Data! Data! Data!

With an increase in the use of IT in each and every field, there is a need for the storing and processing of large data, which is a problem with the traditional approach of data analysis and maintenance. With the increase in use of IT applications in nearly every field, the data capacity reaches from megabytes to terabytes to zettabytes. Nearly 90% of data were generated in the last few years. Consider the example of Facebook, which stores nearly 10 billion photos that take up to 10 petabytes of storage; similarly, Internet archives store around 2 petabytes of data, and it is still growing at the rate of 20 terabytes per month because there are multiple sources of data, including users, Facebook, Internet archive, etc., which keep on adding data to the data source. In 2011, it was assumed that there were nearly 1.8 zettabytes of data, which is constantly booming. There are many initiatives taken to control these data, such as Amazon coming up with public data sets on Amazon web services, Infochimps.org, and the info.org, and all exist to foster the information commons, where data can be shared for anyone to download and analyze. There is a regular need for more and better algorithms for handling the data, and thus Big Data comes into the picture, which overcomes the problem of data storage and analysis.

Thus, such a large amount of data is termed Big Data, data that are too large and too complex to handle with the help of the traditional approach to database management systems because there has been a massive increase in the storage capacity of hard disks with an increase of data, but the processing speeds have not kept up. To read and write data on a single drive is a time-consuming process and takes a large amount of time. So to overcome this problem, one can assume having multiple drive processing in parallel to process the same amount of data and thus can reduce the time consumption in processing. This can be done by splitting the data into small data sets, grouping the data based on matching parameters, and finally storing the data in one location. Using multiple drives is not a solution as it seems to be wasteful, but we can think of storing 100 data sets, each with fixed bytes and providing shared access to them. Thus, provided with this feature, one can reduce the analysis time as the analysis tasks would be spread over time and wouldn't interfere with each other.

Big Data includes data from black box data, including components of jets, airplanes, helicopters, recording of microphones, etc.; social media data, which include data from Twitter, Facebook, etc.; stock exchange data, which include information about buy and sell decisions; power grid data, including the information consumed by a particular node with respect to a base station; and transportation data, including model, capacity, and availability of a vehicle. Thus, using Big Data, processed information can be obtained that can be used for different aspects; for example, using information on social networks, marketing agencies can learn about the response to their advertising media. Using information on social networks, product companies and retail organizations can plan their production. Using information about the power grid, information about usage can be predicted and even power theft can be detected. There are many technologies from different vendors in the market.

Vendors such as Amazon, IBM, and Microsoft are a few that work on Big Data technology. The two types of technology used in Big Data technology are operational Big Data and analytical Big Data. Operational Big Data includes systems, such as MongoDB, that provide operational capabilities in real time. The NoSQL system can provide insights into patterns and trends based on real-time data with minimal coding and without the need for data scientists. Analytical Big Data includes systems such as massive parallel processing database systems and MapReduce that provide analytical capabilities for retrospective and complex analysis that may touch most or all of the data. Big Data is also suffering from many challenges, such as capturing data, curation of data, storage of data, searching of data, sharing of data, transfer of data, analysis of data, and presentation of data.

The data in Big Data can be of three types:

1. Structured data, such as relational data
2. Semistructured data, such as XML data
3. Unstructured data, such as data in word, pdf, text, or media logs

Thus, Big Data is the term used for the collection of data sets that are large and complex and that are difficult to process using on-hand database management tools or traditional data processing applications. These large and complex data suffer with the challenges of capturing, curation, searching, sharing, transferring, analysis, and visualization. Based on characteristics, IBM classifies Big Data into three parts: volume, velocity, and variety. Volume is the amount of data being generated usually in terabytes or zettabytes. Velocity is the speed at which data are generated; for example, Facebook is generating data at the rate of 500 terabytes per day. Variety is the type of data generated, such as video files or click stream; this includes structured and unstructured data.

In this chapter, we support data generation from the power grid and power from households, and based on the real-time analysis of the data of electricity consumption on various parameters using Hadoop technology, Big Data provides suitable solutions for efficient electricity management.

Big Data technology can be used to turn information from smart meters and smart grid projects into meaningful operational insights and insights about company assets and customer behavior. Thus, with this in mind, the SMAASH project is proposed based on Big Data technology, which works on smart meter analysis to overcome the existing problems of service providers and their customers. SMAASH is used to curb energy consumption by analyzing user data and making those insights available to customers in order to show the customer how behavior changes and appliance upgrades reduce energy consumption and enhance direct customer communication. By using Big Data and analytics, data from the smart grid can help utilities get more from existing resources and plan for proactive maintenance and capacity management.

Smart grid is a technology that is advancing at a faster rate. A nascent market is focusing on smart grid installation of more than 310 million smart meters globally. It is expected that this number will triple by 2022, reaching nearly 1.1 billion according to Navigation Research. Represented by fractions of sensors, the grid infrastructure represents a good installation of smart meters and rate of growth of the smart grid. They are termed "smart" as they themselves provide little utility, having the capability of remotely sensing a device state. Collectively these devices generate a huge amount of information. In order to realize the economic, social, and environmental value of the smart grid, utilities need a solution that can aggregate the sum of these data to correlate and scientifically analyze all of the information generated by the smart grid infrastructure in real time. Thus, in order to go to the Big Data solution, Hadoop is used for complex analytic requirements of the smart grid.

8.2 Introduction

With advanced technology, all the data go from a file-based system to computerized data. But with more and more data, managing the data is a challenging task; even processing of scaling data was a challenge to IT professionals. An increase in the size of hard drives can be a solution for storing the large amount of data, but accessing the data is still problematic. Thus, to enhance the speed of accessing the data, a solution can be read from multiple disks all at once. But failure of a single piece of hardware can cause data loss. To overcome this problem, we can use the redundancy concept by replicating the data as done by RAID. Collection of data combined from different sources deals with the problem of performing the collection correctly, which is again a challenge. This problem is more or less solved by Hadoop. The Hadoop architecture framework includes four modules:

1. *Hadoop common*: Hadoop common consists of Java libraries and utilities required by other Hadoop modules.
2. *Hadoop yarn*: Hadoop yarn is a framework for job searching and cluster resource management.
3. *Hadoop distribution file system (HDFS)*: HDFS is a distributed file system that provides high-throughput access to the application data.
4. *Hadoop MapReduce*: Hadoop MapReduce is a new yarn system, which is used for parallel processing of large data sets (Figure 8.1).

White (2013) discusses and helps in understanding the Hadoop and MapReduce technology as MapReduce and HDFS are two important pillars of Hadoop as shown in Figure 8.1. MapReduce processes the entire data set for a whole query, thus having the ability to process ad hoc queries to provide results. MapReduce provides a programing model for abstracting the problem from disk reads and writes and then transforming it into a computation over a set of keys and values. MapReduce is basically a programing model and an associated implementation for processing and generating large data sets with a parallel, distributed algorithm on a cluster. MapReduce thus unlocks the data that were previously archived on tape or disk, whereas HDFS is used to store the data in an organized manner. Thus, Hadoop, on the whole, provides

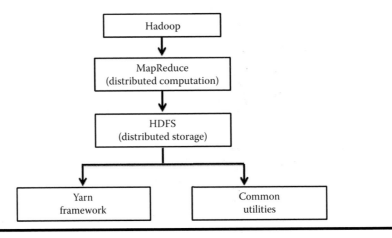

Figure 8.1 Hadoop architecture.

a reliable storage and analysis system for the data, in which storage is provided by HDFS and analysis is provided by MapReduce.

Thus, Hadoop runs an application using MapReduce algorithms with which the data are processed in parallel on different CPU nodes. The working of Hadoop can be classified into three stages:

1. In the first stage, a user application can submit a job to Hadoop for a required process by specifying terms such as the location of the input and output files in the file system, and the Java classes in the form of a jar file containing the implementation of map and reduce functions. The job configuration is done by setting different parameters specific to the job.
2. In the second stage, the Hadoop job client submits the job and configuration to the job tracker, which then assumes the responsibility of distributing the software or configuration to the slave, scheduling the task, and monitoring them.
3. In the third stage, the task tracker on different nodes executes the task as per MapReduce implementation, and output of the reduce function is stored into the output files on the file system.

Thus, it can be concluded that Hadoop is beneficial in the following ways:

1. Hadoop allows a user to quickly write and test distributed systems.
2. Hadoop does not rely on hardware.
3. Servers can be added or removed from the cluster dynamically without interrupting the operation.
4. Hadoop is compatible on all platforms because it is Java based.

8.3 Hadoop

Hadoop is a framework that allows the storage and processing of Big Data in a distributed environment across a cluster of commodity computers using a simple programing model. It uses a cluster of nodes for the processing of Big Data in a distributed environment. Hadoop is an open-source data management tool, which has scale-out storage and distributed processing. The simple programing model for Hadoop is termed MapReduce. Hadoop is a versatile open-source tool having the feature of distributed computing. When working with large data sets, Hadoop reduces costly transmission steps by using distributed storing and transferring code. Hadoop provides redundancy, thus recovering from a situation in the case of failure of a single node. Programing in Hadoop is also easier as it uses the MapReduce framework, which is easier to program. Within Hadoop, the partitioning of data and allocation of the task to the nodes and also communication between the nodes are done automatically. There is no need for manual allocation of these tasks. This leaves the programmer free to focus on the data and logic that need to be implemented.

Hadoop is a collection of open-source tools that are managed by the Apache Software Foundation and are designed for processing Big Data. Hadoop uses MapReduce as its batch processing technique by using it for analysis of large, static, historical data sets. MapReduce performs this task by breaking large data sets into small sets for processing. Thus, parallel processing of these tiny sets is done across multiple machines. In the case of the power system, this might be applied to rate case development, "static" customer segmentation and targeting, energy-saving measure modeling, and other analytics that do not require real-time data. The MapReduce paradigm is used for processing such types of batch workflow and scales very well with large numbers of work items, such as smart meters, as many machines can process the subsets in parallel. The common smart grid requirement is its ability to track thousands of data attributes and to subject those attributes to thousands of computations, matching the frequency with which these computations vary from infrequently (i.e., yearly, monthly, daily, or hourly) in the case of customer energy efficiency programs to millisecond granularity in the case of maintaining grid load stability.

In Hadoop, a user can scale the network up to any number of nodes in a cluster. Hadoop gives us the power to distribute data across a cluster of commodity computers, and these nodes can be as big as 10,000 nodes in which data can be stored and retrieved in parallel, and a lot of parallel processing can be done using the programming model termed MapReduce.

The features supported by Hadoop are as follows:

1. Economical
2. Reliable
3. Flexible
4. Scalable

Hadoop is economical in the sense that there is no need to purchase a license for it as it is an open-source framework. Thus, distribution of Hadoop is free; the only payment will be for its support. Hadoop can be termed as reliable as it is built in such a way that even in the case of failure, data can be retrieved by means of data replication and node replication. Flexibility for Hadoop can be confirmed by the scalability Hadoop supports. Hadoop is free from the constraints of nodes. The number of nodes within Hadoop is scalable—that is, nodes can be added or removed without putting the system down as Hadoop supports an unlimited number of nodes, which gives scalability to Hadoop.

The core of Hadoop consists of the following:

1. HDFS
2. The processing part termed MapReduce

HDFS is used for storing data. It consists of a set of clusters of machines that are combined together for storing data. The cluster consists of two nodes, termed the namenode and datanode. The namenode acts like admin, and the datanode acts as a data store. HDFS is natively redundant, which means that redundancy is built in as all the data of one node are replicated to the other node to avoid failures. Thus, it stores data at multiple locations to prevent data failure.

MapReduce is used for processing of data. It is a programing model that splits the task across processors.

Hadoop breaks the files into smaller blocks of variable size and defines and distributes these data among nodes of the cluster, in which the data get processed in a parallel manner using MapReduce functions. Thus, Hadoop provides a reliable shared storage and analysis system in which the storage is provided by HDFS and analysis is done by MapReduce.

8.3.1 History of Hadoop

The seeds of Hadoop were first planted in 2002 by Internet archive search director Doug Cutting and University of Washington graduate student Mike Cafarella with a view that the world wanted a better open-source search engine. This project was built keeping that era's web in mind, and they termed their project "Nutch." In about a year, Nutch proved to be working pretty well as it was able to crawl and index hundreds of millions of pages. Then, in October 2003, Google released its Google file system paper and, ultimately, in December 2004, released a paper for MapReduce. These papers prove to be revelatory for both engineers building Nutch. Over the course of a month, Cutting and Cafarella built up their underlying file system and processing framework coded in Java and that would become Hadoop, and they ported Nutch on top of it. Because Google MapReduce was using C++, Hadoop proved to be better than Google MapReduce. By 2006, Cutting started working with Yahoo, which influenced the Google file system and MapReduce papers, and planned to build open-source technology based on them. Hadoop was formed by Spuning, the storage and processing part of Nutch, which was named after Cutting's son's stuffed elephant. Hadoop is an open-source Apache Software Foundation project, and the Nutch web crawler remained its own separate project. At Yahoo, the transformation into Hadoop was pretty much completed by 2008. In 2011, Yahoo spun off Hortonworks into a separate Hadoop-focused software company at which the Hadoop infrastructure consisted of 42,000 nodes and hundreds of petabytes of storage. Hadoop became a full-on Apache project that attracts users and contributors from around the world.

8.3.2 Hadoop Ecosystem

Components of Hadoop consist of the following parts (Figure 8.2):

1. *Oozie*—Oozie is a workflow management tool that is used to run a job in parallel.
2. *Hive data warehouse*—Hive is a data warehousing system of Hadoop, which was developed by Facebook.
3. *Pig*—Pig is a data analysis tool developed by Yahoo.
4. *Mahout*—Mahout is a machine learning framework used for analysis, such as recommended system, clustering analysis, etc.

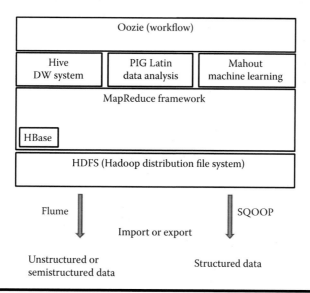

Figure 8.2 Hadoop ecosystem/components of Hadoop.

5. *MapReduce*—MapReduce framework is a programing model that is used to read or write data from a distributed file system.
6. *HBase*—Hbase is used for the database.
7. *HDFS*—HDFS is used for loading data into a database.
8. *SQOOP*—SQOOP is a tool that is used for moving structured data from the relational database management technology (RDBMS) to Hadoop. The name SQOOP is a combination of SQL and Hadoop.
9. *Flume*—Flume is a tool used to import unstructured or semistructured data into Hadoop. The SQOOP and flume are tools used to load real-time data into Hadoop.

All of these are open-source systems. For a reporting tool, one can use R language, which can be used for predicting risk, analytic analysis, predictive analysis, etc.

8.3.3 MapReduce

David De Witt and Stonebraker (2008) defines MapReduce as a processing technique and a programing model that is used for distributed computing based on Java. Basically, the MapReduce algorithm is divided into two important tasks: map and reduce. The map function is used to take a set of data as per the requirement and convert the raw data into another set of data or processed data in which individual elements are broken down into tuples. The reduce function takes the output from a map as an input and combines those tuples into a smaller set of tuples or reduces the data into formatted data as per the requirement of the user. MapReduce is beneficial in the sense that it makes it easy to scale data processing over multiple computing nodes.

Thus, the MapReduce program executes in three stages:

1. *Map stage*: The map or mapper's job is to process the input data, which are in the form of a file or directory and are stored in the Hadoop file system (HDFS).
2. *Reduce stage*: This stage is the combination of the shuffle stage and reduce stage. The reducer's job is to process the data that come from the mapper.
3. *Inputs and outputs*: The MapReduce framework operates on <key values> pairs, i.e, the framework views the input to the job as a set of <key, value> pairs and produces a set of <key, value> pairs as the output of the job. The <key values> can be scalar or composite. For analysis of SMAASH, composite key values have been taken as input. Thus, the <key value> map identifies what we want from the data (Figure 8.3).

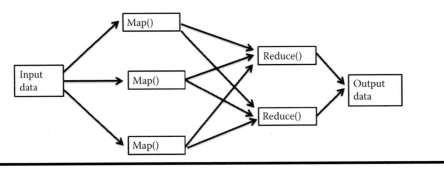

Figure 8.3 MapReduce architecture.

MapReduce consists of Job Tracker, which is a master daemon that distributes a task-to-task tracker. Task Tracker is the program that runs on the datanode. Job Tracker is associated with the master node or namenode, and Task Tracker is associated with the datanode. Thus, it can be said that the datanode is the machine and Task Tracker is the program that runs on these machines.

8.3.4 Hadoop Distributed File System

Fay Chang (2006) discusses HDFS, writing that HDFS was developed using distributed file system design. It runs on commodity hardware. HDFS is better than other distributed file systems in the context that it is highly fault-tolerant and designed using low-cost hardware. It is used to hold a large amount of data and provides easier access. In order to store large amounts of data, the files are stored across multiple machines. These files are stored in a redundant manner to prevent data losses in case of failure. HDFS makes the application available for parallel processing.

For the storing of a data set that outgrows the storage capacity of the single physical machine, partitioning of data needs to be done across a number of separate machines. HDFS is a type of file system that manages the storing of data across a network of machines. Thus, HDFS is used to store large files based on streaming data access patterns, which run on a cluster of commodity hardware. The streaming data access pattern is based on the idea that the most efficient data processing pattern is a write once and read many times pattern. A data set is copied or generated from the source, and by using various parameters, analyses are performed on that data set over time. For cost effectiveness, Hadoop performs better than other software in the sense that Hadoop does not require expensive hardware to run on as it is designed to be run on a cluster of commodity hardware. Apart from using Hadoop on large data and for efficient performance, Hadoop fails in certain fields, including applications that require low-latency access to data, in the tens of milliseconds range. Lots of small files need to be processed. Also, there is no support for multiple writers of a file.

The data are stored in small segments termed a disk. A disk has a small size, which is the minimum amount of data that a disk can read or write. The file system deals with data in blocks, which are an integral multiple of the disk block size. By default, the size of each block in HDFS is 64 MB. The data are broken into chunks and then stored as a separated unit in these blocks. In order to reduce the cost of seeking, the size of the HDFS blocks are kept larger than the size of the disk block. The time for transferring the data from the disk is made larger than the time to seek to the start of the block. The map function performs the map task on each block for operation of the block at a time. The reason for making the unit of abstraction a block rather than a file is to simplify the storage subsystem, especially for a distributed system in which the failure node is so varied. Due to the fixed size block, it becomes easier to calculate the data that can be stored on a given disk and eliminate metadata concerns. Even the block is useful in providing the fault tolerance by replicating the data. "%hadoopfsck/-files –blocks" is the command that is used to list the blocks that make up each file in the file system.

When designing the HDFS cluster, two types of nodes are created that work in a master–worker pattern. The node, which works as master, is termed the namenode, and the nodes that work as workers are termed datanodes. The namenode is used for managing the file system namespace. Namenode maintains the file system tree and metadata for all the files and directories in the tree. The information for this architecture is stored persistently on a local disk in the form of two files named namespace image and editlog. Apart from managing the file system namespace, namenode also regulates the client access to the file and is also used to execute the file system operations, such as renaming, closing, and opening of files and directories. The namenode is also known as data nodes on which all the blocks for given files are located. The datanode performs read–write operations on the file system as per the client request. It also performs operations like block creation, deletion, and replication as per the instruction of the namenode. The datanodes are the workhorses of the file system. A datanode based on the command from a client or namenode stores or retrieves blocks and reports the result back to the namenode periodically with a list of blocks that they are storing. A file system cannot work without a namenode as there would be no way to reconstruct the files from the blocks on the datanode if lost. In order to avoid such types of situations, data backup needs to be maintained. In order to back up the data, a secondary namenode is installed whose main role is to periodically merge the namespace image with the editlog to prevent the editlog from becoming too large. The secondary namenode usually runs on a separate machine because it requires plenty of CPU and as much memory as the namenode to perform the merge. A client accesses the file system on behalf of the user by communicating with the namenode and the datanode.

All the metadata operations that occur in the namenode are represented in Figure 8.4. Metadata are the data that contain information about the list of files; list of blocks for each file; list of datanodes for each block; and file attributes, such as time, replication factor, etc., and they even store transaction logs, such as records of file creation, file deletion, etc. Thus, it can be said that the namenode contains information on the overall file directory structure and places where the data block is stored. The metadata are stored in the main memory of the namenode, and there is no demand paging of FS metadata. The namenode thus contains only metadata, not the actual data. The client interacts with the namenode for metadata operation that is used for extracting information from the datanode, which contains the actual information.

The client can read or write to the datanode through a Java interface or HDFS command line. The end user can get the result through the client. The client can directly read and write to the datanode but gets information on the location of the datanode from the namenode.

Racks are the physical location providing space for multiple datanodes. Multiple racks altogether form clusters. The datanode is commodity hardware, which is divided into blocks, and

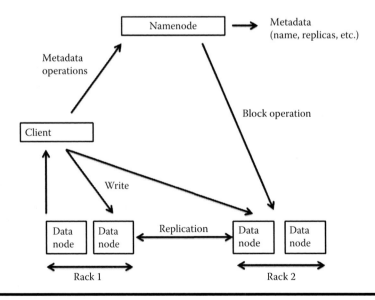

Figure 8.4 HDFS architecture.

each block has a specific size, which varies from 64 to 128 MB. Remote procedure call (RPC) is a protocol that is used for communication among devices with each other.

The namenode is the master of the system. It is a high-quality and high-availability machine that maintains and manages the blocks that are present on the datanode. The namenode is a single point of failure; thus, it is a single machine in the whole cluster. Thus, if the namenode fails, there is no backup for the namenode, and whole systems fail in such a case. A secondary namenode is a solution for disaster recovery. It does not provide redundancy in case the namenode fails; rather, a secondary namenode is used to make a backup of the metadata of the namenode every hour to an external drive. Thus, in case the primary namenode fails, the saved namenode can be used to rebuild a failed namenode. Therefore, a secondary namenode is not a hot standby for the namenode; rather, it is used to connect the namenode every hour for a backup namenode.

Datanodes are slaves that are deployed on each machine and provide actual storage. They are responsible for serving read and write requests for the client. Cheap replicas can be made for datanodes and can be in any number. Datanodes work as a database of the file system; they store and retrieve blocks when they are told by the client or namenode. The datanodes send reports back to the namenode periodically with lists of blocks they are storing.

Thus, the goal of HDFS can be divided into three parts:

1. Fault detection and recovery
2. Huge data sets
3. Hardware at data

The HDFS system is advantageous in the following manner:

1. It is suitable for distributed storage and processing.
2. Hadoop also provides a command interface to interact with HDFS.
3. The built-in servers of the namenode and datanode in HDFS help a user to easily check the status of a cluster.
4. HDFS provides streaming access to file system data.
5. HDFS provides file permission and authentication facilities.

8.4 Smart Metering as a Service Using Hadoop (SMAASH)

The project titled SMAASH aims at analysis of past and present electricity based on data received from smart meters and thus helps in predicting the future analysis of the electricity consumption and taking adequate steps for management of electricity. On monitoring and analyzing the electricity data, parameters, such as climate data, are also taken into consideration along with electricity consumption data, which can be used for prediction of future analysis of electricity and help in providing time of use tariff options to the user.

Brophy-Haney et al. (2009) and Darby (2010) defined a meter or a metering system as smart or advanced regardless of the utility for which it is being used, such as gas, water, or electricity. According to Darby, a meter is termed a smart meter if it can store and transmit measurement at frequent intervals. Smart meters can play a vital role in the collection of registry of end-use electricity consumption on a real-time basis. Advanced electric metering and communication technologies enable data transfer of end-use electricity consumption data; analysis of this high-resolution data can pinpoint unusual patterns caused by electricity consumption. The importance of managing customer electricity consumption data at this high level cannot be underestimated. This information assists in operational management of electricity over the area as it highlights the electricity usage of households with excessive electricity consumption, indicating inefficient use and option for electricity theft, which can be investigated using this technology; this can even be used to determine peak demand and also provide for time to use a tariff option due to lower resolution of logging at hourly intervals.

Britton et al. (2013) and Momoh (2009) discuss that smart metering and associated resource consumption visually displayed technologies enable utility for the customers to access their consumption and compare previous usage. This also enables the electricity distributors to manage the distribution based on the analysis performed. In particular, identifying and communicating theft to customers is something that must be conducted as an ongoing process.

Depuru et al. (2011) discuss smart meters by discussing the working of smart meters; one can say that a smart meter works by communicating directly with the energy suppliers, and they provide accurate reading of the electricity on a real-time basis. Smart meters can also make use of wireless mobile phone type technology for sending the data. Thus, installing a smart meter provides cost-effective meter and data management as well as transparency about pricing and usage.

Many studies reveal that there are three major challenges in customer management, and they are operational efficiencies and reduction of cost to serve, customer satisfaction, and lack of retention of talents. The study also shows that 52% of utilities worldwide expect to outsource the data analysis for their grid operation in 10 years.

SMAASH provides an end-to-end automatic meter and data management solution, which delivers cost savings. It provides meter data collection, processing, and scheduled validated data delivery; SMAASH also provides for metering device management and a single point of contact in a multisupplier environment. Thus, SMAASH is a business process outsourcing tool that includes solutions and life cycle management, giving utilities the flexibility to manage smart metering operations in the best way possible. By using SMAASH, we provide electricity distributors the analysis data of electricity consumption to gain insight into customer usage patterns in order to achieve several target applications, such as time-of-use tariff, demand response management, and billing accuracy. One of the benefits of smart meters is that collection of data in smart meters is on a real-time basis, whereas with old mechanical meters, collection of data is done on an hourly or monthly basis. In order to benefit from the smart grid investment, it is critical that handling the massive amount of data from the smart meters is done efficiently and that it can be used by the grid operators to operate the grid safely, economically, and reliably and to make timely decisions.

The Apache Hadoop framework is used for provisioning this system that allows distributed processing of large data sets across clusters of computers. Hadoop MapReduce is a technology that is based on parallel processing of large data sets, which are then used to achieve the target with respect to the traditional RDBMS approach, which is inefficient and slower in working as compared to the Hadoop framework approach. Thus, for fair economic gain, it is desirable to use smart meters for smart distribution and efficient use of electricity so that the generated power can be used in an efficient manner: a parallel distribution framework using MapReduce for analytics of large amounts of data generated from the smart meters in a faster and efficient manner. SMAASH provides multipurpose beneficial output that includes accurate billing, a time-of-use tariff plan, per user segmentation, area-based segmentation, and type of usage-based segmentation. Thus, SMAASH is implemented using an analytics concept and smart meters with a view to future use.

Smart meters send energy consumption data at regular intervals to the server, generating a huge amount of data. These data are processed using Apache Hadoop, which is an open-source framework used for developing distributed application for processing of such a large amount of data, thus providing a platform for distributed storage and computational capabilities in which a computational tier uses the MapReduce framework and HDFS storage for a distributed file system.

The purpose of this section is to provide details on how the data would be transmitted from various electricity meters installed in consumers' places to the subdistribution system of the electricity plant and from subdistribution. This system identifies the total supply of electricity from the main distribution system to the subdistribution system on an hourly basis and the total electricity supply by subdistribution system to individual or business consumer place. This system provides details on the total electricity misuse between the main distribution system and subdistribution systems by reverse reconciling the consumption, and also identifies the total electricity misuse between the subdistribution system and the individual or business consumer place by reverse reconciling the consumption. The system also identifies the peak usage of electricity on an hourly basis based on individual and business consumer places.

8.5 Benefit of This System

This system will provide information on the theft or misuse of electricity related to each subdistribution system, and if the distribution system is considered a transformer, then it will provide actual information about which transformer theft is happening and how to control theft. Apart from the theft, the SMAASH project is also used for the purpose of finding the load usage pattern of the grid, area, or customer, which can be used to prevent grid failure or avail equal load distribution for a particular area. The SMAASH project can also be used for usage-based analysis, to find out the usage pattern for individual, business purpose usage, etc., which can provide the solution of time-of-use tariffs for customers. The SMAASH project can also be used for finding the usage pattern for different types of purposes, which can be used for electricity, water, gas, or other types of usage and can be used for analysis of these services based on type of purpose.

It also helps in identifying the peak usage of electricity in a real-time, hourly, daily, monthly, or yearly manner, can be used further for setting up new electricity charges based on consumption and time interval; and can also provide other different solutions.

8.6 Case Study

From the background case study, we can conclude that effective measurement of electricity consumption can be performed using smart meters. By means of Big Data technology, we refine the solution for the smart meters, and using computation of data, analysis of the raw data can be done to obtain the processed data.

The benefits of this project can be seen from the facts and figures from the case studies of the smart meter installation project in various European countries.

Austria

In Austria, the EVN smart meter pilot project was started in 2008 and was finished in 2012. This project included installation of smart meters for 300 + 160 customers. Analysis of data was done to simplify the data regarding main costs and benefits. The interfaces used to get access to meter data were web interface, monthly bills, and in-home displays.

The Strommetz smart meter project was another project started in 2009, which was planned to start mass testing, and it will include 400,000 customers by 2020.

Belgium

Belgium started the Eandis smart meter project in 2007, in which 4300 smart meters have been installed in the pilot phase and with a plan to install 40,000 meters in the advanced phase. The communication interfaces available on the data collector are as follows: a power line communication; ethernet interface for home area network, wide area network, and local area network; M-bus interface; RS 485 interface; and optional GPRS or WiFi. This causes a reduction in technical losses of electricity by up to 0.15% per year, reduction in commercial losses up to 4.94% per year, and reduction in maintenance and operations costs up to 5.94% per year.

Finland

Finland started the Fortum smart meter project in November 2007 involving 583 customers. Energy savings calculated for this project were 28% per year, whereas reduction of operation and maintenance costs was 7% per year, and this project also included a reduction in commercial losses such as theft, fraud, etc., up to 1.1%.

Hungary

The EDF Demasz smart meter project was an initiative of Hungary that was started in February 2012. This was a pilot project including 2500 residential customers. A total of 3300 smart meters were expected to be installed for this project with 2800 GPRS communication modules and 530 meters with PCC communication. This project reduced meter reading and operation costs by 9.04%, operation and maintenance costs by 6.43%, electricity technical loss by 3.18%, and commercial losses such as thefts, frauds, etc., by 4.15%.

8.6.1 Data Flow Description

A city is divided into multiple cells based on transmission unit. Each cell has many electricity meters, which are installed for personal or business purposes. Each of these electricity meters for a particular cell will transmit electricity usage to its respective main distribution unit. The main distribution unit will collate all the data for that cell and then transmit the usage information to the main distribution unit (Figure 8.5).

The following information will be captured in this process:

1. Full hourly supply from the main distribution unit to the subdistribution unit
2. Hourly supply received by the subdistribution system

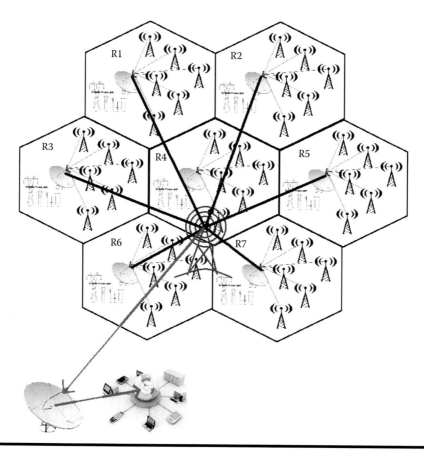

Figure 8.5   Data flow diagram.

3. Hourly supply distributed by subdistribution to consumers
4. Hourly usage by consumer to the subdistribution system
5. Hourly usage by the subdistribution system to the main distribution system

Setup in the main distribution system:

a. The main distribution system will capture meter reading on an hourly basis.
b. Hourly consumption is calculated using the software.

Setup in the subdistribution system:

a. The subdistribution system will capture meter reading on an hourly basis.
b. Hourly consumption is calculated using the software.

Setup in individual or business consumer place:

a. The meter reader will capture meter reading on an hourly basis.
b. Hourly consumption is calculated using the software.

8.6.2 Capturing of Data

The main system will transmit electricity to the subsystem. Meter reading at 00:00 hours is captured at the main system. The meter reading at the main system is MS0000 units. Here MS is the main station at 00:00 hours (Figure 8.6).

All subsystems will also capture the meter reading at 00:00 hours. Electricity is transmitted to individual or business consumers. Let these units be SS10000, SS20000, and so on. Here SS10000 is substation 1 at 00:00; SS20000 is substation 2 at 00:00.

At the individual or business consumer, the meter will capture the reading for 00:00 hours. Let the meter at this time be IMR10000, IMR20000, BMR10000, and so on: IMR10000 is individual meter reading 1 at 00:00, individual meter reading 2 at 00:00, business meter reading 1 at 00:00.

All individual or business consumer meters will transfer these meter readings to their corresponding substation at 00:00 hours. Meter reading would be transferred to the substation using a smart metering device, and the log will be of the form seen in Table 8.1.

The different parameters used for getting the data are as shown in Table 8.1. Here, CustomerID is the customer ID, Sub_Station_ID is the ID of the substation from which the electricity is distributed, Data and Time fields are related with the actual date and time of meter reading,

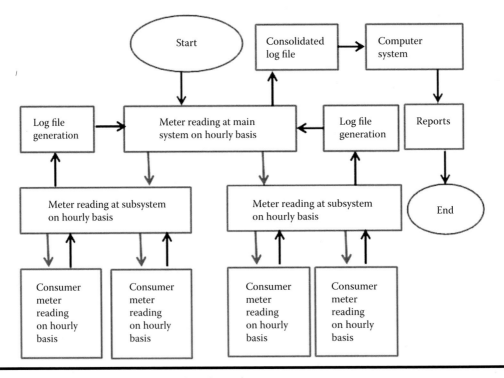

Figure 8.6 Procedure to capture data from the smart meter.

Table 8.1 Attributes from Smart Meter

CustomerID	Sub_Station_ID	Date	Time	Meter_Reading	Purpose_Type	Usage_Type

Purpose_Type is whether it is used for electricity meter purposes, water meter purposes, or gas meter purposes, and Usage_Type is personal or business.

This information from individual meters will be transmitted to the substation. The substation will collate all this information along with its usage and send the information to the main distribution system. The main distribution system will collate all the information from the sub-systems along with its usage and create a single log file every hour and send these log files every hour to the computer system for analysis purpose.

The data sent by individual meters at 00:00 hours is shown in Tables 8.2 through 8.7. The data sent by the substation to the main system is shown in Table 8.8. The data sent by the main station to the computer system at 00:00 hours is shown in Table 8.9.

Table 8.2   Meter Reading (Individual) at 00:00 Hours of Customer C0001

CustomerID	Sub_Station_ID	Date	Time	Meter_Reading	Purpose_Type	Usage_Type
C00001	Sub0001	00102015	0000	87569	EL	IN

Table 8.3   Meter Reading (Individual) at 00:00 Hours of Customer C00032

CustomerID	Sub_Station_ID	Date	Time	Meter_Reading	Purpose_Type	Usage_Type
C00032	Sub0001	00102015	0000	2341	EL	IN

Table 8.4   Meter Reading (Business Unit) at 00:00 Hours of Customer C00231

CustomerID	Sub_Station_ID	Date	Time	Meter_Reading	Purpose_Type	Usage_Type
C00231	Sub0001	00102015	0000	65432	EL	BU

Table 8.5   Meter Reading (Individual) at 00:00 Hours of Customer C00034

CustomerID	Sub_Station_ID	Date	Time	Meter_Reading	Purpose_Type	Usage_Type
C00034	Sub0002	00102015	0000	432111	EL	IN

Table 8.6   Meter Reading (Individual) at 00:00 Hours of Customer C00121

CustomerID	Sub_Station_ID	Date	Time	Meter_Reading	Purpose_Type	Usage_Type
C00121	Sub0002	00102015	0000	212111	EL	IN

Table 8.7 Meter Reading (Business Unit) at 00:00 Hours of Customer C00111

CustomerID	Sub_Station_ID	Date	Time	Meter_Reading	Purpose_Type	Usage_Type
C00111	Sub0002	00102015	0000	202111	EL	BU

Table 8.8 Meter Reading from Substation to Main Station

CustomerID	Sub_Station_ID	Date	Time	Meter_Reading	Purpose_Type	Usage_Type
Sub0002	M00001	00102015	0000	76523109	EL	DP
C00034	Sub0002	00102015	0000	432111	EL	IN
C00121	Sub0002	00102015	0000	212111	EL	IN
C00111	Sub0002	00102015	0000	202111	EL	BU

Table 8.9 Meter Reading from Main Station to Computer System at 00:00 Hours

CustomerID	Sub_Station_ID	Date	Time	Meter_Reading	Purpose_Type	Usage_Type
M00001	M00001	00102015	0000	462378901	EL	MD
Sub0001	M00001	00102015	0000	76533333	EL	DP
C00231	Sub0001	00102015	0000	65432	EL	BU
C00001	Sub0001	00102015	0000	87569	EL	IN
C00032	Sub0001	00102015	0000	2341	EL	IN
Sub0002	M00001	00102015	0000	76523109	EL	DP
C00034	Sub0002	00102015	0000	432111	EL	IN
C00121	Sub0002	00102015	0000	212111	EL	IN
C00111	Sub0002	00102015	0000	202111	EL	BU

Here:

MD is main distribution
DP is distribution purpose
IN is individual use
BU is business use

Similarly, data will be sent from the main system to the computer system at 01:00 hours. The meter reading updated for 01:00 hours is shown in Table 8.10.

Table 8.10   Meter Reading from Main Station to Computer System at 01:00 Hours

CustomerID	Sub_Station_ID	Date	Time	Meter_Reading	Purpose_Type	Usage_Type
M00001	M00001	00102015	0100	462371701	EL	MD
Sub0001	M00001	00102015	0100	76533633	EL	DP
C00231	Sub0001	00102015	0100	65532	EL	BU
C00001	Sub0001	00102015	0100	87669	EL	IN
C00032	Sub0001	00102015	0100	2391	EL	IN
Sub0002	M00001	00102015	0100	76523509	EL	DP
C00034	Sub0002	00102015	0100	432311	EL	IN
C00121	Sub0002	00102015	0100	212161	EL	IN
C00111	Sub0002	00102015	0100	202211	EL	BU

8.6.3 Processing of Data in Computer System

Data can be processed in the computer system by use of HDFS. Calculation of total load for the electricity system for a city with total connection is 100,000. Table 8.11 shows the type of parameters that need to be used for the project and size of data type.

8.6.4 Target Data in Computer System

Raw data after processing will look like those as shown in Table 8.12. Table 8.12 shows the size of data type for different fields that are being used for the project parameters.

These data can be converted to meaningful information using the reporting tool. The reporting tool will process the information as per the requirement based on parameters that

Table 8.11   Parameter Table

Filed Name	Data Type	Data Size
CustomerID	VARCHAR2	50
Sub_Station_ID	VARCHAR2	10
Date	VARCHAR2	8
Time	VARCHAR2	6
Meter_Reading	VARCHAR2	10
Purpose_Type	VARCHAR2	2
Usage_Type	VARCHAR2	2
Rec Size		88

Table 8.12 Data Type and Variable Type

Field Name	Data Type	Data Size
CustomerID	VARCHAR2	50
Sub_Station_ID	VARCHAR2	10
Date	VARCHAR2	8
Purpose_Type	VARCHAR2	2
Usage_Type	VARCHAR2	2
HH_Reading_00	VARCHAR2	10
HH_Reading_01	VARCHAR2	10
HH_Reading_02	VARCHAR2	10
HH_Reading_03	VARCHAR2	10
HH_Reading_04	VARCHAR2	10
HH_Reading_05	VARCHAR2	10
HH_Reading_06	VARCHAR2	10
HH_Reading_07	VARCHAR2	10
HH_Reading_08	VARCHAR2	10
HH_Reading_09	VARCHAR2	10
HH_Reading_10	VARCHAR2	10
HH_Reading_11	VARCHAR2	10
HH_Reading_12	VARCHAR2	10
HH_Reading_13	VARCHAR2	10
HH_Reading_14	VARCHAR2	10
HH_Reading_15	VARCHAR2	10
HH_Reading_16	VARCHAR2	10
HH_Reading_17	VARCHAR2	10
HH_Reading_18	VARCHAR2	10
HH_Reading_19	VARCHAR2	10
HH_Reading_20	VARCHAR2	10
HH_Reading_21	VARCHAR2	10
HH_Reading_22	VARCHAR2	10

(Continued)

Table 8.12 (Continued)   Data Type and Variable Type

Field Name	Data Type	Data Size
HH_Reading_23	VARCHAR2	10
Usage_00_01	VARCHAR2	10
Usage_01_02	VARCHAR2	10
Usage_02_03	VARCHAR2	10
Usage_03_04	VARCHAR2	10
Usage_04_05	VARCHAR2	10
Usage_05_06	VARCHAR2	10
Usage_06_07	VARCHAR2	10
Usage_07_08	VARCHAR2	10
Usage_08_09	VARCHAR2	10
Usage_09_10	VARCHAR2	10
Usage_10_11	VARCHAR2	10
Usage_11_12	VARCHAR2	10
Usage_12_13	VARCHAR2	10
Usage_13_14	VARCHAR2	10
Usage_14_15	VARCHAR2	10
Usage_15_16	VARCHAR2	10
Usage_16_17	VARCHAR2	10
Usage_17_18	VARCHAR2	10
Usage_18_19	VARCHAR2	10
Usage_19_20	VARCHAR2	10

need to be set. The reporting tool can process the information based on usage of a particular customer, which can be selected by using the CustomerID attribute provided by the smart meter, which provides information for each customer's electricity consumption on a real-time basis. The reporting tool can even provide information about the analysis of customer usage patterns on a daily or monthly basis so that customers can see and analyze their usage of electricity on a yearly, monthly, weekly, daily, hourly, or per minute basis and can adjust their electricity usage accordingly.

By using the reporting tool, a user can also distinguish electricity usage based on area-wise segmentation by using the parameter Sub_Station_ID, which will provide information on meter reading in a particular area, and that information can be used for analysis of electricity in a particular area to determine the usage pattern based on area to get a glimpse of electricity usage of the particular area and comparison of electricity usage based on area-wise segmentation. This area-wise segmentation can be done on a real-time basis, an hourly basis, a daily basis, a weekly basis, a monthly basis, or a yearly basis to get the electricity usage of that area and comparison of electricity usage with different areas.

By using the reporting tool, a user can also analyze the electricity usage based on usage type, which can be individual, main distribution, business use, etc., and based on this parameter, the user can have a glimpse of the electricity usage by the type of use of electricity for specific purposes, which can be used to provide the customer with time-of-use tariff flexibility for efficient load management. For example, if electricity usage for business purposes is low in the evening hours, then individual type users can be provided a low tariff electricity opportunity for using their heavy load appliances during odd hours. Thus, management of load can be done based on analysis of electricity usage type patterns.

Apart from all these usage reporting tools, the parameter purpose type can be used for further analysis of electricity metering. Thus, by using the purpose type parameter, a user can analyze electricity, water, or gas type of usage, and based on the type of data required, the analysis of specific purpose type can be calculated and analyzed. These data can also be calculated for water, electricity, gas, etc., on a real-time, hourly, weekly, monthly, or yearly basis, thus providing flexibility and scalability for the analysis of these data, which can be applied for different usage types.

Thus, using the SMAASH project, a user can get the analysis of data of different parameters and different usage patterns, which can be used for analysis of data on a real-time basis and different time-based parameters as per the requirements of the customer.

8.6.5 Advantage of the Project

The input data will be in the form of a meter image file termed the MIF, which is the meter readings sent by the smart meter at regular times in which the consumption will be in kWh to the service provider's local file server.

The expected result will be in the form of a graphical plot between the time (in years) versus expected electricity consumption on the basis of per day, per month, or per year or per user or per area depending on the use of the data requirement, and the predictive analysis of these data can be used to analyze load profile, which gives the result on the basis of load and time, so the user can be allocated a time-of-use tariff, which implies that during odd hours, home users can be provided with cheaper electricity for using heavy load appliances. The data can even be used to make the customer segmentation based on area-wise or type of usage. The analysis can also be used for linearizing the demand supply, which can be used to avoid problems such as grid failures on the basis of predictive data available from the analysis.

When comparing the above system with the current system, it is based on inclusion of manual interpretation of the data, which is hard to analyze as there is no technique to handle such a large amount of data, and interpret data based on prescribed parameters. In the proposed system, the suppliers can predict the consumption pattern of the customer beforehand and can predict the electricity consumption in the future (Figure 8.7).

In order to run this program, what we get is the raw data, and these data need to be processed in a manner that results in the final processed output. The MapReduce function is divided into two phases: the map phase and the reduce phase. Each phase has key value pairs as input and output, the type of which may be chosen by the programmer. These two phases are represented by the map function and the reduce function.

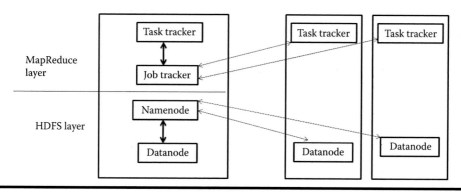

Figure 8.7 High-level architecture of HDFS.

The input to the map function is the raw data of the electricity reading that comes from the smart meter. The map function is just a data preparation phase that takes input from the raw data and pulls out the parameters, such as user type, meter reading, etc., from the raw data. We choose a text input format that gives us each line in the data set as a text value. The key is the offset of the beginning of the line from the beginning of the file because they are of no use, so we can ignore them. The map function is used for extracting customer ID, Sub_Station_ID, Date, Time, Meter_Reading, Purpose_Type, and Usage_Type from the raw data as these are the fields we are interested in. Thus, here the map function is only the data preparation phase, setting up the data in such a way that the reducer function can do its work on it. The map function finds a good place to drop the bad records, which are not needed as per the requirement. The output from the map function is processed by the MapReduce framework before being sent to the reduce function. This processing sorts and groups the key value pairs by key. The reduce function will iterate through the list and pick up the values as per the requirements set by the user, which can be based on customer ID; Sub_Station_ID; hourly, daily, weekly, monthly, or yearly; based on Purpose_Type; or based on Usage_Type. The values will be represented in the form of a graph as per the requirement for predicting the past and present usage, which can be used for predictive analysis of the usage based on the parameter set for the analysis. Comparative analysis based on customer ID will be used for predicting the usage of a particular customer on a per hour, per day, per month, or per year basis, and based on this prediction, the usage or theft of electricity can be determined and also used by the user for comparing his daily, monthly, or yearly usage of electricity. Comparison analysis can be based on Sub_Station_ID or can be by area ID. The average consumption of a particular substation or a particular area can be determined on an hourly, daily, monthly, or yearly basis, which is used for determining the energy consumption of a particular area and can be used for determining the predictive analysis of the usage of that area, which can be used for determining the climatic usage of an area, load analysis of an area, and other requirements. Predictive analysis can be done based on usage type and purpose type, which also can be used for finding the time at which the load is maximum, and based on this analysis, we can make the time-of-use tariff option for the user if load usage for industry purposes is low in the evening hours and then electricity can be provided at lower rates for home usage during those hours so that home users can use heavy appliances during those hours.

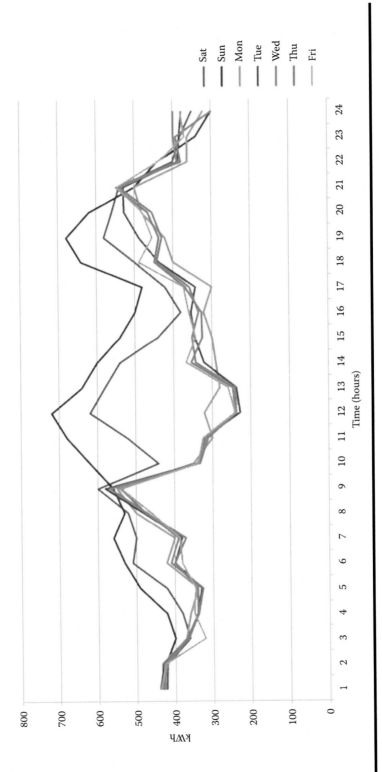

Figure 8.8 Household data consumption pattern.

8.7 Output

Figure 8.8 shows the output for the electricity usage pattern of a customer on an hourly basis for each day, thus providing analysis of the electricity usage pattern from a customer's real-time analysis, which can be used to predict the usage pattern on various days, and the factors that affect the load can be analyzed based on the output parameter.

The output in Figure 8.8 is calculated based on a master–slave pattern arrangement of clusters made by the namenode and datanode, where the namenode acts as master and the datanode acts as slave.

Thus, using a data analytics platform for the smart grid is capable of analyzing slowly and rapidly changing data using a combination of batch and real-time data processing techniques, and is therefore useful in calculating data on a real-time basis on various parameters and can be used for efficient power management.

References

Britton T., 2013, Smart metering: Enable for effective and rapid post meter leakage identification and water loss management, *Journal of Cleaner Production* 54: 166–176.

Brophy-Haney A., Jamasb T., Pollitt M.G., 2009. Smart metering and electricity demand: Technology, economics and international experience, Electricity Policy Research Group Working Paper EPRG003. University of Cambridge, United Kingdom.

Chang F., Dean J., Ghemawat S., Hsieh W.C., Wallach D.A., Burrows M., Chandra T., Fikes A., Gruber R.E., 2006, Bigtable: A Distributed Storage System for Structured Data, OSDI 2006, 1–14.

Darby S., 2010. Smart metering: What potential for householder engagement? Build. Research and Information 38(5), ISSN0961-3281, print/ISSN 1466-4321, online, 2010 Taylor & Francis, 442–457.

De Witt D., Stonebraker M., 2008, MapReduce: A major step backwards, http://databasecolumn.vertica.com/2008/01/mapreduce-a-major-step-back.html, 1–9.

Depuru S.S.S.R., Wang L, Devabhaktuni V., 2011, Smart meters for power grid: Challenges, issues, advantages and status, *Renewable and Sustainable Energy Reviews*, 2736–2742.

Momoh J.A., 2009, Smart grid design for efficient and flexible power networks operation and control. Power System Conference and Exposition, PSCE '09. IEEE/PES, 1–8.

White T., 2013, *Hadoop—The Definitive Guide*, 4th Edition, O' Reilly, ISBN-10: 1491901632, ISBN-13: 978-1491901632.

Chapter 9

Service-Oriented Architecture for Big Data and Business Intelligence Analytics in the Cloud

Muthu Ramachandran

Computing, Creative Technologies, and Engineering School, Faculty of Arts, Environment and Technology, Leeds Beckett University, Leeds, United Kingdom

Contents

Abstract

Service-oriented architecture (SOA) has emerged, supporting scalability and service reuse. At the same time, Big Data analytics has impacted on business services and business process management. However, there is a lack of a systematic engineering approach to Big Data analytics. This chapter provides a systematic approach to SOA design strategies and business process for Big Data analytics. Our approach is based on SOA reference architecture and service component model for Big Data applications, known as softBD and also includes a large-scale, real-world case study demonstrating our approach to SOA for Big Data analytics. SOA Big Data architecture is scalable, generic, and customizable for a variety of data applications. The main contribution of this chapter includes a unique, innovative, and generic softBD framework, service component model, and a generic SOA architecture for large-scale Big Data applications. This chapter also contributes to Big Data metrics, which allows measurement and evaluation when analyzing data.

9.1 Introduction

Distributed systems have been developed and deployed in a traditional software architecture model based on layered architecture. However, this has not able to provide a sustainable IT system that is cost-effective. Therefore, SOA has emerged to address this issue and has emerged with key design principles, such as loose coupling, service reusability, service composability, and service discoverability. The SOA deployment model is based on a service provider publishing its services through a registry and a service requester being able access the published services, compose new services, and request new services. The major challenge of this work is to integrate SOA for Big Data applications. Big Data has emerged to address the challenges faced by the volume, velocity, and veracity of data being received and analyzed in real time. Therefore, we need an SOA model that tackles the required speed and accuracy of data. The model proposed in this chapter aims to achieve these two characteristics. This way, this chapter aims to achieve the merging of two major issues (SOA and Big Data). Zimmermann et al. (2013) emphasize the need for an enterprise SOA architecture for Big Data applications and have proposed the enterprise reference architecture cube (ESARC) for such large-scale application.

Big Data has become a key business improvement indicator for large businesses and the key indicator of success in the cloud and IoT computing technologies. Big Data can be defined as the management of data received from different sources on the use and behavior of a system in real time at the scale of terabytes, petabytes, etc. The size of the data depends on the nature of the systems, such as mobile phone usage, web usage, social media usage, real-time Internet and sensor data received, and streaming media data received and sent. In formal terms, Big Data has been defined as the 5Vs model (volume, velocity, variety, value, and veracity). Value and veracity are two essential characteristics that specify the need for valuable and truthful data (Neves and Bernardino 2016). Therefore, it is important for businesses and organizations to develop a long-term strategy for managing, monitoring, analyzing, and predicting data. We have identified a measure of Big Data value:

$$\text{Value (of data/information)} \propto \sqrt{\text{Number of Business Users (BU)}} \times \text{Number of Business Areas} \quad (9.1)$$

As Equation 9.1 suggests, the value of Big Data is directly proportional (increases in value) to the square root of a number of business users, which is multiplied by the business areas in which they work. The need to integrate business intelligence and business process modeling for Big Data with SOA is the key to achieving business value as suggested by Curko et al. (2007). The SOA concept is a key technology for integration of BI, BPMS, transaction, Big Data, and other IT systems.

However, there is a lack of business intelligence analytics applied to large-scale Big Data that has been received from multiple sources and also a lack of applying intelligence and enterprise architecture for large-scale Big Data that are emerging from multiple business and data sources. In addition, existing approaches (Zimmermann et al. 2013) in this area don't consider applying intelligence analytics for prediction by applying soft computing methods, such as Bayesian theory, fuzzy logic, and neurofuzzy.

This chapter divides into two major sections: an SOA approach for Big Data with SOA reference architecture and a service component model for Big Data applications and, second, a large-scale, real-world case study demonstrating our approach to SOA for Big Data analytics. Our approach is a scalable Big Data architecture model, which is generic and customizable for a variety of data applications. The main contribution of this chapter includes a unique, innovative, and generic softBD framework, a service component model, and a generic SOA architecture for large-scale Big Data applications. This chapter also contributes to Big Data metrics, which allows us to measure and evaluate when analyzing the data.

9.2 SOA-Based Soft Computing Framework for Big Data

One of the key reasons for choosing the soft compute approach is to apply predictions to the large amount of data being generated by IoT, IoE, the cloud system, and other sources, such as user-generated data. Existing approaches in this area have considered architecture data, but have not considered predictive analysis based on the currently collected and previously collected data for the similar situation. SOA has emerged, supporting scalability and service reuse. At the same time, Big Data analytics has impacted on business services. This chapter provides a systematic approach for SOA design strategies and business processes for Big Data analytics. Distributed systems have been developed and deployed in a traditional software architecture model based on layered architecture. However, this has not been able to provide a sustainable IT system that is cost-effective. Therefore, SOA has emerged to address this issue and has emerged with key design principles, such as loose coupling, service reusability, service composability, and service discoverability as shown in Figure 9.1. Thus, this chapter has proposed a reference architecture that is based on SOA and that has the potential to solve the classical problem of customization, composability, interoperability, etc. The major focus of this chapter is to integrate SOA for Big Data applications. Consequently, Big Data have emerged to address the challenges faced by the volume, velocity, and veracity of data being received and analyzed in real time. Therefore, we need an SOA model that tackles the required speed and accuracy of data. The model proposed in this chapter aims to achieve these two characteristics. Earlier studies emphasize the need for an enterprise SOA architecture for Big Data applications and have proposed ESARC for such large-scale applications. Consistent with earlier studies, this research aims to achieve merging two major issues (SOA and Big Data).

Big Data is now a reality for businesses. Examples include Google's Gmail, which is an exabyte of data; Amazon web services, streaming media globally every second; and other real-time life-sensitive data, such as media, weather forecasts, earth monitoring, space application data, etc. However, we need a structured model to select, process, and monitor highly relevant data. In this

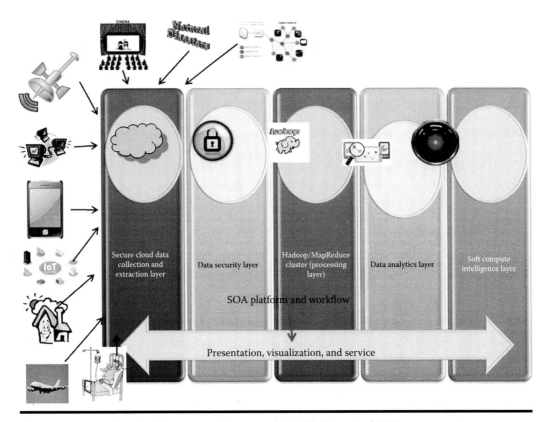

Figure 9.1 SOA-based soft compute framework for Big Data (softBD).

context, Gorton (2013, 2014) describes a lightweight risk reduction approach to Big Data, known as lightweight evaluation and architecture prototyping for Big Data (LEAP4BD). This provides a good starting point for organizations to use a semantic knowledge-based tool for data selection and acquisition. However, it is yet another tool for data extraction. Similarly, Li et al. (2015) has proposed a framework for geoscience Big Data, which is multidimensional data, and Hadoop (HBase) has been adopted for storing and managing multidimensional geoscientific data, and a MapReduce-based parallel algorithm has been used for processing such data. This framework does propose large-scale data extraction, but it lacks in generalization and application of SOA architecture.

Therefore, we have proposed an SOA-based soft compute framework for big data (softBD) with soft compute intelligence algorithms for decision making when collecting, selecting and extracting, validating, and evaluating the data. In addition, soft compute algorithms, such as neurofuzzy and Bayesian theory, allow data prediction based on historical data collected. A softBD framework is shown in Figure 9.1

The softBD starts receiving data continuously with cloud platforms, such as Amazon EC2, Windows Azure, Google, Salesforce, etc. The data can be from multiple sources, including geoscience; entertainment monitoring, selection, and prediction (home, cinema, theater, etc.); aircraft monitoring; IoT devices; health care; mobile, wireless sensor networks (WSNs); and natural disaster areas such as fire, flood, earthquake, and epidemics. The cloud is the most suitable platform as it provides elastic services to store and maintain data globally. The next layer is the data-clustering layer, using the Hadoop platform, which can be part of the chosen cloud platform. This layer does the data processing, categorizing the data into entertainment, geoscience, WSN, etc. The next layer is the data analytics layer, which could include Hadoop/MapReduce algorithms to speed up analyzing the data parallelization. The big challenge in Hadoop is resource allocation and scheduling for parallel high-performance computing. The final layer on the vertical services is our new soft compute intelligence layer, which includes algorithms and models on fuzzy logic, nuerofuzzy, and Bayesian theory. The main purpose of this service layer is to offer prediction models on the categorized and analyzed data. This also covers the data evaluation, assessment, and validation. All of the vertical layers are based on the SOA providing loosely coupled services.

9.2.1 SOA Design Characteristics

SOA has emerged to tackle legacy system design for distributed information system problems and limitations by providing loosely coupled systems in which new business services can be composed and reused. The enterprise of data requirements can be explained by the relation database management system (RDBMS) term. An enterprise that is based on the RDBMS would be willing to adopt dedicated database servers and present query services to SOA components or a database application. These two designs have been accepted for more than five years. This is very successful because of the three dimensions that are query as a service (QaaS). The QaaS is not directly linked to the data storage, but it is mapped to the data storage by a single RDBMS architecture. The major problem of maintaining Big Data is the double entry or duplication; this is easily solved by the single architecture system.

Most Big Data are not maintained in a frequent manner as this would be massive; the data can be nonstructural, nonrelational, or even nonupdated. It is very difficult to abstract it to a query service if it is not in good form. Big Data is not easy to store in an order as it will be in different places where it is connected by networks or the data can be in different formats. These types of problems are handled easily by the two different broad choices in SOA, namely the horizontal and vertical integrated data models.

The horizontal integrated data model uses multiple interfaces to the applications and provides a data management facility with full integrity as the actual data is collected behind an abstract set of data services. The data are not accessed by the components directly, but the process is done in the form of service in the same way as it is done in the single RDBMS architecture. The data management and the application components are kept separate and maintained, not keeping in contact. Although this approach can't create the simple query model of RDBMS for the reasons already given, it at least replicates the simple model of RDBMS that we presented earlier.

The vertically integrated data model links application data services to resources in a more application-specific way, in which the customer relationship management, enterprise resource planning, or dynamic data authentication application is largely separated first at the as-a-service level, and that separation is maintained down to the data infrastructure. In this model, the application most of the time might have the SOA component, which accesses the data storage by itself. To supply well-structured and maintained data integrity, there is a hazard of sacrificing the management service as SOA components that deliver the ability to work on various data systems doing the common task, such as filtering the duplication and matching the integrity, in database-specific ways. This access is easier to conform to the data structure and the application. SOA reference architecture is discussed, in detail, in the later section of this chapter.

Therefore, it is essential to understand the foundations of SOA design that can be tailored for Big Data applications. Figure 9.2 shows the desired design characteristics for solving Big Data

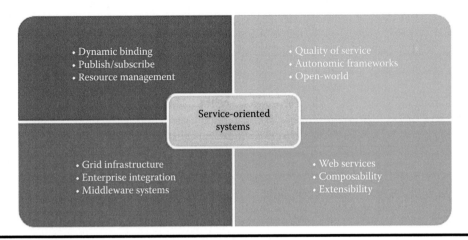

Figure 9.2 SOA design characteristics.

processing requirements. As shown in the figure, the characteristics evolved from the large systematic literature as well as the requirements for Big Data analytics, which are shown in Figure 9.3.

However, there are some fundamental characteristics of SOA presented by Erl (2005) as follows:

- Business-driven.
- Vendor-neutral.
- Enterprise-centric.
- Composition-centric.
- Loosely coupled.
- Every service has a contract.
- Service can be discovered.
- Services are abstract.
- Services are autonomous.
- Services can be composed.
- Services are stateless with respect to complete transactions.
- Services are reusable.

These are essential characteristics of SOA, and SOA-based services are business-driven and should be designed with principles of loose coupling and message-driven services, which are autonomous. Figure 9.3 shows the different approaches to Big Data that have provided us an

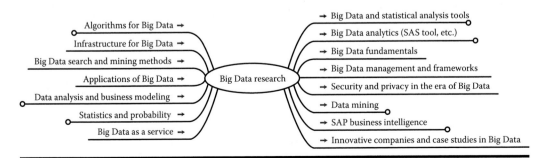

Figure 9.3 Big Data research directions.

insight into developing an SOA reference architecture for Big Data analytics that supports various demands for analytics. We have extended this work to include financial data predictions based on SOA (Chang and Ramachandran 2015).

9.2.2 SOA Reference Architecture and Infrastructure for Big Data Applications

Component-based software engineering has been successful in leveraging large-scale reuse and productivity (Ramachandran 2008, 2011, 2013). Therefore, components-based service development has been a natural choice as it supports service design principles as well as Big Data design principles of security; privacy; and large-scale, real-time processing; and customization. Figure 9.4 provides a service component model for Big Data applications. It is customizable and provides services with two types of interfaces, such as "providers" and "requires." The requires interface is a semi-arc with interfaces on IRealTimeData and ISensorData. The provider interfaces include IDataPreProcessing to IDataCustomisation&Presentation.

Designing relevant architecture is the key for processing and analyzing data at the required scale. Oracle (2013) has proposed a reference architecture for Big Data analytics and discusses that any reference architecture for Big Data should consider including *Any Data Any Source*, a full range of applications and integrated analytic applications. Oracle's proposed reference architecture is based on a layered model and focuses on three main layers of the architecture: universal information management, real-time analytics, and intelligent processes. However, it is based on a traditional layered architecture model, which will have similar problems as the traditional IT

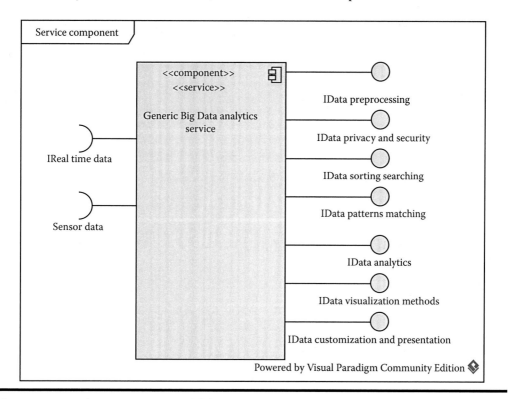

Figure 9.4 Service component model for Big Data.

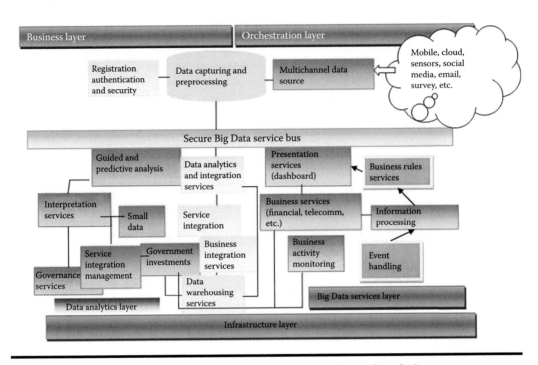

Figure 9.5 SOA reference architecture for Big Data processing and analytics.

systems. Therefore, in this chapter we have proposed a reference architecture that is based on SOA, which is to solve the classical problems of customization, composability, secure Big Data service bus, interoperability, etc. Figure 9.5 shows the SOA reference architecture model for Big Data processing and analytics. As shown in the figure, it is divided into four layers. The first layer consists of business and orchestration in which new business services in Big Data monitoring, analyzing, organizing, and prediction take place. The second layer is the most important layer that integrates and scales Big Data applications and data sources. This is the backbone of the SOA concept: that all communication and data flows through the service bus, which is central to enterprise integration.

The third layer shows data analytics and other Big Data services, such as guided analytics, integration, policies, event handling, business rules, business activity monitoring, etc. This also includes horizontal and vertical data integration.

9.2.3 SOSE Iterative Methodology for Soft Compute Approach for Big Data Analytics

Service computing has emerged to address IT systems development and the maintenance life cycle by reducing cost and improving efficiency and reuse. However, existing approaches to service computing have been ad hoc and opportunistic. This chapter proposes a systematic approach that is based on established software engineering best practices. Figure 9.6 shows the SOSE approach to Big Data analytics. This consists of a number of steps that are interactive, starting from our softBD, which provides data from multiple sources. The next step is to use soft computing models to analyze data and conduct some prediction patterns: knowledge discovery. The next step is to use BPMN models for business intelligence; this process includes developing the UI interface: simulation to validate the business process to make sure they are viable and efficient. The next phase is

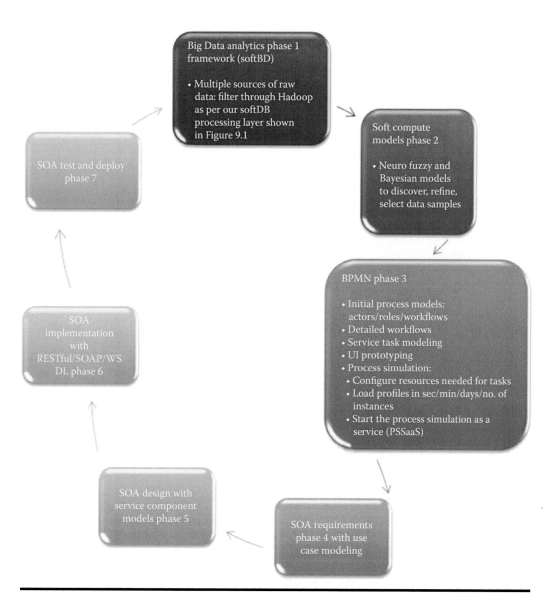

Figure 9.6 SOSE Iterative methodology for soft compute Big Data analytics.

to develop service requirements using traditional requirement engineering processes, such as use cases, story cards, etc. The next step is to start developing a service design in which task modeling approaches can be used and finally test and deployment.

9.3 Case Study: British Energy Power & Energy Trading Ltd. (BEPET)

The concept of service orientation (Erl 2005, p. 291) can be applied to analyze, design, and implement a new system for British Energy Power & Energy Trading Ltd. (BEPET). First, the business process would be modeled using business process model notations, that is, BPMN models (Pant and Juric 2008). The BPMN modeling would be carried out using BonitaSoft (2015a). Using advanced features of the tool, user interfaces would be generated, and a process simulation would be carried out for particular workflows. Services would then be identified to realize these workflows. Next, use case models would be generated using Enterprise Architect (2015). All identified services would be classified (Erl 2005, p. 392; Sommerville 2010), and any nonfunctional requirements would be identified. Next, as a part of the service design, the system architecture comprising the orchestration, business, and application layer services would be identified (Erl 2005, p. 336). Then, the component models would be generated using Enterprise Architect (2015), elaborating how these services would interact with each other. And finally, these services would be implemented in J2EE (Java EE 2015) using SOAP (SOAP specifications 2015) and WSDL (Web Service Definition Language 2015) technologies.

BEPET totally rethought both the way it designs software and its relationships with suppliers as a result of shifting to a service-led model for delivering IT. The energy company moved to a process-driven architecture, deliberately shunning the SOA label to disassociate itself from the hype. The move enabled BEPET to prioritize processes and make IT better serve the business. "Processes are the DNA of our organization. We had to focus on higher-value activities, rather than factory-type programming, to be in good shape for future business. There are no prizes for second place," says Jeremy Lock, IT manager at BEPET in 2017.

Having an SOA would enable the IT department to support value-added processes rather than supporting functionality in a more piecemeal way. In order to facilitate this shift, BEPET divided its business applications into three categories of services, defining a service as a self-contained and independent unit of work. The three categories were a task requiring a human decision, an information service, and a functional service. Technology services supports all of these three categories.

Converting these activities into services has exposed the energy company to some new ways of thinking about intellectual property rights and the execution of design. "Traditionally, we bought packages and did little bespoke development. We would lob our requirements into the marketplace, get bids back, build them, and then accept or reject," Lock says.

However, using an SOA entails a shift in thinking about intellectual property rights. Within the new regime, BEPET looks at the best of breed packages on the market but does not customize. When packages are lacking in functionality, the team writes a service to supplement it. "Whether the service is inside or outside a package, we have to connect to it. And the intellectual property rights of every service have to be captured within our model."

This means that BEPET may own the intellectual property rights of a service within a package, an unusual concept for some software and system integrators. "The big five consultancies all have their own method for implementing packages. And we are now saying to them, 'we want you to do it our way,'" says Lock.

Harvesting reuse, another major objective of the SOA investment, has also called for a radical rethink of the design, says Lock, "You need to design business services at the right atomic level. And an upfront investment in design is crucial if you are going to get reuse later down the line. It really challenges all the normal paradigms of software design and support." Even companies that are compliant with the IT Infrastructure Library (ITIL), breaking everything into a more granular units makes everything more complex by default.

"We have a team of seven supporting 60-odd applications, and when I tell them we are breaking these into services, they are rightly concerned about the risks," says Lock. Governance perhaps represents the biggest expenditure of effort in moving to SOA. "Only 30% of SOA is about development; the rest is about governance and managing services. Working with partners accelerates the adoption rate, but it is important to internalize the lessons and to assume control."

9.3.1 Assumptions

- BEPET sells two types of energy resources—that is, gas and electricity. These are sold to direct customers (B2C) or to other companies (B2B).
- Direct customers of BEPET can be of two types: regular customers or online-only customers.
- The regular customers receive their bills based on meter readings taken by BEPET, and the online customers submit their own meter readings using the customer user interface and thereby receive an online customer discount.
- Direct customers can pay their bills either by direct debit or after the bill has been generated for each billing period either monthly or quarterly.
- Business customers have a dedicated business sales team assigned to them.
- Business customers can buy energy—that is, gas or electricity—from BEPET only after they have entered into a legal contract with BEPET.
- The business sales team, comprising the sales representative and the sales manager, is responsible for creating and maintaining these contracts.
- Business customers need to enter into a separate contract for each energy type—that is, gas and electricity—that they are interested in buying from BEPET.
- Business customer contracts are end-dated only—that is, they are not deleted from the system but are retained for audit purposes.
- After entering into a contract with BEPET, business customers can buy their energy in bulk over a period of time or, in exceptional cases, request an ad hoc energy top up at the rates agreed in their business contracts.
- Business customers can only pay BEPET using CHAPS transfer mechanisms because they deal with significantly large amounts.
- Direct customers can contact the BEPET call center if they have any issues.
- The BEPET call center only deals with the direct customers and not the business customers.
- When customers call the call center, the call center staff would usually take their customer details and use these to search the customer accounts on their internal system. And they can update this system as appropriate.
- The call center staff can also raise a refund request for the customer in exceptional cases. These refund requests need to be approved by their call center managers before they are sent to the accounts team for processing of the refund.
- Only the use cases relevant to the BEPET core energy B2B and B2C businesses have been modeled. For instance, the call center manager would also have additional responsibilities, such as managing the call center team, reporting to management, appraisals, etc. As these are no more relevant to the BEPET core business, they have not been modeled in the use case diagrams.
- Similarly, only the departments within BEPET that directly deal with the core energy business have been considered. For instance, BEPET would have additional departments, such as marketing, sales, HR, etc. As these are not directly involved in the energy business, they have not been considered for this activity.
- Meter readers travel to the local end user premises with handheld devices, which can directly synchronize with the BEPET servers.
- It is assumed that the inventory management system is an existing process written in a low-level language, and it works as expected. Because it very rarely requires updates and due to the prohibitively high cost and potential business impact of migrating it to a new system, BEPET has made a business decision to not migrate it to the new system for now.

9.3.2 Business Process Modeling

To understand the various business workflows, the business processes for BEPET would be modeled using BonitaSoft (2015a). Before the BPMN models are generated, the various actors involved in the business process are identified based on the role that they perform within the business process, and the workflows that these actors would be involved in are shortlisted (Pant and Juric 2008). These actors can either be external actors, such as the direct customer or the business customer, or they can be internal actors such as the call center representative, business sales representative, etc. There are also some automated "system" actors, such as the payment gateway, bank interface, etc.

Table 9.1 presents a list of workflows that has been identified for external actors.

9.3.3 BPMN Process Models for BEPET

Once all the workflows have been identified, the business process models have been generated using the BonitaSoft Community Edition BPM Studio software (BonitaSoft 2015a). As seen from the business process model, the interactions between the various business processes have been captured well. Additionally, the trigger for each business process as well as the exchange of any business messages or notifications has been captured in the BPMN model.

9.3.4 User Interface Screens Using BonitaSoft

The workflow for business sales was used to generate the sample user interface screens for BEPET (BonitaSoft 2015b). The next few screenshots indicate how this process was carried out. To generate these UI screens, the following workflow process was utilized, and the BPMN model for adding a new contract business process is shown in Figure 9.7 and its UI interface is shown in Figure 9.8.

Table 9.1 External Actors

Actors/Roles	Workflows	Workflow Business Processes
Direct customer	Direct customer	Login
	UI interaction	Record readings
	Workflow	View bill
		Pay bill
		Add/Update direct debit details
		Check energy consumption
		View/Modify personal details
Business customer	Business customer	Buy energy in bulk
	Interaction workflow	Ad hoc energy top up
		Make payment

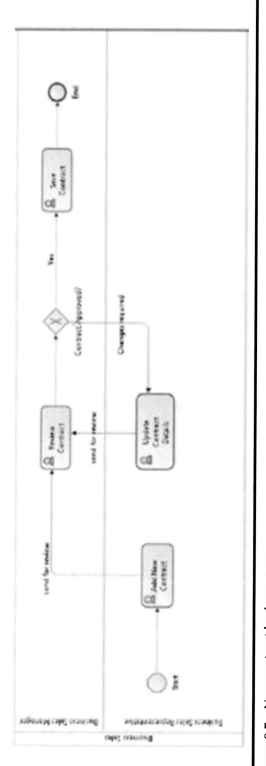

Figure 9.7 New contract business process.

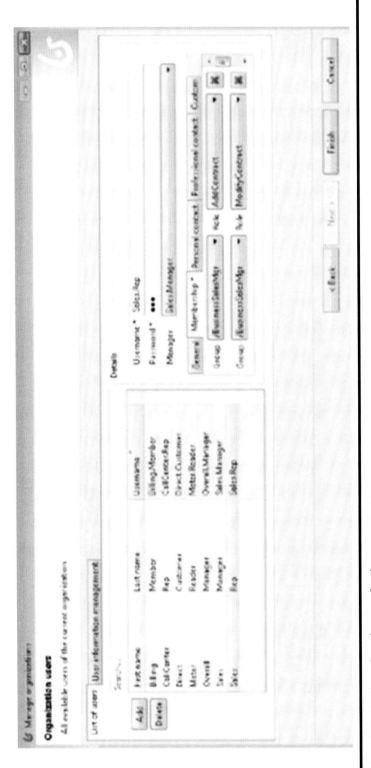

Figure 9.8 UI interface for new business contract.

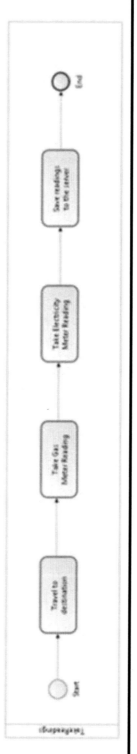

Figure 9.9 Meter reading business process.

The groups, roles, and users in the BEPET organization were created for billing, call center, customer direct, meter reading, overall manager, sales manager, and sales rep.

9.3.5 Process Simulation Using BonitaSoft

The workflow for "Take Meter Reading" was used to perform a process simulation activity in Bonita BPM Studio (BonitaSoft 2015c). This process is used to identify opportunities for process optimization. The next few screenshots indicate how the simulation process was carried out.

To generate these reports using BonitaSoft, the following workflow process was utilized as shown in Figure 9.9. For each task in the workflow, the required time was configured as shown in Figure 9.10. And the resources needed to perform the task were configured as shown in Figure 9.11. Next required load profiles were added as shown in Figure 9.12. And, finally, the simulation process was started as shown in Figure 9.13. This produced the report as shown in Figure 9.14.

9.3.6 Cost Optimization

The cost of providing the "meter reading service" to "regular customers" was identified using this process simulation. This also allowed BEPET to determine the extent of discount that it can offer its "online-only customers." This allowed BEPET to differentiate itself from other similar energy providers by providing additional cost savings. The manpower cost estimates generated are shown in Figure 9.15.

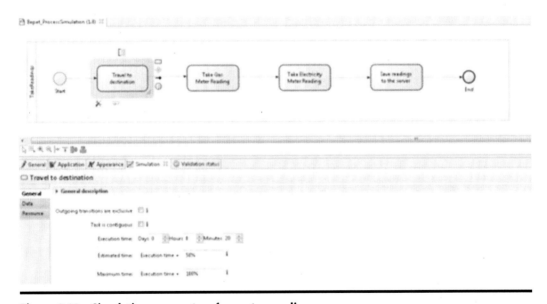

Figure 9.10   Simulation parameters for meter reading.

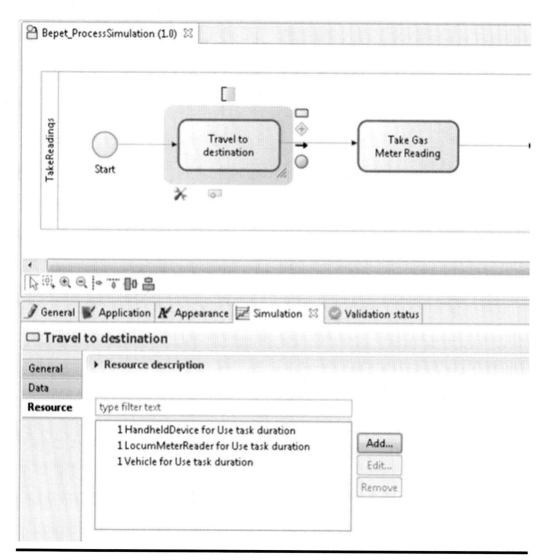

Figure 9.11 Resource configuration simulation parameters.

9.3.7 Resource Profiling

Process simulation also enabled BEPET to identify an optimal resource profile for its meter reading operations. It could identify, using load profiles that varied on the basis of number of customers, how many meter readers it would need to hire and whether it would be advisable to hire locum meter readers or simply hire them as permanent staff. BEPET could also perform a comparative assessment of providing the meter reading services only on weekdays versus throughout the week. As seen from Figure 9.16, the wait time increases over the weekend due to lack of human resources.

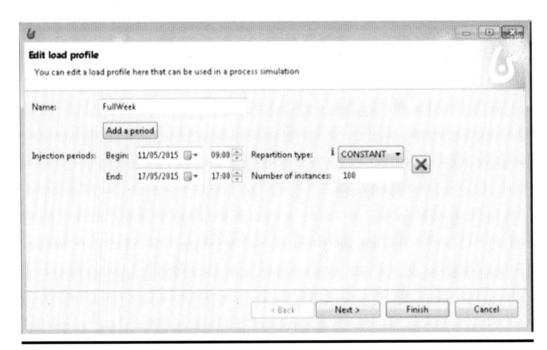

Figure 9.12 Load profile for simulation of meter reading BPMN.

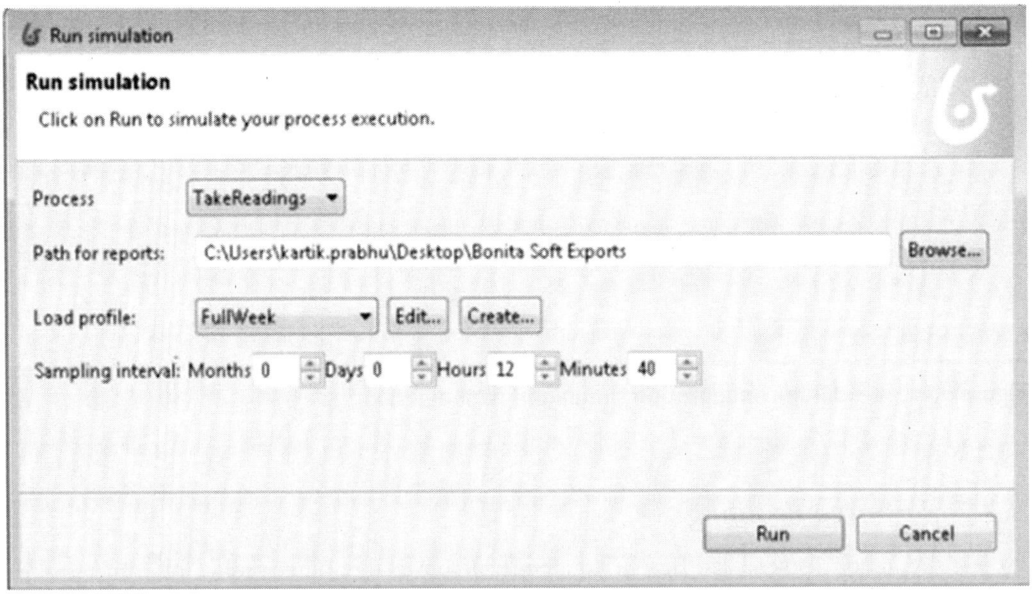

Figure 9.13 Starting the business process simulation.

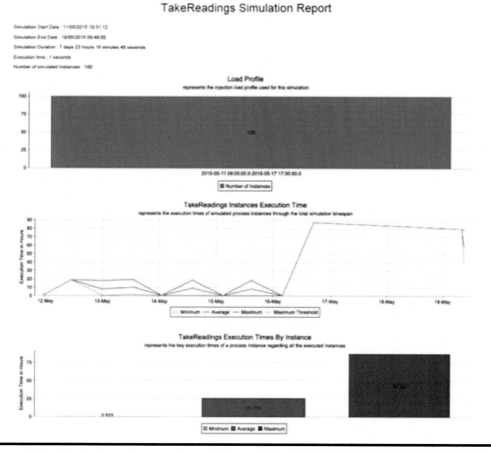

Figure 9.14   Simulation output graphs.

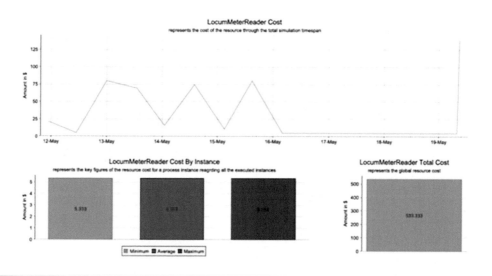

Figure 9.15   Cost optimization for meter reading business process.

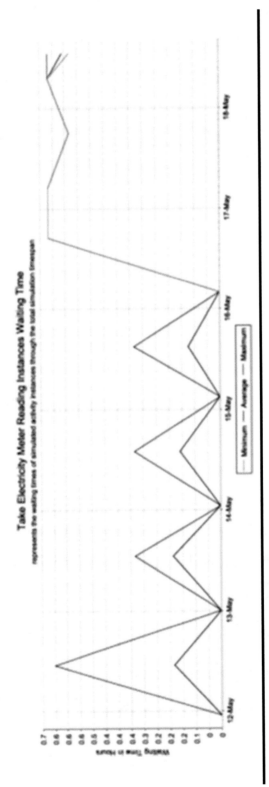

Figure 9.16 Resource profile simulation.

9.4 Conclusion

This chapter has contributed a unique, innovative, and generic softBD framework, service component model, and a generic SOA architecture for large-scale Big Data applications. This chapter has also contributed to Big Data metrics, which allows measurement and evaluation when analyzing the data. Developing a new system for BEPET has made it possible to apply the concept of service orientation. Business process modeling has allowed a better understanding of BEPET's businesses. The application of the various techniques for service analysis and design has enabled a better understanding of the decision-making involved in developing a real-world system. The execution has made it possible to explore the subjects confronted in developing a complex system. The proposed methodologies softBD and SOSE have demonstrated a systematic engineering approach to full life cycle service engineering, which has resulted in high-quality services and assurance.

References

BEPET (2017) Case studies in implementing service oriented architecture (SOA), http://www.computerweekly.com/feature/Case-studies-in-implementing-service-oriented-architecture-SOA. [Accessed January 24, 2017].

BonitaSoft (2015a) BonitaSoft—Open Source Workflow & BPM Software. Available at: http://www.bonitasoft.com/. [Accessed May 5, 2015].

BonitaSoft (2015b) Create and Run Your First Process | BonitaSoft | Open Source Workflow & BPM software. Available at: http://www.bonitasoft.com/for-you-to-read/videos/create-and-run-your-first-process. [Accessed May 3, 2015].

BonitaSoft (2015c) Simulate Processes for Better Optimization | Bonitasoft |Open Source Workflow & BPM software. Available at: http://www.bonitasoft.com/for-you-to-read/videos/simulate-processes-better-optimization. [Accessed May 5, 2015].

Chang, V., and Ramachandran, M. (2015) *Quality of service for financial software as a service,* ESaaSa 2015-CLOSER 2015.

Curko, K., Bach, P. M., and Rodonic, G. (2007) Business intelligence and business process management in banking operations, Proceedings of the ITI 2007 29th Int. Conf. on Information Technology Interfaces, June 25–28, 2007, Cavtat, Croatia.

Enterprise Architect (2015) Enterprise Architect - UML Design Tools and UML CASE tools for software development. Available at: http://www.sparxsystems.com/products/ea/. [Accessed May 6, 2015].

Erl, T. (2005) *Service-oriented architecture: concepts, technology and design.* Prentice Hall.

Gorton, I. (2013) SEI Blogs, Addressing the software engineering challenges of Big Data, Ian Gortan's report. Available at: https://insights.sei.cmu.edu/sei_blog/2013/10/addressing-the-software-engineering-challenges-of-big-data.html.

Gorton, I. (2014) The importance of software architecture in Big Data systems. Available at: https://insights.sei.cmu.edu/sei_blog/2014/01/the-importance-of-software-architecture-in-big-data-systems.html.

Java Platform (2015) Java Platform, Enterprise Edition (Java EE) | Oracle Technology Network | Oracle. Available at: http://www.oracle.com/technetwork/java/javaee/overview/index.html. [Accessed May 10, 2015].

Li, Z. et al. (2015) Enabling big geoscience data analytics with a cloud-based, MapReduce-enabled and service-oriented workflow framework, *PLOS One,* Doi: 10.1371/journal.pone.0116781.

Neves, C. P., and Bernardino, J. (2016) Big Data in the cloud: A survey. *Open Journal of Big Data (OJBD)* Volume 1, Issue 2.

Oracle (2013) Big Data & analytics reference architecture, an Oracle white paper.

Pant, K., and Juric, M. (2008) Business Process Driven SOA using BPMN and BPEL. Packt Publishing.

Ramachandran, M. (2008) *Software components: Guidelines and applications,* Nova Science.

Ramachandran, M. (2011) *Software components for cloud computing architectures and applications,* Springer, Mahmood, Z., and Hill, R. (eds.). www.springer.com/computer/communication+networks /book/978-1-4471-2235-7.

Ramachandran, M. (2013) *Business requirements engineering for developing cloud computing services,* Springer, Software Engineering Frameworks for Cloud Computing Paradigm, Mahmood, Z., and Saeed, S. (eds.), http://www.springer.com/computer/communication+networks/book/978-1-4471-5030-5.

SOAP Specifications (2015) SOAP Specifications. Available at: http://www.w3.org/TR/soap/. [Accessed May 9, 2015].

Sommerville, I. (2010) *Software Engineering, 9th Edition.* Pearson Education.

WSDL (2015) Web Service Definition Language (WSDL). Available at: http://www.w3.org/TR/wsdl .html. [Accessed May 9, 2015].

Zimmermann, A. et al. (2013) Towards service-oriented enterprise architectures for Big Data applications in the cloud, 17th IEEE International Enterprise Distributed Object Computing Conference Workshops.

APPLICATIONS OF COMPUTATIONAL INTELLIGENCE

Chapter 10

Rough Set and Neighborhood Systems in Big Data Analysis

B. K. Tripathy

School of Computing Science and Engineering, VIT University, Vellore, Tamil Nadu, India

Contents

Abstract

The notion of a rough set was introduced by Pawlak, and its extensions have proved themselves to be excellent models to capture imprecision in real-life data sets. However, a rough set has the limitation of being more suitable to handling categorical data than numeric data. The concept of a neighborhood system was introduced by Lin in 1998. It was observed by Hu, who introduced the concept of neighborhood rough sets, that besides being an extension to rough sets, is capable of handling both categorical as well as numeric data sets equally well. Rough sets are widely used for imputing missing values in data sets. Also, they are quite efficient in generating rule sets from given data sets. But another problem with rough sets is that they cannot handle large data sets of their own. As a result, Zhang et al. used techniques such as parallel processing, data reduction, and MapReduce to acquire knowledge from Big Data. However, it still cannot handle heterogeneous data well. In order to solve this problem, recently it has been observed by Hiremath et al. that neighborhood systems are more suitable in this regard. It is our aim in this chapter to present these developments along with some problems for future work on this topic.

10.1 Introduction

Data analysis is a major focus nowadays, and it has formed a huge branch under data mining. Uncertainty in data has become an integral part. As a result, the traditional techniques find themselves not suitable to handle such data sets. With the development of information technology, data are collected from various sensors and devices in multiple formats. Such data processed by independent or connected applications will routinely cross the peta-scale threshold, which would, in turn, increase the computational requirements. The size of data sets follows an ever-increasing trend. There are several models of uncertainty that have been put forth so far. The healthy list of such models includes fuzzy sets introduced by Zadeh in 1965 [1]; rough sets introduced by Pawlak in 1982 [2–4]; intuitionistic fuzzy sets introduced by Atanassov in 1986 [5] and their hybrid models, such as fuzzy rough sets and rough fuzzy sets due to Dubois and Prade in 1990 [6,7]; intuitionistic fuzzy rough sets [8]; and rough intuitionistic fuzzy sets [9]. The basic rough set model and its extensions are excellent tools for categorical data sets. But the same is not true for numeric data sets. Neighborhood systems were introduced by Lin in 1988 [10–12], and they include both the fuzzy sets and rough sets as special cases. Later, it was established by Hu [13] that it is a useful model in handling hybrid data, that is, data sets having both categorical and numeric values. Another problem with rough sets is that they are not efficient in handling large data sets. So a combination of techniques has been found to be useful in handling large data sets [14]. A parallel rough set-based knowledge acquisition technique using MapReduce from Big Data was put forth by Zhang et al. [15]. These techniques were improved by using neighborhood rough sets instead of rough sets very recently by Hiremath et al. [16]. This approach also has some restrictions and needs to be improved further. We present all these in this chapter and also propose some directions of research.

10.2 Uncertainty-Based Models

In this section, we introduce some uncertainty-based models, which are to be referenced during the compilation of this piece of work. Zadeh introduced the concept of fuzzy sets in 1965 [1] to model uncertainty in data by introducing graded membership instead of crisp membership. Let Y be any subset of a universal set V. Then,

Definition 10.2.1 (Fuzzy sets)

Y is said to be a fuzzy subset if it is characterized by a membership function μ_Y, which associates every element x of V with a real number in [0,1].

The basic assumption in fuzzy sets is that the non-membership value of an element x is determined by a function ν_Y such that $\nu_Y(x) = 1 - \mu_Y(x)$, which is not true in general in many real-life situations. This observation prompted Atanassov to introduce the notion of intuitionistic fuzzy sets in 1986 [5] as follows.

Definition 10.2.2 (Intuitionistic fuzzy sets)

Y is said to be an intuitionistic fuzzy subset of V if its nonmembership function $\nu_Y: V \rightarrow [0,1]$ such that $\forall x \in V, 0 \leq \mu_Y(x) + \nu_Y(x) \leq 1$.

Another model of uncertainty that follows the boundary of uncertainty concept due to Frege was introduced by Pawlak in 1982. This is the first model that distinguishes the notions of vagueness and uncertainty.

For any equivalence relation T over V, the generated equivalence classes are denoted by V/T. For any x in V, the equivalence class of x is denoted by $[x]_T$. Let $H = (V, \tau)$ denote a knowledge base, where τ is a family of equivalence relation over V. The indiscernibility relation over W, where $W(\neq \phi) \subseteq \tau$ is the intersection of all equivalence relation in W, and it is represented by IND(W).

Definition 10.2.3

For any subset Y of V and $S \in$ IND(H), two crisp sets, called the S-lower and S-upper approximations of Y, are associated. These are denoted by $\underline{S}Y$ and $\overline{S}Y$, which we define as $\underline{S}Y = \left\{ y \in V \,\middle|\, [y]_S \subseteq Y \right\}$ and $\overline{S}Y = \left\{ y \in V \,\middle|\, [y]_S \cap Y \neq \phi \right\}$, respectively.

The uncertain elements of Y with respect to S are denoted by $BN_S(Y)$ and are the complement of $\underline{S}Y$ in $\overline{S}Y$. Y is said to be rough or undefinable with respect to S if the lower approximation and the upper approximation are unequal; equivalently the boundary is a nonempty set. Otherwise, Y is said to be S-definable.

The lower approximation $\underline{S}Y$ consists of elements that certainly belong to Y with respect to the knowledge provided by S. The elements of the upper approximation are possible elements of Y with respect to S.

10.3 Neighborhood Rough Sets (NRSs)

Rough set theory provides efficient tools for different data mining and artificial intelligence techniques, such as feature selection, rule extraction, and knowledge discovery. Feature subset selection is also used for pattern recognition and machine learning. Much progress has been made on feature subset selection during the past few years. These may be categorized as filter, wrapper, and embedded, supervised or unsupervised. Out of the two approaches under feature selection, the algorithms, in symbolic method all features are considered to be categorical, and under the numerical method, all attributes are considered as real valued variables. In case a data set is heterogeneous—that is, the set is a mixture of categorical as well as numerical attributes—the algorithms are first modified to transform them into a single category, and then the algorithm is applied. In order to apply symbolic methods for numeric attributes, the real valued variables are transformed by using a discretizing algorithm in order to consider them as symbolic features. Similarly, the numeric method code treats the categorical features as numeric attributes after transforming them into a series of numbers. But these approaches have their own drawbacks; for example, the transformation of numeric attributes into categorical ones is likely to cause information loss due to nonconsideration of the membership degrees of numeric values in the transformed discretized ones. Also, the measure of similarity, which has been the Euclidean metric, is not suitable for categorical attributes. The feature subset selection from a heterogeneous feature set was not dealt with fully in any study until Hu et al. proposed an approach by using NRSs [13], which were applied for the reduction of rules, features, and attributes. The closeness of the values within a system is governed by the corresponding neighborhood system [10] using certain characteristics to the effect. In [14], data sets having categorical attributes have been considered for experimentation. On the other hand, an analysis like rough sets is used in [13] by computing the lower and upper approximations, where the attributes have no restrictions to be specifically nominal or categorical. The granules generated here are termed neighborhood granules. The standard deviation is used as the threshold value to compute the size of the neighborhoods. The Minkowsky distance [17] is used to determine the shape and size of the neighborhoods. The reduction in the number of rules is carried out to improve the reasoning time, employing neighborhood covering reduction. The dependency of basic rough sets introduced by Pawlak on equivalence relationships makes it handicapped in the sense that it can only be applicable to categorical attributes. On the contrary, a family of neighborhood granules is generated from numerical attributes using neighborhood relationships. Instead of equivalence granules, neighborhood granules are used to approximate decision classes. These neighborhood granules can be used to approximate decision classes. The NRS model was introduced by Hu et al. [13] in order to study the feature subset selection for heterogeneous attribute data sets.

The NRS model is presented here:

Definition 10.3.1 [18]

Let us take a sample y_i from the database V, E be the set of attributes, and F be a subset of E. The neighborhood information granule (NIG) of y_i in F is defined as

$$\delta_F(y_i) = \left\{ y_j \mid y_j \in V,\ \Delta^F(y_i, y_j) \le \delta \right\} \tag{10.1}$$

where $y_i, y_j \in V$ and Δ is a distance function, which satisfies the following properties:

$$\Delta(y_1, y_2) \ge 0,\ \forall y_1, y_2 \in U \text{ and } \Delta(y_1, y_2) = 0 \text{ iff } y_1 = y_2; \tag{10.2}$$

$$\Delta(y_1, y_2) = \Delta(y_2, y_1), \forall y_1, y_2 \in V; \qquad (10.3)$$

$$\Delta(y_1, y_3) \le \Delta(y_1, y_2) + \Delta(y_2, y_3), \forall y_1, y_2, y_3 \in V. \qquad (10.4)$$

Suppose there are M attributes in a database represented as $B = \{b_1, b_2, \ldots, b_i, \ldots b_M\}$, and the function $g(y, b_i)$ is used to represent the value of the tuple y at the attribute b_i, i = 1, 2, ..., M. Then the Minkowsky distance function over the database elements x, y in V is defined as

$$\Delta(x, y) = \left(\sum_{i=1}^{M} |g(x, a_i) - g(y, a_i)|^p \right)^{1/p}, \ p \ge 1. \qquad (10.5)$$

The Manhattan distance Δ_1 is obtained when $p = 1$ in Equation 10.5 as

$$\Delta_1(x, y) = \sum_{i=1}^{M} |g(x, a_i) - g(y, a_i)| \qquad (10.6)$$

The Euclidean distance Δ_2 is a special case of Equation 10.5, which is obtained by taking $p = 2$. In fact,

$$\Delta_2(x, y) = \left(\sum_{i=1}^{M} |g(x, a_i) - g(y, a_i)|^2 \right)^{1/2}, \qquad (10.7)$$

Definition 10.3.2 [18]

We denote the set of numeric and categorical attributes in E by N and C.
Then, the NIGs of a tuple y induced by E, N, and $E \cup N$ are given by

$$\delta_N(y) = \left\{ y_i \middle| \Delta_N(y, y_i) \le \delta, \ y_i \in V \right\}; \qquad (10.8)$$

$$\delta_C(y) = \left\{ y_i \middle| \Delta_C(y, y_i) = 0, \ y_i \in V \right\}; \qquad (10.9)$$

$$\delta_{N \cup C}(y) = \left\{ y_i \middle| \Delta_N(y, y_i) \le \ \delta \wedge \Delta_C(y, y_i) = 0, \ y_i \in U \right\} \qquad (10.10)$$

Here the Δ represents the "distance function," and $\wedge$ represents the logical "and" operator.

The sets N and C take care of numeric attributes and categorical attributes, respectively. Hence, $N \cup C$ represents a set of hybrid attributes that is a mixture of numeric and categorical attributes. For two numeric elements in the neighborhood granule, they should be identical, and for categorical attributes, they should not be beyond a distance of threshold δ.

Definition 10.3.3 [18]

Given a neighborhood relation M over V and a subset Y of V, we denote the lower and upper neighborhood approximations of Y by $\underline{M}Y$ and $\overline{M}Y$, respectively, and define them as follows:

$$\underline{M}Y = \left\{ y_i \middle| \delta(y_i) \subseteq Y, \; y_i \in V \right\}; \tag{10.11}$$

$$\overline{M}Y = \left\{ y_i \middle| \delta(y_i) \cap Y \neq \phi, \; y_i \in V \right\}; \tag{10.12}$$

The neighborhood boundary of Y is denoted by $BN(Y)$ and is defined as

$$BN(Y) = \overline{M}Y - \underline{M}Y \tag{10.13}$$

In the continuations below, we use $M(y_i)$ in the place of $\delta_M(y_i)$ to avoid complexity in representation.

Definition 10.3.4

We define $M = \{M(y_1), M(y_2)\ldots M(y_m)\}$ as the neighborhood relation over $V = \{y_1, y_2, y_3\ldots, y_m\}$ and the corresponding covering over V as $\bigcup_{i=1}^{m} M(y_i) = V$.

10.4 Use of MapReduce to Extract Knowledge from Big Data Applying Rough Set-Based Techniques in Parallel

Of late, the size of data sets in real-life applications has increased exponentially, and so there is pressure to acquire the inherent useful information from these data sets as quickly as possible. This is one of the various techniques used in Big Data.

In order to analyze a large amount of data by using a group of computers in a distributed environment, a software framework called MapReduce was introduced by Google [19,20], and it has since become a popular and effective technique. Google has been using this in many of its implementations, and people have added this technique to existing methods to enhance their capability to handle large data sets.

10.4.1 Implementation of MapReduce

Apache Hadoop is a software framework that helps in constructing reliable, scalable, distributed systems [21]. Phoenix is a shared-memory implementation of Google's MapReduce model for data-intensive processing tasks [22]. Mars is a MapReduce framework on graphic processors [23]. A twister is a lightweight and iterative MapReduce runtime system [24].

10.4.2 Hybridization of MapReduce

Machine learning algorithms of the Hadoop platform that are scalable can be implemented using Apache Mahout [25]. In [26], one such application for rapid parallel genome indexing is put forth. Also, there we find implementation details for several joint strategies for log processing in MapReduce. In [27], rapid clustering algorithms are proposed by using MapReduce such that the exactness is almost certain. Similarly, it is used in development of graph algorithms and design patterns efficiently [26].

Rough set theory, since its inception, has been extensively used as a fruitful model in the area of data mining in order to discover knowledge from data sets [3,28,29]. It is a profound theory to support extraction of rules [30–33] and attribute reduction, which can also be called attribute selection [18,34,35].

All the abovementioned features of rough sets are confined to small data sets and a single computational device. In order to extend the applicability of these algorithms so that they can handle large data sets and acquire knowledge, some parallel methods were proposed in [1]. MapReduce becomes a very helpful tool in such extensions while the characteristics of the data are being kept in view [36]. The Hadoop platform was used for the development of such algorithms [21].

10.4.3 MapReduce Programming Model

A detailed explanation of this model is as follows: The input and output of this computation model are a set of key/value pairs. The MapReduce libraries are used by specifying the computation of the functions map and reduce with another function, the combination of which is not mandatory.

Definitions of the three functions (compulsory and optional) mentioned above are as follows:

- *Map*: This produces an intermediate set of key/value pairs from an input pair. These corresponding pairs are grouped according to the intermediate keys, and combine/reduce functions are used to transform groupwise.
- *Combine*: Local maps are used to gather keys and their corresponding set of values for merging so that smaller groups of values can be generated by the use of the "reduce" function.
- *Reduce*: The functionality of "reduce" is partially explained above in the combine step. Its function is to form smaller groups by merging the values identified to be associated with a single key. Mostly, binary outputs are produced once this procedure is activated.

10.4.4 Rough Sets and Knowledge Acquisition

Definition 10.4.1

An information system is a fourfold structure $T = (V, B, W, g)$ where

V is a universal set having a nonzero number of elements
B is a set of attributes having a nonzero number of elements
W is the union of all the domains of attributes in B
g is a mapping from $V \times B \to W$ such that $g(y, b) \in W_b$ for $y \in V$ and $b \in B$.

A decision system is an information system $T = (V, B, W, g)$ with $B = E \cup F$, where E is a set of condition attributes, and F is a set of decision attributes such that $E \cap F = \phi$.

Definition 10.4.2 [1]

Let $D = \{d_1, d_2, d_3 \ldots d_\ell\} \subseteq E$ be a set of condition attributes. Then the information set with respect to D for any $y \in V$ by the ℓ-tuple

$$\overrightarrow{y_D} = \left(g(y, d_1), g(y, d_2), \ldots g(y, d_\ell) \right) \tag{10.14}$$

The set of all the attributes D taken together generates a granular structure on V, which is called the indiscernibility relation generated by D denoted as IND(D), where

$$\text{IND}(D) = \left\{ (u, v) \mid (u, v) \in V \times V, \ \overrightarrow{u_D} = \overrightarrow{v_D} \right\} \tag{10.15}$$

This says that two elements u, v in IND(D) cannot be distinguished by considering the attribute set D. Elements in V get decomposed into disjoint equivalence classes with respect to IND(D). The equivalence relation generated is given by

$$V/\text{IND}(D) = \left\{ [y]_D \mid y \in V \right\}, \tag{10.16}$$

where $[y]_D$ denotes the equivalence class determined by y with respect to D, that is

$$[y]_D = \left\{ z \in V \mid (y, z) \in \text{IND}(D) \right\}. \tag{10.17}$$

10.5 Case Study 1

This is a case study to illustrate the concepts introduced above. We use Table 10.1 for this purpose. Let us consider a patient database, in which each patient is assessed with respect to a set of symptoms $\{H, TR, TN, F\}$, where H represents headache, TR represents temperature with respect to rough set criteria, TN represents temperature with respect to NRS criteria, and F represents flu.

Table 10.1   Decision Table

U	H	TR	TN	F
y_1	N	Nr	97.02	N
y_2	N	Hg	101.02	Y
y_3	Y	Nr	99.00	Y
y_4	Y	VHg	103.40	Y
y_5	N	Nr	98.60	N
y_6	Y	Hg	100.60	N
y_7	N	Nr	99.30	N
y_8	N	Hg	101.50	Y
y_9	Y	Hg	100.90	Y
y_{10}	Y	VHg	104.00	Y
y_{11}	N	Nr	97.80	N
y_{12}	Y	Hg	101.50	Y

The set of attributes $E = \{H, TR, TN\}$ denotes the set of condition attributes, and F is the only decision attribute. We select a subset $D = \{H, T\}$ of E. To be concise, we use the abbreviations N = "No" and Y = "Yes."

There are five equivalence classes: P_1, P_2, P_3, P_4, and P_5 where $P_1 = \{y_1, y_5, y_7, y_{11}\}$, $P_2 = \{y_2, y_8\}$, $P_3 = \{y_3\}$, $P_4 = \{y_4, y_{10}\}$, and $P_5 = \{y_6, y_9, y_{12}\}$. We use Nr = normal, Hg = high, and VHg = very high for brevity.

Referring to Table 10.1, we have $(y_{10})_D = \{Y, VHg\}$, $(y_{10})_F = \{Y\}$, and $(y_{10})_{D \cup F} = \{Y, VHg, Y\}$.

Definition 10.5.1

$\{P_1, P_2, \ldots P_N\}$ and $\{Q_1, Q_2, \ldots Q_M\}$ are partitions of E and F, respectively. Then for any two elements, P_i and Q_j, the support (sup), accuracy (ac), and coverage (co) of $P_i \rightarrow Q_j$ are defined as follows:

$$\text{Sup}(E_i \rightarrow D_j) : Sup(D_j|E_i) = \left| E_i \cap D_j \right|;$$

$$\text{Ac}(P_i \rightarrow Q_j) : Ac(Q_j|P_i) = \frac{\left| P_i \cap Q_j \right|}{\left| P_i \right|};$$

$$\text{Co}(P_i \rightarrow Q_j) : Co(Q_j|P_i) = \frac{\left| P_i \cap Q_j \right|}{\left| Q_j \right|}.$$

The following methods are for acquisition of rules using the above concepts.

Definition 10.5.2

When $Ac(Q_j|P_i) = 1$, we say that the rule $P_i \rightarrow Q_j$ is a consistent rule with $Co(Q_j|P_i)$.

Definition 10.5.3

When $Ac(Q_j|P_i) \geq \gamma$ and $Co(Q_j|P_i) \geq \delta$ hold such that $\gamma \in (0.5, 1)$ and $\delta \in (0, 1)$, we say that the rule $P_i \rightarrow Q_j$ is a probabilistic one.

Definition 10.5.4

For some $\gamma', \delta' \in (0, 1)$, if $Ac(Q_j|P_i) = \max_{h=1,2,...M} \{Ac(Q_h|P_i) \geq \gamma'$ and $Co(Q_j|P_i) \geq \delta'$, we say that the rule $P_i \rightarrow Q_j$ is a max-accuracy probabilistic rule.

In [6] using MapReduce, three methods based on parallel techniques were proposed for knowledge acquisition based on rough set theory. The following additional definitions and concepts are needed before introducing these procedures.

Definition 10.5.5

A decision table $T = (V, E \cup F, W, g)$ can be decomposed into a set of decision subtables T_j, $j = 1$, 2,... p such that $T = \bigcup_{j=1}^{p} T_j$ and $T_i = (V_i, E \cup F, W, g)$, and $\{V_j : j = 1, 2,... p\}$ is a decomposition of V into pairwise disjoint subsets.

Result 1: Let P be a set of attributes such that $P \subseteq E$. Suppose P generates two equivalence classes G and H with respect to two subtables of T. Then the two following disjointed cases occur.

1. The case in which $\overrightarrow{G_P} = \overrightarrow{H_P}$, G and H can be combined to form a new equivalence class K with respect to P such that $\overrightarrow{K_P} = \overrightarrow{G_P} = \overrightarrow{H_P}$.
2. Otherwise, G and H cannot be combined to form a new equivalence with respect to P.

It can be derived from the result below that the cardinality of equivalence classes, decision classes, and their union for the subtables can be computed independently, and the results can be combined under suitable conditions. So, the problem of finding the cardinality now boils down to that of a MapReduce one.

Result 2: Let us consider the decision table $T = (V, E \cup F, W, g)$, which is the union of a set of n subtables $T_i = (V_i, E \cup F, W, g)$. Let P be a subset E and $\{F_1, F_2...F_l\}$ be the partition of V corresponding to P. Similarly, $\{F_{k1}, F_{k2},..., F_{kp_k}\}$ is the partitions of V_i corresponding to P, $i = 1, 2, ...,$ l. So, we have $F_{total} = \{F_{11}, F_{12}, ...F_{1p_1}, ...F_{l1}, F_{l2}, ...F_{lp_l}\}$ and $|F_j| = \sum_{C \in F_{total}, \overrightarrow{C_F} = \overrightarrow{F_{jp}}} |C|$.

The following two steps are used in all the proposed knowledge acquisition methods in [21].

Step 1: Since the computation of the cardinalities of G, F, and $G \cap F$ can be carried out in parallel, algorithms can be framed to compute these values using MapReduce/Combine.

Step 2: After the computation of the cardinalities of the three sets in Step 1, Ac($F|P$) and Co($F|P$) can be found out. Next, the three kinds of rules can be generated using 10.5.3–10.5.5.

Note: While the executions in Step 1 are parallel, those in Step 2 are sequential by nature.

10.6 Algorithms

The following algorithms were put forth in [21] in order to implement steps 1 and 2 above.

Algorithm 10.6.1 [21]: Map (key, value)

> **Input:** The name of the document, the values for the subtables, and global variables $P \subseteq E$ are given as input.
> **Output:** Information about the set of objects in the sets of condition, decision, and their union attribute sets is generated.

For each tuple in the subtables V_i, the required information about the objects "y" in it is computed in a variable output_key by using the formulae "output_key = 'EQ'+ y_P," "output_key = 'DE'+ $\overrightarrow{y_F}$," and "output_key = 'AS'+ $\overrightarrow{y_{P \cup F}}$," where "EQ," "DE," and "AS" are flags for the equivalence class, decision class, and association class, respectively. These values are output by calling a function representing it.

Algorithm 10.6.2 [21]: Combine (key, V)

> **Input:** The information about the objects in the subtables P, F, and $P \cup F$ and the list of counts are given as input.
> **Output:** The information about the objects in the subtables P, F, and $P \cup F$, and the count are generated.

Initialize the value to "0" and out_key to key. Then, for each element in the value set, recursively add the values to the initial value. This will generate the total values. Output this value along with the key.

Algorithm 10.6.3 [21]: Reduce (key, W)

> **Input:** The information about the objects in the subtables P, F, and $P \cup F$, and the list of counts are given as input.
> **Output:** The information about the objects in the subtables P, F, and $P \cup F$, and the count are generated.

The output values for out_key and out_value are initialized to the current_key and 0, respectively. The out_value is updated by adding all the values from the domain value. Finally, the out_key and out_value are shown as output.

The parallel method for knowledge acquisition is explained in Figure 10.1.

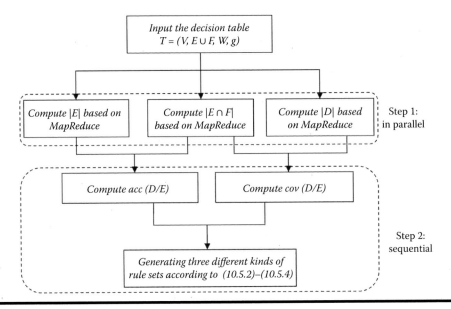

Figure 10.1   Parallel methods for knowledge acquisition.

In Section 10.6.1, some new algorithms are presented, which are to be used in the NRS approach to the above problem.

10.6.1 Use of MapReduce for Knowledge Acquisition through NRSs

As discussed in earlier sections, the rough set-based method is handicapped by the fact that it can handle the categorical attributes well, but it will not be efficient to handle numeric attributes. But, as observed by Hu et al. and also demonstrated by them, the NRS model is very efficient at handling hybrid attributes. So the approach in Section 10.4 was generalized and made more efficient by the introduction of this model of knowledge acquisition by Hiremath et al. [16]. We discuss their approach in this section.

The following additional algorithms were introduced for this purpose.

Algorithm 10.6.4: NSR (involving neighborhood subset reduction)

Neighborhood system concepts are used in order to generate neighborhood subsets from the samples taken in the (E, D) format.

Inputs:

■ $V = \{(E_j, F_j); j = 1, 2, \ldots m\}$, where E and F represent the condition and decision attribute sets, respectively
■ A set of attributes $B = \{b_1, b_2, \ldots b_p\}$ out of which "q" is numeric
■ Samples from V are denoted by $y_j, j = 1, 2, \ldots, m$
■ $g(y_j, b_p)$ is a function generating information from V

Output: A set of neighborhoods $Nbd(y_j)$, $j = 1, 2...m$

1. For each attribute b_j, $j = 1, 2,...p$ and for each sample y_i, $i = 1, 2, ..., m$, the normalized function values $g(y_i, b_j)/\max (g(y_i, b_j))$ are computed, and each $g(y_i, b_j)$ is replaced by the corresponding normalized value.
2. For each $i = 1, 2, ..., m$, the margin of samples $m(y_i)$ and the neighborhoods $Nbd(y_i)$ are computed. It is of note that, in any case, if $m(y_i) < 0$, then it is set to 0.
3. Let Nbd denote the set of all $Nbd(y_i)$, $i = 1, 2, ..., m$ generated in the previous step. Then while (Nbd ≠ φ), the neighborhoods that are subsets of another neighborhood are removed. This process is terminated when there are no neighborhoods satisfying the condition.

Algorithm 10.6.5: COMPUTE (computing support, accuracy, and coverage)

This algorithm provides the intermediate step between the neighborhood generation in the previous step and rule generation, which satisfies the knowledge acquisition process. It computes the support, accuracy, and coverage values for each rule using the definitions given under Definition 4.2.3.

We designate the numeric attributes as $b_{k_1}, b_{k_2}, ...b_{k_p}$ such that for all i, $k_i \leq m$, and $I = \{1, 2, ..., n\} - \{k_1, k_2, ..., k_p\}$.

Inputs:

- The set of neighborhoods obtained in the above algorithm
- The equivalence classes $E_1, E_2,...E_n$ of decision attributes
- The set of all attributes
- The set of categorical attributes

Output: The values of accuracy, coverage, support for each rule.

1. For each element y_i in every neighborhood and each attribute b_j, compute $F_p = \{g(y_i, b_j) \cap Nbd (y_i)\}$, which is a set of equivalence classes and find $F_p \cap E_m$, $m = 1, 2, ..., n$.
2. Next compute support, accuracy, and coverage using the definitions provided in Definition 4.2.3.

The next algorithm is used to compute the neighborhood covering reduction (NCR).

Algorithm 10.6.6 [37]: NCR

Using the margins of individual elements, this algorithm computes the neighborhood covers in a sequential manner.

Inputs:

- A set of training elements $\{(y_j, e_j); j = 1,2...m\}$
- A set of testing elements $\{(y_k, e_k); k = 1,2...p\}$

Output: Set of rules

1. The margins $\text{mar}(y_j)$, $j = 1, 2\ldots m$ are computed, and if any of these values turns out to be negative, then it is set to 0.
2. The neighborhood values $Nbd(y_j)$, $j = 1, 2, \ldots, m$ are computed and put in a set named Nbd, and the rule set is initialized to ϕ.
3. For each of the elements of Nbd, the number of tuples covered by it is computed.
4. While (Nbd $\neq \phi$), select the covering element Nbd(x) covering the largest number of samples and add a rule (y, $m(y)$, z) to S, where z is the decision of y, and remove Nbd (y') if Nbd (y') $\subseteq$ Nbd(y).

10.7 Case Study 2

In [21], the following steps were followed for knowledge acquisition.

Step 1
Using the three Algorithms 10.6.1, 10.6.2, and 10.6.3 to apply the three operations of map, combine, and reduce were done in [21] to generate in parallel the number of elements in F, G, and $F \cap G$. Here, F and G represent the set of equivalence classes for the condition {headache, temperature (rough sets)} and decision {flu} attributes, respectively. For an example, $F_1 = \{N, Nr\} = \{y_1, y_5, y_7, y_{11}\}$. For instance, $G_1 = \{N\} = \{y_1, y_5, y_6, y_7, y_{11}\}$. Also, for $F \cap G$, the attributes {headache, temperature (rough sets), flu} are the union of both the elements in F and G. As an example, $F_1 \cap G_1 = \{N, Nr, N\} = \{y_1, y_5, y_7, y_{11}\}$.

Step 2
Using formulae given in Definition 10.5.1, the values of support, accuracy, and coverage are generated.

Tables 10.2, 10.3, and 10.4 provide the results obtained after Step 1.

Values obtained after the mapper function in which each class is in the form of a <key, value> pair are given in Table 10.2. Each distinct class is identified and assigned a value "1." Next, in Table 10.3, we get the values obtained after the Combine function wherein the values are the cumulative values obtained for each distinct class and those belonging to the same subtable.

Table 10.2   After the Map Function (Rough Sets)

$|F|$	$|G|$	$|F \cap G|$	$|F|$	$|G|$	$|F \cap G|$
(N, Nr), 1	(N), 1	(N, Nr, N), 1	(N, Nr), 1	(N), 1	(N, Nr, N), 1
(N, Hg), 1	(Y), 1	(N, Hg, Y), 1	(N, Hg), 1	(Y), 1	(N, Hg, Y), 1
(Y, Nr), 1	(Y), 1	(Y, Nr, Y), 1	(Y, Hg), 1	(Y), 1	(Y, Hg, Y), 1
(Y, VHg), 1	(Y), 1	(Y, VHg, Y), 1	(Y, VHg), 1	(Y), 1	(Y, VHg, Y), 1
(N, Nr), 1	(N), 1	(N, Nr, N), 1	(N, Nr), 1	(N), 1	(N, Nr, N), 1
(Y, Hg), 1	(N), 1	(Y, Hg, N), 1	(Y, Hg), 1	(Y), 1	(Y, Hg, Y), 1

Table 10.3 After the Combine Function (Rough Sets)

$|F|$	$|G|$	$|F \cap G|$	$|F|$	$|G|$	$|F \cap G|$
(N,Nr), 2	(N), 3	(N, Nr, N), 2	(N, Nr), 2	(N), 2	(N, Nr, N), 2
(N,Hg), 1	(Y), 3	(N, Hg, Y), 1	(N, Hg), 1	(Y), 4	(N, Hg, Y), 1
(Y,Nr), 1		(Y, Nr, Y), 1	(Y, Hg), 2		(Y, Hg, Y), 1
(Y, VHg), 1		(Y, VHg, Y), 1	(Y, VHg), 1		(Y, VHg, Y), 1
(Y, Hg), 1		(Y, Hg, N), 1			

Table 10.4 After the Reduce Function (Rough Sets)

$|F|$	$|G|$	$|F \cap G|$
(N, Nr), 4	(N), 5	(N, Nr, N), 4
(N, Hg), 2	(Y), 7	(N, Hg, Y), 2
(Y, Nr), 1		(Y, Nr, Y), 1
(Y, VHg), 2		(Y, VHg, Y), 2
(Y, Hg), 3		(Y, Hg, N), 1
		(Y, Hg, Y), 2

Finally, in the Reduce function, we get the final values again in the <key, value> form where the value represents the total number of times each distinct class is occurring.

The values of accuracy and coverage are computed using Definition 10.5.1. Then, the accuracy and the coverage of rules are computed, and rule sets are generated as shown in Table 10.5, where ✓ and ✗ mean it is a rule or not, respectively. We can see that the number of rules followed is four, four, and five for these three methods defined in Definitions 10.5.2, 10.5.3, and 10.5.4.

Rough sets are generally used for categorical values and are not competent to handle numerical values. The numerical values in the data set are usually discretized into ranges and converted to categorical attributes before being used.

Table 10.5 Step 2—Accuracy, Coverage, Rules

$F \rightarrow G$	*Acc(F|G)*	*Cove(F|G)*	*Method 1*	*Method 2*	*Method 3*
(N, Nr) → (N)	4/4 = 1.00	4/5 = 0.80	✓	✓	✓
(N, Hg) → (Y)	2/2 = 1.00	2/7 = 0.29	✓	✓	✓
(Y, Nr) → (Y)	1/1 = 1.00	1/7 = 0.14	✓	✗	✓
(Y, VHg) → (Y)	2/2 = 1.00	2/7 = 0.29	✓	✓	✓
(Y, Hg) → (N)	1/3 = 0.33	1/5 = 0.20	✗	✗	✗
(Y, Hg) → (Y)	2/3 = 0.67	2/7 = 0.29	✗	✓	✓

Consider Table 10.6 where we have defined the same attributes as used in Table 10.1 with the exception that instead of using categorical values for all the attributes in the table we are defining the temperature attribute to be the numerical attribute. The range we have considered for temperature varies over

Normal temperature: (97.02–99.5°F)
High temperature: (99.5–101.5°F)
Very high temperature: (101.5–104°F)

The values in the table corresponding to the temperature attribute are normalized using Equation 10.2.

The margin values for the corresponding $g(y_i, T)$ are computed using Equation 10.3.

Using Definitions 10.3.1 and 10.3.4, the neighborhoods of y_i corresponding to the margin values are calculated, and we find the final sets of relatively irreducible neighborhood sets by applying Algorithm 10.6.6. The neighborhood sets that we get are $Nbd'(y) = \{Nbd(y_1), Nbd(y_3), Nbd(y_4), Nbd(y_6), Nbd(y_{10})\}$. Since $Nbd(y_4)$ is similar to $Nbd(y_{10})$, we consider either one of the neighborhoods.

The proximity classes generated are

$$PR_1 = \{y_1, y_{11}\} = \{N\}; PR_2 = \{y_3, y_5, y_6, y_7, y_{11}\} = \{N, Hg\};$$

$$PR_3 = \{y_4, y_8, y_{10}, y_{12}\} = \{Hg, VHg\}; PR_4 = \{y_2, y_6, y_8, y_9, y_{12}\} = \{Hg\}$$

Table 10.6 Decision Table for Neighborhood Systems

V	Temperature (NBRS) $f(x_i, T)$	Normalized Value	Margin $m(x_i)$	Neighborhoods $(N(x_i))$
y_1	97.02	0.933	0.012	$\{y_1, y_{11}\}$
y_2	101.02	0.971	0.003	$\{y_2, y_9\}$
y_3	99.00	0.952	0.015	$\{y_3, y_6, y_7, y_5, y_{11}\}$
y_4	103.40	0.994	0.021	$\{y_4, y_{10}, y_8, y_{12}\}$
y_5	98.60	0.948	0.003	$\{y_5\}$
y_6	100.60	0.967	0.009	$\{y_6, y_8, y_{12}, y_2, y_9\}$
y_7	99.30	0.955	0.004	$\{y_7, y_3\}$
y_8	101.50	0.976	0.009	$\{y_8, y_6, y_9, y_2, y_{12}\}$
y_9	100.90	1.00	0.002	$\{y_2, y_9\}$
y_{11}	97.80	0.940	0.005	$\{y_{11}\}$
y_{12}	101.50	0.976	0.009	$\{y_8, y_6, y_9, y_2, y_{12}\}$

Table 10.7   Accuracy and Coverage for Neighborhood Systems

$F \rightarrow G$	$|F \cap G|$ (Support)	F	$|F|$	G	$|G|$	Accuracy	Coverage
{N, Nr} → N}	2	F_1	2	G_1	5	1	0.4
{N, Nr} → N	3	F_2	3	G_1	5	1	0.6
{Y, Hg} → N	1	F_5	2	G_1	5	0.5	0.2
{Y, Hg} → N	1	F_7	3	G_1	5	0.33	0.2
{N, Hg} → Y	1	F_3	1	G_2	7	1	0.14
{N, Hg} → Y	2	F_4	2	G_2	7	1	0.29
{Y, Nr} → Y	1	F_5	2	G_2	7	0.5	0.14
{Y, Hg} → Y	2	F_7	3	G_2	7	0.667	0.29
[{Y, VHg}, {Y, H}] → Y	3	F_6	3	G_2	7	1	0.428

The decision classes generated are

$$e_{no} = \{y_1, y_5, y_6, y_7, y_{11}\};$$

$$e_{yes} = \{y_2, y_3, y_4, y_8, y_{9}, y_{10}, y_{12}\}$$

The accuracy and coverage values are displayed in Table 10.7, where $F = \{F_1, F_2, F_3, F_4, F_5, F_6, F_7\}$

$F_1 = \{y_1, y_{11}\} = \{N, Nr\};$
$F_2 = \{y_5, y_7, y_{11}\} = \{N, Nr\};$
$F_3 = \{y_8\} = \{N, Hg\};$
$F_4 = \{y_2, y_8\} = \{N, Hg\};$
$F_5 = \{y_3, y_6\} = [\{Y, Hg\}, \{Y, Nr\}];$
$F_6 = \{y_4, y_{10}, y_{12}\} = [\{Y, VHg\}, \{Y, Hg\}];$
$F_7 = \{y_6, y_9, y_{12}\} = \{Y, Hg\}.$

Also, $G_1 = g_{no}$ and $G_2 = g_{yes}$

Here the values of E_i are obtained by taking the intersection of the proximity classes with the categorical attributes. The MapReduce operation is performed on the elements obtained after the intersection. The map function as described in Algorithm 10.6.1 is applied to individual elements of the set, whereas the reduce operation as described in Algorithm 10.6.3 is applied to the set as a whole. Table 10.7, row 9 [{yes, very high}, {yes, high}] means that both these values belong to the same proximity class and are hence represented together. The similar approach has been followed while computing D and $E \cap D$.

10.8   Case Study 3

Let us take $PR_1 = \{y_1, y_{11}\}$ representing normal range. To obtain F_1, Headache$_{no} \cap AR_1$ is performed, which gives the set $\{y_1, y_{11}\}$. Then the map function is applied to the elements to y_1 and

y_{11}, which comprise F_1. At the end of this operation, we get $[\{(y_1), 1\}, \{(y_{11}), 1\}]$. Later, by applying the reduce function, the result $[\{N, Nr\}, 2]$ is obtained as y_1 and y_{11}; both have their values {no, normal}. A similar procedure is followed to derive $|F|$ and $|F \cap G|$.

It is clear from Table 10.7 that if numerical values are taken for some attributes, we get a range of values for accuracy and coverage instead of discrete ones. Crisp values, more often than not, do not represent the cases appropriately. The possibility of occurrence becomes more flexible and provides better representation.

Next, let us apply Algorithm 10.6.6 for NCR, and the computed value is then given as input to Algorithm 10.6.5 for generating the values of accuracy, coverage, and support.

After the covering algorithm defined in Algorithm 10.6.6 is applied, the neighborhoods that we obtain will be

$$\text{Nbd}''(y_1) = \{y_1, y_{11}\};$$

$$\text{Nbd}''(y_2) = \{y_2, y_9\};$$

$$\text{Nbd}''(y_3) = \{y_2, y_3, y_5, y_6, y_7, y_8, y_9, y_{11}, y_{12}\};$$

$$\text{Nbd}''(y_4) = \{y_2, y_4, y_6, y_8, y_9, y_{10}, y_{12}\};$$

$$\text{Nbd}''(y_5) = \{y_5\};$$

$$\text{Nbd}''(y_6) = \{y_2, y_6, y_8, y_9, y_{12}\};$$

$$\text{Nbd}''(y_7) = \{y_3, y_5, y_6, y_7, y_{11}\};$$

$$\text{Nbd}''(y_8) = \{y_2, y_6, y_8, y_9, y_{12}\};$$

$$\text{Nbd}''(y_9) = \{y_2, y_9\};$$

$$\text{Nbd}''(y_{10}) = \{y_2, y_4, y_6, y_8, y_9, y_{10}, y_{12}\};$$

$$\text{Nbd}''(y_{11}) = \{y_{11}\};$$

$$\text{Nbd}''(y_{12}) = \{y_2, y_6, y_8, y_9, y_{12}\}$$

According to Algorithm 10.6.6, the largest covering sample here is $\text{Nbd}''(y_3)$ having cardinality 3. Now, applying Definition 10.3.4, we can find the relative reducible sets. After applying this, we get three classes as follows:

$S = [\{y_3, 0.015, 1\}, \{y_4, 0.021, 1\}, \{y_1, 0.012, 0\}$, with '0' and '1' representing "no" and "yes," respectively.

The class generated for y_3 represents that it is one of the three covers that is not relatively reducible with respect to the other elements in the universe. The margin value computed for y_3 is 0.015, and the element represented by y_3 satisfies the decision {yes}.

Table 10.8 The Number of Elements Obtained from Neighborhood Sets

$F \rightarrow G$	$|F \cap G|$ Support	Accuracy	Coverage
{N, Nr} → N	2	1	0.4
{N, Nr} → N	3	1	0.6
{N, Hg} → N	0	0	0
[{Y, Nr, {Y, Hg}] → N	1	0.5	0.2
{N, Hg} → Y	2	1	0.29
{(Y, Nr), (Y, Hg)} → Y	1	0.5	0.14
{(Y, VHg), (Y, Hg)} → Y	4	1	0.57

Therefore, reduced neighborhood covering or approximate classes that we get are Nbd″ = {Nbd″(y_1), Nbd″(y_3), Nbd″(y_4)}. We follow the same procedure as described in Step 1 of Section 10.7 to find $|F|$, $|G|$, and $|F \cap G|$ and then apply the definitions in 10.5.1 to compute the support, accuracy, and coverage for the rules generated.

In the fourth row of Table 10.8, we find [{Y, Nr}, {Y, Hg}], which indicates that these two values are sufficiently close to each other and so are represented together. In order to compute F and $F \cap G$, a similar procedure is followed.

10.9 Conclusion

In this chapter, we discussed knowledge acquisition from Big Data using two approaches. The first one uses basic rough sets, and the other one uses NRSs for the purpose. Although neighborhood systems have been around for a while, they have not been used for the purpose of computing the accuracy, support, and coverage of decision rules in a decision table. Its application on a data set on which only parallel rough set-based methods were used formerly for the calculation of the values of support, accuracy, and coverage has led to further enhancements as here we show that numerical attributes can also be worked upon and processed to retrieve relevant information. Neighborhood systems, when used, give proximity classes with a certain amount of overlapping in the equivalence sets that, in turn, help to generate a range in the accuracy and coverage values as opposed to the exact values obtained earlier. This gives a certain amount of flexibility, thus giving more accurate results. Moreover, the concept of NCR has led to a decrease in processing time as the number of rules has come down, which becomes quite significant, especially in a Big Data set. But this reduction in the number of rules generated comes at the cost of the values of accuracy and coverage computed.

10.10 Scope for Future Research

It has been observed in the NRS framework that as the number of rules decreases, the accuracy and coverage values tend to be more general than specific.

- So one can work out an approach such that there will be a reduction in the number of rules, but the accuracy and coverage values obtained by the covering technique are similar to those values as in [2] a neighborhood subset model.
- Also, the concepts discussed under the NRS approach can be extended such that they work efficiently with data sets that have a compound attribute defined using both categorical as well as numerical values.

References

1. Zadeh, L. A.: Fuzzy sets, Information and Control, 8 (3), (1965), pp. 338–353.
2. Pawlak, Z.: Theoretical aspects of reasoning about data, Kluwer Academic Publishers (London) (1991).
3. Pawlak, Z., Grzymala-Busse, Slowinski, R., and Ziarko, W.: Rough Sets, Communications of ACM, 38 (11), (1995), pp. 88–95.
4. Pawlak, Z.: Rough sets, *Int. Jour. of Computer and Information Sciences*, 11, (1982), pp. 341–356.
5. Atanassov, K. T.: Intuitionistic fuzzy sets, Fuzzy Sets and Systems, 20, 1 (1986), pp. 87–96.
6. Dubois, D., and Prade, H.: Rough fuzzy sets and fuzzy rough sets, Fuzzy Sets and Systems, 23, (1987), pp. 3–18.
7. Dubois, D., and Prade, H.: Rough fuzzy sets and fuzzy rough sets, International Journal of General Systems, 17, (1990), p. 191–209.
8. Ziarko, W.: Discovery through rough set theory, Communication ACM, 42 (11), (1999), pp. 54–57.
9. Tripathy, B. K., Ghosh, S. K., and Jena, S. P.: Intuitionistic fuzzy rough sets, Notes on Intuitionistic Fuzzy Sets (Bulgaria), 8 (1), (2002), pp. 1–18.
10. Lin, T. Y.: Neighbourhood systems and relational database, in Proceedings of CSC, New York, USA, (1988), p. 725.
11. Lin, T. Y.: Neighbourhood systems: Mathematical models of information granulations, in: IEEE International Conference on Systems, Man and Cybernetics, Washington, D.C., October 5–8 (2003).
12. Lin, T. Y.: Granulation and nearest neighbourhoods: Rough set approach granular computing: An emerging paradigm, Physica-Verlag, Heidelberg (2001), pp. 125–142.
13. Hu, Q., Yu, D., and Liu, J.: Neighbourhood rough set based heterogeneous feature subset selection, Information Sciences, 178 (18) (2008), pp. 3577–3594.
14. Tripathy, B. K., Vishwakarma, H. R., and Kothari, D. P.: Neighbourhood systems based knowledge acquisition using MapReduce from big data over cloud computing, CSIBIG, Proceedings of the Conference on IT in Business, Industry and Government, Indore, M. P., India, (2014), pp. 183–189.
15. Zhang, J., Li, T., and Pan, Y. Parallel rough set based knowledge acquisition using MapReduce from Big Data, in Proceedings of the ACM Big Mine, Beijing, China, (2012), pp. 20–27.
16. Hiremath, S., Chandra, P., Joy, A. M., and Tripathy, B. K.: Neighbourhood rough set model for knowledge acquisition using MapReduce, Int. J. Communication Networks and Distributed Systems, 15 (2/3) (2015), pp. 212–234.
17. Wilson, D. R., and Martinez, T. R.: Improved heterogeneous distance functions, *Journal of Artificial Intelligence Research*, 6, (1997), pp. 1–34.
18. Hu, Q., Pedrycz, W., Yu, D., and Lang, J.: Selecting discrete and continuous features based on neighbourhood decision error minimization, systems, man and cybernetics, *Part B: Cybernetics, IEEE Transactions on*, 40 (1), (2010), pp. 137–150.
19. Dean, J., and Ghemawat, S.: MapReduce: Simplified data processing on large clusters, in: Proceedings of the 6th conference on Symposium on operating systems design & implementation- vol. 6, OSDI'04, (2004), p. 10.
20. Dean, J., and Ghemawat, S.: MapReduce: Simplified data processing on large data clusters, *Communications of ACM*, 51 (1), (2008), pp. 107–113.
21. Hadoop: Open source implementation of MapReduce, http://mahout.apache.org/

22. Ranger, C., Raghu Raman, R. Penmetsa, A., Bradski, G., and Kozyrakis, C.: Evaluating MapReduce for multi-core and multiprocessor system, in: Proceedings of the 2007 IEEE International Symposium on High Performance Computer Architecture, HPCA'07, (2007), pp. 13–24.

23. He, B., Fang, W., Lno, Q., Govindaraju, N. K., and Wang, T.: Mars: A MapReduce framework on graphics processors, in: Proceedings of the 17th International Conference on Parallel Architectures and Compilation Techniques, PACT'08, (2008), pp. 260–269.

24. Ekanayake, J., Li, B., Zhang, B., Gunarathne, T., Bae, S. H., Qiu, J., and Fox, G.: Twister: A runtime for iterative MapReduce, in: Proceedings of the 19th ACM International Symposium on High Performance Distributed Computing, HDPC'10, (2010), pp. 810–818.

25. Mahout: Scalable machine learning and data mining, http://mahout.apache.org/

26. Menon, R. K., Bhat, G. P., and Schatz, M. C.: Rapid parallel genome indexing with MapReduce, in: Proceedings of the Second International Workshop on MapReduce and Its Applications, MapReduce'11, (2011), pp. 51–58.

27. Ene, A., Im, S., and Moseley, B.: Fast clustering using MapReduce, in: Proceedings of the 17th ACM SIGKDD International Conference on Knowledge Discovery and Data Mining, KDD'11, (2011), pp. 681–689.

28. Grzymala-Busse, J. W., and Ziarko, W.: Data mining and rough set theory, *Communications of ACM*, 43(4), (2000), pp. 108–109.

29. Tripathy, B. K.: Rough sets and approximate reasoning, Global Trends in Intelligent Computing Research and Development, B. K. Tripathy and D. P. Acharjya (Eds.), IGI Publications, (2013), pp. 180–228.

30. Kaneiwa, K.: A rough set approach to mining connections from information systems, in: Proceedings of the 2010 ACM Symposium on Applied Computing, SAC'10, (2010), pp. 990–996.

31. Leung, Y., Wu, W. Z., and Zhang, W. X.: Knowledge acquisition in incomplete in formation systems: A rough set approach, *European Journal of Operational Research*, 168 (1), (2006), pp. 164–180.

32. Tsumoto, S.: Automated extraction of medical expert system rules from clinical databases based on rough set theory, *Information Sciences*, 112 (1–4), (1998), pp. 67–84.

33. Han, J., and Kamber, M.: *Data mining: Concepts and techniques*, 2nd edition, Morgan Kaufmann, San Francisco (2006).

34. Hu, Q., Xie, Z., and Yu, D.: Hybrid attribute reduction based on a novel fuzzy-rough model and information granulation, *Pattern Recognition*, 40 (12), (2007), pp. 3509–3521.

35. Qian, Y., Liang, J. Pedrycz, W., and Dang, C.: Positive approximation: An accelerator for attribute reduction in rough set theory, *Artificial Intelligence*, 174 (9–10), (2010), pp. 597–618.

36. Lin, J., and Schatz, M.: Design patterns for efficient graph algorithms in MapReduce, in: Proceedings of the Eighth Workshop on Mining and Learning with Graphs, MLG'10, (2010), pp. 78–85.

37. Blanas, S., Patel, J. M., Ercegovac Rao, J., Shekita, E. J., and Tian, Y.: A comparison of join algorithms for log processing in MapReduce, in: Proceedings of the 2010 international conference on management of data, SIGMOD'10, New York (2010).

Chapter 11

An Investigation of Fuzzy Techniques in Clustering of Big Data

Deepthi P. Hudedagaddi and B. K. Tripathy

School of Computing Science and Engineering, VIT University, Vellore, Tamil Nadu, India

Contents

Abstract

The data clustering algorithms have applications in many areas of data mining, pattern recognition, information retrieval, and image processing. The enormous amount of data generated every day by different sources and their structure and complexity have put forth a major challenge for researchers in the present day for their analysis and mining fruitful rules or finding patterns from them. The traditional clustering algorithms do not have the capability to handle such situations. Developing scalable computing platforms has turned out to be in high demand. The uncertainty hidden in these large data sets has further complicated situations like their counterparts in normal data sets. Researchers are trying to follow the incremental approach in improving the existing data clustering algorithms to make them fit to this challenging situation. However, there have been limited efforts so far. The main objective of this chapter is to present the existing data clustering algorithms available in the literature with a critical review and present some more possibilities in this direction.

11.1 Introduction

The collection of a vast amount of data during the last decade or so has necessitated developing techniques to store and handle them efficiently so that useful information can be obtained for use in the future. But the large volume of these data along with their unstructured nature and other complexities involved has made the process very challenging. Clustering of data has been pursued for nearly 40 years or so. The clustered data granular structure can be used in pattern recognition, information retrieval, rule generation, and many such applications. As is well known, clustering is the process of decomposing the input data set into groups of similar elements such that the elements inside each cluster are closer to each other than those in different clusters. Clustering also solves the data visualization problem in Big Data by grouping data together or binning. Several techniques for cluster analysis, such as K-means, fuzzy C-means, intuitionistic fuzzy C-means, etc., have been enhanced to tackle the Big Data situation and their problems. Their predecessors are either lower in speed of execution or generate poor results.

Several developments with respect to technology and the Internet specifically have forced us to face voluminous data, which is an increasing trend every day. At present, various improvements in existing technologies or introduction of new technologies unknown until very recently have led to the generation of a large amount of data. One of the primary sources of this huge amount of data is from several online services, which are established to provide a wide range of services to their clients. Some of these services include social networks, cloud storage, and sensor networks, which not only produce a lot of data but also have a need to store and reuse these data for several analytical aspects. These services are facing major difficulties in performing operations on these voluminous data. Operations like information retrieval and analytical processes have become highly time-consuming and difficult to handle. One technique of handling these issues is to represent these data in a compact format. This compact format needs the help of clustering the input data such that levels representing the clusters provide relevant information on the entire data. Hence, good clustering techniques are needed to be developed for use. Thereby, researchers are needed to help corporations, which will be profitable as they can provide tools to deal with critical systems.

11.1.1 Big Data

Big Data is a popular expression or a catchphrase these days, one that portrays a large volume of both organized and unstructured data. These data are hugely expansive and are difficult to process using customary database and programming methods. Enormous amounts of information can possibly help organizations enhance operations and make quicker, shrewder choices. Big Data is a term for information sets so substantial or complex that customary techniques for processing are insufficient. Challenges that come with Big Data include examination, capture, information curation, searching, sharing, stocking, exchange, representation, and data security.

Studying of data sets can find novel correlations to spot business trends, prevent diseases, combat crime, etc. Researchers, business administrators, specialists in media and publishing, and governments alike frequently face troubles with expansive data sets in fields including Internet browsing, money, and business informatics. The main challenges faced by Big Data are volume, variety, and velocity [1]. Some of the other challenges include the need for speed, data understanding, data quality, displaying meaningful results, and dealing with outliers [2].

11.1.2 Clustering

Clustering refers to binning a set of objects in such a way that objects in the same group are more similar to each other than to those in other groups. Clustering is being used in many fields, including image analysis, information retrieval, machine learning, pattern recognition, and bioinformatics. It is a very important tool in data mining and also for Big Data analysis. Big Data refers to terabytes and petabytes of data. Clustering algorithms include high computational costs. The research question here is on finding techniques to implement clustering algorithms on Big Data and obtaining the results in a favorable time frame. Clustering is used as an initial tool in order to group data into reasonable components, which are further useful in discovering learning components.

Hard clustering alludes to the partition of data into particular groups, in which every single data component has a place with precisely one cluster. In soft clustering, data components can be part of more than one group, and associated with each element is a set of membership values. These denote the inclusion percentage of the data element in that particular cluster.

The classification of clustering methods is provided in Figure 11.1.

Clustering algorithm				
Partitional	Hierarchical	Density-based	Grid-based	Model-based
-K-means	-BIRCH	-DBSCAN	-Wave	-EM
-K-medoids	-CURE	-OPTICS	-Sting	-COBWEB
-PAM	-ROCK	-DENCLUE	-CLIQUE	-CLASSIT
-CLARANS	-Chameleon		-OptiGrid	-SOMs
-CLARA				

Figure 11.1 Clustering taxonomy.

11.2 Fuzzy Clustering in Big Data

Big Data analytics is separated into three levels. The main level manages the accessing of data and its processing. The second level manages the protection, and the third level manages the data mining algorithms. The principal issue in data mining is to produce global models. Combinations of supervised and unsupervised techniques in the form of clustering and classification help in handling larger data sets. Consensus functions are being applied to clustering ensembles to obtain stable clustering. But application of these functions directly on high dimension data is found to be expensive and also impractical. This indicates that a multistage scheme may be successful. For example, one of the genetic algorithms, namely ant colony optimization, has proven to be a solution for metaheuristic issues. Also, hybrid techniques can be used for clustering large medical data sets. Uncertainty has become a common characteristic of large data sets also. So uncertainty-based techniques are to be developed in order to handle large data sets also. Unfortunately, the existing techniques for normal data sets are found to be wanting. So one can develop new techniques with the large data sets in view or enhance the existing techniques for normal data sets suitably to make them fit to handle the additional problems of large data sets. Efforts have been ongoing since a few years back, but progress has been described as incremental rather than substantial. We describe the extensions of a few well-known algorithms, such as the K-means algorithm and also the fuzzy C-means algorithm (FCM).

The notion of fuzzy sets was introduced by Zadeh [3] in 1965 as an extension of the earlier concept of crisp sets introduced by Cantor. This notion is one of the most fruitful models developed so far as a model of uncertainty and also from the application point of view. It provides graded membership to elements instead of dichotomous membership provided by crisp sets, which is more realistic and also provides space for approximation rather than certainty. Although K-means is the simplest of the clustering algorithms, it cannot handle uncertainty, and the clusters generated are disjointed in contrast to the real-life experience that they may not be so in most cases. FCM takes care of this problem and is the first such algorithm found in the literature. With the size of the solution space being infinitely large, no exhaustive search can be done. As a solution to this, the objective function approach developed by Bezdek is found to be good enough. In fact, this objective function approach, which needs to be optimized, has subsequently become instrumental in the development of many more algorithms for normal data. Obviously, FCM requires a little more computation time. But the advantages of this algorithm outshine this small disadvantage in many ways. FCM handles issues related to pattern matching and classification of noisy data, and provides approximate solutions faster. Several algorithms in the form of rough C-means, intuitionistic FCM (IFCM), and more importantly, algorithms based upon their hybrid models like rough FCM and rough IFCM exist along with their kernelized versions and possibilistic versions. But, as far as large data are concerned, most of these algorithms are yet to be extended to this big setting.

Going by the literature, we find that the single pass FCM algorithm is an algorithm that produces clusters similar to FCM but does not use complicated data reduction techniques or data structures. This algorithm is faster than FCM [4]. Hierarchical techniques of clustering generate partitions in a hierarchical manner [5,6]. The divisive and agglomerative techniques are used in these algorithms. The agglomerative technique generates clusters sequentially by combining clusters produced in a higher level. On the other hand, the divisive technique is the converse of the agglomerative technique. A hierarchical clustering algorithm has been developed [7] for the planning of business systems. Another modification of hierarchical clustering that uses fuzzy-based equivalence relations is introduced in [8]. The fuzzy clustering algorithms used in graph theory are different from their counterpart for normal data due to the fact that data representation in graphs is given by connectivity of nodes. The fuzzy graph notion was introduced in [9], and their characteristics are explained; following this, a cluster analysis technique has been proposed in [10] by using fuzzy graphs.

The frequently used FCM was developed in 1974 [11]. Several modifications have been introduced since then. The Gustafson–Kessel (GK) algorithm [12] is a method that approximates local covariance by partitioning data into subsets that can fit with linear submodels. The Gath–Geva algorithm [13,14] overcomes the fitting problem. The fuzzy C varieties (FCV) [15] algorithm deals with multidimensional prototypes of clusters. Fuzzy clustering algorithms are being applied in the field of image segmentation [16,17]. Coming to the context of large data, in [18], a variation of K-means clustering is developed.

For Big Data clustering, a MapReduce implementation of DBSCAN was introduced in [19]. A MapReduce-based parallel K-means clustering algorithm was developed in [20]. In [1,21,22], approaches with MapReduce-based K-means are developed for document clustering. In order to make it fit for large data sets, a modified self-organizing map (SOM)-based clustering algorithm is proposed in [23]. In [24], the authors applied the MapReduce framework on DISCO (DIStributed CO-clustering with MapReduce). A fast clustering algorithm, including a constant factor, was introduced in [25]. Some other Big Data clustering methods based on MapReduce were proposed in [26,27]. Also, the ant colony optimization approach was used for decomposing Big Data into several partitions.

Fuzziness in Big Data can be handled by using the various fuzzy clustering techniques. But due to the large volume of data, these algorithms perform more slowly. This can be improved by using data division techniques like Spark or Hadoop. After this, clustering algorithms can be applied to each of the components of these divided data so that all the clusters can be unified to provide clusters of the original data set [28,29]. A variant of FCM was developed in the form of fast FCM (FFCM) in [1] and, as expected, takes much less time for processing and generating the clusters.

Some more approaches to clustering big data are the CLARA [30], the CURE [31], and the corset algorithms [32]. Also incremental clustering [33], divide and conquer-based clustering [34–36], BIRCH [37], CLARANS [38], Garden [3], and Cluto [39] were successful in designing algorithms for handling large amounts of data. Although these algorithms work quite well, all these are applicable only to crisp data sets. Hence, their use applicability gets reduced to a large extent due to the inherent uncertainty in large data sets also.

Some of the clustering algorithms, like the FFCM [40] and the multistage random FCM [41], have higher computational speed than the normal FCM for Big Data. Some of the other algorithms mentioned in [2] and [42] also have improved efficiency and are modifications of basic FCM for Big Data. Some deviational algorithms are like the fast kernel FCM [43], which was proposed to work on processing of MRI images.

The nonmembership grades in the case of fuzzy sets are just one complement of their corresponding membership grades. Generalizing the notion of nonmembership grades and making it from this constraint, the model of the intuitionistic fuzzy set was introduced by Atanassov [39] in 1986. This is a better model to handle uncertainty than the fuzzy sets. So, IFCM was proposed and examined experimentally by Chaira and Anand [41] and Tripathy et al. [42]. Basically, she had applied it to medical image data sets and found that the segmentation process generates better images than its fuzzy counterpart.

The rough set model introduced by Pawlak in 1982 [44] is not just another model of uncertainty, but in some facets, it is better than fuzzy sets. It follows the idea of a boundary region of uncertainty proposed by Frege, the father of modern logic in 1883. So we find several rough set-based algorithms for data clustering, starting with that of Lingras et al. in 2004 [45] and improved by Peters in 2006 [46]. Also, it has been established both theoretically and experimentally that hybrid models are better than the individual components from which they have been formulated simply because of the procedure of their framing by taking the strong points of the individual components and hiding or neglecting their weak points through suitable methods of composition. So several hybrid algorithms for data clustering exist in the literature, and they are framed on these hybrid notions. However, we do not find any parallel algorithms for large data sets so far. Moreover, our objective in this chapter is to deal with the clustering algorithms based on fuzzy techniques only in order to make it more exploratory and the concentration specific.

Before describing the fuzzy technique-based algorithms for large data sets, we present below their versions for normal data sets proposed in the literature as these are instrumental in the development of the earlier ones. We start with the FCM.

Although FCM was first proposed by Ruspini in 1967, its version using the objective function approach was developed by James C. Bezdek [40]. For technical reasons, we present the version due to Bezdek below. In this, the data elements can be a member of more than one cluster. Each data element has a corresponding membership value.

11.3 Fuzzy C-Means Algorithm

1. Assign the initial cluster centers.
2. Calculate d_{ik}, which is the Euclidean distance between data objects x_v and centroids

$$v_i d(x, y) = \sqrt{(x_1 - y_1)^2 + (x_2 - y_2)^2 + \ldots + (x_n - y_n)^2}$$ (11.1)

3. Generate membership matrix U:
   If $d_{ij} > 0$, then

$$\mu_{ik} = \frac{1}{\displaystyle\sum_{j=1}^{C} \left(\frac{d_{iv}}{d_{jv}} \right)^{\frac{2}{m-1}}}$$ (11.2)

Or else

$$\mu_{iv} = 1$$

4. The centroids are calculated using the formula

$$V_i = \frac{\displaystyle\sum_{j=1}^{N} (\mu_{ij})^m x_j}{\displaystyle\sum_{j=1}^{N} (\mu_{ij})^m}$$ (11.3)

5. Calculate new U by using Steps 2 and 3.
6. If $\|U^{(r)} - U^{(r+1)}\| < \varepsilon$, stop the process or else start from Step 4 [47].

As explained earlier, IFCM is supposed to handle uncertainty in data in a better way, and in terms of area of application, it has wider areas. This was put forth by Chaira [48]. The algorithm in its original form is presented below.

The hesitation function π_A associated with every intuitionistic fuzzy set A is defined for every element x in the universe of discourse as $\pi_A(x) = 1 - \mu_A(x) - \nu_A(x)$. In the case of fuzzy sets, its value is zero for all x in U, the universe of discourse.

11.3.1 IFCM

1. Initialize cluster centers.
2. Compute Euclidean distances d_{ik} between items y_i and cluster centers w_k.
3. Compute membership matrix $V = (\mu_{ik})$ such that $\mu_{ik} = 1$ if $d_{ik} = 0$, or else μ_{ik} is computed using Equation 11.2.
4. Compute the hesitation matrix π.
5. Calculate the modified membership matrix V' using

$$\mu'_{ik} = \mu_{ik} + \pi_{ik} \tag{11.4}$$

6. Calculate cluster centers using

$$v_i = \frac{\sum_{j=1}^{N} \left(\mu'_{ij}\right)^m y_j}{\sum_{j=1}^{N} \left(\mu'_{ij}\right)^m} \tag{11.5}$$

7. Repeat Steps 2 to 5 for computing the new partition matrix.
8. Stop if $\|V'^{(r)} - V'^{(r+1)}\| < \varepsilon$ or else repeat Steps 4 to 8.

Next, we provide some case studies in connection with the FCM for large amounts of data.

11.4 Case Study 1: Hadoop Intuitionistic Fuzzy C Means (HIFCM)

Direct application of IFCM is cumbersome on Big Data. Hence, a new algorithm was developed by Tripathy et al. [44] with which chunks of data are identified by Hadoop's mapper class. The mapper class takes input as clusters and their centroids and performs an update of centroids after each iteration. This step is done after the chunks of data are merged by the reducer. Hadoop helps in effective computation of clusters and reaches local minina effectively. The algorithm HIFCM is as follows:

1. Allocate centroids randomly based on data set.
2. Mapper class is fed with input data set that contains initial centroid information.
3. Mapper class reads the file and by using appropriate data structures organizes data in chunks.
4. Mapper recomputes nearest centroids using Step 1 to 5 in IFCM. These values are provided to reducer.

5. Reducer then emits updated centroids.
6. It is said to be converged if distance < 0.1. Terminate the process or else repeat from Step 2 utilizing updated centroids.

11.4.1 Experimental Results

Accuracy, sum squares between (SSB), sum squares within (SSW), Dunn–Dunn index (DDI), Davies–Bouldin (DB), and silhouette coefficient (SC) are the metrics used. Accuracy depicts how correctly the clusters were formed.

SSW indicates the closeness of the sample to the center of the cluster. SSB depicts the distance of the sample from a different cluster. DB is a ratio that indicates separation within clusters to that with the different clusters. Lesser DB indicates better clustering. DB determines the compactness and separation of clusters from each other. DDI range lies in [0,∞]. SC determines cluster quality. Its value ranges from –1 to 1 with 1 indicating the best clustering [27,28].

DB index is calculated using

$$DB = \frac{1}{c} \sum_{i=1}^{c} \max_{k \neq i} \left\{ \frac{S(v_i) + S(v_k)}{d(v_i, v_k)} \right\} \quad \text{for } 1 < i, k < c \tag{11.6}$$

D index is calculated using

$$D = \min_{i} \left\{ \min_{k \neq i} \left\{ \frac{d(v_i, v_k)}{\max_{l} S(v_l)} \right\} \right\} \tag{11.7}$$

11.4.2 Results

This algorithm was implemented in Java and was applied on UCI's credit, glass, wine, and Wisconsin data sets. Cluster formation for glass and wine data sets is given in Figures 11.2 and 11.3. From the clustering, it is inferred that HIFCM-produced clusters are distinctive. It has produced dense clusters of high quality.

11.4.3 Execution Time

The execution speed of the developed algorithm in comparison to parallel K-means (PKM) and modified PKM (MPKM) developed by Juby Mathew and Vijayakumar [49] is given in Table 11.1 and represented graphically in Figure 11.4. It is clear from the results that execution time of HIFCM is better than PKM and MPKM.

11.4.4 Performance Metrics

The graphs in Figure 11.5 indicate that the HIFCM algorithm is more accurate when compared to PKM and MPKM.

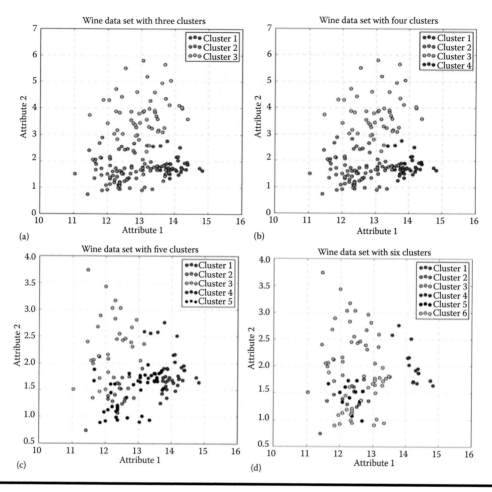

Figure 11.2 **Wine data set clusters: (a) 3 clusters, (b) 4 clusters, (c) 5 clusters, and (d) 6 clusters.**

Table 11.2 gives a clear picture that HIFCM is more efficient than PKM and MPKM. HIFCM has lower dispersion as its DBI value is low. A large value of DI depicts higher intercluster and lower intracluster distance. HIFCM has a higher SC value, which is closer to one.

11.5 Case Study 2: Survey of Clustering Algorithms [45]

11.5.1 BIRCH

The BIRCH algorithm [40] scans the data set and builds a clustering feature (CF) tree. This algorithm works in two phases: scanning the database and building in a memory tree. It is then applied to leaf nodes. The CF tree has two parameters: B, branching factor, and T, threshold. BIRCH uses the concept of radius for controlling the boundary of the cluster. Hence, it does not work well when clusters are not spherical in shape. The algorithm is given in [50].

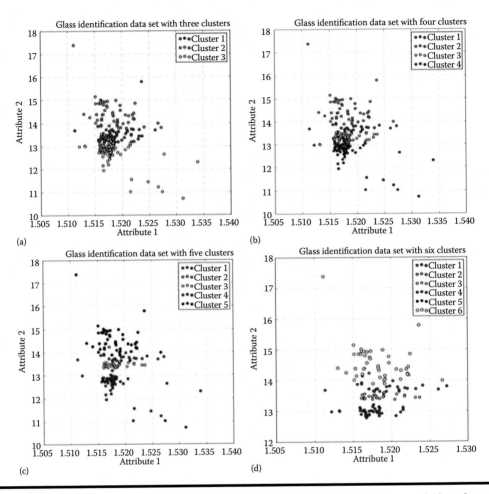

Figure 11.3 **Glass data set clusters : (a) 3 clusters, (b) 4 clusters, (c) 5 clusters, and (d) 6 clusters.**

Table 11.1 **Execution Time of PKM, MPKM, and HIFCM**

Data Set Size N		100K	200K	300K	400K	500K	600K	700K	800K	900K	1000K
Execution Time	PKM	3.12	6.56	10.8	12.9	15.92	19.9	24.2	27.9	29.76	31.43
	MPKM	3.02	6.32	10.4	12.7	15.3	19.4	23.4	26.46	28.67	29.14
	HIFCM	1.65	4.11	6.12	8.78	7.89	11.23	15.23	17.64	18.63	19.76

11.5.2 DENCLUE

The DENCLUE algorithm [19] integrates the data points and influence functions for modeling the distribution of clusters. The influence function depicts the relationship impact of a data point in its neighborhood. This algorithm requires input parameters that have to be selected carefully as they influence quality of clustering results [18]. Some of the properties of DENCLUE are (a) it

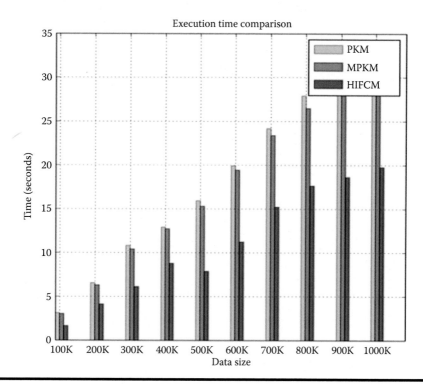

Figure 11.4   Comparison of execution time of PKM, MPKM, and HIFCM.

has a mathematical foundation, (b) it deals with data having noise, and (c) it describes clusters in arbitrary shape mathematically.

The algorithm is given in [50].

11.5.3 *Optimal Grid (OptiGrid)*

The OptiGrid algorithm [20] does partitioning in optimal grids. It uses projections to find the optimal cutting planes. This is achieved by constructing the best cutting hyperplanes through a set of selected projections. These projections are then used to find the optimal cutting planes. OptiGrid makes use of a density function to find the clusters. It is applied in a recursive fashion on the clusters. But this recursion reduces dimensions and hence shows poor performance in low-dimension subspace. In addition, it fails when grid sizes exceed available memory [14]. The algorithm is given in [50].

11.5.4 *Expectation Maximization (EM)*

The EM algorithm [10] approximates the parameters of likelihood in a statistical model in several situations. This uses two steps, the E step and the M step, for approximating the unknown model parameters. Sensitivity in selecting initial parameters is a major disadvantage of the EM algorithm [29]. The algorithm is described in [50].

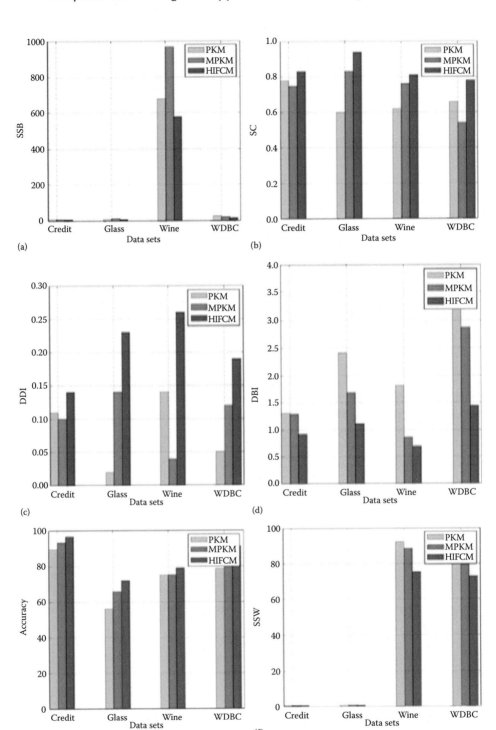

Figure 11.5   Performance metrics comparison of HIFCM with PKM and MPKM: (a) SSB, (b) SC, (c) DDI, (d) DBI, (e) Accuracy, and (f) SSW values of HIFCM with PKM and MPKM.

Table 11.2 Cluster Validity Measures

Data Set	Algorithm	Accuracy	SSW	SSB	DBI	DI	SC
Credit	PKM	89.68%	0.6578	6.89	1.31	0.11	0.78
	MPKM	93.45%	0.6478	6.82	1.29	0.1	0.75
	HIFCM	96.32%	0.61	6.13	0.84	0.14	0.838
Glass	PKM	56.32%	1.1709	7.65	2.41	0.02	0.6
	MPKM	65.89%	1.1821	12.69	1.68	0.14	0.83
	HIFCM	72.32%	1.12	5.22	1.14	0.236	0.956
Wine	PKM	75.34%	92.34	680.2	1.81	0.14	0.62
	MPKM	75.40%	88.45	967.3	0.87	0.04	0.76
	HIFCM	79.39%	78.34	540.628	0.61	0.269	0.827
WDBC	PKM	78.84%	84.22	23.2	3.51	0.05	0.66
	MPKM	78.84%	81.56	19.3	2.87	0.12	0.54
	HIFCM	91.46%	74.43	12.427	1.42	0.19	0.783

11.6 Case Study 3: Incremental Weighted Fuzzy C Means (IWFCM) [4]

Initially data sets are partitioned. Centers are calculated, and membership values are assigned for each partition. The Hadoop environment is used for the implementation of the algorithm. MapReduce decreases the data sets. The output obtained is further processed in the IWFCM environment. The IWFCM algorithm can be seen in [4]. The architecture of IWFCM is provided in Figure 11.6.

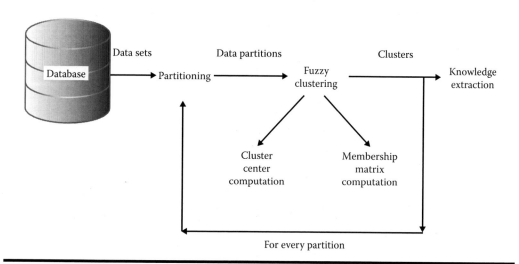

Figure 11.6 Architecture of IWFCM.

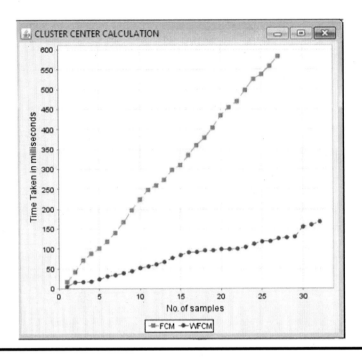

Figure 11.7 Comparison graph.

It is clear from the graph in Figure 11.7 that IWFCM takes lesser time for each iteration when compared to FCM. Since weight is added to every data set, it is more efficient.

11.7 MapReduce-Based FCM Algorithm (MR-FCM)

Previously, message passing interfaces (MPI) [34] or parallel virtual machines (PVM) [35] were used for parallel applications. Parallelization helps in faster processing of Big Data, and hence, researchers are developing new ideas with respect to parallel computing.

Parallel implementation of FCM with MPI was introduced in [36]. This consisted of three master–slave processes. The first computes centroids, the second computes distances and updates the partition matrix and new centroids, and the third computes the validity index. Google has introduced a MapReduce programming paradigm for easier development of parallel applications. This divides large computations into submodules.

The MapReduce model works as follows: The input and output are a set of key value pairs. The map function takes an input pair and returns a set of intermediate key value pairs. All intermediate values are then grouped and associated with the same intermediate key. It is then passed to the reduce function [51].

map (l1, w1) → list (l2, w2)
reduce (l2, list(w2)) → list (w3)

To incorporate FCM to MapReduce, FCM has to be partitioned into two jobs. The first job calculates the centroid matrix, and the second job is necessary since the calculations that follow require complete centroid matrix as input.

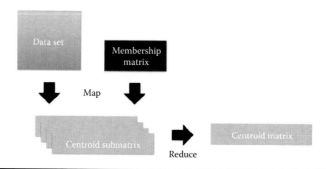

Figure 11.8 First MapReduce job.

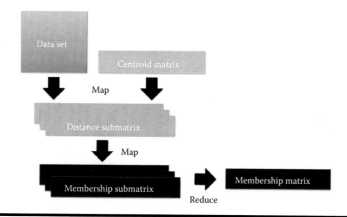

Figure 11.9 Second MapReduce job.

The developed algorithm is shown in Figures 11.8 and 11.9. In the first MapReduce job, a portion of the data set and membership matrix are contained in mappers, and centroid submatrices are produced. The reducer then combines the submatrices into the centroid matrix. The second MapReduce job involves more computations to be executed.

Because centroids have to be calculated before computing the membership matrix, two MapReduce jobs are required.

11.8 Future Directions of Research

The work done so far in the clustering of large data is too meager. So there are a lot of options for future research, including the following:

- So far, the hybrid model-based clustering algorithms have not been developed for large data. This can be handled like in the case of normal data.
- There are variants of the normal uncertainty-based clustering algorithms like the kernelized ones. Research can be done to establish algorithms in this direction.
- Image processing is an important application field for clustering algorithms, leading to image segmentation. Algorithms developed can be applied in this direction for analyzing images to draw conclusions from them in various directions.

11.9 Conclusion

Clustering is a technique to group similar data such that the distance between elements in different groups is larger than that of elements in the same group. In order to handle uncertainty in data, several models exist, and fuzzy sets are one of them. Several FCM algorithms are found in the literature. The extension of FCM is in the form of IFCM. But these basic algorithms are not applicable to large data. So fresh algorithms have been developed to handle the case of large data sets, or the existing algorithms have been extended for the purpose. In this chapter, we provided the basics of crisp and fuzzy technique-based clustering algorithms. Also, we presented all the fuzzy technique-based clustering algorithms developed so far for large data. We find that the research done so far is insufficient in this direction. There is a lot of potential for research in this direction. So it is a fruitful field for future research.

References

1. Zhao, W., H. Ma, and Q. He, Parallel k-means clustering based on MapReduce, in Proceedings of the CloudCom'09, Berlin, Heidelberg, Springer-Verlag, (2009), pp. 674–679.
2. https://www.sas.com/resources/asset/five-big-data-challenges-article.pdf
3. Zadeh, L. A., Fuzzy sets, *Information and Control* 8(3), (1965), pp. 338–353.
4. Prabha, S., and P. K. Sujatha, Reduction of Big Data Sets Using Fuzzy Clustering, *International Journal of Advanced Research in Computer Engineering & Technology (IJARCET)*, 3(6), (2014), pp. 2235–2238.
5. http://searchbusinessanalytics.techtarget.com/definition/Hadoop-cluster
6. http://www.sas.com/resources/asset/five-big-data-challenges-article.pdf
7. Yang, M. S., A survey of fuzzy clustering, *Math. Computer. Modelling*, 18, (1993), pp. 1–16.
8. Lee, H. S., Automatic clustering of business process in business systems planning, *European Journal of Operational Research*, 114, (1999), pp. 354–362.
9. Klir, G. J., and B. Yuan, *Fuzzy Sets and Fuzzy Logic Theory and Application*, Prentice Hall, Upper Saddle River, NJ, (1995).
10. Rosenfeld, A., Fuzzy graphs, in: L. A. Zadeh, K. S. Fu, M. Shimura (Eds.), *Fuzzy Sets and their Applications to Cognitive and Decision Processes*, Academic Press, New York, (1975).
11. Matula, D. W., Cluster analysis via graph theoretic techniques. In R. C. Mullin, K. B. Reid, and D. P. Roselle, editors, Proc. Louisiana Conference on Combinatorics, Graph Theory and Computing, University of Manitoba, Winnipeg, (1970), pp. 199–212.
12. Dunn, J. C., A Fuzzy Relative of the ISODATA Process and Its Use in Detecting Compact Well-Separated Clusters, *Journal of Cybernetics*, 3, (1973), pp. 32–57.
13. Guerrero-Bote, V. P., C. Lopez-Pujalte, F. D. Moya-Anegon, and V. H. Solana, Comparison of neural models for document clustering, *Int. Journal of Approximate Reasoning*, 34, (2003), pp. 287–305.
14. Gath, I., and A. B. Geva, Unsupervised optimal fuzzy clustering, *IEEE Transactions on Pattern Analysis and Machine Intelligence*, 11(7), (1989), pp. 773–781.
15. Bezdek, J. C., C. Coray, R. Gunderson, and J. Watson, Detection and Characterization of Cluster Substructure—Linear Structure, Fuzzy c-Varieties and Convex Combinations Thereof, *SIAM J. Appl. Math.*, 40(2), (1981), pp. 358–372.
16. Yang, Y., and S. Huang, Image Segmentation by Fuzzy C-Means Clustering Algorithm with a Novel Penalty Term, *Computing and Informatics*, 26, (2007), pp. 17–31.
17. Cai, W., S. Chen, and D. Zhang, Fast and robust fuzzy c-means clustering algorithms incorporating local information for image segmentation, *Pattern Recognition*, 40(3), (2007), pp. 825–838.
18. Sarma, T. H., P. Viswanath, and B. E. Reddy, A hybrid approach to speed-up the k-means clustering method, *Int. J. Mach. Learn. & Cyber.* 4, (2013), pp. 107–117.

19. Dean, J., and S. Ghemawat, MapReduce: Simplified data processing on large clusters, in Proceedings of the 6th conference on Symposium on Operating Systems Design & Implementation—Volume 6, OSDI'04, (2004), p. 10.

20. He, Y., H. Tan, W. Luo, S. Feng, and J. Fan, MR-DB scan: A scalable MapReduce-based dB scan algorithm for heavily skewed data, *Frontiers of Computer Science*, 8(1), (2014), pp. 83–99.

21. Zhou, P., J. Lei, and W. Ye, Large-scale data sets clustering based on MapReduce and Hadoop, *Computational Information Systems*, 7(16), (2011), pp. 5956–5963.

22. Li, H. G., G. Q. Wu, X. G. Hu, J. Zhang, L. Li, and X. Wu, K-means clustering with bagging and MapReduce, in Proceedings of the 2011 44th Hawaii International Conference on System Sciences, Washington, DC, USA: IEEE Computer Society, (2011), pp. 1–8.

23. Nair, S., and J. Mehta, Clustering with Apache Hadoop, in Proceedings of the International Conference, Workshop on Emerging Trends in Technology, ICWET'11, New York: ACM, (2011), pp. 505–509.

24. Papadimitriou, S., and J. Sun, Disco: Distributed co-clustering with MapReduce: A case study towards petabyte-scale end-to-end mining, in Proc. of the IEEE ICDM'08, Washington, DC (2008), pp. 512–521.

25. Ene, A., S. Im, and B. Moseley, Fast clustering using MapReduce, in Proceedings of KDD'11, New York, USA: ACM, (2011), pp. 681–689.

26. Yang, J., and X. Li, MapReduce based method for big data semantic clustering, in Proceedings of the 2013 IEEE International Conference on Systems, Man, and Cybernetics, SMC'13, Washington, DC: IEEE Computer Society, (2013), pp. 2814–2819.

27. Cordeiro, F., C. Traina Jr., A. J. M. Traina, J. Lopez, U. Kang, and C. Taloutsos, Clustering very large multi-dimensional datasets with MapReduce, in Proceedings of KDD'11, New York: ACM, (2011), pp. 690–698.

28. Kaufman, L., and P. Rousseeuw, *Finding Groups in Data: An Introduction to Cluster Analysis*. New York: Wiley-Blackwell, (2005).

29. Guha, S., R. Rastogi, and K. Shim, CURE: An efficient clustering algorithm for large databases, *Inf. Syst.*, 26(1), (2001), pp. 35–58.

30. Har-Peled, S., and S. Mazumdar, On core sets for k-means and k-median clustering, in Proc. ACM Symposium on Theory of Computation, (2004), pp. 291–300.

31. Can, F., Incremental clustering for dynamic information processing, *ACM Trans. Inf. Syst.*, 11(2), (1993), pp. 143–164.

32. Can, F., E. Fox, C. Snavely, and R. France, Incremental clustering for very large document databases: Initial MARIAN experience, *Information Sciences*, 84(1–2), (1995), pp. 101–114.

33. Aggarwal, C., J. Han, J. Wang, and P. Yu, A framework for clustering evolving data streams, in: *Proc. Int. Conf. Very Large Databases*, (2003), pp. 81–92.

34. Guha, S., A. Meyerson, N. Mishra, R. Motwani, and L. O'Callaghan, Clustering data streams: Theory and practice, *IEEE Trans. Knowl. Data Eng.*, 15(3), (2003), pp. 515–528.

35. Zhang, T., R. Ramakirshnan, and M. Livny, BIRCH: An efficient data clustering method for very large databases, in: *Proc. ACM SIGMOD International. Conf. Management Data*, (1996), pp. 103–114.

36. Ng, R., and J. Han, CLARANS: A method for clustering objects for spatial data mining, *IEEE Trans. Knowl. Data Eng.*, 14(5), (2002), pp. 1003–1016.

37. Orlandia, R., Y. Lai, and W. Lee, Clustering high-dimensional data using an efficient and effective data space reduction, in: *Proc. ACM Conf. Inf. Knowl. Management*, (2005), pp. 201–208.

38. Karypis, G., CLUTO: A clustering toolkit Technical Report 02-017 Dept. of Computer Science, University of Minnesota (2002). Available at http://www.cs.umn.edu

39. Atanassov, K. T., Intuitionistic Fuzzy Sets, *Fuzzy sets and Systems*, 20(1), (1986), pp. 87–96.

40. Bezdek, J. C., R. Ehrlich, and W. Full, FCM: Fuzzy C-Means Algorithm, *Computers and Geoscience*, 10(2–3), (1984), pp. 191–203.

41. Chaira, T., and S. Anand, A Novel Intuitionistic Fuzzy Approach for Tumor/Hemorrhage Detection in Medical Images. *Journal of Scientific and Industrial Research*, 70(6), (2011), pp. 427–434.

42. Tripathy, B. K., R. Bhargava, A. Tripathy, R. Dhull, E. Verma, and P. Swarnalatha, Rough Intuitionistic Fuzzy C-Means Algorithm and a Comparative Analysis in Proceedings of ACM Compute-2013, VIT University, August 21–22, 2013.

43. Tripathy, B. K., and D. P. Hudedagaddi, Handling Fuzziness in Big Data Using Clustering Technique, NCICT-2015.

44. Pawlak, Z. Rough sets. *International Journal of Parallel Programming*, 11(5), (1982), pp. 341–356.

45. Lingras, P., and C. West, Interval set clustering of web users with rough k-means. *Journal of Intelligent Information Systems*, 23(1), (2004), pp. 5–16.

46. Skowron, A., Ramanna, S., and J. Peters, Conflict analysis and information systems: A rough set approach. *Rough Sets and Knowledge Technology*, (2006), 233–240.

47. Tripathy, B. K., D. Mittal, and D. P. Hudedagaddi, Hadoop with Intuitionistic Fuzzy C-Means for Clustering in Big Data, *Advances in Intelligent Systems and Computing*, Springer, (2016), pp. 599–610.

48. Chaira, T., and A. Panwar, An Atanassov's intuitionistic fuzzy kernel clustering for medical image segmentation. *International Journal of Computational Intelligence Systems*, 7(2), (2014), pp.360–370.

49. Mathew, J., and R. Vijayakumar, Scalable parallel clustering approach for large data using parallel K means and firefly algorithms. High Performance Computing and Applications (ICHPCA), 2014 International Conference on. IEEE, 2014.

50. Fahad, A., A survey of clustering algorithms for big data: Taxonomy and empirical analysis, *IEEE Transactions on Emerging Topics in Computing*, 2(3), (2014), pp. 267–279.

51. Ludwig, S. A., MapReduce-based fuzzy c-means clustering algorithm: Implementation and scalability, *International Journal of Machine Learning and Cybernetics*, 6(6), (2015), pp. 923–934.

Chapter 12

A Survey on Learning Models with Respect to Human Behavior Analysis for Large-Scale Surveillance Videos

M. Sivarathinabala,[1] S. Abirami,[1] and R. Baskaran[2]

[1]*Department of Information Science and Technology, Anna University, Chennai, India*

[2]*Department of Computer Science and Engineering, Anna University, Chennai, India*

Contents

Abstract

Recent advances in pattern recognition have allowed engineers and scientists to jointly address automatic analysis of human behavior via computers. This chapter explores a number of different aspects and open challenges in the field of human behavior analysis (HBA) in the context of Big Data. Human behavior is recognized in different levels with the high-level knowledge in addition to the context. Human pose recognition, action recognition, and interaction recognition are considered as different levels, depending on the number of actors involved. The goal of this chapter is to recognize human behavior analysis in different situations by employing various learning models. Here, the data have been received from the different cameras/locations in streaming; thus, we need an effective learning algorithm that can deal with such situation. Over time, new data become available and the decision structure needs to be revised accordingly. Therefore, different learning models have been identified and studied in the machine learning community under several hierarchies called generative learning, discriminative learning, imitative learning, graphical models, etc. As a result, this chapter addresses the different learning models with respect to HBA for large video data sets, as well as the pros and cons of each learning model. This work also discusses the state-of-the-art learning methodologies that are required to analyze the behavior with respect to Big Data. This chapter also discusses the applications and presents a case study with respect to behavior analysis in large volumes of data.

12.1 Introduction

A video surveillance system is the most recent and important research in the smart environment. In order to enhance safety and privacy protection, surveillance cameras are deployed in all commercial and public places, such as airports, banks, parks, ATMs, retail, etc., and for business intelligence analysis. The widespread use of this technology demanded new functionalities to become smarter surveillance systems. Nowadays, research is mainly focused on multiobject tracking, occlusion handling, event detection, scene analysis, and behavior analysis with respect to surveillance video processing. The objective of this chapter is to recognize human behavior analysis (HBA) in the context of Big Data. The videos from day-to-day activities are recorded and stored. The videos are collected using several surveillance cameras in real time. The video data are of large volume, and they are increasing exponentially over time. The large volume of surveillance videos is collectively known as Big Data with respect to videos, and they need to be analyzed using machine learning approaches for proper exploration (analytics) and analysis. The videos need to be analyzed in order to identify the behavior of the person in the environment.

HBA plays a major role in the video surveillance system. The aim of human activity recognition is to automatically analyze the ongoing activity from an unknown video.

Since the data have been received from different cameras and locations during continuous streaming, we need an effective learning algorithm that can deal with such situations to perform analytics. The data set manipulated in the smart environment grows continuously over time, making the previously constructed classifier obsolete. Indeed, the addition of new records (or deletion of old ones) may potentially invalidate the existing classifier that has been built on the old (still valid) data set. Over time, due to the increase in new data, the decision structures need to be revised further. In most cases, usage of large data sets results in improving the accuracy of the classifier. Thus, the learning model has been identified and studied in the perspective of the machine learning community under several hierarchies, named generative learning, discriminative learning, imitative learning, graphical models, etc. The main focus of this chapter is to address the different learning models with respect to HBA for large video data sets, the pros and cons of each learning model, and the model that can solve the learning problem, and it also discusses the state of the art of learning methodologies that are required to analyze behavior with respect to large-scale video (Big) Data.

Figure 12.1 shows the overview of HBA. Aggarwal and Ryoo (2011) categorized human activities into four different levels based on their complexity: gestures, actions, interactions, and group activities. Gestures are elementary movements of a person's body parts. Actions are the single-person activities that are composed of multiple gestures organized temporally. Concurrent activities are the activities that are performed by multiple persons at the same time. An activity that takes place in the sequence of the actions temporally arranged is called a sequential activity. An activity that takes place repeatedly for some time intervals is also known as a recurrent activity. Interactions are the higher level human activities that happen between two or more persons and/or objects.

Human behavior is modeled as a stochastic sequence of actions. Action recognition is achieved using previously seen actions from the image feature databases. Behavior (Gowsikhaa et al., 2012, 2014) can be represented using the location of the person. The same action sequence can represent

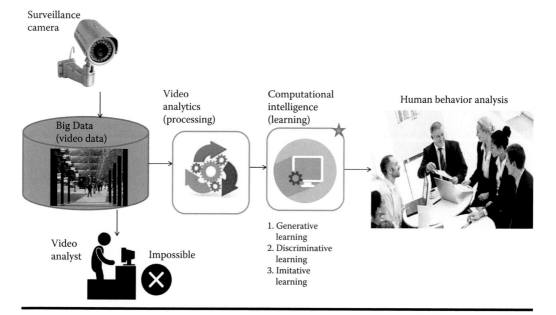

Figure 12.1   Overview of human behavior analysis (HBA) system.

Table 12.1   Behavior with Respect to Activity/Interaction

Action Levels	Semantic Concepts	Behavior Predicted
Activity	Two persons facing each other, person behind one another	Talking, queueing
Interaction	Handshaking, talking, departing	Get together
Recurrent interactions	Kicking, punching, lying down	Fighting
Concurrent interactions	Handshaking, billing (transaction), queueing	Shopping mall scenario

different behavior in different situations. Human behavior can be determined using person interaction with a static object, or person interaction with another person, or interactions between a group of persons. Further, this behavior could be modeled using a suitable learning algorithm to detect abnormalities.

The analysis of human behavior in image sequences consists of three steps:

a. Extract quantitative data from a tracking algorithm
b. Extract qualitative information
c. Predict and classify it into one behavior pattern

Quantitative data from the human behavior system can be obtained by tracking the human using trajectories, body parts of the human, and the face of the human. Qualitative information has been obtained using semantic concepts. Hence, some prior knowledge about the scenario must be provided in order to deal with the semantic gap in every system devoted to extracting qualitative information from numerical data. The system cannot understand the semantic terms—that is, those semantic terms are given by human beings with respect to their representation in natural language. The semantic gap is present in both learning and recognition of behaviors. Then, by combining quantitative and qualitative data, the system interprets and classifies the behavior pattern of the human. With respect to activity and interaction, the possible behaviors are listed in Table 12.1.

Example of Semantic Gap
Given the quantitative input as a trajectory, two possible interpretations can be done:

1. The agent is searching his parked car (considered to be *normal* behavior).
2. The agent is kicking the car (or) trying to steal a car (*suspicious* behavior).

For this given situation, no possible behavior can be identified until prior information is obtained or provided beforehand.

12.2 Open Research Issues in HBA

HBA involves stages such as preprocessing, tracking of humans, extraction of features, estimating the pose of the body, and understanding human behaviors from the sequence of images. It is the major application in surveillance and behavior analysis in the sports domain, etc. The task of tracking has been done using filtering approaches. Mainly, particle filter-based methods are used so as to maintain multiple probabilistic hypotheses with respect to body posture. Pose estimation can be performed using stick figure models or motion history image features.

The challenges that exist in the preprocessing stage are background clutter, dynamic backgrounds or environment (indoor and outdoor), illumination change, camera movements, etc. During the tracking and feature extraction stages, the prevailing challenges are suitable feature selection, low-level feature extraction, occlusion analysis, etc. In the pose estimation, motion analysis, saliency computation, changes in body shape and pose, different dressing style, camera view angles, multicamera, fusion, etc., are considered. The main problem is with the temporal classification of the sequential images. As a more focused challenge, the performance of the system heavily depends on the automatic classification of or learning human behavior from the large volume of video data, and this is discussed in detail in this chapter. Behavior pattern learning and understanding may be considered to be the classification of time-varying feature data. The fundamental problem of behavior understanding is to learn the reference behavior sequences from training samples and to devise both training and testing methods effectively with small variations of the feature data within each class of features.

Existing approaches for learning video data are generative learning, discriminative learning, and imitative learning. Generative learning makes stronger assumptions about the data, and when these assumptions are correct, we can achieve good results when compared to other models. Also generative models need less data for training purposes. Discriminative learning lacks prior knowledge, structure, and uncertainty. Discriminative classifiers overcome the limitation of generative learning, and it has alterations for penalty functions, regularization, and kernel functions. The relationship between the variables is not explicit in the classifiers. Discriminative learning cannot be used if there are no labeled data. The combination of a generative and discriminative pair is known as imitative learning. If the features are conditionally independent, both the models improve the results along with additional features. It is known that graphical models (Kaneko et al., 2012) are the best to model many variables that are interdependent. Some of the challenges that occur in undirected graphical models are the following: Even with complete data, the partition function can introduce dependencies between the parameters. Although maximum likelihood learning is adequate when there are enough data, in general, it is necessary to approximate the average over the parameters. Usually, non-Bayesian methods use averaging methods to avoid overfitting. Figure 12.2 shows the framework of the learning model.

- A model that mathematically relates the visual data x to the world state w. The model specifies a family of relationships that depends on parameters θ.
- A learning algorithm fits parameters θ from paired training examples X_i, W_i.
- An inference algorithm uses the model to return $Pr(w|x)$ given new observed data x.

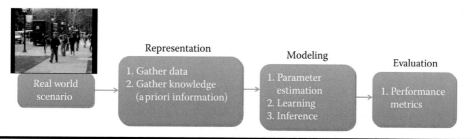

Figure 12.2   A framework of the learning model.

A well-defined learning problem is described in three ways: A computer program is said to learn from experience E. Learning takes place with respect to class of tasks T and performance measure P. The performance at tasks T, as measured by P, improves with experience E. For example, learning is to recognize the human behavior in the scene. Tasks T: Recognize the human behavior. Training E: Sequence of images is recorded while observing the human. Performance measure P: Error happened as judged by the human observer.

It is better to have a machine that learns from a large data set. In learning, rule-based expert systems are replaced by probabilistic models. A key challenge in behavior modeling is model selection, how to choose a model at different levels of complexity. Rule-based and manually driven models are replaced by probabilistic data-driven models. The classification of learning models along with the references is shown in Figure 12.3.

Example: In the sequential learning problem from Cheng (2013), the construction of a classifier h contains a set of labeled sequences from a training set. Every position in a sequence has an observation vector X_T and a discrete label Y_T, where T is the index into the sequence. For time series data, T represents a discrete time step in the sequence. The observation vector X_T contains one or more variables that either are discrete or real valued. The labels Y_T are drawn from a finite set of discrete values, and the size of the label set is represented as $|Y_T|$.

All observations in a sequence are referred to as $X = \{X_1, X_2, X_3,......X_T\}$, where T is the length of the sequence. Similarly, we refer to the labels for a single sequence as $Y = \{Y_1, Y_2, Y_3,......Y_T\}$. A labeled sequence is the pair (X, Y), and the training set of n labeled sequences is defined as $D = \left\{ (X,Y)^i \right\}_{i=1}^{n}$. While T is used to denote the length of arbitrary sequences, it does not necessarily hold that the length of $((X, Y)^{(i)}) \in D$ is equal to the length of $((X, Y)^{(j)}) \in D$ when $i \neq j$. Furthermore, while h is trained on labeled sequences, the label sequence is unavailable at test time, and the trained classifier h maps from X to Y. That is, given a sequence of observations X, h predicts a corresponding label sequence $\hat{Y}$.

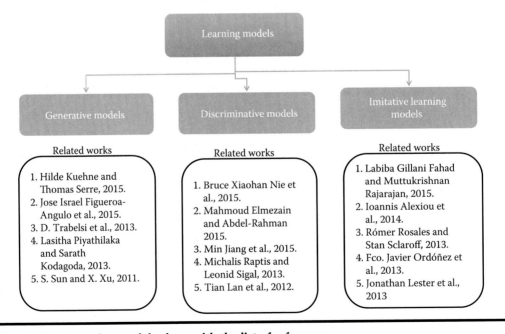

Figure 12.3   Learning models along with the list of references.

Based on the current trend, in order to predict a single label y from a single observation vector x, we assume that individual observation label pairs (X, Y) in the data are independent and identically distributed (IID). In the sequential classification problem, the data are assumed to be IID at the level of entire sequences. That is, all of the variables in $((X, Y)^{(i)}$ are independent of the variables in $((X, Y)^{(j)}$ for $i \neq j$, but there is no assumption about the relationship between the variables within a single sequence X_T and Y_T. When defining the learning problem, no independence assumptions are made within a sequence to predict the solution.

12.3 Generative Probabilistic Models

Generative methods model the joint probability distribution and prior probability and describe the data using structured probabilistic models. The observations are random variables whose distribution depends on model parameters. The generative model allows the imposition of prior knowledge specified by the user. This is called "generative" because when the samples are drawn from the model, they generate new data. Generative models require making assumptions on both the correlation of data and the way in which data are distributed given the activity state. The risk is that the assumptions may not reflect the true attributes of the data. It is hard to integrate complex features in this model. Some of the popular generative models are Naïve Bayes (NB), Gaussian, mixture of Gaussians, and the hidden Markov model (HMM).

Example: Consider a classification problem in which we want to learn to distinguish between a zebra ($y = 1$) and nonzebra ($y = 0$) based on some features of the image. Given a training set, a classification algorithm tries to find elephants and zebras. To classify a new animal as either zebra or nonzebra, the algorithm checks the decision boundary where it falls and makes the prediction accordingly.

Here's a generative approach. First, looking at a zebra, a model is built on what a zebra looks like. Then, looking at a zebra, a separate model is built on what a nonzebra looks like. Finally, to classify a new animal, we can match the new animal against the zebra model and match it against the nonzebra model, to see whether the new animal looks more like the zebra or more like the nonzebra in the training set.

For instance, if y indicates whether an example is a nonzebra (0) or a zebra (1), then $p(x|y = 0)$ models the distribution of nonzebra features, and $p(x|y = 1)$ models the distribution of zebra features. After modeling $p(y)$ (called the class priors) and $p(x|y)$, our algorithm uses Bayes' rule to derive the posterior distribution on y given x:

$$p\left(y|x\right) = \frac{p\left(x|y\right)p(y)}{p(x)} \tag{12.1}$$

$$\arg\max{}_y\, p\left(y|x\right) = \arg\max{}_y\, p\left(x|y\right)p(y) \tag{12.2}$$

12.3.1 Example of Generative Model

12.3.1.1 Gaussian Mixture Models for Representing Images

A Gaussian mixture model (Westerveld et al., 2007; Sun and Xu, 2011) is the model that captures the main characteristics of the image. An image sample is generated by a mixture of Gaussian sources, and the number of Gaussian components is fixed for all images.

For example, in a particular image, feature vectors are extracted, and from the feature vectors, a Gaussian mixture with three components is estimated. The mean vector, covariance matrices, and the prior probability of the components describe the resulting model in the high dimensional feature space. Three Gaussian components are used, but that is not necessarily enough to capture all the information in an image. Any distribution can be approximated closely by a mixture of Gaussians. If the number of components in the mixture is high, then the approximation can be better.

12.3.1.2 Gaussian Mixture Models in HBA

Human behavior is represented in a hierarchical manner, such as person-centered actions, actions with spatiotemporal context, action sequences, and finally behavior. An approach to recognize the behavior has been proposed by Robertson and Reid (2006). The current action sequence has been explained by the set of predefined HMM and by computing likelihood from the set. In the upper levels, they used Bayesian networks and belief propagation; the lowest level used nonparametric sampling from a previously learned database of actions. At each time step, the most likely action was computed. The sequence of actions and their likelihoods over a number of time steps is used to find the most likely behavior by computing the likelihoods of predefined behavior HMMs explaining the current action sequence.

Human actions are a collection of different human body poses moving sequentially at different time intervals. Piyathilaka and Kodagoda (2013) proposed a Gaussian Mixture Model (GMM)-based HMM for human activity detection. In this work, the authors used only skeleton features provided by a RGB-D camera. Gaussian mixtures are useful in clustering data into different groups as a collection of multinomial Gaussian distributions. Therefore, each body pose can be described as a collection of multinomial distributions, and HMM can model the intraslice dependencies between each time period.

Each skeleton joint is separately considered for each activity in the data set and trained with single-stream HMM with GMM output. The K-mean algorithm was used to initialize the mixture components and Gaussian parameters. The optimum sequence of the hidden joint states is determined using the Viterbi algorithm. This process is repeated for each joint, and optimum joint state sequences are added together to form a new feature vector for a given activity. Again, the feature vector is clustered using the K-mean algorithm according to the number of states of the proposed GMM-based HMM. Then the new sequence of observation vectors was obtained by concatenating the observation vectors assigned to each state. For each and every state set of the pose nodes, mixture parameters and Gaussian parameters were initialized using the K-means algorithm. Finally, with the initial parameters, the expectation maximization (EM) algorithm was applied.

Kuehne and Serre (2015) focused on understanding long action sequences to recognize human daily activities. The authors proposed a method that uses reduced Fisher vectors (FVs) in conjunction with structured temporal models for the recognition of video sequences. It shows that the overall generative properties of FVs make them especially suitable for a combination of generative models like Gaussian mixtures. As the resulting FV representation is too high dimensional to be processed in a generative framework, principal component analysis (PCA) is used to reduce the dimensionality of the feature vector. In order to improve the accuracy of recognition of activities, the authors combined the compact video representation based on FVs with HMMs.

12.3.1.3 Learning and Inference in GMM

To train the generative models from data, the maximum likelihood approach is used. The parameter settings of a model describing an image are those that maximize the likelihood of observing that image. The maximum likelihood estimate cannot differentiate the characteristics that are common for many images in a collection and characteristics that are typical of a particular image. For retrieval, this distinction is very important. Therefore, the model is interpolated with a background model, describing the main characteristics shared by many images in the collection. This interpolation will reduce the influence of common characteristics and thus improve retrieval results. Finally, the modeling of textual information in the same generative model can be adapted to describe video documents.

12.4 Discriminative Probabilistic Models

Discriminate methods are models directed by the posterior probabilities (Fahad and Rajarajan, 2015). This model focuses on the computational resources of a given task in order to provide better performance. It is more expensive to learn, and you need to run decoding (Viterbi method) during training and usually multiple times for an example. It is easy to integrate features in this model and focus only on modeling the posterior probability regardless of how the data are distributed. Discriminative models usually provide less accuracy for small data sets. Some of the popular models are logistic regression, support vector machine (SVM), nearest neighbor, conditional random field (CRF), and neural networks.

12.4.1 Examples of Discriminative Models

12.4.1.1 SVM Classifier

SVM performs classification using linear decision hyperplanes in the feature space. The hyperplanes are calculated during training, and they are used to separate the training data with different labels. Using the kernel function, SVM has many extensions, such as regression, density estimation, and kernel PCA. If the training data are not linearly separable, the kernel function is used to transform the data into a new space. SVMs (Manosha Chathuramali and Rodrigo, 2012) scale well for very large training sets and perform well and produce better results. When the number of training samples increases, the complexity in training also increases.

12.4.1.2 Discriminative Models in HBA

Zheng et al. (2015) presented a different approach for human activity recognition. This paper uses a hierarchical method to recognize 10 activity classes. In this work, 10 classes were divided into five different classification problems. The Least Squares SVM (LS-SVM) and NB algorithm have been used to classify the different activity classes. The activities are recognized based on the features, such as mean, variance, entropy of magnitude, and the angle between triaxial accelerometer signal features.

The authors recognized 10 activities, and these 10 activities are grouped into four different activities, such as 2-D walking, 3-D walking, walking activities, and static activities. To achieve higher scalability than the single-layer framework, a multilayer classification framework was presented. In this method of activity recognition, three layers have been designed. The walking-related activities are recognized in the first layer, static activities are recognized in the second layer, and 2-D and 3-D activities are recognized using the third layer. Using this methodology, 10 activities have been recognized with an accuracy of 95.6%.

However, many classifiers face the problem of long training time and large size of the feature vector. These problems in human activity recognition are solved using the SVM classifier along with spatiotemporal feature descriptors. Manosha Chathuramali and Rodrigo (2012) proposed human activity recognition using SVM. Their system is compared with existing classifiers using two standard data sets, and their results were good. Due to the imbalance in training examples, the computation time is less.

Yu et al. (2014) proposed an approach based on weighted feature trajectories to recognize the activity. The SIFT and particle BOFs are combined, and weighted spatiotemporal descriptors are used for action recognition. SVM is used for action classification.

A data set $D = \left\{ X_i, Y_i \right\}_{i=1}^{s}$ is given along with $Y_i = \{-1, +1\}$, $X_i \in \mathbb{R}^s$. The SVM algorithm calculates a hyperplane that can separate the data by reducing the following equation:

$$\int (\theta, \varepsilon) = \frac{1}{2} \left\| \theta \right\|^2 + C \sum_{i=1}^{s} \varepsilon_i \tag{12.3}$$

$$Y_i (\theta . X_i + b) \geq 1 - \varepsilon_i, \quad \varepsilon_i \geq 0 \tag{12.4}$$

where θ is the weight vector, and $C > 0$ is the coefficient for constraint violation. For multiclass classification, the one-against-rest approach is used. A multichannel χ^2 kernel is employed to train SVM.

Kapsouras and Nikolaidis (2014) introduced a novel method for action recognition in motion capture data. The motion capture sequence is represented using the joint orientation angles and the forward differences of these angles in different temporal scales. Initially, K-means is applied on training data to discover the most representative sequence on the motion capture data. The periodic nature of angular data is applied on the K-means variant. Each frame is then assigned to one or more of these informative patterns and histograms that describe how many times the same sequence occurs for each movement. The nearest neighbor and SVM methods of classification have been used in this work to classify the actions. This method has been tested using motion capture data. It is very clear that SVM χ^2 classification provides better results. This χ^2 kernel takes the codebook or histogram into consideration.

12.5 Learning and Inference in SVM

In general, SVM is a binary classifier and discriminative model. Given training data (X_i, Y_i) for $i = 1, 2, \ldots, N$, with $X_i \in \mathbb{R}^D$, $Y_i = \{-1, +1\}$ learns a classifier $f(x)$ such that $f(X_i) = \left\{ \begin{array}{ll} \geq 0 & y_i = +1 \\ \leq 0 & y_i = -1 \end{array} \right\}$ —

that is, $y_i f(X_i) > 0$ for correct classification. A linear classifier has the form $f(x) = W^T X + b$ in 2-D. W is the weight vector for the linear classifier, and it is normal to the line. b is the bias. The training data are used to learn the parameter W. Only W is needed to classify the new data.

Learning an SVM has been formulated as an unconstrained optimization problem over W and ε $\min_{W \in \mathbb{R}^D, \varepsilon_i \in \mathbb{R}} \left\| W \right\|^2 + c \sum_{i}^{N} \varepsilon_i$ subject to $Y_i (W^T X_i + b) \geq 1 - \varepsilon_i$ for $i = 1, 2, \ldots, N$. The constraint $Y_i (W^T X_i + b) \geq 1 - \varepsilon_i$ can be written more concisely as $y_i f(X_i) \geq 1 - \varepsilon_i$, which together with $\varepsilon_i \geq 0$ is equivalent to $\varepsilon_i = \max (0, 1, -y_i f(X_i))$.

$$\min_{W \in \mathbb{R}^D} \left\| W \right\|^2 + c \sum_{i}^{N} \max\left(0, 1, -y_i \, f(X_i)\right) \tag{12.5}$$

where $\max(0, 1, -y_i f(X_i))$ is the loss function, and $\left\| W \right\|^2$ is the regularization parameter. If $y_i f(X_i) > 1$ and $y_i f(X_i) = 1$ represent the points outside the margin, then this will not contribute to loss. If $y_i f(X_i) < 1$ represents the points violating the margin constraints, then this will contribute to loss.

12.6 Probabilistic Graphical Models in HBA

A graphical model is a probabilistic model in which the graph is specified to determine the conditional dependency between the variables. Graphical models provide a flexible framework for modeling a large collection of variables with complex interactions (Koller and Friedman, 2009).

12.6.1 Directed and Undirected Graphs

An undirected graph (undirected network) has a set of objects that are connected together, and the objects are vertices and edges. In the undirected graph, all the edges are connected bidirectionally. However, in the directed graph, the edges are pointed in a particular direction. When drawing an undirected graph, the edges are typically drawn as lines between pairs of nodes as illustrated in Figure 12.4. Each edge represents the dependency as shown in the figure. An example of an undirected graph is the Markov Random Field (MRF). Undirected graphs are represented as factor graphs. Examples of directed graphs are Bayesian networks. This is the Directed Acyclic Graph (DAG). Bayesian networks are not compatible with undirected graphs or factor graphs. CRF is the discriminative undirected graphical model. This is widely used in the sequence labeling task. CRF is used to encode the known relationship between observations and construct the interpretations in sequential data.

12.6.2 Generative Graphical Model

An HMM is the most important generative graphical model that models sequential data or time-series data. HMM is used in many applications, such as speech recognition, protein/DNA sequence analysis, robot control, and information extraction from text data. HMM depends on the formulations whether to "generate" the output from a state or a transition. We assume that an output symbol is always generated from a state and that any state can be a starting state or ending state.

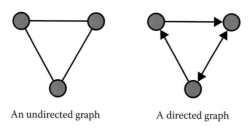

An undirected graph   A directed graph

Figure 12.4   Undirected and directed graphs.

HMM plays a vital role in determining activities that are vision based. Research (Yamato et al., 1992; Li et al., 2008b; Aggarwal and Ryoo, 2011; Figueroa-Angulo et al., 2015) proves that HMM is one of the most appropriate models for person activity prediction. Li et al. (2008a) proposed a graphical model for learning and recognizing human actions. In order to encode actions in a weighted directed graph, known as an action graph, nodes of the graph represent salient postures. The transitional probability between the two postures is represented by the weights between two nodes. An action is encoded using an action graph, and the postures are encoded using a GMM. The pose and actions are learned from the training samples through unsupervised clustering and an EM algorithm. Oliver et al. (2004) stated that, "a layered hidden Markov model (LHMM) can obtain different levels of temporal details while recognizing human activity. The LHMM is a cascade of HMMs, in which each HMM has different observation probabilities processed with different time intervals." Hu et al. (2013) have proposed an LHMM as a statistical model, which is derived from the HMM.

In the context of HBA, Li et al. (2014) proposed a novel technique for automatic activity recognition based on multisensor data. An offline adaptive HMM is proposed to utilize the data efficiently and overcome the Big Data problem. A sensor selection scheme based on an improved Viterbi algorithm is presented. The series of hidden states are used to capture the temporal evolution of an activity, and the hidden states are observed from appearance and/or motion observations. For example, Yamato et al. (1992) proposed an HMM to recognize the activity that observes a sequence of symbols over the video frames in varying time intervals. Once a particular activity is trained, the model assigns higher probabilities to a sequence of symbols that more closely match the learned activity.

Lv and Nevatia (2006) performed key pose matching with sequence alignment via Viterbi decoding. Xu et al. (2013) extended HMMs to model the duration of each state in the temporal evolution of activities. During execution, these models are highly robust to time shifts as well as time variance in activities. However, this model lacks information about the spatial structure. This spatial structure can be crucial for making recognition; for example, spatial structure makes the decision in understanding whether a motion comes from the upper or lower body or whether the two parts meet or miss each other in a relative motion. Trabelsi et al. (2012) proposed a method that takes into account the sequential appearance of the data. The sequential appearance of the data has been considered for temporal acceleration data to accurately detect activities. The observed acceleration data are multidimensional. As an extension of standard HMM, HMM regression is presented. Each segment is described by a regression model while preserving the Markov process in modeling the sequence of unknown (hidden) activities. The standard HMM-based approaches use simple Gaussian densities as density of observation.

HMM is the most successful approach to modeling and classifying dynamic behaviors. Human action recognition (Brand et al., 1997) has been done using three-layered HMM. Their system was capable of recognizing six distinct actions, including raising the right arm, raising the left arm, stretching, waving the right arm, waving the left arm, and clapping. From the observations made in the survey process, most of the previous work centered on identification of particular activities in a particular scenario, and less effort has been put into recognizing interactions. The LHMM and Coupled Hidden Markov Model (CHMM) are the major attempts to enhance the robustness of the interaction analysis system by reducing the training parameters. An effective learning process has been carried out by combining the max-belief algorithm and the Baum–Welch algorithm (McCallum et al., 2006). The max-belief algorithm is used to derive the most likely sequence of results in observation activities, and the Baum–Welch algorithm reduces the inference errors.

12.6.3 Discriminative Graphical Model

CRF was proposed by Lafferty et al. (2001) and is a discriminatively trained model for structured classification. Activity recognition, with which the observations and labels arrive in a sequence over time, is a structured domain, and CRFs are well suited for activity recognition. Sutton and McCallum (2010) introduced CRFs as undirected graphical models, in which the graph structure encodes independence relationships between labels. The term "conditional" refers to that condition on the observations. In other words, the structure of the graph encodes independence relationships between labels and not the observations. The CRF model assumes no independence relationships between observations, and inference in CRFs remains tractable even when the relationships are complex and the observations have arbitrary features.

Lan et al. (2012) proposed CRF to model group activities. For example, for the group activity of talking, ideally the people want to keep the interactions with people facing each other but eliminate the noisy interactions, such as people facing the same direction, which will confuse talking with queuing.

From Figure 12.5, the group activity class is represented by Y, which are indices of classes, such as talking, standing in a queue, and so on. Actions are represented by h. For both activity y and actions h, they have used feature level descriptions, denoted by x. In this case, they used HOG. The model is an MRF model, which encodes the joint likelihood as the summation of the clique weights and the clique potentials. The first set of cliques encodes the co-occurrence relationship between activity and actions. The next set of cliques is the co-occurrence between pairs of actions. The dashed line has been used to indicate the connectivity. This is because the structures of this layer have been treated as a latent variable in the model and automatically infer it during learning and inference. They are not using a fully connected model here; only a set of actions that are closely interacted will be connected to each other. For learning the hidden structures, standard Integer Linear Programming (ILP) has been used and a graph sparsity constraint in the objective function. Also making the graph sparse will make the inference more suitable. This is one of the challenges in the learning problem involving hidden variables, structured learning, and parameter estimation.

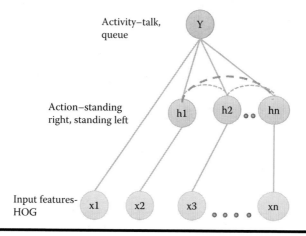

Figure 12.5 Conditional random field (CRF) model representation. (Adapted from T. Lan, L. Sigal, and G. Mori, Social roles in hierarchical models for human activity recognition, in: IEEE International Conference CVPR, 2012.)

12.7 Learning and Inference Methods Used in HBA

Graphical models are mainly used for pose estimation, action recognition, interaction recognition, and behavior recognition. These models represent the relationships between different body parts and performers. Poses are usually denoted as nodes in the graph, and edges depict specific relationships between poses. In the Bayesian network, the conditional distribution of a set of nodes is given as $V' = \{v_1, v_2, \ldots \ldots v_i\}$ and another set of nodes $W' = \{w_1, w_2, \ldots \ldots w_i\}$ in the MRF by summing over all possible assignments to $u \notin V', W'$; this is called exact inference. However, exact inference is a P complete problem. Markov chain Monte Carlo and loopy belief propagation are the approximation techniques that are mostly used in practice.

Mukherjee et al. (2014) proposed a graphical approach to recognize interactions. They generated the dominating poses of each person and used these as nodes of the graph. All possible combinations of dominating poses of two persons and doublets are created for each interaction. Ranking is done using a graph to produce dominating pose doublets. The corresponding interaction is represented as a selected set of dominant pose doublet. Another new graphical approach known as 2.5-D graph representation was proposed by Yao and Li (2012) to recognize actions from single images. The key joints of the body parts are represented as graph nodes, and spatial relationships between key joints are represented as graph edges. Each key joint is represented by 2-D appearance features and 3-D positions. An exemplar-based representation is used to classify actions. The similarity between actions is measured by matching their corresponding 2.5-D graphs.

Many approaches model human poses by localizing body joints. The poses are represented using spatial configuration of body joints. Lan et al. (2010) proposed action recognition in videos. The authors modeled the spatial pose structure as well as temporal pose evolution using body joints. They estimated human joint locations and calculated the best estimated joints for each frame. Then the estimated joints are grouped into five body parts and sets of selective co-occurring pose sequences of body parts in spatial and temporal domains were obtained. For example, the "lifting" action involves the right and left arms moving up concurrently. In the testing phase, histograms of detected body parts are created as inputs of SVM classifiers. Meng et al. (2012) used the locations of the body joints to recognize human interactions. They have recognized intraperson and interperson interactions between the parts of the same person and between the parts of different persons, respectively. In order to learn the model, joint relative locations are represented as semantic spatial relational features.

CRF is the framework of labeling and segmenting structured data, and it is able to deal with various features in a single unified model. Specifically, in order to handle the "multiscale" relationships, fully connected CRFs have been introduced by Kaneko et al. (2012). Instead of specifying the range of human relationships, this approach describes human relationships in position, size, movement, and time sequence as potentials so as to deal with various types, sizes, and shapes of groups. The unary only, adjacently connected, and fully connected models are the various models in CRF. The features extracted from the detected persons and the observed data are defined as $x = \{x_1, x_2, \ldots \ldots x_N\}$, where x_i is the observed data from the ith person, and N is the number of detected persons. The corresponding activity labels are $= \{y_1, y_2, \ldots \ldots y_N\}$; each variable y_i is the set of labels $L = \{l_1, y_2, \ldots \ldots l_k\}$, where k is the class of labels. A CRF $\{x, y\}$ is characterized by a Gibbs distribution.

$$P(y|x) = \frac{1}{Z(x)} \exp(-\big(E\big(y\big)\big)) \tag{12.6}$$

where $Z(x)$ is the partition function, and $E(y)$ is the Gibbs energy.

$$E(y) = \sum_i \psi_u(y_i) + \sum_i \sum_{j>1} \psi_p(y_i, y_j) \tag{12.7}$$

where ψ_u and ψ_p are the unary potential and pairwise potential. In inference, the maximum a posteriori (MAP) labeling of the random field is estimated.

$$\vec{y} = \arg\max_{y \in L^N} P(y|x) \tag{12.8}$$

Since it is intractable to compute the exact distribution $P(y|x)$ for all the sets of labels L^N, this model uses a mean field approximation. The mean field approximation is calculated. However, the pairwise potential in this model is defined by the gaussian kernel; therefore, it is possible to use a highly efficient approximated inference algorithm via high-dimensional filtering. The calculation complexity is reduced from quadratic to linear in the number of variables N. In learning, the kernel parameters are defined with respect to size, position, and motion. The collective activities, such as queuing, talking, walking, and gathering, are recognized.

12.8 Imitative Learning (Generative or Discriminative Paired Model)

Imitative learning is simply the generative–discriminative paired model (Cheng, 2013). The popular model is NB–logistic regression pair and HMM and CRF. The generative–discriminative paired model is shown in Figure 12.6. The meaning of the paired model is that they have the same form as a linear classifier, but the parameter has been estimated in different ways. For feature x and label y, NB estimates a joint probability $p(x,y) = p(y){*}p(x|y)$ from the training data and uses the bayes rule to predict $p(y|x)$ for the new test instances. On the other hand, logistic regression estimates $p(y|x)$ directly from the training data by minimizing an error function. These differences have inference for error rate:

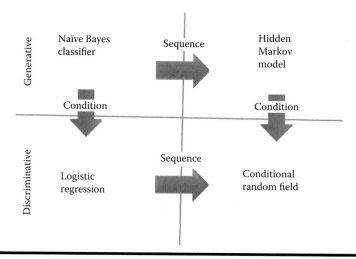

Figure 12.6　Generative–discriminative pair.

1. When there are very few training samples, an overfit problem occurs in logistic regression because there are not enough data to estimate $p(y|x)$ reliably. NB can do it better because it models the entire joint distribution.
2. When a large-scale data set is used, the NB classifier might "double count" features that are correlated with each other because it assumes that each $p(x|y)$ event is independent when they are not. Logistic regression can provide good results by naturally "splitting the difference" among these correlated features.

If the features are mostly conditionally independent, both models might improve with more and more features, provided there are enough data instances. The problem arises when the training set size is small relative to the number of features. In these cases, priors on NB feature parameters or regularization methods for logistic regression are useful.

Ordóñez et al. (2013) proposed the combination of the discriminative capabilities of an artificial neural network (ANN) or an SVM, and the dynamic time warping abilities of HMM can achieve better results for dynamic problems. The model proposed in this paper is denoted as a hybrid HMM approach, in which the temporal characteristics of the data are modeled by HMM state transitions, and an ANN is used to model HMM state distributions. The different types of hybrid HMM systems have successfully been applied in a large-scale video data set; particularly, the popular approach is to combine HMMs with ANNs. The authors have applied a hybrid HMM/ANN methodology to predict time series data, obtaining a model that gave a much better segmentation of the series. Models based on a hybrid ANN framework have been also widely used for various recognition tasks, namely, speech recognition, handwritten text recognition, sentence recognition, and digit recognition.

Lester et al. (2013) presented a hybrid approach to recognize activities, which combines the useful features and ensemble of static classifiers to recognize different activities with HMMs to capture the temporal regularities and smoothness of activities. The activities people perform have certain natural regularities and temporal smoothness—for example, people do not abruptly change between walking and driving a car; thus, the recent observations can help in predicting the present. From the instantaneous classifiers, the sequence of posterior probabilities is computed and used to train HMMs that significantly improve the performance of the recognition system. By incorporating the static classification results, we overcome the weakness of HMMs as effective classifiers. The proposed model succeeded in identifying a small set of maximally informative features and was able to identify 10 different human activities with an accuracy of 95%.

12.9 Summary

Activities can be recognized (Aggarwal and Ryoo, 2011) as single layered approaches and in hierarchical approaches. Single layer approaches are suitable to recognize human activities based on image sequences, and they are suitable for gesture or action recognition. In contrast, hierarchical approaches recognize high-level activities, which are complex in nature. It has been observed from the literature that the hierarchical approach is well suited to recognize high-level activities (interactions). Thus, many researchers proposed a different level of graphical models as hierarchical HMM, semi-HMM, 2-D HMM, factorial HMM, coupled HMM, asynchronous IO HMM, fully connected CRF, tree CRF, hidden CRF, layered CRF, etc. The activity recognition models that are used in large-scale data sets are summarized in Table 12.2.

Table 12.2   Activity Recognition Models in Large-Scale Video Data Sets

Author, Year	*Learning Methods Used*	*Inference Used*	*Activities Recognized*
Generative Models			
Hilde Kuehne and Thomas Serre, 2015	Combination of generative framework FV and Gaussian mixtures	For mice behavior, Bigram model—parsing technique, Viterbi algorithm—FV encoding	Activities recognized from the data sets: ADL, Olympic, Toy Assembly, CMUMMAC, MPIICooking, 50 Salads, Breakfast, and CRIM13
Jose Israel Figueroa-Angulo et al., 2015	Compound HMM	Viterbi learning algorithm	Sit still, stand still, stand up, sit down, walk
D. Trabelsi et al., 2013	HMM in a multiple regression context—multiple HMM regression (MHMMR)	EM algorithm	(a) Climbing stairs down, (b) climbing stairs up, (c) walking, (d) sitting, (e) standing up, (f) sitting on the ground
Lasitha Piyathilaka and Sarath Kodagoda, 2013	GMM-based HMM model	EM algorithm	Twelve unique activities done in five different environments: office, kitchen, bedroom, bathroom, and living room
Hejin Yuan et al., 2015	Semisupervised learning: k-means clustering, skeleton features (cumulative skeleton image, silhouette history image)	Nearest neighbor-based classification	Weizmann data set (10 basic actions): bend, jump, jump, jack, wave, wave 1, wave 2, side, walk, run
Discriminative Models			
Bruce Xiaohan Nie et al., 2015	Spatiotemporal and/or graph model; learning coarse and fine level parameters—coarse level—linear SVM; fine level—structure latent SVM	Dynamic programming	Sub-JHMDB data set: baseball pinch, baseball swing, bench press, bowl, clean and jerk, golf swing

(Continued)

Table 12.2 (Continued)   Activity Recognition Models in Large-Scale Video Data Sets

Author, Year	Learning Methods Used	Inference Used	Activities Recognized
Mahmoud Elmezain and Abdel-Rahman 2015	Latent Dynamic Conditional Random Field (LDCRF)	Gradient ascent with the BFGS optimization technique	Walk, run, jog, box, clap, wave
Michalis Raptis and Leonid Sigal, 2013	Max-margin learning framework	Structured SVM	UT interaction data set
Generative/Discriminative Pair			
Rómer Rosales and Stan Sclaroff, 2006	EM Algorithm—maximum likelihood parameter estimation	Deterministic approximation for inference, the mean output solution (MO)	Pose estimation
Fco. Javier Ordóñez et al., 2013	Hybrid scheme: ANN and HMM	Viterbi algorithm	Leaving, toileting, showering, sleeping, breakfast, dinner, drink
Jonathan Lester et al., 2013	Adaboost algorithm—feature extraction; ensemble of classifier—decision stumps (discriminative) and HMM (generative)	EM Algorithm	Sitting, walking, jogging, entering a building, driving a car
Yuhuang Zheng, 2015	Hierarchical classification—four different classifiers, least square support vector machine (LS-SVM) and NB classifier	Maximum likelihood estimation	Ten activities, such as walking (forward, left, and right), walking (upstairs, downstairs), jumping, running, standing, sitting, and sleeping
Graphical Models			
Ninghang Hu et al., 2014	Latent CRF—hidden latent conditional random field (LCRF)	Max margin approach—learning parameters; exact inference—dynamic programming; learning—structural SVM	Reaching, moving, pouring, eating, drinking, opening, closing, placing, scrubbing, and null

(Continued)

Table 12.2 (Continued)   Activity Recognition Models in Large-Scale Video Data Sets

Author, Year	Learning Methods Used	Inference Used	Activities Recognized
Tian Lan et al., 2012	Max-margin learning framework	Exact inference—belief propagation	UT interaction data set (handshake, hug, kiss)
Takuhiro Kaneko et al., 2012	Fully connected conditional random field (CRF)	Gaussian kernel—kernel parameters, (multiscale relationship)	Collective activities—queuing, walking, talking, gathering, crossing
Sunyoung Cho et al., 2013	Visual and textual information—features undirected graphical model using structured learning with latent variables	Nonconvex minization procedure	High five, handshake, hug, and kiss

12.10 Applications

Graphical models have been applied to a variety of domains, including text processing, computer vision, and bioinformatics. MRFs are used in image processing to generate textures as they can be used to generate flexible and stochastic image models. In image modeling, the task is to find a suitable intensity distribution of a given image, for which suitability depends on the type of application. Application of MRF includes image and texture synthesis, image compression and restoration, image segmentation, surface reconstruction, image registration, texture synthesis, super-resolution, stereo matching, and information retrieval. They can be used to solve various computer vision problems, which can be posed as energy minimization problems. The different regions have to be distinguished using a set of discriminating features within an MRF framework to predict the category of the region.

The different graphical structures that occur in the literature have different applications. One of the first large-scale applications of CRFs was by Sha and Pereira (2003) to segment noun phrases in text. Then, graphical models have been applied to many problems in HBA at various levels, including pose recognition (Rosales and Sclaroff, 2006; Eweiwi et al., 2011; Raptis and Sigal, 2013; Wang et al., 2013), action recognition (Lv and Nevatia, 2006; Yao and Li, 2012; Jain et al., 2013; Jiang et al., 2015; Lan et al., 2015), interaction recognition (Kaneko et al., 2012; Cho et al., 2013; Sener and Ikizler-Cinbis, 2015), behavior recognition (Lan et al., 2010, 2012; Elmezain and Abdel-Rahman, 2015; Nie et al., 2015; Ziaeefard and Bergevin, 2015), and many others.

Another application is to multilabel classification, in which each instance can have multiple class labels. Rather than learning an independent classifier for each category, Ghamrawi and McCallum (2005) proposed a CRF that can learn the dependencies between the variables, and classification performance has been improved. Finally, the skip-chain CRF is a general CRF that represents long-distance dependencies in information extraction. The collective activity recognition problem can be solved using a new graphical CRF structure using a fully connected CRF using a piecewise learning model (Kaneko et al., 2012).

12.11 Performance Metrics

Every system has been evaluated using statistical metrics to measure the performance of the system. The study of these metrics gives more details about the strength and weakness of the system. The performance evaluation metrics are described as follows:

True Positive (TP), True Negative (TN), False Positive (FP), and False Negative (FN) are called frame-based metrics, where,
TP – correct identification
TN – correct rejection
FP – incorrect identification
FN – incorrect rejection
Precision (Positive Predictive Value [PPV])
Precision is defined as the number of TPs relative to the sum of the TPs and the FPs—that is, precision is the fraction of correctly detected items.

$$Precision = TP / (TP + FP)$$

Recall (sensitivity or TP rate)
Recall is defined as the number of TPs relative to the sum of the TPs and the FNs. Recall = TP/(TP + FN).
Specificity (TN rate)
Specificity is defined as the TNs relative to the sum of the TNs and the FPs.

$$TNR = TN / (TN + FP).$$

$$FP \ rate \ (FPR) = 1 - specificity = FP/(FP + TN)$$

$$FN \ rate = 1 - sensitivity = FN / (TP + FN)$$

$$Negative \ predictive \ value \ (NPV) = TN/(TN + FN)$$

Precision recall curve
The system evaluation can be done using precision and recall measures based on the correct behavior predicted. The precision and recall curve identifies the system that maximizes recall for a given precision.
F-Score
The F-score can be used as a single measure of performance test for the positive class. The F-score is the harmonic mean of precision and recall and is given as

$$F\text{-}Score = 2 * (Recall * Precision)/(Recall + Precision)$$

Table 12.3 Performance Metrics Used in Recent Research

Reference	Performance Metrics
Acampora et al., 2015	Precision, recall, F-score, ROC curve
Sener and Ikizler-Cinbis, 2015	Accuracy
Fahad and Rajarajan, 2015	Precision, recall, F1-score, accuracy
Kapsouras and Nikolaidis, 2014	Correct classification rate (CCR)
Yu et al., 2014	Mean average precision, accuracy
Ordóñez et al., 2013	F-measure, precision and recall
Cheng, 2013	Precision, recall, F1-score, accuracy
Lester et al., 2013	Precision and recall

Accuracy

Accuracy is defined as the sum of the TPs and the TNs relative to the total number of ground truth objects. This is a measure of the actual performance of the system with regard to both correctly detecting and correctly rejecting target behavior.

$$\text{Accuracy} = (TP + TN)/(TP + TN + FP + FN)$$

Some of the metrics play a major role in measuring performance of the HBA system. The extracted features have been used in the experiments to analyze the behavior of the person. Receiver Operating Characteristic (ROC) and Correct Classification Rate (CCR) are some of the important metrics that are defined below, and the performance metrics that are used in recent research are tabulated in Table 12.3.

ROC Curve

HBA performance is evaluated using ROC curve. The ROC curve denotes a trade-off curve between a FPR and TP Rate (TPR) in the *x*- and *y*-axes, respectively, when the acceptance threshold is varied by a receiver.

Correct Classification Rate

The CCR is defined as the rate at which the correct behavior recognition is done by the system.

12.12 Case Study: HBA Using Neurofuzzy Systems (Acampora et al., 2015)

This chapter has been especially devoted to the study of HBA. The authors intended to design a new architecture to recognize human behavior in normal and abnormal situations from videos. The uncertainty and vagueness of the video data becomes difficult to analyze, and it is hard to design and develop from everyday human activities. In order to overcome this difficulty, the authors (Acampora et al., 2015) propose a novel hybrid architecture, an HBA model with different computational intelligence methodologies. This HBA model provides more scalable and effective behavior detection. The effectiveness of the system has been tested using the CAVIAR data set. The system can recognize the normal and abnormal behavior of the person in the ATM scenario. The behaviors, such as meeting, walking, money withdrawing, bag leaving, and fighting, are recognized using the system.

The behavior learning has been done using a combination of the Time Delay Neural Networks (TDNN) and a Fuzzy Inference System (FIS). The novel hybrid architecture has been modeled using lower and higher layers. The lower layer is based on the TDNN, and the higher layer is based on the fuzzy inference engines based on the tracking algorithm. The primitive behaviors, such as walking, running, stopping, and loitering, are recognized from the tracking algorithm data in the lower layer. From these primitive behaviors, a context-aware process has been added using fuzzy inference engines, and high-level behaviors, such as meeting, walking, money withdrawing, and dangerous situations, are recognized in an effective manner.

The features, such as horizontal position, vertical position, and speed, are given as input to the channels 1, 2, and 3. TDNN has been designed in such a way that it has two hidden layers, and each layer has 15 neurons. FIS has been designed using contextual rules that provide contextual features. Assuming both O1 and O2 are humans, the contextual rule is given as

IF (distance O1; O2 is small) AND (loitering1 is yes)
AND (loitering2 is yes) THEN (output is fighting)

The labels are represented as distance O1; O2; loitering1; loitering2 and output, respectively, the distance between the human O1 and the human O2, the micro behavior related to the human O1 is loitering, the micro behavior related to the human O2 is loitering, and the inferred group behavior is fighting in this case. The performance of the system has been measured using precision, recall, F-score, and accuracy of the behavior detector.

12.13 Conclusions

In this chapter, the problem with respect to the learning method in large data sets from big video data has been discussed. Mainly, this work focuses on the different learning approaches that can handle big video data synchronously. Performing classification of such data sets requires techniques that limit access to the secondary storage in order to reduce substantially the overall execution time. Big video data in the context of a smart environment aim to improve accuracy in HBA. In learning large and entire data sets, classification or learning techniques are used. The generative model, discriminative model, imitative or paired model, and graphical model are used based on the applications. The pros and cons of each learning techniques are discussed. Features that link the observations to transitions or incorporate observations from several time steps are often required for good classification accuracy in activity recognition tasks. As a model, CRFs do not make independence assumptions between the observations; they can link a particular observation (or any function computed on the observation sequence) to state transitions, and as discriminatively trained models, they will often have lower error rates than the corresponding generative model. It is then identified that conditional random fields are suitable models for large-scale data.

References

Acampora, G., Foggia, P., Saggese, A., and Vento, M., 2015. A hierarchical neuro-fuzzy architecture for human behavior analysis, *Information Sciences,* 310, pp. 130–148.

Aggarwal, J. K., and Ryoo, M. S., 2011. Human activity analysis: A review, *ACM Computing Survey.* 43, 3, Article 16.

Brand, M., Oliver, N., and Pentland, A., 1997. Coupled hidden Markov models for complex activity recognition. Proceedings of CVPR.

Cheng, H.-T., 2013. Learning and recognizing the hierarchical and sequential structure of human activities, PHD Thesis, Carnegie Mellon University, Pittsburgh, PA.

Cho, S., Kwak, S., and Byun, H., 2013. Recognizing human-human interaction activities using visual and textual information, *Pattern Recognition Letters,* 34 (15), pp. 1840–1848.

Elmezain, M. and Abdel-Rahman, E. O., 2015. Human activity recognition: Discriminative models using statistical chord-length and optical flow motion features, *Applied Mathematics & Information Sciences,* 9 (6), pp. 3063–3072.

Eweiwi, A., Cheema, S., Thurau, C., and Bauckhage, C., 2011. Temporal key poses for human action recognition, in: IEEE International Conference on Computer Vision Workshops (ICCVW), 2011, pp. 1310–1317.

Fahad, L. G. and Rajarajan, M., 2015. Integration of discriminative and generative models for activity recognition in smart homes. *Applied Soft Computing,* 37, pp. 992–1001.

Figueroa-Angulo, J. I. et al., 2015. Compound hidden Markov model for activity labeling, *International Journal of Intelligence Science,* 5, pp. 177–195.

Ghamrawi, N. and McCallum, A., 2005. *Collective Multi-Label Classification.* CIKM'05, Bremen, Germany.

Gowsikhaa, D., Manjunath, and Abirami, S., 2012. Suspicious human activity detection from surveillance videos. *International Journal on Internet and Distributed Computing Systems,* 2 (2), pp. 141–149.

Gowsikhaa, D., Abirami, S., and Baskaran, R., 2014. Automated human behavior analysis from surveillance videos: A survey. *Artificial Intelligence Review,* 42 (4), pp. 747–765.

Hu, W., Tian, G., Li, X., and Maybank, S., 2013. An improved hierarchical Dirichlet process-hidden Markov model and Its application to trajectory modeling and retrieval, *International Journal of Computer Vision,* 105, pp. 246–268.

Jain, M., Jegou, H., and Bouthemy, P., 2013. Better exploiting motion for better action recognition, in: IEEE Conference on CVPR, pp. 2555–2562.

Jiang, M., Kong, J., Bebis, G., and Huo, H., 2015. Informative joints based human action recognition using skeleton contexts, *Signal Processing: Image Communication,* 33, pp. 29–40.

Kaneko, T., Shimosaka, M., Odashima, S., Fukui, R., and Sato, T., 2012. Consistent collective activity recognition with fully connected CRFs. IEEE Conference on ICPR, pp. 2792–2795.

Kapsouras, I. and Nikolaidis, N., 2014. Action recognition on motion capture data using a dynemes and forward differences representation. *Journal of Visual Communication and Image Representation,* 25 (6), pp. 1432–1445.

Koller, D. and Friedman, N., 2009. *Probabilistic Graphical Models—Principles and Techniques.* Cambridge, MA: MIT Press.

Kuehne, H. and Serre, T., 2015. Towards a generative approach to activity recognition and segmentation. CoRR abs/1509.01947.

Lafferty, J., McCallum, A., and Pereira, F., 2001. Conditional random fields: Probabilistic models for segmenting and labeling sequence data. Proc. 18th International Conf. On Machine Learning. Morgan Kaufmann. pp. 282–289.

Lan, T., Wang, Y., Yang, W., and Mori, G., 2010. Beyond actions: Discriminative models for contextual group activities. International Conference on Advances in Neural Information Processing Systems (NIPS), pp. 1–9.

Lan, T., Sigal, L., and Mori, G., 2012. Social roles in hierarchical models for human activity recognition. IEEE International Conference CVPR.

Lan, T., Zhu, Y., Zamir, A. R., and Savarese, S., 2015. Action recognition by hierarchical mid-level action elements. International Conference on Computer Vision (ICCV), pp. 4552–4560.

Lester, J., Choudhury, T., Kern, N., Borriello, G., and Hannaford, B., 2013. A hybrid discriminative/generative approach for modeling human activities, *IJCAI*, 5, pp. 766–772.

Li, W., Zhang, Z., and Liu, Z., 2008a. Graphical modeling and decoding of human actions. International Workshop on Multimedia Signal Processing (MMSP), Cairns, Queensland, Australia, October 8–10, pp. 175–180.

Li, W., Zhang, Z., and Liu, Z., 2008b. Expandable data-driven graphical modeling of human actions based on salient postures, *IEEE Transaction on Circuits and Systems for Video Technology*, 18 (11), pp. 1499–1510.

Li ,Y., Shi, D., Ding, B., Liu, D. 2014. Unsupervised Feature Learning for Human Activity Recognition Using Smartphone Sensors. In: Prasath R., O'Reilly P., Kathirvalavakumar T. (eds) Mining Intelligence and Knowledge Exploration. Lecture Notes in Computer Science, vol 8891. Springer, Cham.

Lv, F. and Nevatia, R., 2006. Recognition and segmentation of 3D human action using HMM and multi class ADABOOST. European Conference on Computer Vision–ECCV, pp. 359–372.

Manosha Chathuramali, K. G. and Rodrigo, R., 2012. Faster human activity recognition with SVM. International Conference on Advances in ICT for Emerging Regions (ICTer), pp. 197–203.

McCallum, A., Pal, C., Druck, G., and Wang, X., 2006. HMM multi-conditional learning: Generative/discriminative training for clustering and classification. AAAI'06 Proceedings of the 21st National Conference on Artificial Intelligence, pp. 433–439.

Meng, L., Qing, L., Yang, P., Miao, J., Chen, X., and Metaxas, D. N., 2012. Activity recognition based on semantic spatial relation. IEEE International Conference on Pattern Recognition (ICPR), pp. 609–612.

Mukherjee, S., Biswas, S. K., and Mukherjee, D. P., 2014. Recognizing interactions between human performers by "Dominating Pose Doublet." *Machine Vision and Applications*, 25, pp. 1033–1052.

Nie, B. X., Xiong, C., and Zhu, S.-C., 2015. Joint action recognition and pose estimation from video. IEEE Conference on Computer Vision and Pattern Recognition (CVPR), pp. 1293–1301.

Oliver, N., Garg, A., and Horvitz, E., 2004. Layered representations for learning and inferring office activity from multiple sensor channels. *Computer Vision and Image Understanding*, 96, pp. 163–180.

Ordóñez, F. J., de Toledo, P., and Sanchis, A., 2013. Activity recognition using hybrid generative/discriminative models on home environments using binary sensors, *Sensors*, 13 (5), 5460–5477.

Piyathilaka, L. and Kodagoda, S., 2013. "Gaussian mixture based HMM for human daily activity recognition using 3D skeleton features," *2013 IEEE 8th Conference on Industrial Electronics and Applications (ICIEA)*, Melbourne, VIC, pp. 567–572.

Raptis, M. and Sigal, L., 2013. Poselet key-framing: A model for human activity recognition. IEEE International Conference on CVPR, pp. 2650–2657.

Robertson, N. and Reid, I., 2006. A general method for human activity recognition in video, *Journal of Computer Vision and Image Understanding,* 104 (2), pp. 232–248.

Rosales, R. and Sclaroff, S., 2006. Combining generative and discriminative models in a framework for articulated pose estimation, *International Journal of Computer Vision*, 67 (3), 251–276.

Sener, F. and Ikizler-Cinbis, N., 2015. Two person interaction recognition via spatial multiple instance embedding. *Journal of Visual Communication and Image Representation*, 32, pp. 63–73.

Sha, F. and Pereira, F., 2003. Shallow parsing with conditional random fields. NAACL '03 Proceedings of the Conference of the North American Chapter of the Association for Computational Linguistics on Human Language Technology, 1, pp. 134–141.

Sun, S. and Xu, X., 2011. Variational inference for infinite mixtures of Gaussian processes with applications to traffic flow prediction, *IEEE Transactions on Intelligent Transportation Systems*, 12 (2), pp. 466–475.

Sutton, C. and McCallum, A., 2010. An introduction to conditional random fields. arXiv:1011.4088.

Trabelsi, D. et al., 2012. Belle Colloboration, arxiv.1301.2033. CKM 2012, Cincinnati, OH, USA.

Trabelsi, D., Mohammed, S., Chamroukhi, F., Oukhellou, L. and Amirat, Y., 2013. An Unsupervised Approach for Automatic Activity Recognition Based on Hidden Markov Model Regression, *IEEE Transactions on Automation Science and Engineering*, 10 (3), pp. 829–835.

Wang, C., Wang, Y., and Yuille, A. L., 2013. An approach to pose-based action recognition. IEEE Conference on Computer Vision and Pattern Recognition (CVPR), pp. 915–922.

Westerveld, T., de Vries, A., and de Jong, F., 2007. Generative Probabilistic Models, Centrum voor Wiskunde en Informatica. University of Twente, Enschede, Netherlands.

Xu, X., Tang, J., Zhang, X., Liu, X., Zhang, H., and Qiu, Y., 2013. Exploring techniques for vision based human activity recognition: Methods, systems, and evaluation. *Sensors (Basel).* Jan 25; 13 (2), pp. 1635–1650.

Yamato, J., Ohya, J., and Iishi, K., 1992. Recognizing human action in time-sequential images using hidden Markov model. IEEE Computer Society Conference on Computer Vision and Pattern Recognition, pp. 379–385.

Yao, B. and Li, F.-F., 2012. Action recognition with exemplar based 2.5D graph matching. European Conference on Computer Vision (ECCV), pp. 173–186.

Yu, J., Jeon, M., and Pedrycz, W., 2014. Weighted feature trajectories and concatenated bag-of-features for action recognition, *NeuroComputing*, 131, pp. 200–207.

Zheng, Y., 2015. Human activity recognition based on the hierarchical feature selection and classification framework. *Journal of Electrical and Computer Engineering*, 2015: 140820:1–140820:9.

Ziaeefard, M. and Bergevin, R., 2015. Semantic human activity recognition: A literature review, *Pattern Recognition*, 48, pp. 2329–2345.

Chapter 13

Mining Unstructured Big Data for Competitive Intelligence and Business Intelligence

Anass El Haddadi,[1] Amine El Haddadi,[2]
Zakaria Boulouard, Fadwa Bouhafer, Nihal Chouati,[3]
Abdelhadi Fennan,[4] and Bernard Dousset[5]

[1]*Department of Computer Sciences, ENSA of Al-Hoceima, Ctre Ait Youssef Ou Ali, Morocco*

[2]*Paul Sabatier University Toulouse, France and Faculty of Sciences and Technologies, Tangier, Morocco*

[3]*National School of Applied Sciences, Tangier, Morocco*

[4]*Abdelmalek Essaâdi University, Tétouan, Morocco*

[5]*Paul Sabatier University, Toulouse, France*

Contents

Abstract

In the information era, people's lives are deeply impacted by IT due to exposure to social networks, emails, RSS feeds, chats, white papers, web pages, etc. Such data are considered very valuable for companies nowadays since they will help them improve their strategies, for example, by analyzing their customers' trends or their competitors' marketing interventions. Several decisional tools have been developed in the past few years, but they still faced a big challenge. Being mostly based on relational databases, it was difficult to use them to analyze unstructured data, which represent nowadays more than 85% of the available data. Thus, there is a rising need for a suitable management process for unstructured data through collecting, managing, transferring, and transforming them into meaningful informed data. In this chapter, we explore a new analytical model of big unstructured data for the competitive intelligence system XEW.

13.1 Introduction

People nowadays rely on information technologies in their everyday lives, resulting in petabytes of shared data. This can present a huge opportunity for companies in order to evolve and improve their presence in the market as well as their strategy as a whole. The use of traditional decision tools, mostly based on relational databases, has shown its limits in analyzing such data. According to Merrill Lynch, more than 85% of all business information exists as unstructured data commonly appearing in emails, memos, notes from call centers and support operations, news, user groups, chats, reports, letters, surveys, white papers, marketing material, research, presentations, and web pages (Blumberg and Atre 2003). Plejic et al. (2008) claimed that unstructured data are often part of a document's text body, content not included in structured data management systems. Common examples in which we can find unstructured data are emails, maps, reports, contracts, images, movies, spreadsheets, web content, and presentations. As we can see, unstructured data also come in different forms. Thus, the user will encounter many issues in handling these data that will require extra programming and coding (Yafooz et al. 2011). In this study, we explored several ways to deal with unstructured data, which all agree on the necessity of extracting the data and structuring them for later use. Then, synthetic information often takes a relational form based on the connections between actors, semantic networks, etc. Representing this information as a graph may ease its analysis for nonexperts since understanding a network's (graph's) structure helps in understanding the way its components interact.

It is worth mentioning that visualization in existing systems is not satisfactory when it comes to readability; it would be in the global structure or in the detailed analysis of local communities, especially when it comes to complex networks. Two approaches may be chosen: simplifying the network to a reduced graph in which each node represents a group or exploding the graph into subgraphs.

This new approach we have adopted in our competitive intelligence system XEW resides in incremental clustering. This technique helps to represent each class by its most significant node. It is modified in order to randomize the number of classes. Yet it is not sufficient when it comes to evolving data. The total graph can be divided into several period graphs when the time dimension is taken into account. With these two solutions, each class may first be analyzed separately on the reduced graph and then on a specific time slice.

The rest of the chapter is structured as follows: Section 13.2 presents the problem of Big Data; Section 13.3 discusses the methods of managing unstructured data, and Section 13.4 introduces the approach proposed in our solution, the competitive intelligence system XEW in mining and visualizing unstructured data. In Section 13.5, XEW will be tested in a case study in which we will extract up-to-date data from the online database BioSpace and visualize the strategic alliances between biotechnology companies.

13.2 Big Data

The growing amount of data has made researchers as well as professionals set standards defining what we call Big Data (Zikopoulos et al. 2012). Until recently, this trend has been defined as in Figure 13.1.

This model has been extended to 5 Vs more recently, which was explained by Lomotey and Deters (2013) as follows:

- *Volume*: The actual size of data keeps growing at an exponential rate. It is believed that the amount of data produced within the last two years is more than the total electronic data ever created.
- *Variety*: The data being generated come in heterogeneous formats and from multiple sources. Besides, the data have no standard schema to contain semistructured or unstructured data.
- *Velocity*: The concept of data sets (batches) is very fast moving to data streams due to the speed of data coming in and going out.
- *Value*: To remove the frequent confusion in the definition of the value between either quality or cost, Lomotey and Deters (2013) have identified it as the cost, adopting the fact that enterprises are in possession of various data that have different price values.
- *Veracity*: Getting the "noise" out of the data will guarantee its quality and will make sure that the data we get are what we want.

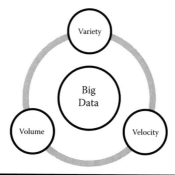

Figure 13.1   Initial 3 Vs of Big Data.

13.3 Significance and Methods of Managing Unstructured Data

Today's business routine cases require analyzing gigabytes of documentary data (Big Data) on a daily basis. The need arises due to these facts (Geetha and Mala 2012):

■ 80% of all entity data are unstructured.
■ The amount of unstructured data is doubling every 2 months.
■ A computer's inability to manage content-based data still remains a problem.
■ Most sophisticated artificial intelligence tools are still unable to realize proper analysis.
■ Text analysis technologies seem better at data reduction than actual data analysis.

In this section, we present several methods of managing unstructured data, especially textual and image data.

13.3.1 Using Relational Databases

The relational database management system (RDBMS) has a powerful and robust data structure for managing, organizing, and retrieving structured data (Doan et al. 2009), which has made it the most preferred way to manage data in the business world for more than 30 years. Yet the exponential growth of unstructured data has made it difficult for the RDBMS to keep up with it since, besides their enormous size, they come in different shapes and store the data without any constraints or rules, such as textual documents in directories, emails, reports, and online news articles. Gupta and Lehal (2009) pointed out that 80% of information is often stored in text documents, thus the urgent need for a suitable management process for unstructured data.

Most of the techniques proposed so far are based on mapping the unstructured data to structured data.

Abdullah and Ahmad (2013) suggested that this mapping should be according to the following four steps:

■ *Extraction*: This is about identifying the format and source of unstructured data. It has two main activities:
  – *Entity extraction*: This is the process of extracting entities found within unstructured data, such as names, dates, places, etc.
  – *Fact extraction*: This is the process of understanding the information about the facts from the unstructured data (contacts, issues, content, etc.), which is important for integration purposes.
■ *Classification*: This is a process in which unstructured data are classified or categorized according to the nature and format of the same group. Four main data classes have been identified (text, image, audio, and video).
■ *Repository development*: The main activity in this process is the preparation and development of individual repositories to store all identified unstructured data.
■ *Data mapping*: This has two main activities:
  – *Preparation of the subject*: This comes from the study of the business needs and the organizational interests.
  – *Mapping*: This requires involving metadata as a linkage to create an association between unstructured data with the thematic topic. The content of the metadata is defined earlier based on the organizational needs.

Meanwhile, Yafooz et al. (2013) pointed out three methods for managing unstructured data using a relational database approach: by creating a database schema, by developing a new data model, or by query search.

13.3.1.1 Database Scheme

A database scheme is a description of the entities in a database.

Mansuri and Sarawagi (2006) have proposed a technique that establishes a connection among unstructured data in a relational database. Their technique is based on two stages: First, the named entities are extracted. Second, the extracted entities are matched with an entity that already exists in the database table or in the same table.

Similarly, Tari et al. (2010) have proposed an intermediate repository for an incremental information extraction framework with an RDBMS to avoid repeating several information extraction processes in biomedical textual articles. Figure 13.2 shows the system architecture of an incremental repository.

Chu et al. (2007) developed an extraction architecture based on a database scheme that incrementally extracts structured information from textual data for further queries.

13.3.1.2 Data Model

A data model is a data structure used to organize data. Doan et al. (2009) have introduced the unstructured database management system (UDMS), which is based on a data model called data generation and exploitation (DGE). DGE interacts with three main elements: system, data, and users. Liu et al. (2011) developed an advanced unstructured data repository (AUDR), which focuses on managing multimedia files based on a tetrahedral data model.

Commercial database vendors have two methods:

- *Traditional*: Storing textual data in a variable with a link to the file stored separately
- *Modern*: Introducing binary large objects (Oracle) and file streams (Microsoft)

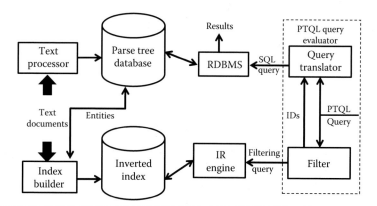

Figure 13.2   System architecture of incremental repository.

13.3.1.3 Query-Based Approach

This is a front-end database technique used to retrieve data from a text database.

There are attempts to run SQL queries on unstructured data (extract then query, query then extract, and keyword search).

- *Extract then query*: This is an offline process that focuses on extracting structured data from text files, then storing them in the database.
- *Query then extract*: This retrieves only the relevant document.
- *Keyword search*: This is utilized to search for a term or a word in a text document or a search engine.

13.3.2 Using XML

Abidin et al. (2010) have proposed an approach for capturing unstructured data in web pages, classifying them, transforming them into XML format, and then saving them into a multimedia database. Their prototype was built based on a framework of five layers:

- **User.**
- **Interface:** This is an interaction medium between the source and the user that allows manipulating the data in the web page.
- **Source:** This consists of a huge amount of useful data in the form of structured, semistructured, or unstructured web pages.
- **XML:** In this layer, the results of the classification process will be placed into a structured XML document.
- **Storage:** The storage system used in this layer is a multimedia database.

They have considered classification as the most important step in the process, especially when it comes to the data extraction. They have identified four classes (text, image, video, and audio), and each of these classes has several subclasses, which represent the detailed category of particular data.

The classification process was based on the DOM tree technique in order to find the correct data in the HTML document. Some of the unnecessary nodes, such as script, style, or other customized nodes, were filtered, which has minimized the unnecessary information during the extraction process.

13.3.3 Using NoSQL

NoSQL is a new generation of database management systems introduced to solve the problems and limitations of RDBMS, such as performance and managing large amounts of data. They are designed to be implemented in a distributed environment; the workload is thus divided among several machines.

It is worth considering that although Yafooz et al. (2013) have considered NoSQL management systems, they are still unable to replace the RDBMS since their databases lack the most important database properties, namely being atomic, consistent, isolated, and durable (ACID). The databases known as ACID are guaranteed to achieve successful database transactions. Sequeda and Miranker (2012) add to that the fact that NoSQL databases are products of different vendors, so their query styles vary, and in order to aggregate the data from all of these sources, a mash-up service has to be deployed, obliging the developer to study different API and deal with different structures of returned data.

On the other hand, Lomotey and Deters (2013) believed in the potentials of NoSQL and suggested that it just needs proper data mining tools based on it. They have proposed a tool based on two algorithms: parallel search and bloom filtering.

13.4 Mining Unstructured Data Approach in the Competitive Intelligence Systems XEW

After the great number of strategic analyses that we have already conducted using the software Tétralogie and Xplor V1, we realized that the final users of analysis products need, along with the macroscopic view, some microscopic analyses on the already identified elements (competitiveness, markets, new products or processes, potential partners, etc.) or to discover others. In hindsight, many experts or decision makers need more details on the traditional elements of their environment, especially concerning their specific vocabulary, the actors and markets around them, as well as the alliances they plan.

So what we propose is to keep adopting the proposed Xplor model and to complete its macroscopic analyses by an advanced online model XEW that enhances the obtained information using statistical overlaps, incremental classifications, or multidimensional analyses. Our goal is to favor the information's extraction according to the general context and nonexclusively by decrypting the contents of separate documents. This makes it possible to retrieve, from a known element (actor, keyword), all or some of its related information (teams, collaboration, concepts, rises, associate keyword, etc.) using advanced filtering concepts.

The XEW prototype helps running strategic analyses on information corpuses coming from various sources, such as online bases (scientific publications, patents, portals, directories), CDs, the visible and invisible web, newspapers, internal bases, RSS feeds, social networks, etc., and gives the decision makers the possibility to run their own investigations without the assistance of a senior analyst or expert.

Its applications are very diverse:

- Identification of themes and actors in the field
- Demonstrating development and cooperation strategies
- Proposing scenarios for the technologic evolution (innovation)
- Extracting weak signals
- Consulting updated information in real time thanks to the web services
- Make-up "field" information during salons, customer visits, or meetings
- Asking for urgent specific information to be online

The CI model XEW relies on a four-level decisional architecture, presented in Figure 13.3:

A. *XEW Sourcing Service (XEW-SS)*

This service allows searching, collecting, and processing the data from different sources. This requires consideration of a multimodal fusion able to consider the heterogeneity, the imprecision, and the uncertainty of multisource data. This fusion awareness ensures

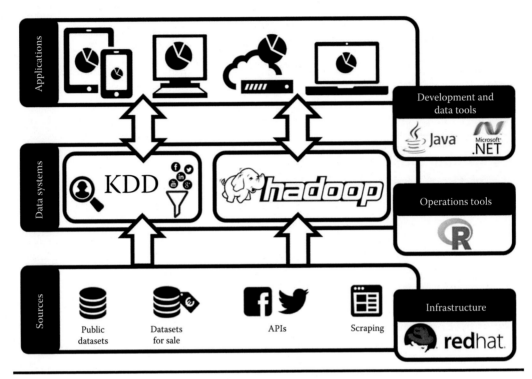

Figure 13.3 XEW architecture.

mastering the knowledge and the information and, consequently, eases the decision making. XEW-SS processes the information heterogeneity from different sides:

- Semantic content: scientific, technical, etc.
- Structural: from highly structured (patents) to unstructured (emails)
- Language (multilingualism): Chinese, Arabic, etc.
- Support format: Word, HTML, PDF, etc.
- Size: definition of the information unit to be analyzed (information granularity)

This architectural level's objective is to provide a complete description of the multisource data process. The techniques used in this level rely on web services dedicated to every source of information.

B. *Meta-Model of Unstructured Data*

The multidimensional model aims to identify all the relationships of existing dependences between different variables from the subject of analysis. These relationships are defined by co-occurrence matrices, which indicate the simultaneous presence of the methods of two qualitative variables in a document.

We have altered these matrices by introducing a third temporal variable (year, month, days, hours), which consists of indicating the presence of a certain relationship in a certain moment.

Example. Figure 13.4 presents a formed multidimensional presentation of collaborations between scientists in cells and of three edges graduated respectively according to the sets of their research themes, the organizations they are affiliated to, and the publication dates of their

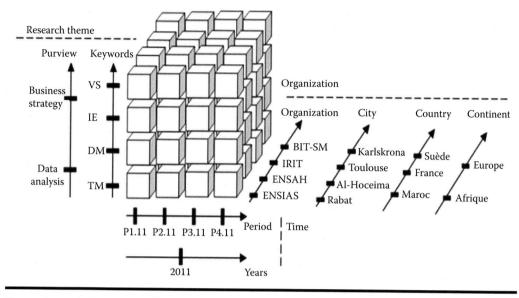

Figure 13.4 Laboratory collaboration.

respective articles. This presentation is not limited to three axes but spreads into a meta-meta-model in which the number of axes is able to go to several tens.

13.4.1 Homogenization of the Information Sources

The final objective is to obtain a unified view over the collected sources, which will be used throughout the process of analysis. This view must be

- Homogeneous: shared by the various data whatever their sources
- Reduced: to facilitate and accelerate the treatment of information
- Able to facilitate the analysis of any type of information and to restore it within very short times in order to answer to the competitive intelligence requirements

This unified view associated with the targeted corpus corresponds to a logical structured representation, presenting its whole collection in the form of a warehouse of strategic data.

The data homogenization process is described in Figure 13.5.

This service is a storage space called "XEW Data Warehousing Services – XEW-DWS," which allows, on its first level, to have a unified view of the target corpus, extraction, and storage of incoming data, would they be structured, semistructured, or unstructured and represent them a multidimensional form. The second level is about the data warehouse creation processes from the classical SQL to NoSQL (MongoDB, Neo4j, GraphDB, HBase, etc.).

13.4.2 XEW Big Data Analytics Service (XEW–BDAS)

This service allows making multidimensional analyses by adapting data mining algorithms to Big Data. It is based on the parallelism of the algorithms developed in the XEW system as well as other open-source tools, such as Weka or R.

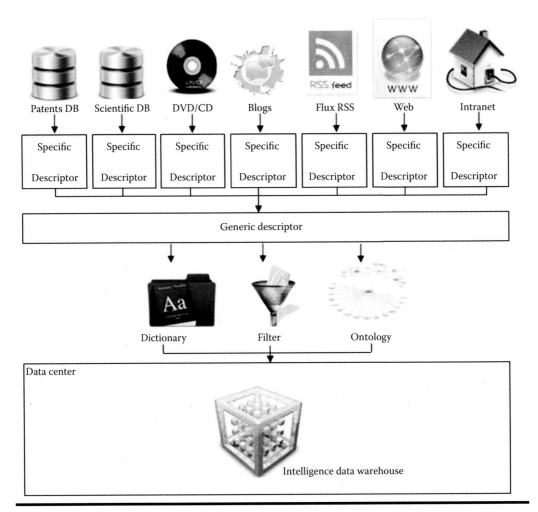

Figure 13.5 Information processing subsystem.

13.4.2.1 Graph Visualization in CIS XEW

Competitive intelligence (CI) is a set of coordinated actions of search, treatment, and distribution of useful information helping stakeholders in the process of decision making. In the opposite of industrial espionage, CI is a legal process of competitiveness in which the source of information is the external business environment.

The concept of CI is a bit wide, and it is necessary to define a specific framework based on a multidisciplinary approach. In our research team, we define the CI process according to three concepts:

- Strategic analysis: Defines the information needs of a company on its environment in order to ease decision making.
- Environment analysis: The process of collecting, treating, analyzing, and diffusing the useful information in order to respond to the expressed needs.
- Information system: Used as a support to the activities of data collection, analysis, and reporting.

Graphs are considered among the most powerful tools when it comes to visualizing trends. They can display any type of information and thus can respond to the needs of competitive intelligence.

It is worth mentioning that, opposite to the typical business intelligence (BI) graphs, which are based on structured data, CI graphs are based on unstructured, even massive, data. This makes it necessary to define layout algorithms or solutions that may be able to visualize a large amount of data and, in other words, large graphs.

A study conducted by Hu and Shi (2015) has proven several techniques of large graph visualization and categorized them into four different major models:

- *Spring–electric model*: This model includes force directed placement along with the algorithms deriving from Eads' work (1984). When it comes to visualizing massive data, FDP tends to fall into local minima due to the great amount of nodes and the repulsive charges they emit. Several solutions were proposed in order to address this problem, especially the approaches of Tunkelang (1999) and Quigley (2001) along with the multilevel approach in which a sequence of smaller and smaller graphs is generated from the original graph. Every one of these graphs captures the information concerning the connectivity of its parent. Once the smallest graph possible is generated, it gets refined and adjusted.
- *Stress model*: In this model, instead of minimizing the attractive or repulsive energy within nodes, we try to minimize it within the edges (represented as springs). As an example, Kamada and Kawai (1989) have proposed an algorithm that minimizes the stress energy within the edges by bringing the distance between the nodes to the ideal length of the spring connecting them, and because the latter depends on the distances between all the couples of nodes, they should all be calculated by finding the shortest paths between all these couples. In this case, scaling would be extremely expansive. Several teams tried to solve this problem, such as Hadany and Harel (2001), who proposed a solution to improve the speed of the Kamada–Kawai (1989) algorithm by accelerating its convergence, and Gajer et al. (2000) have proposed a multilevel approach similar to this one.
- *High dimensional embedding*: This algorithm, also known as (HDE) affects coordinates to nodes in k-dimension space, then projects it into a regular 2-D or 3-D space.
- *Algorithms based on the spectral information of the Laplacian*: Hall (1970) remarked that several node positioning problems could be brought back to problems of defining positions which would minimize the weighted sum of the squared distances between the nodes. Hu and Shi (2015) have mathematically represented this proposition using this notation:

$$\sum_{i \leftrightarrow j} w_{ij} \left\| x_i - x_j \right\|^2, \text{ such as } \sum_{k=1}^{|V|} x_k^2 = 1 \tag{13.1}$$

where x_i is the 1-D coordinate of the node i.

This function can also be rewritten as

$$\sum_{i \leftrightarrow j} w_{ij} \left\| x_i - x_j \right\|^2 = x^T L_w x , \tag{13.2}$$

such as $x = \{x_1, x_2, \ldots, x_{|V|}\}$ and L_w is the weighted Laplacian matrix.

The solution x to this minimization problem is the eigenvector, which has the smallest positive eigenvalue of the weighted Laplacian matrix (L_w).

Koren et al. (2002) have proposed an algorithm that brings a quick solution to this problem based on a multilevel approach, but it still keeps the weakness of Hall's algorithm regarding sparse graphs.

In XEW, massive data are collected, analyzed, and organized according to the steps mentioned above. The connected data are later filtered and stored in a graph-oriented data mart, which will be the source of our graphs.

13.4.3 Graph Visualization

According to Purchase (1998), a well-spread graph should provide an explicit vision of the relationships between the presented entities, which may help the decision maker have a quick understanding of the graph and extract the useful information from it.

In order to respond to this growing need, several graph representations (or layouts) have been suggested. Tutte (1963), as one of the pioneers of this field, proposed to lay down the first nodes on a plan, then the later ones on the barycenters of their neighbors. Eads (1984) has suggested a model called the "spring layout" in which the nodes are given an initial positioning and then the edges (represented as springs) would bring the nodes back to an equilibrium position corresponding to a global energy minimum. This work was improved later on by Fruchterman and Reingold (1991), who introduced the force directed placement (FDP) in which the attractive force of the spring between two neighboring nodes is proportional to the squared distance between them. The attraction force is then expressed as

$$F_a = -\frac{d^2(n_1, n_2)}{K} \tag{13.3}$$

where K is a parameter related to the nominal edge length of the final layout.

On the other hand, the repulsive force between any nodes on any other node is inversely proportional to the distance between these two nodes. It is expressed as

$$F_r = -\frac{K^2}{d(n_1, n_2)} \tag{13.4}$$

Fruchterman and Reingold thought later about reducing the complexity of this algorithm by partitioning the drawing space into a cell grid in order to calculate the local repulsive energy between nodes in a neighboring cell. This procedure could cause several calculation errors because it neglects the repulsive forces that may exist between non-neighboring nodes.

Tunkelang (1999) and Quigley (2001) could find a solution to this problem by introducing quad trees. A quad tree is a grouping of nodes that could be presented as a "supernode" with which we can approximate the total repulsive force of the nodes it contains. If a group of nodes is far enough from a certain node, the group of nodes is then considered a supernode. Other methods were proposed, such as minimizing the spring energy between links, etc.

13.4.4 Benchmarking

Several trials for algorithms have been launched in order to have a better graph visualization in a CI context, but those which attracted our attention were Gephi and VisuGraph.

13.4.4.1 Gephi

Gephi (Jacomy et al. 2014) is free software for analyzing and visualizing data in the form of graphs. It helps you get maximum information from the data, isolate their most important factors, detect inconsistencies and errors, etc. It imports data from different sources and displays them in the form of graphs.

This tool comes as an executable and offers a plug-in management system, programming APIs, and a graph visualization based on the most common algorithms.

The main visualization algorithm adopted by Gephi as mentioned in Jacomy et al. (2014) is ForceAtlas 2 (FA2). It is a force directed layout (FDL) algorithm developed by the Gephi team. It simulates a graph as a physical system in which nodes repel each other (repulsive force) while links attract back the connected nodes (attraction force).

The basic expression of the attractive force (F_a) between two connected nodes, according to the model adopted by the Gephi team, is equal to the distance between these nodes, which would be represented as

$$F_a = d\left(n_1, n_2\right)$$

(13.5)

The repulsive force (F_r) between two nodes, according to the same model, depends on the node degrees. This allows the highly connected nodes to be more centered, and the less connected ones (called leaves) are repelled to the suburbs. The repulsive force is expressed as

$$F_r = K_r \frac{\deg\left(n_1 + 1\right) * \deg\left(n_2 + 1\right)}{d(n_1, n_2)}$$

(13.6)

K_r can be fixed by the settings and the (+1), different from Noack's expression (Noack 2007), which is added in order to make sure that even the nodes with a zero degree can have a repulsive force.

The combination of these two forces creates a movement that converges to an equilibrium position, which would help in interpreting the data. A node's position depends on the other nodes and on the links connecting it with them. This algorithm eases the visual interpretation of the data structure under study. However, it does not take the nodes' attributes under consideration during the positioning process, which would be a problem if those attributes were actually meant to be initial coordinates. Figure 13.6 displays a person's friendship network on Facebook visualized using Gephi.

13.4.4.2 VisuGraph

VisuGraph (Loubier 2009) particularly interested us by its approach regarding mass data visualization. This approach can be subdivided into two principal axes (Figure 13.7):

- Graph visualization
- Evolutionary aspect: By taking the time variable into consideration while drawing the graph

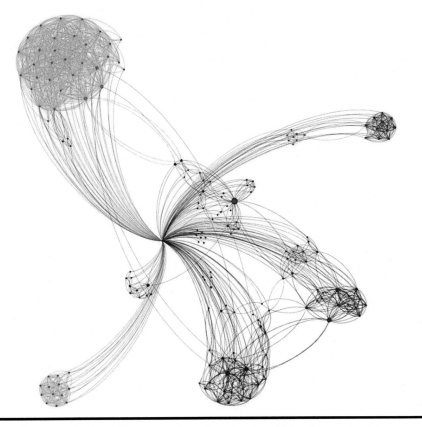

Figure 13.6   A person's friendship network on Facebook displayed using Gephi.

a. *Graph Visualization*

Loubier has proposed a slight modification of the FDP by setting the attraction and repulsion forces as follows.

The attraction force:

$$F_a(u,v) = \frac{\beta * d_{uv}^{\alpha_a}}{K} \qquad (13.7)$$

where β is a constant parameter; d_{uv} is the distance between the nodes u and v; α_a is a parameter used to increase or decrease the attraction between the two precited nodes; K is calculated according to the dimensions of the drawing space: $K = \sqrt{\dfrac{L * l}{N}}$; and L is the window's length, and l is its width.

The repulsion force:

$$F_r(u,v) = \frac{\alpha_r * K^2}{d_{uv}^c} \qquad (13.8)$$

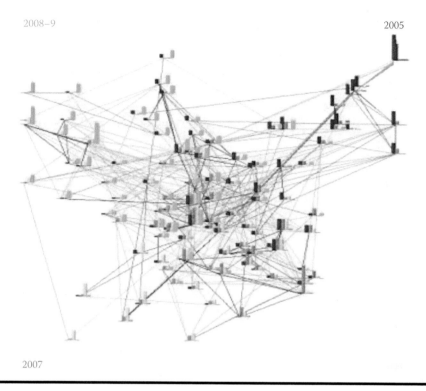

2008–9   2005

2007

Figure 13.7   Screenshot of VisuGraph.

where *c* is a constant parameter; and α_r is a parameter used to increase or decrease the repulsion between the nodes *u* and *v*.

b. *Evolutionary Aspect: Time Slices*

Loubier has remarked that when the analysis is time-dependent, a graph can send mixed signals or mis-interpretable information. Thus, she proposed a graph presentation based on "time slices." Every slice represents a certain period of time.

Taking the temporal dimension into account, the graph visualization goes in two steps:

– First, a global graph of all periods concerned is drawn.

– Second, some virtual nodes representing the time slices are scattered in the drawing space, and the graph nodes are positioned near the virtual nodes, which represent the time slice they belong to.

13.4.5 XEWGraph

Our team has introduced XEWGraph, a new module for the CI system Xplor EveryWhere dedicated to visualizing Big Data in the form of graphs representing, for instance, social networks, semantic networks, or even strategic alliance networks.

Our main objective with this tool is to give the decision makers a better user experience when it comes to large graph visualization. Thus, we have adopted several different approaches in our work.

First, we adopted the FDP as defined by Fruchterman and Reingold (1991), and we improved it using an approach inspired by the hypergraphs as explained in Boulouard et al. (2015), which gave us an "out of the box" categorization.

The need for that approach came from the fact that XEWGraph, being a part of Xplor EveryWhere, which is web- and mobile-oriented, has suffered from many problems when the graphs get larger.

The hypergraph approach has helped for sure, but it was not enough. For that reason, we proposed an amelioration in which we couple it with a multilevel approach similar to the ones proposed by Tunkelang (1999) and Quigley (2001) so that the nodes would be clustered or expanded according to the hyperedges they belong to and, in other terms, to their categories.

Figure 13.8 describes a clustered (a) then expanded (b) hypergraph representing the collaboration between research teams that have published papers within previous editions of the colloquium on Scientific and Technological Strategic Intelligence (Boulouard et al. 2015).

This approach gave us two advantages: The first one is to be able to draw a smaller graph with a general view and then have a deeper view on more specific details according to the decision makers' needs. The second advantage is the ability to display these graphs within smaller screens, such as smartphones.

Loubier's work on the "time slices" inspired us to come up with another approach when it comes to taking the time variable into consideration. Indeed, we proposed a slider that gets the time periods from the data and then takes the decision maker on a "time travel" as he or she slides through the time periods, which will give him or her an idea of the evolution of, for example, the collaboration between research teams throughout the last decade.

In Figures 13.9 and 13.10, you see screenshots of the previous graph with a time slider but taken from smartphones.

Another approach was adopted in order to improve the execution of the FDP within XEWGraph, which is prepositioning. Indeed, if the server gives the nodes some coordinates that

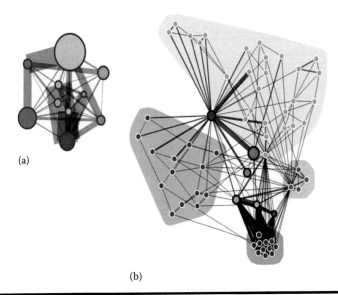

(a)

(b)

Figure 13.8 Clustered (a) then expanded (b) hypergraph.

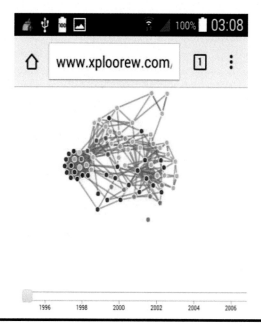

Figure 13.9   The global graph.

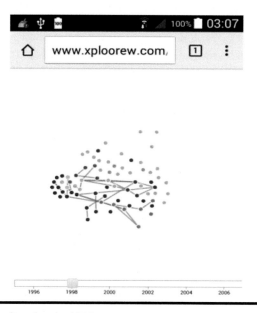

Figure 13.10   The graph situation in 1998.

would bring them to a close to best position, it would ease the FDP's process, which is executed client-side, and have a better visualization.

The proposed prepositioning method is a hybridization between the FDP and the genetic algorithm by taking as a fitness evaluation criterion the minimum of the spring electrical model's global energy function, as defined by Noack (2004):

$$E(x) = \sum_{i \leftrightarrow j} \left\| x_i - x_j \right\|^3 / (3K) - \sum_{i \neq j} K^2 \ln\left(\left\| x_i - x_j \right\| \right) \tag{13.9}$$

where x is a vector of nodes, x_i and x_j are nodes of x, and K is a parameter related to the nominal edge of the final layout.

This prepositioning approach made us go further by adding a third coordinate and thus proposing a 3-D representation of our graph by taking advantage of the WebGL engine as in Figure 13.11.

13.5 Case Study: Strategic Alliances between Biotechnology Companies

This case study introduces an experiment made by our research team in order to evaluate the performances of the competitive intelligence system XEW.

In this experiment, we extract up-to-date data from the online database Bio Space, analyze them, and then visualize the current strategic alliances between world-leading biotechnology companies.

13.5.1 Bio Space

Bio Space is a leading online resource dedicated to health-related news. For more than 30 years, Bio Space has provided quality information for professionals in the biotechnology and pharmaceutical industries. In addition, Bio Space offers a means of communication between business and scientific leaders in the biopharmaceutical market and allows them to stay up to date with the latest discoveries regarding the matter.

Figure 13.11 Screenshot of the 3-D graph.

The platform BioSpace.com provides daily biotechnology-related news feeds. These feeds will be the data sources on which we will perform our tests.

13.5.2 Data Extraction and Storage

The first step is the data collection. It is ensured by the XEW sourcing service (XEW-SS). This service starts by comparing the structure of the news feed with the essential data that the user needs to extract. It then provides a model of the needed data. This model is later transferred to the XEW-SS scraper, which will extract the data accordingly.

In our case, the information needed will be the biotechnology companies' names, the strategic alliances between them, and their dates of occurrence. The resulting model will contain those variables, and the scraper will extract the data related to these variables and discard the unrelated data.

The collected data are converted into JSON, the unified communication medium between XEW's different services, and then transferred to the second step of the process, the storage. It is ensured by the XEW data warehousing service (XEW-DWS). This service will store the data in its NoSQL data warehouse. In our case, the expected data are related, so the data warehouse will be a graph-oriented one, which will ease the communication with the XEW graph visualization service (XEWGraph).

13.5.3 Graph-Oriented Data Visualization

The final step is the data visualization. In our case, we need to visualize the strategic alliances connecting biotechnology companies. The best method to represent this connection is through a graph in which the nodes represent the companies and the links represent the strategic alliances between them.

XEWGraph will read the data stored in the data warehouse through the JSON communication medium. After that, it will visualize the related graph according to the user's preferences, ranging from 2-D to 3-D, global or time-sliced graphs.

Figure 13.12 presents the 3-D global graph describing the strategic alliances between biotechnology companies up to May 20, 2016 (the date of the experiment).

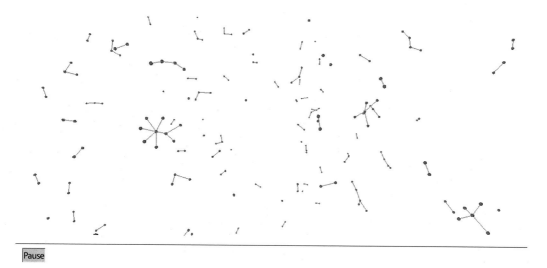

Pause

Figure 13.12　Screenshot of the 3-D graph.

The users can activate or deactivate the rotation of the 3-D graph using the "play/pause" toggle button and can zoom in or out of it using their mouse wheel or simply their fingers if they were using their smartphone or tablet.

13.6 Conclusion and Future Research

This chapter has provided a study on the state-of-the-art methods concerning mining unstructured data and large graph visualization. It has also described the current works led by the XEW research team regarding the matter, by way of explanation, the competitive intelligence system XEW. This system operates according to four principal steps, each with a dedicated service:

- *XEW sourcing service (XEW-SS)*: This allows searching, collecting, and processing the data from different sources.
- *XEW data warehousing services (XEW-DWS)*: This brings a unified view of the target corpus and then, creates a data warehouse accessible from the analytics and visualization services.
- *XEW big data analytics service (XEW-BDAS)*: This allows making multidimensional analyses by adapting data mining algorithms to Big Data.
- *XEW graph visualization service (XEWGraph)*: This allows visualizing Big Data in the form of graphs representing, for instance, social networks, semantic networks, strategic alliances networks, etc.

This chapter has also introduced a case study representing the performance of XEW. In this case study, we have presented the ability of XEW to extract up-to-date data from the BioSpace online database, analyze their contents, and then display the current strategic alliances between biotechnology companies as a 3-D graph.

Future works on the competitive intelligence system XEW will include enhanced clustering and analysis processes, an improvement in the data collection process, as well as more refined large graph visualization.

References

Abdullah, M. F. and Ahmad, K., 2013. "The Mapping Process of Unstructured Data to Structured Data." *Research and Innovation in Information Systems, 3rd Conference on. ICRIIS*.

Abidin, S. Z. Z., Idris, N. M. and Husain, A. H., 2010. "Extraction and Classification of Unstructured Data in Web Pages for Structured Multimedia Database via XML." IEEE.

Blumberg, R. and S. Atre, 2003. "The Problem with Unstructured Data." *DM Review*, February, pp. 42–46.

Boulouard, Z., El Haddadi, A., El Haddadi, A., Koutti, L. and Fennan, A., 2015. "XEWGraph: A tool for visualization and analysis of hypergraphs for a competitive intelligence system. *Proceedings of the 6th International Conference on Information Systems and Economic Intelligence (SIIE)*, Hammamet, Tunisia, pp. 66–70.

Chu, E., Baid, A., Chen, T., Doan, A. and Naughton, J., 2007. "A Relational Approach to Incrementally Extracting and Querying Structure in Unstructured Data." *Proceedings of the 33rd International Conference on Very Large Databases*, vol. VLDB Endowment.

Doan, A., Naughton, J. F., Baid, A., Chai, X., Chen, F., Chen, T., Chu, E., DeRose, P., Gao, B., Gokhale, C., Huang, J., Shen, W. and Vuong, B. Q., 2009. "The Case for a Structured Approach to Managing Unstructured Data." arXiv preprint arXiv:0909.1783.

Eads, P., 1984. "A heuristic for graph drawing." *Congressus Numerantium* 42, pp. 149–160.

Fruchterman, T. M. J. and Reingold, E. M., 1991. "Graph drawing by force-directed placement." *Software: Practice and Experience* 21, pp. 1129–1164.

Gajer, P., Goodrich, M. T. and Kobourov, S. G., 2000. "A fast multidimensional algorithm for drawing large graphs." *Lecture Notes on Computer Sciences*, Springer, pp. 211–221.

Geetha, S. and Mala, G. S. A., 2012. "Effectual Extraction of Data Relations from unstructured Data." Sustainable Energy and Intelligent System, 3rd International Conference on. VCTW.

Gupta, V. and Lehal, G. S., 2009. "A Survey of Text Mining Technics and Applications." *Journal of Emerging Technologies in Web Intelligence* 1 (1), 60–76.

Hadany, R. and Harel, D., 2001. "A multi-scale algorithm for drawing graphs nicely." *Discrete Applied Mathematics* 113, pp. 3–21.

Hall, K. M., 1970. "An r-dimensional quadratic placement algorithm." *Management Science, Informs Journal on Computing*, pp. 219–229.

Hu, Y. and Shi, L., 2015. "Visualizing large graphs." *WIREs: Computational Statistics* 7, pp. 115–136.

Jacomy, M., Venturini, T., Heymann, S. and M. Bastian, 2014. ForceAtlas2, a Continuous Graph "Layout Algorithm for Handy Network Visualization Designed for the Gephi Software." *PLoS ONE* 9.

Kamada, T. and Kawai, S., 1989. "An algorithm for drawing general undirected graphs." *Information Processing Letters* 31, pp. 7–15.

Koren, Y., Carmel, L. and Harel, D., 2002. Ace: "A fast multiscale eigenvectors computation for drawing huge graphs." In *Proceedings of the IEEE Symposium on Information Visualization* (InfoVis'02), pp. 137–144.

Liu, X., Lang, B., Yu, W., Luo, J. and Huang, L., 2011. "AUDR: An Advanced Unstructured Data Repository." Pervasive Computing and Applications (ICPCA), 6th International Conference on. IEEE.

Lomotey, R. K. and Deters, R., 2013. "Topics and Terms Mining in Unstructured Data Stores." Computational Science and Engineering, 16th International Conference on. IEEE.

Loubier, E., 2009. "Analyse et visualisation de données relationnelles par morphing de graphe prenant en compte la dimension temporelle." Ph.D. Thesis, IRIT, Paul Sabatier University.

Mansuri, I. R. and Sarawagi, S., 2006. "Integrating Unstructured Data into Relational Databases." *Data Engineering, ICDE'06, Proceedings of the 22nd International Conference on*. IEEE.

Noack, A., 2004. "An energy model for visual graph clustering." *Proceedings of the 11th International Symposium on Graph Drawing* (GD 2003), volume 2912 of LNCS, Springer, pp. 425–436.

Noack, A., 2007. "Energy Models for Graph Clustering." *Journal of Graph Algorithms and Applications* 11 (2), pp. 453–480.

Plejic, B., Vujnovic, B., and Penco, R. 2008. "Transforming unstructured data from scattered sources into knowledge." Knowledge Acquisition and Modeling Workshop, 2008. KAM Workshop 2008. IEEE International Symposium on, pp. 924–927.

Purchase, H. C., 1998. "Performance of Layout Algorithms: Comprehension, not Computation." *Journal of Visual Languages and Computing* 9 (6), pp. 647–657.

Quigley, A., 2001. "Large scale relational information visualization, clustering, and abstraction." Ph.D. Thesis, Department of Computer Science and Software Engineering, University of Newcastle, Australia.

Sequeda, J. and Miranker, D. P., 2012. "Linked Data." Linked Data tutorial at Semtech. Available: http://fr.slideshare.net/juansequeda/linked-data-tutorial-at-semtech-2012

Tari, L., Tu, P. H., Hakenberg, J., Chen, Y., Son, T. C., Gonzalez, G. and Baral, C., 2010. "Parse Tree Database for Information Extraction." *IEEE Transactions on Knowledge and Data Engineering*.

Tunkelang, D., 1999. "A numerical optimization approach to general graph drawing." Ph.D. Thesis, Carnegie Mellon University.

Tutte, W. T., 1963. "How to draw a graph." *Proceedings of the London Mathematical Society* 13, pp. 743–767.

Yafooz, W. M. S., Abidin, S. Z. Z. and Omar, N., 2011. "Towards automatic column-based data object clustering for multilingual databases." Control System, Computing and Engineering (ICCSCE), IEEE International Conference on. IEEE.

Yafooz, W. M. S., Abidin, S. Z. Z., Omar, N. and Idrus, Z., 2013. "Managing Unstructured Data in Relational Database." Systems, Process & Control (ICSPC), Conference on. IEEE.

Zikopoulos, P. C., Eaton, C., DeRoos, D., Deutsch, T. and Lapis, G., 2012. *Understanding Big Data: Analytics for Enterprise Class Hadoop and Streaming Data.* New York: McGraw-Hill.

Index

Page numbers followed by f and t indicate figures and tables, respectively.